Emerging Tools and Strategies for Financial Management

Begoña Álvarez-García
Universidade da Coruña, Spain

José-Pablo Abeal-Vázquez
Universidade da Coruña, Spain

A volume in the Advances in Finance, Accounting, and Economics (AFAE) Book Series

Published in the United States of America by
IGI Global
Business Science Reference (an imprint of IGI Global)
701 E. Chocolate Avenue
Hershey PA, USA 17033
Tel: 717-533-8845
Fax: 717-533-8661
E-mail: cust@igi-global.com
Web site: http://www.igi-global.com

Copyright © 2020 by IGI Global. All rights reserved. No part of this publication may be reproduced, stored or distributed in any form or by any means, electronic or mechanical, including photocopying, without written permission from the publisher.
Product or company names used in this set are for identification purposes only. Inclusion of the names of the products or companies does not indicate a claim of ownership by IGI Global of the trademark or registered trademark.

Library of Congress Cataloging-in-Publication Data

Names: Álvarez García, Begoña, editor. | Abeal-Vázquez, José-Pablo, 1977- editor.
Title: Emerging tools and strategies for financial management / Begoña Álvarez-García and José-Pablo Abeal-Vázquez, editors.
Description: Hershey : Business Science Reference, 2020. | Includes bibliographical references and index. | Summary: ""This book explores practical and theoretical perspectives on the evolution of financial management"--Provided by publisher"-- Provided by publisher.
Identifiers: LCCN 2019039291 (print) | LCCN 2019039292 (ebook) | ISBN 9781799824404 (hardcover) | ISBN 9781799824435 (paperback) | ISBN 9781799824411 (ebook)
Subjects: LCSH: Finance--Management.
Classification: LCC HG173 .E54 2020 (print) | LCC HG173 (ebook) | DDC 658.15--dc23
LC record available at https://lccn.loc.gov/2019039291
LC ebook record available at https://lccn.loc.gov/2019039292

This book is published in the IGI Global book series Advances in Finance, Accounting, and Economics (AFAE) (ISSN: 2327-5677; eISSN: 2327-5685)

British Cataloguing in Publication Data
A Cataloguing in Publication record for this book is available from the British Library.

All work contributed to this book is new, previously-unpublished material.
The views expressed in this book are those of the authors, but not necessarily of the publisher.

For electronic access to this publication, please contact: eresources@igi-global.com.

Advances in Finance, Accounting, and Economics (AFAE) Book Series

ISSN:2327-5677
EISSN:2327-5685

Editor-in-Chief: Ahmed Driouchi, Al Akhawayn University, Morocco

MISSION

In our changing economic and business environment, it is important to consider the financial changes occurring internationally as well as within individual organizations and business environments. Understanding these changes as well as the factors that influence them is crucial in preparing for our financial future and ensuring economic sustainability and growth.

The **Advances in Finance, Accounting, and Economics (AFAE)** book series aims to publish comprehensive and informative titles in all areas of economics and economic theory, finance, and accounting to assist in advancing the available knowledge and providing for further research development in these dynamic fields.

COVERAGE

- E-finance
- Stock Market
- Economic Downturn
- Labor Economics
- Finance
- Environmental and Social Accounting
- Auditing
- Taxes
- Corporate Finance
- Economic Policy

IGI Global is currently accepting manuscripts for publication within this series. To submit a proposal for a volume in this series, please contact our Acquisition Editors at Acquisitions@igi-global.com or visit: http://www.igi-global.com/publish/.

The Advances in Finance, Accounting, and Economics (AFAE) Book Series (ISSN 2327-5677) is published by IGI Global, 701 E. Chocolate Avenue, Hershey, PA 17033-1240, USA, www.igi-global.com. This series is composed of titles available for purchase individually; each title is edited to be contextually exclusive from any other title within the series. For pricing and ordering information please visit http://www.igi-global.com/book-series/advances-finance-accounting-economics/73685. Postmaster: Send all address changes to above address. Copyright © 2020 IGI Global. All rights, including translation in other languages reserved by the publisher. No part of this series may be reproduced or used in any form or by any means – graphics, electronic, or mechanical, including photocopying, recording, taping, or information and retrieval systems – without written permission from the publisher, except for non commercial, educational use, including classroom teaching purposes. The views expressed in this series are those of the authors, but not necessarily of IGI Global.

Titles in this Series

For a list of additional titles in this series, please visit:
http://www.igi-global.com/book-series/advances-finance-accounting-economics/73685

Mapping, Managing, and Crafting Sustainable Business Strategies for the Circular Economy
Susana Serrano Rodrigues (Polytechnic Institute of Leiria, Portugal) Paulo Jorge Almeida (Polytechnic Institute of Leiria, Portugal) and Nuno Miguel Castaheira Almeida (Polytechnic Institute of Leiria, Portugal)
Business Science Reference • ©2020 • 280pp • H/C (ISBN: 9781522598855) • US $195.00

Growth and Emerging Prospects of International Islamic Banking
Abdul Rafay (University of Management and Technology, Pakistan)
Business Science Reference • ©2020 • 500pp • H/C (ISBN: 9781799816119) • US $215.00

Economics, Business, and Islamic Finance in ASEAN Economics Community
Patricia Ordoñez de Pablos (The University of Oviedo, Spain) Mohammad Nabil Almunawar (Universiti Brunei Darussalam, Brunei) and Muhamad Abduh (Universiti Brunei Darussalam, Brunei)
Business Science Reference • ©2020 • 374pp • H/C (ISBN: 9781799822578) • US $215.00

Handbook of Research on Theory and Practice of Global Islamic Finance
Abdul Rafay (University of Management and Technology, Pakistan)
Business Science Reference • ©2020 • 888pp • H/C (ISBN: 9781799802181) • US $445.00

Challenges and Impacts of Religious Endowments on Global Economics and Finance
Buerhan Saiti (Istanbul Sabahattin Zaim University, Turkey) and Adel Sarea (Ahlia University, Bahrain)
Business Science Reference • ©2020 • 350pp • H/C (ISBN: 9781799812456) • US $225.00

Regional Trade and Development Strategies in the Era of Globalization
Akhilesh Chandra Prabhakar (Lovely Professional University, India) Gurpreet Kaur (Lovely Professional University, India) and Vasilii Erokhin (Harbin Engineering University, China)
Business Science Reference • ©2020 • 325pp • H/C (ISBN: 9781799817307) • US $225.00

For an entire list of titles in this series, please visit:
http://www.igi-global.com/book-series/advances-finance-accounting-economics/73685

701 East Chocolate Avenue, Hershey, PA 17033, USA
Tel: 717-533-8845 x100 • Fax: 717-533-8661
E-Mail: cust@igi-global.com • www.igi-global.com

Editorial Advisory Board

Lucía Boedo Vilabella, *University of A Coruña, Spain*
Gustavo Díaz Valencia, *University of Santo Tomás, Colombia*
Joaquín Enríquez-Díaz, *University of A Coruña, Spain*
Ángel S. Fernández Castro, *University of A Coruña, Spain*
Antonio Grandío Dopico, *University of A Coruña, Spain*
Susana Iglesias Antelo, *University of A Coruña, Spain*
María Dolores Lagoa Varela, *University of A Coruña, Spain*
Pablo de Llano-Monelos, *University of A Coruña, Spain*
George Leal Jamil, *FUMEC University, Brazil*
Jesús Mirás Araujo, *University of A Coruña, Spain*
Ariadna Monje Amor, *University of A Coruña, Spain*
Estefanía Mourelle Espasandín, *University of A Coruña, Spain*
Carlos Piñeiro Sánchez, *University of A Coruña, Spain*
Fernando Ruíz Lamas, *University of A Coruña, Spain*
José Manuel Sánchez Santos, *University of A Coruña, Spain*
Isabel Suárez Massa, *University of A Coruña, Spain*
Álvaro Andrés Vernazza Páez, *University of Santo Tomás, Spain*

Table of Contents

Preface xv

Section 1
Finance and New Technologies

Chapter 1
Financial Risk and Financial Imbalances: Does Information Technology Matter? 1
    Carlos Piñeiro Sanchez, Universidade da Coruña, Spain
    Pablo de Llano-Monelos, Universidade da Coruña, Spain

Chapter 2
Tokens and Tokenization: Still a Gordian Knot for the Future of FinTech?........32
    Carlos Fernandez-Herraiz, Grant Thornton, Spain
    Sara Esclapes-Membrives, Grant Thornton, Spain
    Antonio Javier Prado-Dominguez, Universidade da Coruña, Spain

Chapter 3
The Financial Function in Era 4.0: Challenges of Digital Transformation in SMEs...59
    José Pablo Abeal Vázquez, Universidade da Coruña, Spain

Section 2
Financial Management, Funding, and Economic Cycle

Chapter 4
Effect of Venture Capital on the Growth of Information and Communication Technology University Spin-Offs: Venture Capital Effect on the Growth of ICT-USOs 82
    María Jesús Rodríguez-Gulías, Universidade da Coruña, Spain
    Sara Fernández-López, Universidade de Santiago de Compostela, Spain
    David Rodeiro-Pazos, Universidade de Santiago de Compostela, Spain
    Ana Paula Faria, Universidade do Minho, Portugal
    Natalia Barbosa, Universidade do Minho, Portugal

Chapter 5
Are the New Sources for Financing SMEs a Reality or a Chimera? The Spanish Case Study 106
    José Pablo Abeal Vázquez, Universidade da Coruña, Spain
    Begoña Alvarez García, Universidade da Coruña, Spain
    Lucía Boedo Vilabella, Universidade da Coruña, Spain

Chapter 6
Shadow Banking: A Practical Approach 131
    Antonio Javier Grandío Dopico, Universidade da Coruña, Spain
    José Álvarez Cobelas, ANJOCA, Spain

Chapter 7
Recent Developments in Mortgage Loans in Spain and the Effects of the Subsequent Legislative Reforms 152
    Lucía Boedo Vilabella, Universidade da Coruña, Spain
    Begoña Alvarez García, Universidade da Coruña, Spain

Chapter 8
Financial Contagion and Shock Transmission During the Global Financial Crisis: A Review of the Literature 173
    Thomas J. Flavin, Maynooth University, Ireland
    Dolores Lagoa-Varela, Universidade da Coruña, Spain

Section 3
Financial Education and Inclusion

Chapter 9
The Economic and Social Value of Financial Literacy 199
    José Manuel Sánchez Santos, Universidade da Coruña, Spain

Chapter 10
Tool for the Financial Inclusion of Informal Retailers in Colombia 227
    Gustavo Adolfo Diaz, Universidad Santo Tomás, Colombia
    Olga Marina García Norato, Universidad Santo Tomás, Colombia
    Alvaro Andrés Vernazza Páez, Universidad Santo Tomás, Colombia
    Oscar A. Arcos Palma, Universidad Santo Tomás, Colombia

Chapter 11
The Role of Financial Inclusion: Does Financial Inclusion Matter? 248
    Ulkem Basdas, Philip Morris International, Portugal

Chapter 12
Evaluating Financial and Fiscal Knowledge for an Inclusive Society 280
    Laura Varela-Candamio, Universidade da Coruña, Spain
    Joaquín Enríquez-Díaz, Universidade da Coruña, Spain

Compilation of References 301

About the Contributors 350

Index 355

Detailed Table of Contents

Preface xv

Section 1
Finance and New Technologies

Chapter 1
Financial Risk and Financial Imbalances: Does Information Technology Matter? 1
    Carlos Piñeiro Sanchez, Universidade da Coruña, Spain
    Pablo de Llano-Monelos, Universidade da Coruña, Spain

The study of the financial imbalances of companies is a common topic for academics and practitioners because bankruptcy affects financial stability and modifies the investors' behavior. Since the 1960s, financial ratios have been used as diagnostic tools and also as independent variables within models aimed at quantifying firms' financial risk (e.g., Altman's Z-Score). In parallel, the strategic theory has developed theoretical constructs to explain why competitiveness is empirically heterogeneous. The resource-based view argues that companies can outperform rivals if they manage scarce, expensive, and hard-to-imitate resources. Ultimately, outperformers should be able to avoid (or overcome) financial imbalances. This chapter intends to analyze whether IT resources modify firm performance and financial risk. To do that, the authors collected data from a random sample of Galician SMEs, combining questionnaires, focused interviews, and public financial data. Hypotheses are explored by applying parametric statistical methods.

Chapter 2
Tokens and Tokenization: Still a Gordian Knot for the Future of FinTech? 32
    Carlos Fernandez-Herraiz, Grant Thornton, Spain
    Sara Esclapes-Membrives, Grant Thornton, Spain
    Antonio Javier Prado-Dominguez, Universidade da Coruña, Spain

The authors have carried out an examination of the status of tokens and tokenization in financial markets with regulatory problems, which lack proposals for solutions based on a generalized consensus. Overall, it seems to authors that cutting the Gordian knot of tokenization and tokens is the essential need to achieve a consensual and efficient protocol of unequivocal attribution of legal responsibility to obtain satisfactory levels of transparency and reliability in all transactions. In particular, tokens that claim to be money appear to have a more complicated potential development than the rest, since there is a controversy between the pressures of the sector agents and the specific restrictions indicated by Knapp and Ingham and maintained by the states and regulators with respect to its exclusive regulatory capacity over money as a means of payment of a wide and reliable acceptance.

Chapter 3
The Financial Function in Era 4.0: Challenges of Digital Transformation in
SMEs 59
    José Pablo Abeal Vázquez, Universidade da Coruña, Spain

The global system evolves at high speed. Megatrends emerge, and they develop, interact, multiply, and transform into a continuous and increasingly crazy movement. Companies have to dance this rhythm. It's not just about adapting, but about doing it the right way. SMEs also share these similarities even if they have their own casuistry. Due to the important weight that SMEs have in the globalized global economy, there is a growing interest in studying them and the way they create value. In this context, the figure of the financial director has acquired great relevance. The last major financial crisis has confirmed its important work in SMEs and also that his role is evolving to become an essential key to increase the value of the company. In this chapter, the authors discuss the role of the financial director and the challenges they have to take on in the new technological context.

Section 2
Financial Management, Funding, and Economic Cycle

Chapter 4
Effect of Venture Capital on the Growth of Information and Communication Technology University Spin-Offs: Venture Capital Effect on the Growth of
ICT-USOs 82
    María Jesús Rodríguez-Gulías, Universidade da Coruña, Spain
    Sara Fernández-López, Universidade de Santiago de Compostela, Spain
    David Rodeiro-Pazos, Universidade de Santiago de Compostela, Spain
    Ana Paula Faria, Universidade do Minho, Portugal
    Natalia Barbosa, Universidade do Minho, Portugal

The creation of university spin-off firms (USOs) to commercialize the academic research outputs contributes to the economic development of the regions. These firms are often resource-constrained, which may hamper their growth. However, the involvement of venture capital (VC) partners in their management can partly counterbalance their traditional lack of resources. Within the USOs created in Portugal and Spain, around one-third operate in the information and communication technology industry (ICT-USOs). This chapter aims to explore the effect of VC partners on the ICT-USOs' growth by using a sample of 127 Spanish and 176 Portuguese ICT-USOs over the period 2007–2013. The results show that the effect of VC on the ICT-USOs' growth depends not only on the country, but also on how firm growth is measured; whereas a weak positive effect on the sales growth is found, a negative one is obtained in the case of the employment growth.

Chapter 5
Are the New Sources for Financing SMEs a Reality or a Chimera? The Spanish Case Study..106
    José Pablo Abeal Vázquez, Universidade da Coruña, Spain
    Begoña Alvarez García, Universidade da Coruña, Spain
    Lucía Boedo Vilabella, Universidade da Coruña, Spain

Small and medium-sized enterprises (SMEs) are a key pillar of the European economy because they play an important role in generating growth, employment, and value added. However, SMEs cannot access funding from sources such as issuing securities because they do not meet the listing requirements of official markets. This is why these firms are forced to cover their financial needs by borrowing from banks and reinvesting profits. For this reason, several alternative markets have been launched in Europe. In the Spanish case, two alternative markets have been created (one equity trading market and one debt market). In this chapter, these markets are presented for the purpose of analyzing to what extent they are a real solution to the financing problems faced by Spanish SMEs. This research shows that these two markets follow different paths, although for the time being, they are not capable of reaching a large number of companies.

Chapter 6
Shadow Banking: A Practical Approach 131
    Antonio Javier Grandío Dopico, Universidade da Coruña, Spain
    José Álvarez Cobelas, ANJOCA, Spain

Shadow banking has gained prominence in recent years, and especially after the world financial and economic crisis because, on the one hand, it favours the funding of firms that have difficulty accessing the tradicional banking system, and, on the other hand, it offers to investors alternatives to the traditional bank deposits. However, shadow banking involves risks because it is subject to a lower level of regulation than the traditional system and it is clearly pro-cyclical, contributing to worsening the economic climate in times of recession. The chapter shows in detail how the shadow banking works and what the advantages and disadvantages of this alternative system are. In addition, reference is made to the debate about the possibility of reinforcing the regulation of this sector, although so far, the supervisory authorities prefer maintaining a vigilant attitude while not imposing strict requirements, which would lead to limit the role played by shadow banking.

Chapter 7
Recent Developments in Mortgage Loans in Spain and the Effects of the
Subsequent Legislative Reforms 152
    Lucía Boedo Vilabella, Universidade da Coruña, Spain
    Begoña Alvarez García, Universidade da Coruña, Spain

This chapter analyses the evolution of the mortgage loan in Spain during the present century. The economic development of Spain is described with its great connection to mortgages. The text centres on the new conditions incorporated in the loans in the years before the crisis, which were subsequently demonstrated to be unfair terms and caused serious problems for consumers and a lack of confidence in the financial sector. This provoked the reaction of legislators. This chapter studies the effectiveness of the subsequent mortgage laws in their intention to minimize the asymmetrical positions that the lender and the borrower occupy in the contractual relationship. Among the conclusions of the chapter, the authors highlight how each law is more precise but its effectiveness is lacking if the banking culture is not changed in terms of the relationship between to clients.

Chapter 8
Financial Contagion and Shock Transmission During the Global Financial
Crisis: A Review of the Literature 173
    Thomas J. Flavin, Maynooth University, Ireland
    Dolores Lagoa-Varela, Universidade da Coruña, Spain

After the recent financial crisis, the analysis of shock transmission across the financial system has received a great deal of attention. In particular, the role of financial contagion as a shock propagation mechanism has been studied in detail. The globalisation of financial and banking markets has increased the connections and relationship between them. Hence, recent crises have spread all around the world. The stability of linkages between financial assets across different market conditions cast doubt upon the benefits of portfolio diversification. This chapter reviews the extant literature on financial contagion during the global financial crisis and thus provides information for both portfolio managers (when optimizing their investment portfolios) and policymakers (when designing their strategies in order to mitigate spillover effects during crisis periods).

Section 3
Financial Education and Inclusion

Chapter 9
The Economic and Social Value of Financial Literacy..................................199
    José Manuel Sánchez Santos, Universidade da Coruña, Spain

The main objective of this chapter is to provide new insights into the economic and social value that financial literacy has for individuals and societies. Financial literacy has implications that are relevant both at a micro (especially for households) and macro-level (for the financial system and for the national economy as a whole). On the one hand, a lack of financial literacy put households a risk from making sub-optimal financial decisions and prevent them to maximize their wellbeing. On the other hand, financial literacy favors a better allocation of resources, reduces the risks associated with episodes of financial instability, and therefore, contributes to the increase of social welfare. The analysis and the empirical evidence showing the benefits (costs) of financial literacy (illiteracy) allows to conclude that policymakers have a key role to play implementing initiatives aiming to improve financial literacy of the population at all stages of life.

Chapter 10
Tool for the Financial Inclusion of Informal Retailers in Colombia..................227
    Gustavo Adolfo Diaz, Universidad Santo Tomás, Colombia
    Olga Marina García Norato, Universidad Santo Tomás, Colombia
    Alvaro Andrés Vernazza Páez, Universidad Santo Tomás, Colombia
    Oscar A. Arcos Palma, Universidad Santo Tomás, Colombia

One of the structural problems in Colombia is the informality of economic activities. Indeed, there is a high proportion of informal retailers in large cities of the country. This chapter propounds a tool, Credit Scoring, for the financial inclusion of this population. The tool is designed for obtaining resources at lower financial costs, and it aims at improving the commercial activities of these agents. In this way, informal financing, which increases poverty, is avoided. Also, in connection with this subject, surveys conducted among a thousand informal retailers in five Colombian cities—Bogotá, Cúcuta, Ibagué, Villavicencio and Arauca—were taken into account.

Chapter 11
The Role of Financial Inclusion: Does Financial Inclusion Matter?.................248
    Ulkem Basdas, Philip Morris International, Portugal

This chapter highlights the importance of financial education, its link with financial decision-making process, comparative status of different countries, and efforts to improve current situation. Unfortunately, there is no standard definition for neither financial education nor measures to quantify it. Therefore, this chapter first aims to provide a comprehensive definition in order to explain how financial knowledge affects the decision-making process. Then, financial literacy measures from previous studies over different countries would be discussed to show financial illiteracy problem is global. Lastly, solutions and recommendations would be discussed at three different levels: younger people, individuals, and national strategies.

Chapter 12
Evaluating Financial and Fiscal Knowledge for an Inclusive Society 280
 Laura Varela-Candamio, Universidade da Coruña, Spain
 Joaquín Enríquez-Díaz, Universidade da Coruña, Spain

Financial education and fiscal awareness are considered two fundamental branches of knowledge in the training of citizens from the first stages of learning. Thus, it is necessary to teach them in order to know the different savings products that can be acquired in a bank, to understand the basic information related to savings and the means of payment, or to differentiate between investment and risk. This work seeks to analyze the factors that determine the degree of financial knowledge and also fiscal knowledge of the current population. As a case study, the authors have selected a small sample of young people between 9 and 19 years at middle schools in the region of A Coruna (Spain). Findings reveal the low level of both financial and fiscal knowledge of the youngest population.

Compilation of References 301

About the Contributors 350

Index 355

Preface

OVERVIEW

The economic and financial environment has changed dramatically in recent decades due to the remarkable effect of phenomena such as globalization, the significant expansion of ICTs, and the increase in international competitiveness. These macro-phenomena have a major impact on the behavior of individuals and businesses and even on the relationships that occur between them. On the individuals' side, it is observed that they increasingly use ICTs in their daily activities and they are permanently interconnected through communication networks. On the corporate side, it is observed that more and more companies are entering the technology race because the managers at the highest level (whether managing directors or chief financial officers) try to take advantage of the benefits of technological innovation. In fact, the digitization and the expansion of ICTs are helping many companies to improve the productive processes, save costs, improve the quality of products, and allow these companies to relate to customers in a much more direct and personalized way without geographical or time limits. Companies are aware of the importance of proper information management and are increasingly focusing on the digital strategy, in which financial solutions go hand in hand with technological innovations.

However, there are not only advantages. As the global financial crisis, triggered in the year 2008, has shown, the risks to which companies, markets and financial systems are subjected are increasing and spreading more rapidly, causing serious social imbalances and serious effects on the real economy. Additionally, the authorities and citizens themselves are also aware that financial information is becoming more and more abundant and sophisticated and that they are not always well equipped to make basic decisions (such as buying a home, signing for a pension plan, choosing between investment or savings alternatives, etc.). Therefore, financial education is perceived as an opportunity to empower financial consumers and many countries are making significant efforts to promote and develop financial education programs and initiatives.

In this context of technological changes and challenges, it is important to open the debate and gain in-depth knowledge, at both theoretical and practical levels, of the new risks and opportunities that companies and citizens must face. Likewise, it is important to find a space for thinking of the strategies they can put into practice to transform these challenges into opportunities for improvement. For this reason, this book provides fertile ground for understanding the impacts that macro-phenomena (such as globalization, the digital revolution, and the international competitiveness) are having on corporate financial management and the sources of financing. In addition, this book is a space for analyzing the importance of improving the financial and fiscal education of the citizens of the 21th century.

The book is structured around three main areas of debate. The first one (chapters 1 to 3) begins with a joint reflection on how digital transformation is changing the financial management and the elements involved in the corporate chain value. The second one (chapters 4 to 8) focuses on analyzing the sources of funding used by firms. Reference is also made to the financial crisis and the importance of the contagion effect in a globalized world. The financial crisis had a devastating effect on the capacity of companies to get external financing and, as a result, alternative sources of funding have begun to emerge in recent years. The third one (chapters 9 to 12) puts emphasis on financial education and its importance in improving the economic and social inclusion of citizens.

TARGET AUDIENCE

The target audience of this book is wide. Includes scientific researchers of areas such as Management Science, Economics, Information Science, Technological Innovation, Marketing, Engineering, Law Studies, Sociology, among many others. It is also useful for financial managers who wish to deepen their knowledge and students in degrees related to Management, Economics, Computer Science and Social Sciences in general. It also contribute to practical implementations, allowing business decision makers, strategic planners, and consultants to develop their ideas, and understanding of financial management challenges and outlook on the future.

DETAILED ORGANIZATION OF THE BOOK

Chapter 1, "Financial Risk and Financial Imbalances: Does Information Technology Matter?" authored by Carlos Piñeiro Sánchez and Pablo de Llano-Monelos, analyses whether the corporate investments in Information Technology (IT) have influence on company performance and financial risk. For this purpose, the authors examine

Preface

105 firms from a random sample of Spanish small and medium enterprises (SMEs). They use questionnaires, personal interviews with Chief Executive Officers (CFOs) and Chief Information Officers (CIOs), and financial information obtained from public records to explore the initial hypothesis of their research. The results achieved confirm that the absence of both IT assets and the necessary capabilities may lead to an erosion of competitiveness and have influence on the assessment of failure risk. Likewise, the results highlight the great importance of internal capacities, particularly experience and managerial skills. In addition, the authors conclude that the synergistic interactions between resources and capabilities are complex and bidirectional.

Chapter 2, "Tokens and Tokenization: Still a Gordian Knot for the Future of FinTech?" authored by Carlos Fernández-Herráiz, Sara Esclapes-Membrives, and Javier Prado-Domínguez, examines the current status of tokens and tokenization in financial markets. This chapter discusses an emerging area of research that is directly related to the impact that technological innovation is having on the financial sphere. The authors introduce and explain in detail important concepts such as blockchain, cryptocurrencies, the distributed ledger technologies (DLT), Initial Coin Offerings (ICOs), or Initial Exchange Offering (IEO). Likewise, the authors identify the most relevant issues and challenges related to the regulation of tokens and tokenization and the main economic implications. Finally, they made several useful recommendations and present a basic framework for a regulatory strategy.

Chapter 3, "The Financial Function in Era 4.0: Challenges of Digital Transformation in SMEs," authored by José Pablo Abeal Vázquez, focuses on the role played by the financial function (and, specifically, by Chief Financial Officers- CFOs) in the context of the current economy that is heavily influenced by, among other factors, the development of the information and communication technologies (ICTs). The author explains that the increasingly complexity of global economy and the new technological paradigm lead to the transformation of the financial function, and he proposes to explore these issues from a double perspective, professional and academic. The author firstly describes the current economic and social reality, together with the challenges that companies (and, in particular, SMEs) must face. Subsequently, the author characterizes the role of SMEs in the disruptive paradigm drawn by ICTs and Industry 4. 0. This characterization serves to configure the figure of CFOs against the objective of generating value. To meet this objective it is necessary to know thoroughly the needs and define the appropriate tools. In this respect, the financial information becomes an essential asset that favors all the processes of the companies. This is why, the CFO's profile will have an increasingly open and multidisciplinary character that will help these professionals to face the strategic and technological changes and constantly adapt themselves to new functions in the company.

Chapter 4, "Effect of Venture Capital on the Growth of Information and Communication Technology University Spin-Offs," authored by María Jesús Rodríguez-Gulías, Sara Fernández-López, David Rodeiro-Pazos, Ana Paula Faria, and Natalia Barbosa, focuses on verifying the hypothesis that the presence of Venture Capital (VC) partners has a positive effect on the growth of University spin-off firms (ICT-USOs). The creation of USOs is one of the formulas used by Universities to direct their technological developments to society, thus promoting the generation of economic value and a virtuous process of growth among universities, businesses and the society as a whole. In this research the authors use a longitudinal dataset from 127 Spanish and 176 Portuguese ICT-USOs for the period 2007 to 2013. The results obtained show that the influence of VC on the ICT-USOs' growth has slight differences in these two countries. Moreover, the chapter shows different effects on the growth of sales and employment, with a weak positive effect on sales growth and negative on employment growth. Therefore, venture capitalists would prioritize the increase in sales to the detriment of job creation. In addition, the authors point out that VC could have a positive effect on knowledge, technological, and R&D spillovers.

Chapter 5, "Are the New Sources for Financing SMEs a Reality or a Chimera? The Spanish Case Study," authored by José Pablo Abeal Vázquez, Begoña Álvarez García, and Lucía Boedo Vilabella, focuses on analyzing the alternative markets that are emerging over recent decades as a new way of financing small and medium size enterprises (SMEs). The authors explain that SMEs are a key part of the economy because of their contribution to the generation of employment and wealth. However, a multitude of factors constantly threaten their survival, financial constraints being one of the most relevant. The barriers that SMEs have to raise financing make them, in many cases, dependent on bank funding and highly vulnerable to the ups and downs of the economic cycle and crises. This is why two new markets were recently created in Spain for SMEs: one is an equity trading market (the Spanish Alternative Equity Market), and the other is a debt market (the Spanish Alternative Fixed-Income Market). Even though these markets share common elements, the chapter shows that they have followed two different paths. In addition, the chapter shows the reasons that have justified the launch of these markets and the main characteristics of the companies listed in them.

Chapter 6, "Financial Banking: A Practical Approach," authored by Antonio Grandío Dopico and José Álvarez Cobelas, explains the functioning of shadow banking and the main advantages and disadvantages of this means of alternative funding. This is a banking system complementary to the traditional one, which operates in a different way. The authors explain that this complementary banking system entails many risks, although it also contributes to wealth creation (indeed, the EU shadow banking represented 40% of the European financial system at the year 2007). Additionally, the authors show several important conclusions. One

Preface

of them is that shadow banking plays an important role in the financial world. In fact, shadow banking finances projects that may be excluded from the traditional banking system. Another important conclusion is that there are many links between shadow banking and the traditional banking system and both of them interrelate bidirectionally. Another conclusion is that a greater regulation of shadow banking may not be the most beneficial option for fostering economic growth. Finally, the authors indicate that transparency and information are two essential elements in shadow banking, because it is necessary to know and understand all the characteristics of the products to invest in them.

Chapter 7, "Recent Developments in Mortgage Loans in Spain and the Effects of the Subsequent Legislative Reforms," authored by Lucía Boedo Vilabella and Begoña Álvarez García, focuses on analyzing the evolution of mortgage loans in Spain over the last years. The authors study how the mortgage contracts have varied over time and highlights the economic and social consequences of incorporating some clauses into these contracts. The authors explain that the relationship between banking and its customers has become increasingly asymmetric. They also indicate that the vocabulary, concepts, and calculations used in banking products (such as mortgage loans) are difficult to understand for a large part of the population. This is why the authors consider that mortgage loan complexity is not justified and contracts should be written in a simple and easy to understand manner. Additionally, the authors note that financial entities should adapt the mortgages to the profile of each client and advise them not only in accordance with what is convenient for the entity but looking for a more personable face to face partnership with the clients.

Chapter 8, "Financial Contagion and Shock Transmission During the Global Financial Crisis: A Review of the Literature," authored by Thomas J. Flavin and Dolores Lagoa Varela, presents a detailed and profound revision of the literature on financial contagion during the last global financial crisis. The main aim of this revision is to learn from what happened and provide information to managers, investors, and policy makers. Evidence seems to indicate that the financial crisis generated a contagion effect in different sectors. Research also provides evidence of contagion during the global financial crisis within the United States, the Eurozone and internationally. The authors analyze the crucial role that the United States played in transmission within its financial system. Likewise, the authors study the importance of the banking sector in the transmission of the crisis and its extension to non-financial companies. The authors also pay attention to several contagion channels during the financial crisis, such as international bank, stock, and bond markets. Finally, the authors offer several useful recommendations for investors and policy makers. In the case of investors, the financial contagion may threaten the effectiveness of the portfolio diversification. This is why is advisable to take into account the empirical properties of contagion effects for asset allocation and risk management strategies. In the case of policy makers, the chapter stress the importance of facilitating the access of companies to markets (specially small and medium sized companies).

Chapter 9, "The Economic and Social Value of Financial Literacy," authored by José Manuel Sánchez Santos, shows the importance of financial literacy from a social and economic point of view. It focuses on studying how financial literacy contributes to improve the economic outcomes of financial decisions and the well-being of the people who make them. It also analyzes the effect of financial education on issues of great relevance, such as savings, wealth accumulation and inequality, personal finance management, financial inclusion, financial markets efficiency, financial stability, and labor markets competitiveness. The outcomes of many previous studies on this subject reveal that financial illiteracy is a relevant problem that is detected in a wide range of countries and even in specific segments of each of them. The results obtained confirm the need for political intervention in this area because financial illiteracy has negative implications from both the individual and social spheres. This is why the chapter proposes many important recommendations for policymakers to design policy interventions.

Chapter 10, "Tool for the Financial Inclusion of Informal Retailers in Colombia," authored by Gustavo Adolfo Díaz, Olga Marina García Norato, Álvaro Andrés Vernazza Páez, and Oscar Arcos Palma, addresses two relevant issues that characterize the Colombian economy: the informality of many economic activities and the low level of financial inclusion of low-income households. To this end, the authors explain the main reasons why informal retailers use informal financing resources and present the opinions of 489 informal retailers obtained from surveys carried out in Colombia in the year 2018. Likewise, the authors suggest applying a scoring model for the allocation of credits to informal retailers and they use the Analytical Hierarchy Processs (AHP) model to design the criteria for the approval of credits. The application of the scoring tool is based on a study on informal retailing carried out in key sectors of the Colombian cities of Bogotá, Cúcuta, Ibagué Villavicencio, and Arauca. The authors believe that implementing the Credit Scoring tool would contribute to the integration of many informal retailers into the formal financial system, which in turn can relieve the financial needs of this population and promote a change from informality to formality.

Chapter 11, "The Role of Financial Education," authored by Ulkem Basdas, highlights the relevant role of financial education and explores the links between financial literacy and financial decisions. The chapter puts emphasis on analyzing how to measure financial literacy and how financial literacy would affect financial actions through different ways. For this reason, the author firstly reviews some definitions of financial literacy in order to identify the different aspects or skills that are taken into account in definitions. This is important because if some skill

Preface

is prioritized in a definition, the measure could be biased to that direction as well. Subsequently, the chapter shows a comprehensive survey of different measures of financial literacy presented in literature. In addition, it addresses the comparative situation in several countries and the actions to improve the existing situation. The author explains that, even if financial education is an issue that is being given more and more attention, financial knowledge is necessary but not sufficient to implement the relevant actions. Therefore, the link between financial education and financial decisions becomes a key element in the analysis. Finally, the author offers some important recommendations at three different levels: the first one, is focused on younger people, the second one on individuals and the third one on the national level.

Chapter 12, "Evaluating Financial and Fiscal Knowledge for an Inclusive Society," authored by Joaquín Enríquez-Díaz and Laura Varela-Candamio, study which are the elements that determine the level of financial and fiscal knowledge of the current population. To meet this objective, the authors first refer to the importance of both the financial and public sectors, and then they show the relevance that financial and fiscal education have for the improvement of citizens' literacy and social inclusion. The authors carry out a complete review of literature that show that an improvement in knowledge is directly related to more positive financial behaviors in activities in which financial knowledge is required (such as cash withdrawal, cash flow management, investment in financial assets, sing up for a pension plan, etc.). Subsequently, the authors perform a descriptive analysis of the determinants of the degree of financial and fiscal literacy and, finally, they conduct a case study by analyzing the opinions and knowledge of 472 young students from the region of A Coruña (Spain). The students were aged between 9 and 19. The results show that even if in Spain the access to financial services is certainly high, the degree of financial knowledge is not yet sufficient to guarantee positive behavior in financial decision making. In fact, students have problems calculating financial income, as well as to understand basic concepts such as the interest rate or the inflation. Therefore, there is a clear need to implement, from middle school to college, continuous programs of financial and fiscal education that may help consumers to create enhanced financial habits at an early age.

Begoña Álvarez-García
Universidade da Coruña, Spain

José-Pablo Abeal-Vázquez
Universidade da Coruña, Spain

Section 1
Finance and New Technologies

Chapter 1
Financial Risk and Financial Imbalances:
Does Information Technology Matter?

Carlos Piñeiro Sanchez
Universidade da Coruña, Spain

Pablo de Llano-Monelos
Universidade da Coruña, Spain

ABSTRACT

The study of the financial imbalances of companies is a common topic for academics and practitioners because bankruptcy affects financial stability and modifies the investors' behavior. Since the 1960s, financial ratios have been used as diagnostic tools and also as independent variables within models aimed at quantifying firms' financial risk (e.g., Altman's Z-Score). In parallel, the strategic theory has developed theoretical constructs to explain why competitiveness is empirically heterogeneous. The resource-based view argues that companies can outperform rivals if they manage scarce, expensive, and hard-to-imitate resources. Ultimately, outperformers should be able to avoid (or overcome) financial imbalances. This chapter intends to analyze whether IT resources modify firm performance and financial risk. To do that, the authors collected data from a random sample of Galician SMEs, combining questionnaires, focused interviews, and public financial data. Hypotheses are explored by applying parametric statistical methods.

DOI: 10.4018/978-1-7998-2440-4.ch001

INTRODUCTION

As Argenti (1976) stated, bankruptcy is the final stage of a predictable sequence of facts. All companies suffer from weaknesses, often caused by restrictions on access to resources and limited capabilities. When erroneous decisions are also made, these weaknesses become more serious and tend to become chronic over time. At some point, symptoms of imbalance arise, but it is often too late to take corrective action. As Knight (1921) stated, *"Hence it is our imperfect knowledge of the future (...) which is crucial for our understanding of our problem"* (p. 198).

In his pioneering work, Beaver (1966) offered solid statistical evidence that financial ratios took on different values in failed enterprises. Taking these findings as a starting point, Altman (1968) formulated what is recognized as the first quantitative model capable of scoring financial risk and classifying companies that are likely to go bankrupt.

Altman's model is in line with Argenti's approach and allows bankruptcy to be interpreted as a temporal sequence: preexisting operational anomalies reduce the capacity to generate resources and self-finance, and force companies to increase their indebtedness; at the same time, they try to increase their chances of survival by reducing expenses. Often these decisions lead to a feedback process that exacerbates financial tensions and leads to failure.

MDA has been extensively used to classify healthy and failed firms (e.g. Altman, 1968 Altman, Haldeman & Narayanan, 1977). Within the parametric models, the main alternative to the discriminant analysis is the logistic regression (Martin 1977, Ohlson, 1980; Zmijewski, 1984); however, many machine-learning techniques have been also suggested: recursive partitioning (Frydman, Altman & Kao, 1985) expert systems, and artificial neural networks (Messier & Hansen, 1988; Bell, Ribar & Verchio, 1990, Hansen & Messier, 1991, Serrano & Martin, 1993; Koh & Tan, 1999, Brockett, Golden, Jang & Yang, 2006). Some forecasting models are built upon fuzzy set theory and fuzzy logic (Dubois & Prade, 1992, Slowinski & Zopounidis, 1995, McKee & Lensberg, 2002). Recently, multicriteria analysis models have been developed, combining group decision support systems (GDSS) and the Analytic Hierarchy Process (AHP) (Sun & Li, 2009).

Most of these models rely on financial ratios to diagnose the situation of the company and measure financial risk; however, there is little agreement about which are the relevant independent variables. Many forecasting models are not strictly generalizable, as they must be recalibrated before they are applied in different countries and/or time horizons.

Some researchers have explored the use of additional variables, e.g. macroeconomic conditions (Rose, Andrews & Giroux, 1982) and evidence from external audit

(Piñeiro, de Llano & Rodríguez, 2012). However, the use of variables complementary to financial ratios is largely an unexplored path.

Let us return to the approach of Argenti (1976), who stressed that failure is the synergistic effect of multiple internal dysfunctions that include both decision errors and lack of resources: companies do not fail *because* their financial indicators are inadequate. Rather, financial indicators are the external manifestation of underlying anomalies.

Companies use different resources: financial, human, organizational, etc. The point of interest of this work are information technology-based resources, e.g. assets and infrastructure (equipment, software), human skills (management abilities), and organizational capabilities (relational capital, flexibility, etc.). IT can be viewed as enabling resources, as far as they provide companies with tools to deploy processes and business strategies that would be impossible (or less efficient) without them; as a consequence, the effect of ICT on financial indicators is rather indirect. On the other hand, these effects appear to be contingent, and depend on the presence of other contextual factors, as well as on synergies with other complementary resources and capacities.

However, ICT *should* have measurable effects on the financial health of the firms. As many recent papers, we draw on the *resource-based view of the firm* (RBV) to explore how resources interact to create a sustainable competitive advantage.

The article is structured as follows. First, previous research is revised to summarize the state-of-the-art; then we describe our assumptions and methodology, paying particular attention to the definition of the variables. After discussing our results, we offer our main conclusions and suggestions for future research.

BACKGROUND

The evaluation of IT investments has been a common topic for researchers and practitioners since the eighties. IT assets were expected to increase productivity, as the steam engine and electricity had done in the past (David, 1989). However, many researchers concluded that financial improvements were marginal, or even non-inexistent (Morrison & Berndt, 1990; Strassman, 1990; Noyelle, 1990; Bakos, 1991; Siegel & Griliches, 1991; Roach, 1991; Osterman, 1991; Brynjolfsson & Hitt, 1993; Loveman, 1994).

Many hypothesis were suggested to explain this results. Most of them emphasized that IT are just enabling resources, and the need to introduce additional changes in organizational structures and business processes. Drawing on this idea, the contingency approach proposes that the outcomes of IT investments depend on context factors, i.e., they are not automatic nor systematic.

Recent research has found evidence of effects on firm value, shareholders' wealth (dos Santos, Peffers, & Mauer, 1993; Im, Dow & Grover, 2001; Bharadwaj, Bharadwaj, & Konsynski, 1999), production, sales, profitability, and value added (Weill, 1992; Brynjolfsson & Hitt, 1993; Brynjolfsson & Hitt, 1996; Lehr & Lichtenberg, 1998; Kudyba & Diwan, 2002; Pereira, 2003). IT also enables new structural designs and business models (Drucker, 1988; Osterman, 1991; Phan, 2003; Gratzer & Winiwarter, 2003; Gharavi, Love & Cheng, 2004; Bourlakis & Bourlakis, 2006), helps to mitigate operational and financial risks (Bharadwaj et al., 1999; Otim, Dow, Grover & Wong, 2012), and leverages intangible assets (Itami & Roehl, 1991; Nonaka & Takeuchi, 1995).

Recently, some new experimental designs have been put forward. *Event studies* explore the behaviour of stock prices when relevant news on IT investments are disseminated (dos Santos et al., 1993; Bharadwaj et al., 1999; Dehning, Richardson & Stratopoulos, 2005; Otim et al., 2012). Tobin's q has also been used to jointly assess the expected cash flows, the timing of investment (current vs. future investment) and the amount of funding (Tam, 1998; Bharadwaj et al., 1999). These models assume that prices are the best indicator of the value of the shares and the company, hence they assume the efficient market hypothesis (EMH) to be true. Prices are appealing because they summarize the expected cash flows of current assets and the planned investments, hence real options can be considered; however, as EMH is imperfect (Fama & French, 1988; Poterba & Summers, 1988; Peters, 1991; Mandelbrot & Hudson, 2004), model risk must be considered.

Overall, research findings are more haphazard than expected. For example, Weill (1992) noted that transactional investments substantially changed the performance of manufacturing activities, while strategic projects were generally neutral in the short term. R&D expenses (Boulding & Staelin, 1990; Jacobson, 1990; Bharadwaj et al., 1999; Mao & Palvia, 2008; Holsapple & Wu, 2011) and innovative investments (Chatterjee et al., 2001; Wang et al., 2012) increased firms' value by adding real options (Fichman, 2004); however, the value of these opportunities were firm-dependant (Dos Santos et al., 1993; Im et al., 2001; Fargher & Weigand, 1998).

The available evidence suggests that the impact of IT on the value of the company is highly contingent (Dos Santos et al., 1993; Im et al., 2001; Quan, Hu, & Hart, 2003). Researchers descry a complex underlying financial dynamic with time lags, cumulative effects (Cron & Sobol, 1983; Kudyba & Diwan, 2002), synergistic interactions, and moderating factors: business processes (Dehning & Richardson, 2002; Melville, Kraemer, & Gurbaxani, 2004), knowledge (Sambamurthy, Bharadwaj, & Grover, 2003), IT management skills, previous experience with IT (Damanpour & Ewan, 1984; Mingfan & Ye, 1999; Brynjolfsson, Hitt, & Yang, 2002; Neirotti & Paolucci, 2012), organizational capabilities (Nevo & Wade, 2010; Ravinchandran

& Lertwongsatien, 2005), dynamic capabilities (Lee, Barua & Whinston, 1997) and financial capacity (Cron & Sobol, 1983; Harris & Kaatz, 1989, Dehning et al., 2005).

The synergistic hypothesis argues that companies cannot fully capture the profits from their IT investments unless they count with certain intangible resources and complementary skills (Brynjolfsson et al., 2002; Pereira, 2003; Bhatt, Emdad, Roberts, & Grover, 2010, Holsapple & Wu, 2011). Since technology and resources are imitable (Barney, 1991; Carr, 2003), the heterogeneous diffusion (Peteraf, 1993) observed in the competitive impact is explained by the presence (or absence) of invisible resources (Mata et al., 1995), namely the capabilities required to use them effectively (Mingfang & Ye, 1999). The resource-based view (Barney, 1991; Mahoney & Pandian, 1992; Amit & Schoemaker, 1993; Peteraf, 1993; Lado & Wilson, 1994), provides a sound theoretical basis to explore the influence of IT on the competitiveness of the firms (Bharadwaj, 2000; Olson, 2006; Mao & Palvia, 2008; Melville et al., 2004; Ravinchandran & Lertwongsatien, 2005; Gu & Hung, 2013).

Synergies must be considered within the resource-based view of the firm (RBV). According to the RBV, the firm is a bundle of heterogeneous resources, i.e., assets and capabilities (Barney, 1991). Capabilities are skills developed over time, that allow to coordinate and effectively exploit the available resources (Prahalad & Hamel, 1990; Amit & Shoemaker, 1993; Wade & Hulland, 2004); some relevant capabilities are management quality (Souder & Jenssen, 1999), the ability to manage complex contractual structure of the company (Grover & Kohli, 2012), and dynamic capabilities (Teece, Pisano & Shuen, 1997; Newman, 2000; Helfat & Raubitscek, 2000)]. From this point of view, the competitive heterogeneity of companies would be explained by the rigidities of its resources (Barney, 1991; Mahoney & Pandian, 1992, Carroll, 1993; Peteraf, 1993; Rumelt, 1991; Dierickx & Cool, 1989).

The RBV has been extensively used to put together the results of the research on competitive advantage. In what concerns to our work, the RBV predicts that the differences in competitive performance can be explained by the resources that companies have (or can access), and by the effect of some unidentified moderating factors.

The focus of our work are IT-based resources, and the moderating effect of financial conditions. Our aim is to clarify whether the availability of IT assets and capabilities significantly modifies the risk a company goes bankrupt, and whether the availability of those resources is moderated by the financial situation of the firm

MAIN FOCUS OF THE CHAPTER

The advances in information systems theory have been made in parallel with the progress that financial theory has made to improve the prediction of financial failure. Researchers have devoted effort to develop a more comprehensive view of the causes and drivers of financial distress, discovering new links with financial decisions (e.g. leverage; Modigliani & Miller, 1958, 1963), shareholders' wealth and corporate value (Baxter, 1967; Altman, 1969; Gordon, 1971, Scott, 1977). Sound and reliable forecasting models were developed to measure the risk a company goes bankrupt (Altman, 1968, 1977, 2000). A new concept was coined (the *risk of ruin*) to support the view of bankruptcy as the final stage of an ongoing degradation of financial performance (Dambolena & Khoury, 1980). Failure has a time-structure (Hing-Ling, 1987) and is driven by previous firm's decisions. Currently, researchers are trying to build a comprehensive picture of financial distress by combining several elements from financial and organization theory, e.g. management quality (Rose et al., 1982; Lajili & Zéghal, 2011), external audit (Kahl, 2002; Piñeiro et al., 2012), market risk premium (Merton, 1974; Longstaff & Schwartz, 1995; Collin-Dufresne & Goldstein, 2001; Bakshi et al., 2006), accruals and financial manipulation (Lennox, 2000; Arnedo, Lizarraga & Sánchez, 2008) and real options (Hotchkiss & Mooradian, 1997; Kahl, 2002).

Issues, Controversies, Problems

Overall, researchers agree that financial failure is a complex process driven (and moderated) by operational facts (e.g., sales and profitability) and context factors (e.g. management abilities, flexibility and market responsiveness). As enabling resources, IT resources allow firms to develop agile business processes, to collect and analyse market data, to coordinate asynchronous/disperse activities, to enhance information flows, to build intangibles (e.,g. reputation and customer loyalty), etc. However, as we stated earlier, these effects are unclear and mostly contingent on other factors.

We suggest a conceptual model linking the risk of bankruptcy to several IT-based resources, and considering the moderating effect of financial conditions (Figure 1). Our research hypothesis are the following:

Hypothesis One. The availability of IT resources is not related to the financial situation of the company. Most IT assets - equipment, network infrastructure, etc. – are accessible and cheap, and can be viewed as a tactical need - essential means to perform business operations -. Therefore they are expected to be substantially similar in all companies, regardless of their financial situation.

Hypothesis Two. The availability of IT resources (considered in insolation from each other) does not substantially modify the financial risk of the firm. Competitive advantages arise from cost savings (Mukhopadhyay, Kekre, & Kalathur, 1995), innovation, and network economies driven by the combination of complementary assets and capabilities (Nevo & Wade, 2010; Muhanna &

Stoel, 2010). Recent empirical evidence suggest that capabilities help explain the value of the firms, and are unbiased predictors of future cash flows (dos Santos et al., 1993; Bharadwaj, 2000; Gu & Hung, 2013; Wade & Hulland, 2004). Management quality, IT skills and online information capabilities (OIC) (Barua, Konana & Whinston, 2004) are potential sources of competitive advantage because they are embedded in corporate culture (Barney, 1991) and / or are subject to path dependencies (Dierickx & Cool, 1989), so they cannot be transferred nor imitated (Mata, Fuerst & Barney, 1995). Flexibility and organizational features are also relevant (Eisenhardt & Martin, 2000; Teece et al., 1997; Hameed, Counsell, & Swift, 2012) emphasize the importance of a favourable organizational context.

Hypothesis Three. Flexible IT resources are negatively correlated with financial risk. The core of the strategy is the ability to manage activities along the value chain (Porter, 1999). Available resources should support operations, learning processes, and innovation; they should also be cohesive and flexible (Clemons & Row, 1991; Li, 1995; Melville et al., 2004; Bhatt et al., 2010; Grover & Kohli, 2012; Prasad, Green & Heales, 2013).

Several features can be considered as external signs of flexibility: decentralization and autonomy (Sprague, 1980; Gul & Chia, 1994; Choe, 1998; Chang et al., 2003), scalability (Guinard et al., 2011), relational capital (Bhatt et al., 2010), and teamwork (Garfield & Dennis, 2012). In this context IT plays three roles: first, they must provide effective means for communication, sharing of information and knowledge, generation of ideas, integrating judgments by means of decision models, and the remaining tasks concerning teamwork and virtual teams; this is the field of work of group decision support systems (GDSS). Secondly, it promotes group performance, offering appropriate decision routines (Garfield & Dennis, 2012). Finally, IT facilitates (and simultaneously induces) changes in the structure and processes of the organization, to improve the fit between resources and strategy, provide flexibility to the structure, and create synergistic value (Milgrom & Roberts, 1995).

Delegation and autonomy increase firm's flexibility (Milgrom & Roberts, 1995), but they are also support the development of mental models and knowledge transfer (Jarvenpaa & Ives, 1991; Chang et al., 2003). Previous works report a positive relationship between decentralization and financial performance (Leifer, 1988; Zeffane, 1992; Jordan, 1994; Rai, Patnayakuni & Patnayakuni, 1997). Software is also a key enabler for flexibility (Schwarz & Takhteyev, 2010; Campbell-Kelly & Garcia-Swartz, 2012).

Hypothesis Four. The intensity of use of the Internet is inversely associated with financial risk.

Figure 1. IT resources and financial risk: a conceptual model

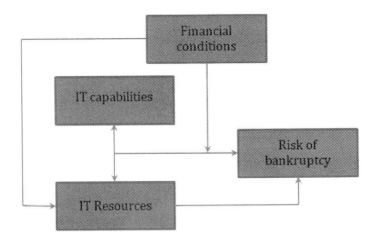

Digitization has been associated with higher levels of competitiveness and higher odds of surviving as a going concern (Phan, 2003; Bhatt et al., 2010; Chang, Chang, & Paper, 2003; Poon & Swatman, 1995; Teo & Pian, 2003). The Internet technology plays a key role in both operations and competitive effort, because it allows channelling large amounts of rich information (Daft & Lengel, 1986; Daft, Lengel, & Trevino, 1987). The Net-enabled business transformation (Straub & Watson, 2001) involves radical changes in internal processes and its relationships with the environment (Bourlakis & Bourlakis, 2006; Choy, Lau, Kwok, & Stuart, 2007; Gharavi et al., 2004). At the same time, digitization may cause the development of relevant intermediate resources (Amit & Shoemaker, 1993), such as online information capabilities (OIC) (Barua et al., 2004).

However, as basic internet technology is cheap and accessible, the contribution of value would be given by the development of unique and non-replicable business applications (Kim, Ow, & Jun, 2008). To do that, firms need to leverage internal skills and raise barriers against imitation, e.g. embeddedness, path dependency, or intangibles. For example, the use of Internet technology in customer relationship tends to strengthen firm's reputation (Alba et al., 2010; Chatterjee, Grewal, & Sambamurthy, 2002).

Solutions and Recommendations

We explore these hypothesis using the data collected from a random sample of Spanish SMEs (private companies with less than 250 employees); we initially

Financial Risk and Financial Imbalances

Table 1. Population and sample, per industry

	Population	Initial sample	Final sample
Agric. & fishing	3.0%	3.0%	1.9%
Extractive & building	18.7%	18.6%	20.0%
Industry	18.2%	18.4%	21.9%
Commerce	40.3%	40.3%	38.1%
Services	19.8%	19.7%	18.1%
	100.0%	100.0%	100.0%

selected 370 firms but only 105 cases were valid for our study – many of them refused to participate, because they felt that IT investments were strictly confidential –; answer rate (28%) is similar to that reported by previous studies on SMEs, e.g. Teo & Pian (2003). The overall composition of the final sample is representative of the population of interest (Table 1).

Financial data was obtained from public records, and IT resources were identified through questionnaires and personal interviews with CEOs and CIOs.

Our dependent variable is binary. It equals one if the company has filed for bankruptcy, and zero otherwise. Independent variables are grouped into two categories: financial measures, and IT resources.

A logistic regression (logit) is fitted to assess our hypothesis. The logit model allows linking a binary variable (healthy vs. bankruptcy) with scale and categorical variables; unlike other methodologies, multivariate normal distribution is not required. The model to estimate is

$$p = P(Y_j = 1) = \frac{1}{1 + e^{-[\beta_o + \beta_1 \cdot X_2 + \beta_2 \cdot X_{2j} + ... + \beta m - X_{nj}]}}$$

where Y_j is a binary variable that expresses the financial situation of the company J (healthy vs. bankrupt); X_{hj} is the value of the attribute h, and the vector $X_j = \{X_{1j}, X_{2J} ... X_{nj}\}$ expresses the IT profile of the company.

Table 2. Percentage of failed companies, per industry

	Agric & fishing	Extractive & building	Industry	Commerce	Services	Sample
No. companies	2	21	23	40	19	105
% bankrupted	50%	24%	30%	33%	16%	27.6%

Independent variables (Table 3) were designed considering previous works, and the transversal structure of our work - variables must make sense in any organization and industry (Poon & Swatman, 1995) -. We considered IT infrastructure (equipment and software), human assets (management skills, IT experience), IT-based applications (CRM, MRP, DSS, etc.) and organizational attributes (e.g., flexibility, decentralization).

Several financial measures have been considered, bearing in mind previous research on financial distress and bankruptcy: size (assets, equity funds), leverage, liquidity, profitability, and volatility (as measured by the standard deviation of Earnings before Interests and Taxes, EBIT). R&D expenses were not been considered because most of the sampled firms SMEs issued simplified financial statements, and these charges are not detailed.

The financial situation is expected to affect both financial risk and the availability of IT resources (Helfat & Raubitscek, 2000; Teece & Pisano, 1994). Some IT resources might be more accessible for healthy business, if they are expensive and/or require additional enablers (e.g. skills or a specific corporate structure). Hence, financial situation may be considered a confounding factor (Xiang, 1993). To control for confounding factors, interactions are included along with the independent variables (Riegelmen, 2005; Anderson et al., 2009); this also guarantees that estimates of the main effects are unbiased.

Results

27.6% of companies surveyed went bankrupt between 2003 and 2012. Financial theory explains that these events were driven by long-lasting imbalances, and predicts that failed firms will share some common financial attributes, e.g. high leverage and weak ability to generate cash flows. The RBV also predicts that distressed firms lack some critical resources, and/or have been unable to develop the synergies needed to face competitive challenges.

Before considering whether IT resources are or not a relevant explanation for business failure, it is necessary to clarify whether the availability of IT assets and capabilities is moderated by the financial conditions of the firm. A preliminary analysis (Table 4 and Table 5) suggests that the availability of basic IT resources is essentially homogeneous, despite the financial situation of the firms; this finding is not unexpected, as IT assets are cheap and affordable. However, healthy companies have been using IT resources for longer periods (i.e., they can be viewed as pioneers); their internal infrastructure is more decentralized, runs commercial software and is tightly linked to the environment through several Internet services. Some evidences also suggest that they owe more sophisticated management skills and more flexible business processes.

Financial Risk and Financial Imbalances

Table 3. Independent variables

Variable	Meaning		Content
assts	Book value of assets	Continuous	Financial situation
shfnd	Book value of the firm		
levg	Leverage		
liq	Liquidity		
roa	Return on Assets		
indus	Industry	Categorical (5)	
nsha	Number of shareholders	Continuous	Management quality
age	Age		Management experience and skills; environmental responsiveness
lan	Local area network	Binary	Enabling resources: manage the information resources; flexibility, channelling information, business-environment links
term	Intelligent / dumb terminals		
decen	Decentralization	Categorical (4)	
int	Internet access	Binary	
email	e-mail		
sw	Source of software	Categorical (4)	Capabilities: flexibility; malleability; innovation
auton	Distribution / delegation		
group	Group and/or collaborative practices	Binary	Capabilities: transferring and sharing knowledge, building a shared view of the business; coordination
grper	Permanent, stable, teams		
exptic	Time from 1st relevant IT investment	Continuous	Abilities: experience, management skills, ability to perceive opportunities, ability to deploy effective IT projects
exptic/age	Ratio of IT experience to age		
imptic	Importance of IT for business	Categorical (4)	
impint	Degree of Internet use		
intad	Using the internet to disseminate business information	Binary	Internal capabilities: market responsiveness, sensitivity to innovation opportunities, ability to rearrange the resources
b2c	B2C activities		
b2b	B2B (EDI / e-marketplaces)		
risk	Financial risk (standard deviation of net income)	Continuous	Technical uncertainty

Besides that, bankrupt companies are smaller and younger, and more indebted (LEVG); they have a relatively small number of different shareholders (NSHA), and they underperform in terms of profitability (ROA). Although they are in line

Table 4. Chi-square tests of equality of means for categorical variables: bankruptcy x independent variable

Variable	χ^2	α	Variable	χ^2	α
indus	2.552	0.635	int	0.042	0.505
auton	4.3	0.03*	impint	8.074	0.003**
group	6.818	0.011*	lan	0.391	0.347
grper	0.353	0.354	term	0.107	0.482
b2c	0.403	0.423	decen	12.39	0.000**
b2b	0.76	0.266	email	0.225	0.4
intad	0.598	0.309	sw	13.221	0.001**

** Significant at p£0,01; * significant at p£0,05

with the literature on financial distress, these results stress the need to control for confounding effects.

To explore whether financial situation and/or industry can be a source of confusion, we performed a Mantel-Haenszel test (Table 6). Overall, we do not find evidence to refuse our hypothesis (H1) that the availability of IT resources is essentially homogeneous, whatever the financial situation of the firm is. Weak significance was found for with assets, leverage, and shareholders' funds; however, aside from

Table 5. Welch's t-tests of equality of means for continuous variables

	Average		Standard deviation		Welch	Sig.
	Healthy	Bankrupt	Healthy	Bankrupt		
nsha	4.58	1.14	11.95	1.85	5.93	0.017*
age	27.36	20.87	16.16	8.97	6.78	0.011*
assts	40047.30	9926.88	163675.58	17624.23	2.50	0.118
shfnd	14858.23	2180.82	47301.97	3471.01	5.38	0.023*
emply	104.08	28.20	281.22	24.55	5.42	0.022*
levg	58.45	77.09	20.74	18.92	19.30	0.000**
liq	3.86	1.34	11.84	0.52	3.42	0.068
roa	7.17	1.96	7.67	9.25	7.31	0.010*
risk	5262.04	425.24	22391.10	889.77	3.53	0.064
exptic	19.58	17.10	6.66	4.85	4.40	0.040*
exptic/age	0.81	0.87	0.23	0.17	1.92	0.171

(financial magnitudes in thousand Euros)
** Significant at p£0,01; * significant at p£0,05

Financial Risk and Financial Imbalances

Table 6. *Significant interactions between financials and IT resources*

Financial	IT resource		Mantel-Haenszel	Sig.
Asset (ASSTS)	Teamwork	group	5.961	0.015
	Importance of IT	imptic	4.862	0.027
	Software	sw	11.757	0.001**
Leverage (LEVG)	Autonomy	auton	3.243	0.072
	Teamwork	group	8.732	0.003**
	Importance of IT	imptic	6.914	0.009**
	Importance of the NET	impint	4.187	0.041
	Decentralization	decen	8.563	0.003**
	Software	sw	9.533	0.02
Equity Capital (SHFND)	Autonomy	auton	3.081	0.079
	Teamwork	group	5.975	0.015
	Importance of IT	imptic	2.998	0.083
	Importance of the NET	impint	3.901	0.048
	Decentralization	decen	9.463	0.002**
Activity (INDUS)	Importance of IT	imptic	3.047	0.081
	Importance of internet	impint	5.745	0.017
	Decentralization	decen	9.288	0.002**
	Software	sw	9.608	0.002**

** Significant at $p \leq 0.01$ (non-significant interactions omitted for brevity)

being statistically weak, these relationships appear to be financially inconsistent. For example, the stratified analysis suggests that debt and centralization are associated; to our knowledge, there is no financial and/or organizational reason to support such statement. In fact, a decentralized structure can be developed with standard, affordable and accessible resources: it is difficult to argue that centralization is the result of financial constraints. In our opinion, it is more reasonable to consider centralization, the passive use of the Internet, the absence of collaborative strategies, etc. as an outcome of a more conservative corporate culture, focused on control and maybe reluctant to create space for creativity and innovation. Similarly, as far as we know, there are no reasons to relate the industry to the type of software or the level of decentralization; however, it is possible that ICT and Internet have different operational and strategic importance in different sectors. To rule out any uncontrolled effect, interaction terms were considered when fitting the logit model (Riegelmen, 2005; Anderson et al., 2009).

Table 8. Hit rate

		Predicted Status		hit rate
		Healthy	Bankrupt	
True Status	Healthy	73	3	96.05%
	Bankrupt	4	25	86.21%
		Average		93.33%

The logit model was fitted using stepwise regression, to guarantee parsimony without compromising statistical significance; confusion was controlled by testing the significance of the interactions listed in Table 6 (Riegelmen, 2005). The model fitting is satisfactory (Nagelkerke's $R^2 = 0,741$; Hosmer and Lemeshow test suggests no evidence of lack of fit: $\grave{A}^2 = 2.516$; $\alpha^* = 0.961$), and 93.3% of companies are correctly classified (Table 8.)

Five main effects and an interaction are found to be significant (Table 7). The coefficients on independent variables take on the expected signs (positive for leverage, and negative for variables indicating the availability of resources and / or capabilities). The remaining variables do not help explain financial distress; hence, our hypothesis H2 that the availability of *individual* IT resources does not modify firm's risk, was supported. In particular, financial variables (except indebtedness) and their interactions with IT resources and capabilities were not significant: financial imbalances (low profitability, indebtedness, shortage of cash flow, etc.) are the outward expression of underlying strategic and competitive anomalies, e.g. investment policy, R&D, and internal skills (Argenti, 1976).

Table 7. Estimates of the logit model

	B	σ	Wald	df	Sig.	e^B	C.I. 95% for e^B	
							Low	High
levg	0.093	0.028	11.060	1	0.001	1.098	1.039	1.160
age	-0.148	0.052	8.095	1	0.004	0.862	0.778	0.955
decen	-1.751	0.836	4.389	1	0.036	0.174	0.034	0.893
imptic	-3.029	1.181	6.576	1	0.010	0.048	0.005	0.490
intad	2.516	1.044	5.803	1	0.016	12.374	1.598	95.803
exptic/age x sw	-5.015	1.350	13.805	1	0.000	0.007	0.000	0.094
exptic/age	-4.617	1.501	9.465	1	0.002	0.010	0.001	0.187
Intercept	1.222	2.174	0.316	1	0.574	3.394		

Decentralization of IT resources (DECEN) has, as expected, a negative influence on firm's risk (B = 1.751 and $e^{-1.751} = 0.174 < 0$). Higher levels of decentralization correspond to lower risk, and vice versa. Ceteris paribus, the adoption of flexible, decentralized configurations (DECEN = 1 vs. DECEN = 0) reduces the odds of bankruptcy by 82%.

Previous works suggest that decentralization and the use of commercial software are associated with higher levels of flexibility. For example Rai et al. (1997) found a positive relationship between investment in client-server systems, the ROA and productivity. Proprietary software is less flexible because implies high development and switching costs, but it may be suitable for core activities (Campbell-Kelly & Garcia-Swartz, 2012). On the contrary, Schwarz & Takhteyev (2010) point out the economic advantages of using commercial software. Our results suggest that the use of commercial software may lead to a risk mitigation, if specific IT skills are also present. This combination is associated with a sharp reduction in financial risk, (B = 5.015 and $e^{-5.015} = 0.007$). These results are also in line with our hypothesis No. 3 that flexible IT resources are negatively correlated with financial risk.

IMPTIC is found to be significant at 1% level. As noted earlier, this variable expresses the importance of IT resources to perform the operations and deploy the strategy, as measured by guided interview responses. The estimate has the expected negative sign, indicating that high assimilation levels are associated with a lower financial risk, in average. It might be inferred that these firms have leveraged their IT resources to meet their operational needs and strategic challenges. However, managers' view of the business value of their IT resources may also be an ex-post judgement – satisfied managers are expected to express a more positive and optimistic view of the contribution of their IT resources -. In wide terms, IMPTIC expresses the ability of the company to design an IT aligned, efficient and effective IT infrastructure to handle opportunities and challenges. Companies that have achieved this goal have lower risk levels, compared to those with lower degrees of digitization (Barua et al., 2004). On average, their odds of *surviving* are $1 / 0.048 = 20.8$ times higher. These results strongly support our hypothesis No. 4 that the intensity of use of the Internet is inversely associated with financial risk.

We have found that management expertise exerts a strong effect on firm's financial risk. EXPTIC / AGE measures the technological skills of the firm, once adjusted for age. We assume that firms and individuals acquire experience and skills by the operations route (Itami & Roehl, 1991), i.e. *learning by doing* (Brynjolfsson & Hitt, 1993). The estimate has the expected negative sign and $e^B = 0.0099$ indicates that each additional year of IT skills accumulation dramatically reduces a firm's risk of going bankrupt. Although striking, this finding emphasizes the importance of the cultural factors that make learning, collaboration, and innovation effort possible. The critical issue is not just "developing R&D", but being able to keep ahead of the market and systematically explore new opportunities. The explosive growth of social networks has driven dramatic changes in the relations with the environment; we feel it is a clear example of how quickly changes may occur.

The empirical evidence strongly support this hypothesis. Pioneering companies – those who made their first relevant IT investments in the seventies - have nowadays more decentralized information systems, and make an intensive use of the Internet technology to channel corporate information and/or support the operations; from a financial point of view, most of them are healthy firms. Many younger companies have not been able to catch up with the pioneers, although they are expected to be more flexible. The lack of internal skills appears to be decisive. As Cron & Sobol (1983) reported, the adoption of IT seems to strengthen the initial competitive advantage (or disadvantage) of each company.

The age of the firm may be seen as a proxy for general management abilities. This variable is found to be significant at 1% level, although the effect on financial risk is just moderate: each additional year of life reduces the risk of failure about 13%.

Leverage (LEVG) has an estimated effect of 0.093; therefore, if a company increased its leverage from 1 to 2, the average risk of failure would be increased by $e^{0.093} = 9.8\%$. As a matter of fact, financial distress is caused by an inability to meet payments; hence, LEVG must be significant. Let us note that financial variables are intentionally present in our model to control for financial situation and assure that the remaining estimates are unbiased.

We haven't found evidence that e-commerce activities have any relevant effect on firm's financial risk. Several previous studies (e.g. Barua et al., 2004; Teo & Pian, 2003) reported that the adoption of the Internet modifies firms' competitiveness. Our results indicate that healthy and bankrupt companies have made similar decisions regarding their presence on the Internet, e.g. B2B/B2C projects and social networks. There is no evidence that healthy companies have been pioneers in the development of e-business models. Nor have we found signs that distressed companies (affected by more severe financial constraints) had systematically rejected these projects. However, it must be noted that Spanish firms began to use the Internet in the first nineties; digitization began somewhat later than in other countries. In 2003, 30% of Spanish firms were making EDI on value-added networks, but only 47% had Internet access and only 5% were performing B2B. Apparently, online skills (Barua et al., 2004) were still imperfect and/or market opportunities were unclear. Finally, it must be noted that successful companies have an incentive to be discreet and preserve the confidentiality of their projects (Teo & Pian, 1003); on the contrary, those firms whose projects failed have an incentive to hide their weakness.

In any case, these findings do not mean that investments in Internet technology have been neutral. These resources can drive several tangible profits, e.g. as time and cost efficiencies (Rai et al., 1997) and improvements in productivity, EBITDA,

Figure 2. Summary of hypotheses and results

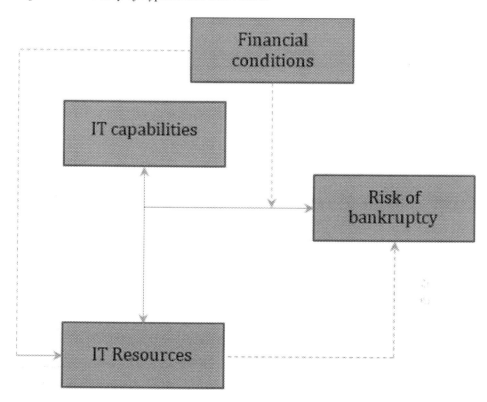

intangible value, and working capital. We have not find evidence that distressed firms had followed a risk-seeking strategy, as we could infer from the *Prospect theory* (Kahneman & Tversky, 1979). Underperformers may be forced to accept risky projects to increase the likelihood of achieving their financial goals (Fiegenbaum & Thomas, 1988; Lehner, 2000) and/or catching up with rivals. However, as we noted earlier, healthy and distressed firms have followed a similar investment pattern.

FUTURE RESEARCH DIRECTIONS

The use of bankruptcy as dependent variable enriches the strategic approach, and allows to establish logical connections with the financial literature on financial bankruptcy. It provides a novel experimental design based on long-term observation and it allows to consider the time lags reported by the literature on IT. However, as with any research, a number of limitations must be considered. Our experimental design requires a large volume of detailed information, and a close collaboration with companies. This reduces the sample size and makes it extremely difficult the use of pairing strategies. It should be recalled that the RBV implicitly assumes that the company is optimizing the use of each and every one of its resources and capabilities. These are extremely restrictive conditions, especially if organizational changes are required, and/or competencies are generated over long periods of time. We feel that our understanding of the role of *time* in bankruptcy is still incomplete; future research might explore the temporal dynamics of IT investment, and the relationship with the average life of companies.

It would also be useful to extend the study to collaborative IT investments, i.e. investments made by companies to manage partnerships and contractual relationships with other organizations. These relationships have been studied from different points of view (i.e. cost savings, the impact on competitiveness, etc.) but to our knowledge, research has never dealt with its possible influence on the bankruptcy, either as cause or as a moderator of the risk.

CONCLUSION

Our work explores whether IT resources exert a measurable influence on firm's financial risk. Globally, the results support the hypothesis that the lack of IT assets and/or the absence of the required capabilities may erode competitiveness and exert a quantifiable influence on failure risk assessment. Neither the financial situation of the firm nor the industry in which the firm operates significantly modify these influence: the observed heterogeneity of IT resources can be explained by the specific operational and/or strategic requirements of each sector.

Flexibility - the ability to rearrange electronic linkages, business processes, and the assignment of tasks within the firm – is a key determinant of the business value of IT. Empirical evidence suggests that flexibility is driven by both organizational and logical attributes: decentralization is found to increase malleability, and so does the use of commercial software when complementary IT skills are also present. Apparently, standard software allows developing customized information structures in an efficient manner, but specific IT management skills are required to deliver successful projects.

Our results highlight the critical importance of internal capabilities, particularly experience and management skills. We believe that synergistic effects between resources and capabilities are complex and bidirectional: some capabilities are an *ex ante* requirement for deploying effective IT investments; however, skills are also built by *active learning*, i.e., they are an outcome of the operations route.

Previous positive (negative) experience increases (reduces) the probability that a company will be involved in an uncertain investment project. Some evidences also suggest that financially distressed companies follow a *risk-seeking* behaviour. Healthy firms usually have higher financial capacity, more internal expertise and more sophisticated management abilities; on the contrary, distressed firms usually are limited by more severe financial restrictions, they are impelled to prioritize the allocation of their resources and their R&D budget is usually smaller. However, the prevalence of e-commerce projects and e-marketing activities is essentially similar in both healthy and failed firms. Perhaps healthy firms have behaved more conservatively, but alternative hypothesis must be also considered. In particular, the prospect theory predicts that distressed firms could implement more aggressive survival strategies, which could involve the acceptance of riskier projects.

REFERENCES

Alba, J., Lynch, J., Weitz, B., Janiszewski, C., Lutz, C., & Swyer, A. (2010). Interactive home shopping: Consumer, retailer, and manufacturer incentives to participate in electronic marketplaces. *Journal of Marketing, 61*(3), 38–53. doi:10.1177/002224299706100303

Altman, E. (1968). Financial Ratios, Discriminant Analysis and Prediction of Corporate Bankruptcy. *The Journal of Finance, 23*(4), 589–609. doi:10.1111/j.1540-6261.1968.tb00843.x

Altman, E. (1969). Corporate bankruptcy potential, stockholder returns, and share valuation. *The Journal of Finance, 24*(5), 887–904. doi:10.1111/j.1540-6261.1969.tb01700.x

Altman, E. (1977, Oct.). Some estimates of the cost of lending errors for commercial banks. *Journal of Commercial Bank Lending*.

Altman, E. I. (2000). *Predicting Financial Distress of Companies: Revisiting the Z-Score and ZETA© Models*. NYU Salomon Center.

Altman, E. I., Haldeman, R. C., & Narayanan, P. (1977). ZETA Analysis. A New Model to Identify Bankruptcy Risk Corporations. *Journal of Banking & Finance, 1*(June), 29–54. doi:10.1016/0378-4266(77)90017-6

Amit, R., & Shoemaker, P. (1993). Strategic Assets and Organizational Rent. *Strategic Management Journal, 14*(1), 33–46. doi:10.1002mj.4250140105

Anderson, S. R., Auquier, A., Hauck, W. W., Oakes, D., Vandaele, W., & Weisberg, H. I. (2009). *Statistical Methods for Comparative Studies: Techniques for Bias Reduction*. New York: Wiley.

Argenti, J. (1976). *Corporate Collapse: The Causes and Symptoms*. London: McGraw – Hill.

Arnedo, L., Lizarraga, F., & Sánchez, S. (2008). Going-concern Uncertainties in Prebankrupt Audit Reports: New Evidence Regarding Discretionary Accruals and Wording Ambiguity. *International Journal of Auditing, 12*(1), 25–44. doi:10.1111/j.1099-1123.2008.00368.x

Bakos, Y. (1991). A strategic analysis of electronic marketplaces. *Management Information Systems Quarterly, 15*(3), 295–312. doi:10.2307/249641

Bakshi, G., Madan, D., & Xiaoling, F. (2006). Investigating the role of systematic and firm-specific factors indefault risk: Lessons from empirically evaluating credit risk models. *The Journal of Business, 79*(4), 1955–1987. doi:10.1086/503653

Barney, J. (1991). Firm resources and sustained competitive advantage. *Journal of Management, 17*(1), 99–120. doi:10.1177/014920639101700108

Barua, A., Konana, P., Whinston, A., & Yin, F. (2004). An empirical investigation of the Net-enabled business value. *Management Information Systems Quarterly, 28*(4), 585–620. doi:10.2307/25148656

Baxter, N. (1967). Leverage, risk of ruin, and the cost of capital. *The Journal of Finance, 22*, 395–404.

Bharadwaj, A., Bharadwaj, S., & Konsynski, B. (1999). Information Technology Effects on Firm Performance as Measured by Tobin's q. *Management Science, 45*(7), 1008–1024. doi:10.1287/mnsc.45.7.1008

Bharadwaj, A. S. (2000). A resource-based perspective on information technology capability and firm performance: An empirical investigation. *Management Information Systems Quarterly, 24*(1), 169–196. doi:10.2307/3250983

Bhatt, G., Emdad, A., Roberts, N., & Grover, V. (2010). Building and leveraging information in dynamic environments: The role of IT infrastructure flexibility as enabler of organizational responsiveness and competitive advantage. *Information & Management, 47*(7–8), 341–349. doi:10.1016/j.im.2010.08.001

Boulding, W., & Staelin, R. (1990). Environment, market share and market power. *Management Science, 36*(10), 1160–1177. doi:10.1287/mnsc.36.10.1160

Bourlakis, M., & Bourlakis, C. (2006). Integrating Logistics and Information Technology Strategies for Sustainable Competitive Advantage. *Journal of Enterprise Information Management, 19*(4), 389–402. doi:10.1108/17410390610678313

Brockett, P., Golden, L., Jang, J., & Yang, C. (2006). A comparison of neural network, statistical methods, and variable choice for life insurers' financial distress prediction. *The Journal of Risk and Insurance, 73*(3), 397–419. doi:10.1111/j.1539-6975.2006.00181.x

Brynjolfsson, E., & Hitt, L. (1993). Is information systems spending productive? New evidence and new results. *International Conference on Information Systems.*

Brynjolfsson, E., & Hitt, L. (1996). Paradox lost? Firm-level evidence on the returns to information systems spending. *Management Science, 42*(4), 541–558. doi:10.1287/mnsc.42.4.541

Brynjolfsson, E., Hitt, L., & Yang, S. (2002). Intangible assets: Computers and organizational capital. *Brookings Papers on Economic Activity, 1*(1), 137–191. doi:10.1353/eca.2002.0003

Campbell-Kelly, M., & Garcia-Swartz, D. (2012). The Move to the Middle: Convergence of the Open-Source and Proprietary Software Industries. *International Journal of the Economics of Business, 17*(2), 223–252. doi:10.1080/13571516.2010.483091

Carr, N. (2003). IT doesn't matter. *Harvard Business Review, 81*, 41–50. PMID:12747161

Carroll, G. R. (1993). A sociological view on why firms differ. *Strategic Management Journal, 14*(4), 237–249. doi:10.1002mj.4250140402

Chang, R., Chang, Y., & Paper, D. (2003). The effect of task uncertainty, decentralization and AIS characteristics on the performance of AIS: An empirical case in Taiwan. *Information & Management, 40*(7), 691–703. doi:10.1016/S0378-7206(02)00097-6

Chatterjee, C., Grewal, R., & Sambamurthy, V. (2002). Shaping Up for e-commerce: Institutional enablers of the organizational assimilation of web technologies. *Management Information Systems Quarterly, 26*(2), 65–89. doi:10.2307/4132321

Chatterjee, D., Richardson, V., & Zmud, R. (2001). Examining the shareholder wealth effects of new CIO position announcements. *Management Information Systems Quarterly, 25*(1), 43–70. doi:10.2307/3250958

Choe, J. M. (1998). The effects of user participation on the design of accounting information systems. *Information & Management, 34*(3), 185–198. doi:10.1016/S0378-7206(98)00055-X

Choy, K., Lau, H., Kwok, S., & Stuart, C. (2007). Using Radio Frequency Identification Technology in Distribution Management: A Case Study on Third-Party Logistics. *International Journal of Manufacturing Technology and Management*, *10*(1), 19–32. doi:10.1504/IJMTM.2007.011399

Clemons, E. K., & Row, M. C. (1991). Sustaining IT advantage: The role of structural differences. *Management Information Systems Quarterly*, *15*(September), 275–292. doi:10.2307/249639

Collin-Dufresne, P., & Goldstein, R. (2001). Do credit spreads reflect stationary leverage? Reconciling structural and reduced-form frameworks. *The Journal of Finance*, *56*(5), 1929–1957. doi:10.1111/0022-1082.00395

Cron, W. I., & Sobol, M. G. (1983). The relationship between computerization and performance: A strategy for maximizing the economic benefits of computerization. *Journal of International Management*, *6*, 171–181.

Daft, R. L., & Lengel, R. H. (1986). Organizational Information Requirements. Media Richness and Structural Design. *Management Science*, *32*(5), 554–571. doi:10.1287/mnsc.32.5.554

Daft, R. L., Lengel, R. H., & Trevino, L. K. (1987). Message Equivocality, Media Selection, and Manager Performance: Implications for Information Systems. *Management Information Systems Quarterly*, *11*(3), 355–366. doi:10.2307/248682

Damanpour, F., & Evan, W. M. (1984). Organizational Innovation and Performance: The Problem of Organizational Lag. *Administrative Science Quarterly*, *29*(3), 392–409. doi:10.2307/2393031

Dambolena, I., & Khoury, S. (1980). Ratio stability and corporate failure. *The Journal of Finance*, *35*(4), 1017–1026. doi:10.1111/j.1540-6261.1980.tb03517.x

David, P. A. (1989). *Computer and dynamo: the modern productivity paradox in a not-too-distant mirror*. Stanford, CA: Center for Economic Policy Research.

Dehning, B., & Richardson, V. (2002). Returns on investments in information technology: A research synthesis. *Journal of Information Systems*, *16*(1), 7–30. doi:10.2308/jis.2002.16.1.7

Dehning, B., Richardson, V., & Stratopoulos, T. (2005). Information technology investments and firm value. *Information & Management*, *42*(7), 989–1008. doi:10.1016/j.im.2004.11.003

Dierickx, I., & Cool, K. (1989). Asset Stock Accumulation and Sustainability of Competitive Advantage. *Management Science, 35*(12), 1504–1511. doi:10.1287/mnsc.35.12.1504

dos Santos, B. L., Peffers, K., & Mauer, D. C. (1993). The impact of information technology investment announcements on the market value of the firm. *Information Systems Research, 4*(1), 1–23. doi:10.1287/isre.4.1.1

Drucker, P. (1988). The Coming of the New Organization. *Harvard Business Review, 66*(1), 3–11.

Eisenhardt, K. M., & Martin, J. (2000). Dynamic Capabilities: What Are They? *Strategic Management Journal, 21*(10-11), 1105–1121. doi:10.1002/1097-0266(200010/11)21:10/11<1105::AID-SMJ133>3.0.CO;2-E

Fama, E., & French, K. R. (1988). Permanent and temporary components of stock prices. *Journal of Political Economy, 96*(2), 246–273. doi:10.1086/261535

Fargher, N. L., & Weigand, R. A. (1998). Changes in the stock price reaction of small firms to common information. *Journal of Financial Research, 21*(1), 105–121.

Fichman, R. (2004). Real Options and IT Platform Adoption: Implications for Theory and Practice. *Information Systems Research, 15*(2), 132–154. doi:10.1287/isre.1040.0021

Fiegenbaum, A., & Thomas, H. (1988). Attitudes Toward Risk and the Risk-Return Paradox: Prospect Theory Explanations. *Academy of Management Journal, 31,* 85–106.

Frydman, H., Altman, E., & Kao, D. (1985). Introducing Recursive Partitioning for Financial Classification: The Case of Financial Distress. *The Journal of Finance, XL*(1), 269–291. doi:10.1111/j.1540-6261.1985.tb04949.x

Garfield, M., & Dennis, A. (2012). Toward an Integrated Model of Group Development: Disruption of Routines by Technology-Induced Change. *Journal of Management Information Systems, 29*(3), 43–86. doi:10.2753/MIS0742-1222290302

Gharavi, H., Love, P., & Cheng, E. (2004). Information and Communication Technology in the Stockbroking Industry: An Evolutionary Approach to the Diffusion of Innovation. *Industrial Management & Data Systems, 104*(9), 756–765. doi:10.1108/02635570410567748

Gordon, M. (1971). Towards a theory of financial distress. *The Journal of Finance, 25*(2), 347–356. doi:10.1111/j.1540-6261.1971.tb00902.x

Gratzer, M., & Winiwarter, W. (2003). A Framework for Competitive Advantage in eTourism. In *Proceedings of the 10th International Conference on Information Technology and Travel and Tourism*. Berlin: Springer-Verlag.

Grover, V., & Kohli, R. (2012). Cocreating IT value: New capabilities and metrics for multiform environments. *Management Information Systems Quarterly, 36*(1), 225–232. doi:10.2307/41410415

Gu, J., & Jung, H. (2013). The effects of IS resources, capabilities, and qualities on organizational performance: An integrated approach. *Information & Management, 50*(2-3), 87–97. doi:10.1016/j.im.2013.02.001

Guinard, F., Trifa, V., Mattern, F., & Wilde, E. (2011). From the Internet of Things to the Web of Things: Resource-oriented Architecture and Best Practices. In D. Uckelmann, M. Harrison, & F. Michahelles (Eds.), *Architecting the Internet of things* (pp. 97–129). New York: Springer – Verlag. doi:10.1007/978-3-642-19157-2_5

Gul, F. A., & Chia, Y. M. (1994). The effect of management accounting systems, perceived environment uncertainty and decentralization on managerial performance: A test of three-way interaction. *Accounting, Organizations and Society, 19*(4), 413–426. doi:10.1016/0361-3682(94)90005-1

Hameed, M., Counsell, S., & Swift, S. (2012). A meta-analysis of relationships between organizational characteristics and IT innovation adoption in organizations. *Information & Management, 49*(5), 218–232. doi:10.1016/j.im.2012.05.002

Harris, S. E., & Kaatz, L. (1989). Predicting organizational performance using information technology managerial control ratios. *Proceedings of the 22nd Hawaiian International Conference on System Science*. 10.1109/HICSS.1989.48122

Helfat, C. E., & Raubitscek, R. S. (2000). Product sequencing: Co-evolution of knowledge, capabilities and products. *Strategic Management Journal, 21*(10-11), 961–979. doi:10.1002/1097-0266(200010/11)21:10/11<961::AID-SMJ132>3.0.CO;2-E

Hing-Ling, A. (1987). A five-state financial distress prediction model. *Journal of Accounting Research, 25*(1), 127–138. doi:10.2307/2491262

Holsapple, C., & Wu, J. (2011). An elusive antecedent of superior firm performance: The knowledge management factor. *Decision Support Systems, 52*(1), 271–283. doi:10.1016/j.dss.2011.08.003

Hotchkiss, E., & Mooradian, R. (1997). Vulture investors and the market for control of distressed firms. *Journal of Financial Economics, 43*(3), 401–432. doi:10.1016/S0304-405X(96)00900-2

Im, K., Dow, V., & Grover, V. (2001). Research Report: A Re-examination of IT Investment and the Market Value of the Firm - An Event Study Methodology. *Information Systems Research, 12*(1), 103–117. doi:10.1287/isre.12.1.103.9718

Itami, I., & Roehl, R. (1991). *Mobilizing Invisible Assets.* Cambridge, MA: Harvard University Press.

Jacobson, R. (1990). What really determines business performance? Unobservable effects – The key to profitability. *Management Science, 9,* 74–85.

Jarvenpaa, S. L., & Ives, B. (1991). Executive involvement and participation in the management of information technology. *Management Information Systems Quarterly, 15*(2), 205–227. doi:10.2307/249382

Jordan, E. (1994). Information strategy and organization structure. *Information Systems Journal, 4*(4), 253–270. doi:10.1111/j.1365-2575.1994.tb00055.x

Kahl, M. (2002). Economic Distress, Financial Distress, and Dynamic Liquidation. *The Journal of Finance, 57*(1), 135–168. doi:10.1111/1540-6261.00418

Kahneman, D., & Tversky, A. (1979). Prospect Theory: An Analysis of Decision Under Risk. *Econometrica, 47*(2), 263–291. doi:10.2307/1914185

Kim, D., Ow, T., & Jun, M. (2008). SME strategies. An assessment of high vs. low performers. *Communications of the ACM, 51*(11), 113–117. doi:10.1145/1400214.1400237

Knight, F. H. (1921). *Risk, uncertainty and profit.* Boston: Houghton Mifflin.

Kudyba, S., & Diwan, R. (2002). Research report: Increasing returns to information technology. *Information Systems Research, 13*(1), 104–111. doi:10.1287/isre.13.1.104.98

Lado, A., & Wilson, M. (1994). Human resource system and sustained competitive advantage: Competency-based perspective. *Academy of Management Review, 19*(4), 699–727. doi:10.5465/amr.1994.9412190216

Lajili, K., & Zéghal, D. (2011). Corporate governance and bankruptcy filing decisions. *Journal of General Management, 35*(4), 3–26. doi:10.1177/030630701003500401

Lee, B., Barua, A., & Whinston, A. (1997). Discovery and representation of causal relationships: A methodological framework. *Management Information Systems Quarterly, 12*(1), 109–136. doi:10.2307/249744

Lehner, J. M. (2000). Shifts of Reference Points for Framing of Strategic Decisions and Changing Risk-Return Associations. *Management Science*, *46*(1), 63–76. doi:10.1287/mnsc.46.1.63.15130

Lehr, W., & Lichtenberg, F. (1998). Computer use and productivity growth in US Federal Government agencies. *The Journal of Industrial Economics*, *XLVI*(2), 257–279. doi:10.1111/1467-6451.00071

Leifer, R. (1988). Matching computer – based information systems with organizational structures. *Management Information Systems Quarterly*, *12*(1), 63–73. doi:10.2307/248805

Lennox, C. (2000). Do companies successfully engage in opinion - shopping? Evidence from the UK. *Journal of Accounting and Economics*, *29*(3), 321–337. doi:10.1016/S0165-4101(00)00025-2

Li, F. (1995). *The Geography of Business Information*. Chichester, UK: John Wiley and Sons.

Longstaff, F., & Schwartz, E. (1995). A simple approach to valuing risky fixed and floating rate debt. *The Journal of Finance*, *50*(3), 789–819. doi:10.1111/j.1540-6261.1995.tb04037.x

Loveman, G. W. (1994). An assessment of the productivity impact on information technologies. In T. J. Allen & M. S. Morton (Eds.), *Information Technology and the Corporation of the 1990s*. Cambridge, MA: Information Technology Press.

Mahoney, J. T., & Pandian, J. R. (1992). The Resource-based View within the Conversation of Strategic Management. *Strategic Management Journal*, *13*(5), 363–380. doi:10.1002mj.4250130505

Mandelbrot, B., & Hudson, R. (2004). *The (mis)behavior of markets. A fractal view of risk, ruin & reward*. New York: Basic Books.

Mao, E., & Palvia, P. (2008). Exploring the effects of direct experience on IT use: An organizational field study. *Information & Management*, *45*(4), 249–256. doi:10.1016/j.im.2008.02.007

Mata, F., Fuerst, W., & Barney, J. (1995). Information technology and sustained competitive advantage: A resource-based analysis. *Management Information Systems Quarterly*, *19*(4), 487–505. doi:10.2307/249630

Melville, N., Kraemer, K., & Gurbaxani, V. (2004). Information Technology and Organizational Performance: An Integrative Model of IT Business Value. *Management Information Systems Quarterly*, *28*(2), 283–322. doi:10.2307/25148636

Merton, R. (1974). On the pricing of corporate debt. The risk structure of interest rates. *The Journal of Finance*, *29*, 449–470.

Milgrom, P., & Roberts, J. (1995). Complementarities and Fit Strategy, structure, and organizational change in manufacturing. *Journal of Accounting and Economics*, *19*(2-3), 179–208. doi:10.1016/0165-4101(94)00382-F

Mingfang, L., & Ye, R. (1999). Information technology and firm performance: Linking with environmental, strategic and managerial contexts. *Information & Management*, *35*(1), 43–51. doi:10.1016/S0378-7206(98)00075-5

Modigliani, F., & Miller, M. (1958). The cost of capital, corporation finance, and the theory of investment. *The American Economic Review*, *48*(3), 261–297.

Modigliani, F., & Miller, M. (1963). Corporate Income Taxes and the Cost of Capital: A correction. *The American Economic Review*, *53*(3), 433–443.

Morrison, C. J., & Berndt, E. R. (1990). *Assessing the productivity of information technology equipment in the US manufacturing industries*. National Bureau of Economic Research Working Paper No. 3.582.

Muhanna, W., & Stoel, M. (2010). How Do Investors Value IT? An Empirical Investigation of the Value Relevance of IT Capability and IT Spending Across Industries. *Journal of Information Systems*, *24*(1), 43–66. doi:10.2308/jis.2010.24.1.43

Mukhopadhyay, T., Kekre, S., & Kalathur, S. (1995). Business Value of Information Technology: A Study of Electronic Data Interchange. *Management Information Systems Quarterly*, *19*(2), 137–156. doi:10.2307/249685

Neirotti, P., & Paolucci, E. (2012). Assessing the importance of industry in the adoption and assimilation of IT: Evidence from Italian enterprises. *Information & Management*, *48*(7), 249–259. doi:10.1016/j.im.2011.06.004

Nevo, S., & Wade, M. (2010). The formation and value of IT-enabled resources: Antecedents and consequences of synergistic relationships. *Management Information Systems Quarterly*, *34*(1), 163–183. doi:10.2307/20721419

Newman, K. L. (2000). Organizational transformation during institutional upheaval. *Academy of Management Review*, *25*(3), 602–619. doi:10.5465/amr.2000.3363525

Nonaka, I., & Takeuchi, H. (1995). *The Knowledge-Creating Company*. Oxford, UK: Oxford University Press.

Noyelle, T. (1990). *Skills, wages and productivity in the service sector*. Boulder, CO: Westview Press.

Olson, E. (2006). Not by Technology Alone: Sustaining Winning Strategies. *The Journal of Business Strategy, 27*(84), 33–42. doi:10.1108/02756660610701003

Osterman, P. (1991). Impact of IT on Jobs and Skills. In M. S. Scott Morton (Ed.), *The Corporation of the 1990's. Information Technology and Organizational Transformation* (pp. 221–243). Oxford, UK: Oxford University Press.

Otim, S., Dow, K., Grover, V., & Wong, J. (2012). The Impact of Information Technology Investments on Downside Risk of the Firm: Alternative Measurement of the Business Value of IT. *Journal of Management Information Systems, 29*(1), 159–193. doi:10.2753/MIS0742-1222290105

Pereira, M. J. (2003). Impacts of information systems and technology on productivity and competitiveness of the Portuguese banking sector: An empirical study. *International Transactions in Operational Research, 11*(1), 43–62. doi:10.1111/j.1475-3995.2004.00439.x

Peteraf, M. (1993). The Cornerstones of Competitive Advantage: A Resource-based View. *Strategic Management Journal, 14*(3), 179–191. doi:10.1002mj.4250140303

Peters, E. (1991). *Chaos and order in capital markets. A new view of cycles, prices, and market volatility*. New York: Wiley.

Phan, D. D. (2003). E-business development for competitive advantages: A case study. *Information & Management, 40*(6), 581–590. doi:10.1016/S0378-7206(02)00089-7

Piñeiro, C., de Llano, P., & Rodríguez, M. (2012). Evaluation of the likelihood of financial failure. Empirical contrast of the informational content of the audit of accounts. *Spanish Journal of Finance and Accounting, XLI*(156), 565–588.

Poon, S., & Swatman, P. (1995). The Internet for Small Business: an enabling infrastructure for competitiveness. INET'95 Proceedings.

Porter, M. (1999). Creating advantage. *Executive Excellence, 6*(1), 13–14.

Poterba, J. M., & Summers, L. H. (1988). Mean reversion in stock prices: Evidence and implications. *Journal of Financial Economics, 22*(1), 27–59. doi:10.1016/0304-405X(88)90021-9

Prahalad, C. K., & Hamel, G. (1990). The core competence of the corporation. *Harvard Business Review, 68*(3), 79–91.

Prasad, A., Green, P., & Heales, J. (2013). On Governing Collaborative Information Technology (IT). A Relational Perspective. *Journal of Information Systems, 27*(1), 237–259. doi:10.2308/isys-50326

Quan, J., Hu, Q., & Hart, P. J. (2003). Information Technology Investments and Firms' Performance: A Duopoly Perspective. *Journal of Management Information Systems, 20*(3), 121–158. doi:10.1080/07421222.2003.11045773

Rai, A., Patnayakuni, R., & Patnayakuni, N. (1997). Technology investment and business performance. *Communications of the ACM, 40*(7), 89–97. doi:10.1145/256175.256191

Ravinchandran, T., & Lertwongsatien, C. (2005). Effect of Information Systems Resources and Capabilities on Firm Performance: A Resource-Based Perspective. *Journal of Management Information Systems, 21*(4), 237–276. doi:10.1080/07421 222.2005.11045820

Riegelmen, R. K. (2005). *Studying a Study and Testing a Test: How to Read the Medical Evidence*. Philadelphia: Lippincott Williams & Wilkins.

Roach, S. S. (1991). Services under siege – The restructuring imperative. *Harvard Business Review, 69*(5), 82–91. PMID:10113914

Rose, P. S., Andrews, W. T., & Giroux, G. A. (1982). Predicting Business Failure: A Macroeconomic Perspective. *Journal of Accounting, Auditing & Finance, 6*(1), 20–31.

Rumelt, R. P. (1991). How much does industry matter? *Strategic Management Journal, 12*(3), 167–185. doi:10.1002mj.4250120302

Sambamurthy, V., Bharadwaj, A., & Grover, V. (2003). Shaping agility through digital options: Reconceptualizing the role of information technology in contemporary Firms. *Management Information Systems Quarterly, 27*(2), 237–263. doi:10.2307/30036530

Schwarz, M., & Takhteyev, Y. (2010). Half a Century of Public Software Institutions: Open Source as a Solution to Hold-Up Problem. *Journal of Public Economic Theory, 12*(4), 609–639. doi:10.1111/j.1467-9779.2010.01467.x

Scott, J. Jr. (1977). Bankruptcy, secured debt, and optimal capital structure. *The Journal of Finance, 32*(1), 1–19. doi:10.1111/j.1540-6261.1977.tb03237.x

Siegel, D., & Griliches, Z. (1991). *Purchased services, outsourcing, computers and productivity in manufacturing*. National Bureau of Economic Research Working Paper No. 3.678.

Souder, W. E., & Jenssen, S. A. (1999). Management practices influencing new product success and failure in the United States and Scandivavia: A cross-cultural comparative study. *Journal of Product Innovation Management, 16*(2), 183–203. doi:10.1111/1540-5885.1620183

Sprague, R. H. (1980). A Framework for the Development of Decision Support Systems. *Management Information Systems Quarterly, 4*(4), 1–26. doi:10.2307/248957

Strassman, P. A. (1990). *The business value of computers.* Information Economics Press.

Straub, D. W., & Watson, R. T. (2001). Research Commentary: Transformational issues in Researching IS and Net-Enabled Organizations. *Information Systems Research, 12*(4), 337–345. doi:10.1287/isre.12.4.337.9706

Tam, K. (1998). The Impact of Information Technology Investments on Firm Performance and Evaluation: Evidence from Newly Industrialized Economies. *Information Systems Research, 9*(1), 85–98. doi:10.1287/isre.9.1.85

Teece, D., & Pisano, G. (1994). The dynamic capabilities of firms: An introduction. *Industrial and Corporate Change, 3*(3), 537–556. doi:10.1093/icc/3.3.537-a

Teece, D. J., Pisano, G., & Shuen, A. (1997). Dynamic Capabilities and Strategic Management. *Strategic Management Journal, 18*(7), 509–533. doi:10.1002/(SICI)1097-0266(199708)18:7<509::AID-SMJ882>3.0.CO;2-Z

Teo, T. S., & Pian, Y. (2003). A contingency perspective on Internet adoption and competitive advantage. *European Journal of Information Systems, 12*(2), 78–92. doi:10.1057/palgrave.ejis.3000448

Wade, M., & Hulland, J. (2004). The Resource-Based View and Information Systems Research: Review, Extension, and Suggestions for Future Research. *Management Information Systems Quarterly, 28*(1), 107–142. doi:10.2307/25148626

Wang, N., Liang, H., Zhong, W., Xue, Y., & Xiao, J. (2012). Resource Structuring or Capability Building? An Empirical Study of the Business Value of Information Technology. *Journal of Management Information Systems, 29*(2), 325–367. doi:10.2753/MIS0742-1222290211

Weill, P. (1992). The relationship between investment in information technology and firm performance: A study of the value manufacturing sector. *Information Systems Research, 3*(4), 307–333. doi:10.1287/isre.3.4.307

Xiang, B. (1993). The choice of return-generating models and cross-sectional dependence in event studies. *Contemporary Accounting Research, 9*(2), 365–394. doi:10.1111/j.1911-3846.1993.tb00887.x

Zeffane, R. (1992). Patterns of structural control in high and low computer user organizations. *Information & Management, 23*(3), 159–170. doi:10.1016/0378-7206(92)90040-M

ADDITIONAL READING

Kraaijenbrink, J., Spender, J. C. & Groen, A. (2009). *The resource-based view: A review and assessment of its critiques*. MPRA Paper No. 21442.

Lim, J., Dehning, B., Richardson, V., & Smith, R. (2011). A Meta-Analysis of the Effects of IT Investment on Firm Financial Performance. *Journal of Information Systems*, 25(2), 145–169. doi:10.2308/isys-10125

Robson, W. (1994). *Strategic management and information systems an integrated approach*. London: Pitman.

KEY TERMS AND DEFINITIONS

Capability: An ability allowing the firm to execute plans and/or activities with an abnormally high performance.

Financial Distress: A set of imbalances that reduce the capacity to generate cash flows, make current payments difficult, and may lead to an insolvency.

Performance: A measure of how well a company is doing, often measured against competitive goals or rivals' achievements.

Resource: A tangible or intangible mean to which value is attributed because it is required to perform an activity.

Risk: The inability to make perfect forecasts about future facts, e.g. the outcomes of an investment or the consequences of a decision, because available information is incomplete.

Chapter 2
Tokens and Tokenization:
Still a Gordian Knot for the Future of FinTech?

Carlos Fernandez-Herraiz
Grant Thornton, Spain

Sara Esclapes-Membrives
Grant Thornton, Spain

Antonio Javier Prado-Dominguez
Universidade da Coruña, Spain

ABSTRACT

The authors have carried out an examination of the status of tokens and tokenization in financial markets with regulatory problems, which lack proposals for solutions based on a generalized consensus. Overall, it seems to authors that cutting the Gordian knot of tokenization and tokens is the essential need to achieve a consensual and efficient protocol of unequivocal attribution of legal responsibility to obtain satisfactory levels of transparency and reliability in all transactions. In particular, tokens that claim to be money appear to have a more complicated potential development than the rest, since there is a controversy between the pressures of the sector agents and the specific restrictions indicated by Knapp and Ingham and maintained by the states and regulators with respect to its exclusive regulatory capacity over money as a means of payment of a wide and reliable acceptance.

DOI: 10.4018/978-1-7998-2440-4.ch002

INTRODUCTION

The emergence of communication protocols that structure information as chains of blocks of information linked in a cryptographic way represents a profound technological-instrumental innovation for the financial system. These protocols are generically referred to as blockchains. However, blockchain is only a part of a larger set, commonly known as distributed ledger technologies (DLT), whose aim is to enable a group of parties to manage a non-centralized database. Authors acknowledge the different definitions available for DLTs and blockchains however, in this document, both terms will be used interchangeably.

DLTs admit and foster the representation and transfer of previously existing goods and rights, the creation of new goods and rights and the natural experimentation and evolution on market mechanisms. Such possibilities entail the development of reward and punishment models associated with the positioning of market participants' interests. A process that can be expected to be intense, but in some way similar to those already experienced in the past, as a consequence of other significant procedural advances in financial system.

Main, but not exclusively, DLTs are built with the aim of not depending on the role of a trusted intermediary or third party in the process of representation and transmission of value. The ability to maintain and transmit value as well as the ability to dispense with third parties could be considered as the two main aspects in the solution given by these technologies.

Regarding representation and transfer of value, blockchain makes possible to create units of account or complex financial products, digitally represent real assets or any right, and transfer them with great ease. These units of account are commonly known as "tokens", and its transfer is simple since all the agents participating in a system fed by this technology have either the same duplicated information, or mechanisms to indirectly verify the good purpose and existence of the transactions executed in the network.

The first DLT arose to support a new means of digital payment, known as Bitcoin (considered a type of token), which was formulated as the first means of payment capable of overcoming the problem of double spending in the transfer of purchasing power by electronic means. Thus, the original Bitcoin white paper by Nakamoto (2008) allude to "digital cash", proposing a system that supports the exchange of purchasing power with the same guarantees as a physical transaction, but dematerializing the means of payment and making remote transfer possible.

This leads to the second aspect of the solution given by distributed ledger technologies: absence of trusted third parties. The existence of the problem of double expenditure in the transmission of value is one of the main reasons that determine the role of trusted third parties in the payments function and, in general, in the transmission of value in the current financial system. Trusted third parties, or reliable intermediaries, fully process the registration, maintenance and updating of purchasing power records, securities registers or financial contract registers. They do so within the framework of a system of guarantees based on the regulation and control of their activity.

This process has been historically absorbed by financial institutions, due to feedback between convenience for users, regulatory barriers and competitive advantages for the banking institutions themselves. The coexistence between payment function and credit function allows institutions to expand their balance sheet and create money supply, based on their risk appetite and within the framework of regulatory compliance.

Due to the fact that DLTs are communication protocols that, in turn, lay on internet communication protocols, there should not be appreciable difference between transferring value using that protocol between users who are closer or more distant in geographical terms. This also implies another revolution compared to current value transfer systems. Today's payment systems are multi-local, so the transmission of purchasing power between different parties located around the world is not a trivial problem. Blockchain-based payment systems simplify this problem by sending units of account with the same simplicity as sending units of information. The challenge is how to articulate these units of account from an economic and legal point of view as well as the system that support them: blockchain, and this question inevitably invokes the concept of money.

We can define "money" as the reliable and accepted means to provide solutions to the human space-time equation when completing a transaction (acquisition or enjoyment of goods and services), in a multitude of ways. Consequently, it could be said that, throughout history, the successful money models have been, and continue to be, directly linked to the task of improving the asymptotic approximation of such equation to the solution of zero-space and zero-time in human transactions. It is not intended to suggest that there is a deterministic direction with no ups and downs in said equation, but models with a technology able to improve such asymptotic approach have been, from a historical perspective, systematically more successful. This statement is also valid for the current processes we are studying in this document. In the mix of means classifiable as money under this definition, it is possible to identify, at present, different types of money coexisting, and actors that continue being subject to different restrictions in the use of one or another type of money, as has historically happened.

The movement of goods and rights and their negotiation in global markets broadens the potential definition of means of payment, establishing different levels of risk, profitability and associated liquidity. In short, the conversion of means of payment into financial assets and financial assets into means of payment. In line with the above definition of money, tokens could represent a seemingly optimal solution to the convergence of both aspects. The reason is that, due to the possibility of representing and transferring value in an easy, immediate and safe way, (and without prejudice of the legal considerations that will be addressed below) the assets represented in Blockchain become so liquid that could be considered equivalent to money.

In his 1980 article, "Banking in the theory of finance", Fama (1980) makes a prescient analysis of the function of bank payments. From the perspective of 1980, Fama already stated that payments function consisted fundamentally in the maintenance of an accounting record system in which transfers of purchasing power were carried out by means of book entries. In his final considerations, Fama argued that a financial system based on the updating of accounting records, not limited by regulation, could lead to different banking or non-banking providers competing for enough reserves and liquidity to meet the provision of payments. In addition, Fama's registry model allowed the collateralization of those units of account linked to the registries by means of any set of securitizable assets or rights. Today, we can affirm that this vision has crystallized in the potential evolution of asset representation models in token format.

In fact, the current model of book entries, or ledger records, allows the representation of multiple instruments of greater complexity than a unit of account. The book-entry model includes the representation of securities, financial contracts and other securitized assets or rights. In this context, it is possible to propose the reconstruction of the book-entry model, valid for value representations transmissible today in financial system, by means of a cryptographic representation in a specific implementation of blockchain technology. This solution involves a merge between means of payment and financial asset. Something that, as we have been able to discover in the form of an economic experiment, has occurred with Bitcoin and other cryptocurrencies.

The flexibility of the means of representation offered by this technology allows us to emphasize different aspects when building potential financial products. Thus, for example, the wave of project financing through the issuance of tokens reminds in its characteristics to the practice of crowdfunding. In crowdfunding, a multitude of agents decide to support a project by offering financing in exchange for: a) a reward, for example a unit of the finished product, b) a share in the terminal value of the project (shares) or c) a future promise of payment (debt) or even without pro bono (donation).

The aim of this document is to examine the status of tokens and tokenization in financial markets, clearly identityfying the main regulatory and economic challenges involved and approaching potential ways to overcome them. Section two will define and detail the concepts of token, tokenization and the legal and economic approaches to these concepts. Section three will cover how selected key regulators are addressing the multiple issues regarding this emerging financial paradigm and the market initiatives and responses. Section four draws several recommendations and define the product problem and the market problem, the asset tokens and the representative tokens, a convenient framework for regulatory, legal and economic design advances. Finally, we introduce potential avenues for research and conclusion.

BACKGROUND

Blockchain literature starts with the well-known Nakamoto (2008) white paper about Bitcoin, a new electronic cash system. This paper is the foundation of the blockchain movement and the first use case of this technology: decentralized electronic cash. Although the Bitcoin network created "programmed" money, and started a global movement of dozens of cryptocurrencies, current implementations based on full scope smart contracts have been generalized and enhanced after the development of Ethereum. Buterin (2014) defines Ethereum as a "Blockchain with a fully-fledged turing-complete programming language" (p. 1) and Wood (2014) formalized the approach as a "generalized singleton machine with shared-state" (p.1). It was Ethereum the harbinger of tokenization and tokenomics efforts.

Since then, the technology and its possibilities have grown in interest. During 2015 World Economic Forum, a survey covering potential impact of emerging technologies, showed respondents pointing to a 10% of global GDP potentially tokenized by 2027 (World Economic Forum, 2015). The number has appeared in different commercial reports and is one of the benchmarks of the potential interest in the development of the technology. In a recent post, Finoa (2018) uses that reference to project the potential level of assets tokenized in 2027, coming up with a figure around 24 trillion of us dollars.

The spread of use cases among industries is enormous, having created a sort of "blockchain hype" during the last years. Recent surveys of general blockchain applications and use cases are reviewed in Konstantinidis et al (2018) and Casino, Dasaklis, and Patsakis (2019), where it is possible to find use cases and applications in several economic and industrial activities: from healthcare to logistics, from energy to the financial sector.

Bibliometric studies on blockchain (Zeng & Ni, 2018) and Bitcoin (Merediz-Sola & Bariviera, 2019) literature show also a significant and growing academic interest in the topic.

Blockchain technology cannot be properly understood without introducing the concept of token. A token is a fragment of code that represents value in a digital form, that is, an asset created or represented within a blockchain network. Through these fractions of code, tokenization seeks to establish how to convert traditional assets into tokens, defining the processes, parameters and functionalities that these tokens must represent, as well as the legal requirements that said assets must meet in order to be tokenized.

The Tokenization Standards Association defines token as "a digital unit resulting from the records in blockchain or other type of distributed leger" and offers a classic technical taxonomy for tokens. Tokens "may be generated on the ground of a protocol (protocol token), application (application token), a smart contract or other technology" (TSA, 2018). The advantage of tokens is the ability to issue, distribute and make easily transferable digital assets, that allow these atomic rights to be exchanged.

We would argue that, beyond cryptocurrencies, most of tokens are not protocol tokens, but run over existing protocols as an application specific token or a smart contract driven token. Also, application tokens use smart contracts.

Smart contracts are pieces of code stored in blockchain and executed according to previously defined and scheduled rules. This implies the possibility of automating value exchanges in a network once the conditions that were established take place. This execution does not need validation by any traditional third party, due to the decentralized and immutable nature of blockchain technology.

The best-known example of token within a blockchain are cryptocurrencies, protocol tokens whose function resembles quasi-moneys or means of payment, but in a digitized environment. However, there are several types of tokens that represent value, sometimes also serving as a mean of exchange within a blockchain, like utility tokens that will be defined below. In this context, it is worth mentioning tokens representing shares, participations, voting rights, loyalty points, financial or real estate assets, intangible assets such as storage space or software developments, or even access to services.

Cryptocurrencies, a type of token, introduced again in debate the definition, properties and boundaries of money both at the academic and practitioner levels and the potential for Central Bank Digital Currencies (Bech & Garrat, 2017). The classic definition of means of payment, store of value and unit of account; the topics about it issuance (private or public); commodity, physical, electronic, …; centralized or decentralized, and other… helped first comers to create basic frameworks for analyzing these new assets, and even think about future avenues for applying the underlying technology to private banks or central banks money creation and management, like Central Bank Digital Currencies (CDBC). Barontini & Holden (2019), survey of 63 central banks from around the world, representing 80% of world´s population and 90% of world economic output. "70% of the respondents are currently (or will soon be) engaged in CBDC work".

But the topic of this article goes beyond new crowdfunding implementations or discussions about more efficient ways of representing money, or quasi-money. There is a new field of decentralized and securitized assets and rights implied in the concept of "tokenization". Tokenization is understood as the possibility of digitally represent already existing assets, that is, as tokens. Kim, Sarin & Virdi (2018) discuss crypto-assets as an emerging assets class.

Therefore, the term tokenization implies the creation of a token representing either a good or a right over an underlying asset whose properties are verified by a blockchain protocol. Tokenization is, in consequence, the process of establishing the correspondence of the value of an asset, tangible or intangible, into tokens that can be recorded, exchanged and stored in a blockchain system. Janulek (2018), discusses the potential of tokens as new forms of payment and valuation.

The tokenization of an asset or a right with economic value, allows its exchange in a faster and safer way, it increases the liquidity of the underlying asset, which, in turn, generates benefits such as:

- Potentially greater commercialization capacity, as it makes possible the exchange of assets that, due to their low liquidity, were costly to trade.
- Improvement in the streaming of business models by reducing the risk associated with ownership.
- Market access for new agents and, therefore, access to greater capital, since digitalization of value enables elimination of restrictions based on location.

In this context, and as a way of encompassing this new figure, the concept of crypto-asset begins to emerge, addressed by different authorities, among others, by the European Central Bank. ECB (2019) defines crypto-asset as "any asset recorded in digital form that is not and does not represent either a financial claim on, or a financial liability of, any natural or legal person, and which does not embody a proprietary right against an entity" (p.7) Therefore, a crypto-asset is considered valuable by its users (an asset) as an investment and/or means of exchange.

Valuation of tokens and crypto assets is still an emerging field. A first approach from Burniske (2017), took basic money equations from Fisher and Metcalfe´s network effects to imagine how to value a crypto-asset. Hargrave, Sahdev & Feldmeier (2018) enter a proposed economic token taxonomy and experimental qualitative and quantitative models, including the potential value of the network effect, and the "framework for token confidence". Catalini & Gangs (2018) develop a theoretical framework in order to address the entrepreneur incentives to finance a new venture using tokens versus traditional forms of finance, but also point to some of the issues regarding token finance. For example, the tension between retaining value and issuing more tokens to fund platform development. Cong, Li & Wang (2019) develop a dynamic asset pricing model for tokens based on users demand instead of classic cashflow discounts.

Figure 1, offers a basic approach to token taxonomy based on the source of value and the type of value of the tokens, including some real examples. It is a basic approach based on The Tokenist (2019) proposed taxonomy and Funcas (2019, 2018) reports. As any potential classification, there are grey zones and tokens that could be potentially classified in different ways, depending on the point of view. For instance, Bitcoin is clearly a payment token, but due to the limited issuance and network effect, it has become a store of value asset and not a quasi-money instrument. We are not saying that Bitcoin does not work as a means of payment, but most of its value today comes from being perceived as an emerging store of value.

Source of value is also an important question, because methodologies to understand and measure the network source of value for tokens are still in its infancy. Figure 1 also clarifies that tokenized assets and rights derive their value primarily from the issuer or the underlying asset or financial contract.

Intrinsically linked to tokens, is the concept of ICO. ICOs (Initial Coin Offerings) have emerged as a new alternative for fundraising. Actors within the blockchain ecosystem had globally issued tokens representing a variety of rights to finance their projects. Howell, Niessner & Yermack (2018) explore the ICO landscape and find that ICO success is linked to reduction in information asymmetry and a viable blockchain business model. Investors acquire such tokens in exchange for existing cryptocurrencies or even traditional cash. Adhami, Giudici & Martinazzi (2018) explore the potential determinants of success of ICOs. Gileborg (2018), explores the ICO phenomenon and its implications for behavioral economics, the issue of potential lack of regulation and the situation of investors. Finally, once the ICO is completed and the project is launched, sponsors try to list their tokens in various exchanges of crypto-assets. Due to the development of a regulatory body and the application of some basic financial regulatory standards, the picture is much richer today. Hacker & Tomale (2018) address some of the issues and drawbacks of current financial regulation to support tokenized finance and offer a rich crypto-asset taxonomy. We will come back to the ICO space later.

Optimal economic design of tokens is also an emerging field of interest. Tan (2019) proposes strategies for sound token designs pointing to the intersection between market design, mechanism design, including governance and non-financial incentives, and token design.

Figure 1. Basic token source and type of value taxonomy
Source: Authors elaboration based in The Tokenist (2018) and FUNCAS-ODF, Several Numbers.

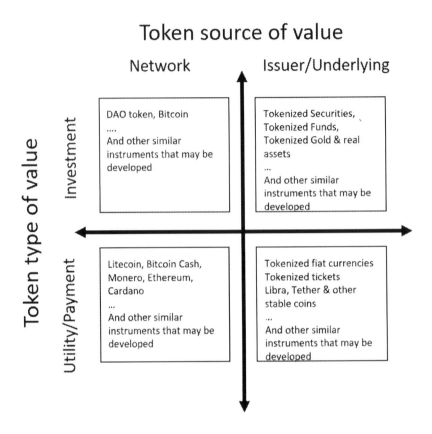

APPROACH TO THE REGULATION OF TOKENS, TOKENIZATION AND ECONOMIC IMPLICATIONS

The Regulatory and Comparative Approach: Issues and Controversies

Today, the most relevant barriers for representing financial instruments by means of tokens lie on two main aspects. The first one is the necessary regulatory changes so that transactions and custody of traditional and potentially new types of financial instruments are done through blockchain networks. The second one has to do with defining the role of intermediaries linked to such networks, if they exist.

Regarding the first barrier, the real challenge for financial authorities lies on those tokens that represent new ways of introducing liquidity in the market, such as utility tokens, payment tokens and, specially, asset tokens digitalizing new tradable "assets" or hybrid tokens (Annunziata, 2019). When we open the scope of tokenization to all kinds of goods, services, rights, etc..., there are possibilities, even unexplored, for the trading of practically anything. This is what we call a "product challenge". The essence of product challenge lies, therefore, on the concept of token and the immense possibilities of creating and representing value in a digital, secure and independent way.

This leads to the issue of how to deal with two conflicting interests: creation of new products representing any kind of good or service in a platform vs. how to regulate them in order to protect consumers from eventual bad practices. To accomplish this task, asking some questions is required. What are the legal interests involved in each category? What legal interest should be protected for each case? Do we need more standardization?

Most of financial authorities work to answer these questions, but not always addressing the real core of the challenge. Creating tokens with intrinsic value requires either a completely new regulation for these new financial products (if applicable) or, at least, some changes in current regulation able to address the challenges derived from these new ways of creating value. On the other hand, representing existing goods or rights in a DLT, only (from a strictly product perspective) shows natural evolution in the way of representing assets.

However, the answer of most of authorities to the questions stated above are aimed to create its own classifications of tokens with its relevant legal treatment, most of times, fitting them in current regulation and without a clear distinction between new assets and tokenized assets.

In this regard, the Financial Conduct Authority (FCA) of the United Kingdom published guidelines on the legal framework applicable to crypto-assets in January 2019 (FCA, 2019). In this consultation paper, the FCA uses the term crypto-asset broadly, i.e. as a concept that encompasses tokens of any nature. In this context, although the purpose of the British regulator is to dissociate the term crypto-asset or token from the term cryptocurrency, it is not clear whether the representation of an existing asset through a token would fall into any of the categories identified by FCA.

The use of the term crypto-asset or virtual asset in a generic way to refer to tokens of different nature is also carried out by the US Securities and Exchange Commission. Its Strategic Hub for Innovation and Financial Technology (2019) commented on different guidelines on the framework applicable to virtual assets used in investment contracts. In these guidelines, the group uses the term "digital asset" in reference to an asset issued and transferred using a distributed registry or blockchain technology including, but not limited to, cryptocurrencies, coins and tokens.

The main concern of the U.S. supervisor is that securities market regulation is enforced if the token meets the conditions of the Howey Test. In this sense, the

Securities Exchange Commission (SEC) categorizes tokens into two large groups: security tokens and utility tokens. In this case, the question of the possibility of representing existing assets in the form of tokens remains again somewhat open and, based on the above classification, it could be understood that this possibility would be imbued in the category of security tokens. However, the American regulator is concerned to have a clear distinction, a basic working rule, to decide whether we are talking about securities that should be properly regulated and supervised according to the legislation in force, in order to protect the general public. The alternative is that these tokens represent a prepayment of future goods and services, in the same line as some of the first crowdfunding models.

One of the most recognized token taxonomies is the one established by the Swiss financial authority (FINMA) which clearly establishes that the possibility of representing existing assets in physical reality through tokens falls within the category of asset tokens. The Federal Council (2019) draws a clear and precise distinction between payment tokens, or cryptocurrencies, clearly the tokens used as a means of payment. On the other hand, utility tokens, i.e. the pre-payment of a service provision or the acquisition of a good or license. And finally, asset tokens that support a wide range of financial instruments including, of course, securities, and the digital representation of assets (tokenization). In that sense, the Swiss classification is the clearest from the point of view of the taxonomy of tokens, given that it is possible to fit any token currently existing within one of the three typologies proposed by the regulator.

European Securities Market Authority (ESMA, 2019) defines crypto-asset as "a type of private asset that depends primarily on cryptography and Distributed Ledger Technology as part of their perceived or inherent value" (p.7). According to ESMA (2019) "there is a wide variety of crypto-assets, from virtual currencies such as Bitcoin to so-called "digital tokens", also issued through Initial Coin Offerings (ICOs)"(p.4). In addition, ESMA (2019) defines digital tokens as "any digital representation of an interest, which may be of value, a right to receive a benefit or perform specified functions or may not have a specified purpose or use"(p.42).

ESMA, establishes a detailed taxonomy of "digital assets", incorporating within the figure of the "asset token" a wide variety of flavors for different types of financial contracts, not necessarily securities, and also indicating that a token could be built as a combination of several of these properties. Thus, ESMA establishes eight different categories of possible "utility" or "asset token", depending on the possibility of trading or not on the secondary market, of securities with economic or political rights and, of course, of various types of financial contracts that may or may not be linked to underlying assets of all types, including commodities.

As can be observed, ESMA and other authorities do not clearly specify the distinction between creating an asset in blockchain and representing an existing asset in blockchain. Then, their token taxonomies could reflect unintended legal consequences, as we will analyze later. On the other hand, authorities introduce nuances aimed to solve other problems not directly related to the product itself but to its movement in the market. In this regard, authorities are making decisions on a case by case basis (Blandin et al, 2019) which, given the rate of growth of the market, evidences the future inefficiency of this method and therefore the need and urgency of at least some guidance about legal treatment of issuing and moving tokens.

In order to accomplish this task, it is necessary to widen the context and not focus only on the product or service that is being tokenized or created, but in the framework that surrounds it. This, in turn, leads to another important issue: liability. Is the issuance of tokens a crowdfunding – like mechanism? How do we deal with the potential decentralization of liabilities in open and permissioned blockchains? Likewise, there are significant challenges like product origination and market distribution in primary markets and trading in secondary markets.

This leads to the second main legal challenge that should be developed: the decentralized market, i.e. the way of issuing, distributing and trading tokens in decentralized platforms. Several implications follow: new ways of trading without a central supervisory point, with no territorial limits, in a digital ecosystem and with new operators that, at present, are not regulated. This is what we call a "market challenge".

The essence of market challenge lies on the decentralization of the network in which tokens are registered, the emergence (or changes) of new liabilities and the change of role (or even the absence) of trusted third parties or intermediaries. Each of one has numerous edges, from the need of reconsidering KYC procedures (already addressed by some regulators) to data protection aspects, tax or corporate issues, also related to the kind of token subject to the analysis.

The Market Approach

Tokens and tokenization started as a highly unregulated market, back in 2013, difficult to handle due to the decentralized nature, the ubiquity of the proposition and the global reach offered by the internal design. The market for Initial Coin Offerings (ICOs), has gain increasing popularity for financing innovation projects since its awakening in 2016. Previous ICOs were launched during 2013, 2014 and 2015, but the issued amount and the public impact was negligible.

During the second part of 2016 and the first part of 2017, the first regulatory investigation was developed by the Securities and Exchange Commission, regarding the Decentralized Autonomous Organization (DAO) Project. The investigation ended with a report (SEC, 2017) regarding the robbery of 50 M US dollars from the DAO

Table 1. Token Issuance

Token Issuance Million USD	Strategy&	Coinschedule	Inwara	Coindesk	Icodata	IcoBench
2013	0.8					
2014	30.5			30.43	16.03	
2015	9.9			8.61	6.08	
2016	252	256.92		256.41	90.25	
2017	7,043.30	6,557.84		5,481.97	6,226.60	10,062.39
2018	19,689.30	21,644.52		14,295 (June)	7,812.15	11,596.38
2019 (June)	3,263 (may)	2,643.70	3,378.30			

Source: Authors elaboration with data from Strategy&, Coinschedule, Inwara, Coindesk, Icodata, Icobench, 2019.

smart contract. That first case drew attention from the authorities and regulators to the new tokenized finance issue and started the rush to regulate tokens and tokenization.

The growth in regulation impacted the ability to launch successful ICOs and issuers and intermediaries were forced to evolve, at least in part, to new models of token finance. During the last two years, the concept of STO (Security Token Offering) emerged in the market as a regulatory compliant approach to raise funds using tokens for venture businesses. The STO concept implies properly regulated securities issuance, employing tokens as the representation of the security.

During the last year, a new concept evolved and has gain traction during 2019: The IEO (Initial Exchange Offering), which is an ICO launched within a crypto exchange. The IEO covers the KYC and AML processes, because issued tokens are distributed among the clients of a crypto exchange. In that sense, it appears more regulatory friendly that the classical ICO with low costs, no investor rights and global scope, but lack of clear regulation. At the same time, is far away from the concept of STO, the strongest regulated form of token finance.

Table 1 offers some insights regarding token issuance during the last years. As can be observed, token finance is a young, emerging phenomenon. Increasing levels of token offerings since 2016 are closely related to the emergence of the Ethereum blockchain. Conversely, the "crypto winter" or crypto bear market of the second half of 2018 and an increased scrutiny from regulators impacted the figures for the first half of 2019.

There is a huge dispersion in numbers regarding the money raised from token finance depending on the reference source. Those discrepancies are clear in table 1 and they could have arisen due to different reasons: ICO market coverage of the

Table 2. The emerging of the era of regulated token finance. Token Issuance 2019 (June)

Token Issuance 2019. Million USD	Strategy&	Coinschedule	Inwara
ICO	1,480	988	1,329.3
IEO	1,542	1,546	1,630
STO	241	108,76	419
Total	3,263	2,642.76	3,378.30

Source: Authors elaboration with data from Strategy&, Coinschedule, Inwara, 2019.

different analysis, inclusion or not of special offerings, like Telegram restricted token offering during 2018, the high volatility of the cryptos used for payments, and so on.

In Table 2, the emergence of the IEO token issuance is clear, although there is a big outlier of around 1 billion US dollars: the Bittfinex IEO. Even discarding it, the amount issued more than doubles the amount in STOs during the period. This evolution could be related to the high regulatory standards of STOs, the difficulties to put STOs in place and the highly convenient issuing method of IEOs. Apparently, IEOs could replace a significant part of the traditional ICO space during the following periods. Anyway, authors recognize that it is probably too early to draw conclusions on this emerging situation within an emerging market.

In our view, IEOs solve only part of the problem, by providing proper identification to the investors in a token issuance. But there are still many risks and issues to handle. The quality of the issuances, consumer and investor protection, and so on. On the other side, STOs are still a complex mechanism, not easy and flexible enough and highly dependent on the jurisdiction, something that also has implications in terms of assets raised.

SOLUTIONS AND RECOMMENDATIONS

The reflection about token finance regulation and market approach in previous sections uncovers how volatile and challenging is the state of the field today. Token finance represents a multifaceted and complex new financial paradigm, that is still in its infancy. A paradigm that evolves naturally from new technologies, a classical financial innovation trigger, and that may lead to the adaptation of some of the roles of traditional financial markets stakeholders.

The authors will try to draw some recommendations regarding the topic, including a basic framework for regulatory strategy, the impact of selected challenges in different types of tokens, the recognition of the unresolved issue of evolved ICOs or the dual nature of many tokens as quasi-money and assets.

First recommendation: Basic framework for a sound regulatory strategy. Product challenge and market challenge. Asset tokens and representative tokens.

First, the recognition and analysis of the product challenge and the market challenge is paramount. The product challenge focuses on the definition and adequacy of legal interests protected by a financial contract and their technical representation by means of a token. The market challenge arises from the interaction of the actors in a distributed ledger protocol, the protection of the weakest users and the adaptation of the token transmission rules to the legal standards required by the regulations applicable to financial markets, whether organized or over the counter.

Second, confusing the asset with a representation in the form of a token implies confusing the legal interests protected by each regime. The different nature and rights to be protected in the case of asset tokens and representative tokens must be addressed. Asset tokens are those that have an intrinsic value for themselves and therefore, can be considered products. This category includes all tokens whose value is determined by their nature, either because they are used at the incentive level within a network, or because their value depends on the value of the network in which they operate. Representative tokens are those tokens that reflect, refer to or symbolize in a DLT environment (tokenize) a good or a right that has its origin out of the blockchain.

Although this is a starting point for an economic, legal and regulatory analysis, authors recognize that the plasticity of these new financial instruments creates fuzzy states that may require further developments. Regulators started to suffer this problem in token taxonomy efforts. There are dual tokens offering new asset characteristics and, at the same time, including a representation of out of the blockchain assets or rights.

In addition, the market challenge is heavily interconnected with the product challenge, a classic problem in traditional finance. A balance approach between the product challenge and the market challenge must be addressed. The current focus on token taxonomy, the product challenge, is creating a profound asymmetry and opportunities for regulatory arbitrage. At the same time, those regulatory imbalances constrain the evolution of a new wave of tokenized assets and rights unachievable in many investor portfolios today.

Second recommendation: Create the proper regulation to solve the product challenge, especially for asset tokens.

Many regulators are actively engaged in solving the product challenge, both for new or existing assets and rights represented by tokens. The first efforts are focused in token or crypto-asset taxonomy.

Product challenge is of particular relevance with regard to asset tokens, that is, new assets whose value has its origin in the blockchain. Legal interests involved in that newly created financial products, asset tokens, should be properly understood and protected. To do so, nature of the asset must be analyzed and questions like what type of product is a cryptocurrency or a token whose value comes from its use in the blockchain protocol should be solved, defining conveniently the characteristics of that product.

On the other hand, product challenge also becomes important when representing rights over goods or rights represented in blockchain, but existing outside it, that have not been traded in traditional financial markets, or at least have not been widely traded. For example, what type of product is a token that represents a ticket (a ticket to a show) that can be traded on a secondary resale market, etc... Again, asking the question about legal interests that should be protected is essential.

Finally, tokenization of an existent financial instrument must protect the same legal assets and grant the same rights to the parties as a book entry or title representing that very instrument. In that case, the product challenge is much simpler: The legal definition and regulatory framework for the product already exist, it is the asset that the token represents, not the token itself, that should be analyzed. The product challenge is reduced to a fiduciary challenge, checking the proper implementation via token of the rights and responsibilities derived from the existence of that instrument. To clarify the problem with an example, equities represented by a token do not present a product challenge, because equity shares protected rights and responsibilities are properly defined.

Opposite to the taxonomy proposition of several regulators, it is not possible to include all token modalities under the concept of "crypto-asset", or asset token, since a token could represent either a good or right existing out of blockchain (in which case tokens is a convenient technological solution for an asset registry and transfer, and not an asset itself), or be an asset itself. .

This distinction, in many cases not covered by legislators, can lead to regulatory errors. Among these errors, the most common in the context of financial markets, has to do with mixing the rules applicable to the representation of financial assets with the rules applicable to the financial assets themselves.

Third recommendation: Circumvent the confusion between asset and representative tokens protected rights and regulatory responses needed.

Solving the product challenge for asset tokens is not only about classifying some of those tokens as utility tokens, for example, and consider them out of the financial regulatory scope. The important issue is to provide investors with information on which to base their decision to invest or not in them. This is where regulation should focus. The protected legal interest is therefore the rights of the investor. But today there are not generally accepted models for utility token valuation, and so it is difficult to address what information should be material and relevant.

The object of protection in case of representative tokens is the movement of the asset represented in the market, with the aim of assuring acquirer and the transferor rights. In that sense, it will be necessary that, in order to represent and transmit value in accordance with the law, the blockchain platform is able to fulfill the above objective. In addition, the nature of the asset or right they represent in terms of protection of the investor's must be analyzed.

In short, the problem of asset tokens is a problem that lies on the need to define new non-existent instruments and either classify them in an existing category or create new laws to regulate them. On the other hand, tokenizing, that is, creating a representation of assets and rights using a blockchain network, is simply the natural evolution of the virtual representation of assets.

Fourth recommendation: Focus on framing the market challenge for representative tokens.

In the view of the authors, the market challenge is much more complex and implies the proper definition and taxonomy of the different stakeholders of a tokenized or DLT based financial market, including new roles for financial intermediaries. Blockchain is a decentralized infrastructure, which clashes head-on with the existing market structure today. To see how the market challenge impacts the evolution of the tokenized finance field let´s take the example of an equity security. Today, equities represented by means of tokens, instead of being represented by means of a book entry, are not public securities according to many of current regulatory frameworks. Then, the representation of public securities in the form of tokens is not properly addressed by existent regulation. But tokens, and thus representative tokens, cannot be dissociated from the infrastructure in which they operate, that is, a blockchain platform, by nature decentralized, disintermediated and different from a custodian ledger.

Therefore, the reason to not represent public securities using tokens, has nothing to do with the Law's requirements that such securities should be represented through book entries. The reason is that in order to represent a public security through a token, a blockchain platform must necessarily be used. So, it is the blockchain infrastructure that clashes with the articulation of the market.

In fact, there is no reason to refuse the representation of a security admitted to secondary market through a token, if the infrastructure continues ensuring the protection of the legal interest collected in Law. This can be done in many ways, not necessarily by fitting the technology into the existing centralized structure, which prevents using blockchain's potential.

But other aspects are also important in the market challenge. Main public blockchains would be hardly "compliant" with the KYC and AML rules required of intermediaries vis-à-vis their clients. How do we prevent the transmission of a token representing a share within the Ethereum network to a new holder who is in another jurisdiction or who has not been identified? There are initial responses from the market, like the white lists. White lists imply the creation of standards that limit the transmissibility of tokens only to wallets that have gone through an accreditation process. The IEOs partially solve this problem but only to a point, offering the KYC and AML procedures for the primary market, that is, the issuance of the token. But there is still a challenge for properly identifying the counterparties in the secondary market trading of the tokens.

Fifth recommendation: Recognize that IEOs are only a partial solution and STOs do not solve the market problem.

IEOs offer more comfort to regulators, due to the KYC and AML procedures offered by the issuance, but only solve part of the problem. In fact, IEOs introduce several agency problems overcame by the current financial market regulation. In an IEO, the exchange acts as the broker in charge of issuing the security and as the market in which this security is going to be traded, at the same time.

STOs try to follow current securities regulation to issue tokens. This type of tokens are representative tokens by nature, because their value is derived from the underlying value of the existing rights and assets they represent. A typical STO may imply equity, debt or mezzanine securities represented by means of a token. Tokens issued by an STO imply little product challenges, but at the same time are caught in the market challenge. Due to the low regulatory progress made in solving the market challenge, these type of security issuances are relegated to the less regulated and more flexible security issuance procedures, restricted to institutional investors.

Sixth recommendation: Recognize the dual role of (many) tokens as asset/ representation of an asset and medium of exchange.

In "A Treatise on Money", Keynes (1930) distinguishes between the "money of account" and "money" by stating that "the money of account is the description or title and the money is the thing which answers to the description", and continues "if the same thing always answered to the same description, the distinction would have no practical interest. But if the thing can change, whilst the description remains the same, then the distinction can be highly significant".

Tokens are easily transferable, and interchangeable for other tokens or even legal tender monetary units by means of the exchanges enabled for it, in a secure and traceable manner. From the point of view of utility tokens, an accounting registration system on rights of use on service platforms, which are also interchangeable/ exchangeable, can only be defined as commodity money, in the sense that the usability and demand for such services turns these tokens into a desired and accepted exchange mechanism. Minsky (2008) says that "Everyone can create money; the problem is to get it accepted" (p. 255), and we would add, that "accepted" is the key term, which has a very broad, complex and dynamic meaning because it is subject to transforming dynamic forces, before, now and in the future.

But if the fundamental role of an exchange system is to maintain an accounting record of rights and obligations (Fama, 1980), and if the rights derived from the possession of a token are demanded by a sufficiently large group of users, who also have simple and convenient methods to access or exchange those rights; could we say that a cryptocurrency or a utility token, for example, fulfil a function similar to a digital means of payment? And if that service were sufficiently demanded to constitute a system of relative value compared to other units of account, could it not be considered a unit of account, even if it did not have the legal backing of a state in the "chartalist" sense (Knapp, 1924). Consider the Facebook Libra project. Facebook had more than 2,4 billion monthly users as of June 30 (Facebook, 2019). If that project progresses, is it not going to be "accepted money" in the Minskean sense?

The answer to this question requires deepening the "accepted" key and we had to consider, simultaneously, that money always signifies a chartal means of payment. Chartalism is often identified with the proposition that legal tender laws determine that which must be accepted as means of payment. However, Knapp's analysis (1924) went further. If we have already declared in the beginning that money is a creation of law, this is not to be interpreted in the narrower sense that it is a creation of jurisprudence, but in the larger sense that it is a creation of the legislative activity of the state, a creation of legislative policy. And what is the nature of this "legislative activity" that determines what will be the chartalist money accepted within the jurisdiction of the state?

Precisely, that lack of a satisfactory integration between the unit of account and the means of payment is still an open question and without a generalized consensus regarding tokens with claims to be considered money. Finally, at this point, it should not be forgotten that money is "one of those normative ideas that obey the norms that they themselves represent." (Ingham, 2013).

FUTURE RESEARCH DIRECTIONS

Tokens and tokenization are still emerging forces within the financial industry, so different avenues for research are open to academics and practitioners. Legal definition of asset tokens and regulatory developments regarding both asset tokens and representative tokens are fertile fields for further investigation. Research on regulatory comparisons and potential regulatory arbitrage, financial policy and protected rights for globally tradeable tokens imply deep considerations for economic policy, political economy, regulatory strategy, fiscal policy and state sovereignty, among multiple others.

Future research should cover the potential options for tokenizing any kind of instrument, asset or right, present or future, in a digital form. The huge plasticity of representative tokens leads us foresee markets for multiple alternative asset classes, like real assets, collectives or art, or even new alternative assets classes, like curated data, patents, identities, and so on.

The easier and more secure access to the market that this new technology entails could enhance financial inclusion. This development may have economic, social, regulatory and even political consequences whose dimensions require further analysis.

CONCLUSION

The authors have carried out an examination with the aim of clarifying the economic consequences of the state of tokens and tokenization in financial markets. This has made it essential to re-identify the most relevant regulatory challenges and the economic consequences of the current situations of tokens and tokenization. Both groups of issues are still emerging fields of study, so it may not surprise the dispersion of measures that the different regulators studied have applied in the various strategies implemented, which, without doubt, will create opportunities for regulatory arbitrage.

The uncertainties indicated in the previous point considerably limit the potential activity of most regulated financial services companies by hindering the development of new types of intermediaries and by delaying the emergence of traditional intermediaries in this new business activity. In this sense, at a general level, it seems to us that cutting the Gordian knot of tokenization and tokens is the essential need to achieve a consensual and efficient protocol of unequivocal attribution of legal liability with which to give this new industry transparency and satisfactory reliability in all transactions.

Currently, there seem to be large differences between tokens with the objective of being considered "money" with the rest of tokens that do not have that claim. The expansion of the latter seems a bit clearer of obstacles as a review of the literature shows that the obstacles are linked to specific regulatory or legal issues, which, although not having a satisfactory development, are mitigated by regulators with the KYC and AML type regulatory protocols contest.

On the other hand, tokens with claims to be money seem to have a potential development even more complicated than the previous ones, since there is a great disparity of positions between the chartalist pressures of the members of the sector and the restrictions maintained by states and regulators in the sense of Knapp and Ingham, in regard to their normative and monopolistic capacity over money as a means of payment of widespread and reliable acceptance.

We defined a product challenge, focused on the features of tokens and the goods and rights that they represent, that lead us to clarify the definition of token, tokenization and crypto-asset. The value represented by a token could have its origin out of the network (representative token) or within the network (asset token). Legal approach should differ depending on the category on which the token fits, since the legal interests protected in each case are different.

Thus, a token could be either no more than a convenient technological solution for an asset registry and transfer (in case of representative tokens), or an asset itself (in case of asset tokens). This distinction, in many cases not covered by legislators, can lead inefficiencies and regulatory failures, which are inherent in a Flawed State negative situations and imply that the effects of regulatory intervention far from solving the problems indicated increase them and, even, generate new ones of very difficult solution. The most common has to do with mixing the rules applicable to the representation of financial assets with the rules applicable to the financial assets themselves.

Intrinsically linked to the product challenge is the market challenge. The decentralized infrastructure of blockchain, even in "trusted third party friendly" implementations, like permissioned networks, clashes head-on with the existing market structure. On the one side, off chain governance issues, interoperability, market uses, privacy, among other many challenges, prevent regulators from candidly embrace the potential advantages of applying blockchain with full legal effects. In addition, protecting the same legal interests does not mean using the same mechanisms existing today to guarantee them. In fact, some of them might be ensured by the nature of blockchain technology.

Market dynamics have created ICOs as a new financing instrument, but the rush for regulation produced innovative solutions, like IEOs and STOs. IEOs solve the lack of reliable KYC and AML procedures, but introduced agency problems and moral hazard issues well known to market practitioners and researchers. STOs take token issuance to a traditional regulatory environment for securities, but do not solve the market problem.

Authors understand that the dual nature of many tokens, as asset/representation of as asset and, at the same time, as "moneys" following our definition in the introduction of this chapter, may bring back the old debate on public versus private issue of money or quasi-money instruments. But today, money is an issue of the state. So, calling Minsky back: everybody can create money, but it must be accepted.

Finally, a balanced approach between the market decentralization and change of roles of trusted third parties has become a pending task for regulatory efforts and developments. It is necessary to put more emphasis on the problem of attribution of liabilities under decentralization schemes. Today, we miss a generally accepted, successful and efficient framework for the proper attribution of liabilities across this new decentralized and innovative ecosystem. It is not only a question of financial liabilities, but also the full scope of legal areas that may be involved: taxation, labor, corporate, commercial and many others.

ACKNOWLEDGMENT

This research received no specific grant from any funding agency in the public, commercial, or not-for-profit sectors.

REFERENCES

Adhami, S., Giudici, G., & Martinazzi, S. (2018). Why do businesses go crypto? An empirical analysis of initial coin offerings. *Journal of Economics and Business*, *100*, 64–75. doi:10.1016/j.jeconbus.2018.04.001

Annunziata, F. (2019). *Speak if you can. What are you? An alternative approach to the qualifications of tokens and Initial Coin Offerings.* Bocconi Legal Studies Research Paper Series, n 2636561.

Barontini, C. & Holden, H. (2019). *Proceeding with caution – a survey on central bank digital currency*. BIS Papers No 101.

Bech, M. L., & Garratt, R. (2017). Central Bank Cryptocurrencies. *BIS Quarterly Review*. Retrieved from SSRN: https://ssrn.com/abstract=3041906

Blandin, A., Cloots, A. S., Hussain, H., Rauchs, M., Saleuddin, R., Allen, J. G., . . . Cloud, K. (2019) *Global Cryptoasset Regulatory Landscape Study*. Retrieved from SSRN: https://ssrn.com/abstract=3379219

Burniske, C. (2017, Sep 24). *Cryptoasset valuation*. Retrieved from https://medium.com/@cburniske/cryptoasset-valuations-ac83479ffca7

Buterin, V. (2013). *Ethereum: A Next-Generation Smart Contract and Decentralized Application Platform*. Retrieved from https://github.com/ethereum/wiki/wiki/White-Paper

Casino, F., Dasaklis, T. K., & Patsakis, C. (2019). A systematic literature review of blockchain-based applications: Current status, classification and open issues. *Telematics and Informatics, 36*, 55–81. doi:10.1016/j.tele.2018.11.006

Catalini, C., & Gans, J. S. (2019). *Initial Coin Offerings and the Value of Crypto Tokens*. NBER Working Paper No. w24418.

Coindesk. (n.d.). Retrieved from https://www.coindesk.com/ico-tracker

Coinschedule. (n.d.). Retrieved from https://www.coinschedule.com/stats

Cong, L., Li, Y., & Wang, N. (2019). *Tokenomics: Dynamic Adoption and Valuation*. Columbia Business School Research Paper No. 18-46.

ECB. (2019). *Crypto-Assets: Implications for financial stability, monetary policy, and payments and market infrastructures*. Occasional Paper Series, 223.

ESMA. (2019). *Advice. Initial Coin Offerings and Crypto-Assets*. ESMA50-157-1391. Retrieved from https://www.esma.europa.eu/sites/default/files/library/esma50-157-1391_crypto_advice.pdf

Facebook. (2019). *Facebook Q2 Earnings Release*. Retrieved from https://s21.q4cdn.com/399680738/files/doc_financials/2019/Q2/FB-Q2-2019-Earnings-Release.pdf

Fama, E. F. (1980). Banking in the theory of finance. *Journal of Monetary Economics, 6*(1), 39–57. doi:10.1016/0304-3932(80)90017-3

FCA. (2019). *Guidance on Cryptoassets*. Consultation paper CP19/3. Retrieved from https://www.fca.org.uk/publication/consultation/cp19-03.pdf

Finoa. (2018, Oct 27). *The Era of tokenization – market outlook on a $24trn business opportunity*. Retrieved from https://medium.com/finoa-banking/market-outlook-on-tokenized-assets-a-usd24trn-opportunity-9bac0c4dfefb

FUNCAS-ODF. (2018a). *Informe Criptomercados y Blockchain, primer trimestre*. Retrieved from www.funcas.es/_obsdigi_/DownLoadObs.aspx?Id=1177

FUNCAS-ODF. (2018b). *Informe Criptomercados y Blockchain, cuarto trimestre*. Retrieved from www.funcas.es/_obsdigi_/DownLoadObs.aspx?Id=1237

FUNCAS-ODF. (2019). *Informe Criptomercados y Blockchain, primer semestre.* Retrieved from www.funcas.es/_obsdigi_/DownLoadObs.aspx?Id=1290

Gileborg, R. (2018). *Initial token offerings, friend or foe?* (Master of Science Thesis Dissertation). TRITA-ITM-EX; 2018:445.

Hacker, P., & Thomale, C. (2018). Crypto-Securities Regulation: ICOs, Token Sales and Cryptocurrencies under EU Financial Law. *European Company and Financial Law Review, 15*(4), 645–696. doi:10.1515/ecfr-2018-0021

Hargrave, J., Sahdev, N., & Feldmeier, O. (2019). How value is created in tokenized assets. In M. Swan, J. Potts, S. Takagi, F. Witte, & P. Tasca (Eds.), *Blockchain economics: Implications of distributed ledgers* (pp. 125–143). London: World Scientific. doi:10.1142/9781786346391_0007

Howell, S. T., Niessner, M., & Yermack, D. (2019). *Initial Coin Offerings: Financing Growth with Cryptocurrency Token Sales.* NBER Working Paper No. 24774.

Icobench. (2019). *ICO market analysis 2018.* Retrieved from https://icobench.com/reports/ ICO_Market_Analysis_2018.pdf

Icodata. (n.d.). Retrieved from https://www.icodata.io/ stats/2018

Ingham, G. (2013). Revisiting the Credit Theory of Money and Trust. In J. Pixley (Ed.), New Perspectives on Emotions in Finance (pp. 121-139). London: Routledge.

Inwara. (2019). *Half-Yearly Report. H1 2019. Deciphering token offerings – IEOs, STOs and ICOs.* Retrieved from https://www.inwara.com

Janulek, P. (2018). *Tokenization as a Form of Payment and Valuation Professional, Scientific, Specialist and Technical Activities.* Available at SSRN: https://ssrn.com/abstract=3307180

Keynes, J. M. (2011). *A Treatise on Money.* Martino Fine Books. (Original work published 1930)

Kim, S., Sarin, A., & Virdi, D. (2018). *Crypto-Assets Unencrypted.* Retrieved from SSRN: https://ssrn.com/abstract=3117859

Knapp, G. F. (1973). *The State Theory of Money.* Clifton, NY: Augustus M. Kelley. (Original work published 1924)

Konstantinidis, I., Siaminos, G., Timplalexis, C., Zervas, P., Peristeras, V., & Decker, S. (2018). *Blockchain for Business Applications: A Systematic Literature Review.* BIS.

Merediz-Solá, I., & Barriviera, A. F. (2019). A bibliometric analysis of Bitcoin scientific production. *Research in International Business and Finance*, *50*, 294–305. doi:10.1016/j.ribaf.2019.06.008

Minsky, H. P. (2008). *Stabilizing an unstable economy*. Mc Graw Hill.

Nakamoto, S. (2008). *Bitcoin: A peer-to-peer electronic cash system*. Retrieved from https://Bitcoin.org/Bitcoin.pdf

Savelyev, A. (2018). Some risks of tokenization and blockchainizaition of private law. *Computer Law & Security Review*, *34*(4), 863–869. doi:10.1016/j.clsr.2018.05.010

SEC. (2017). Report of investigation pursuant to Section 21(a) of the Securities Exchange Act of 1934: The DAO. *Release No.*, *81207*(July), 25.

Strategic Hub for Innovation and Financial Technology. (2019). *Framework for "Investment Contract" Analysis of Digital Assets*. Retrieved from https://www.sec.gov/corpfin/framework-investment-contract-analysis-digital-assets

Strategy. (2019). *5th ICO/STO Report. A strategic perspective*. Retrieved from https://www.pwc.ch/en/insights/fs/5th-ico-sto-report.html

Tan, L. (2019). *Token economics framework*. Retrieved from SSRN: https://ssrn.com/abstract=3381452

The Federal Council. (2018). *Legal framework for distributed ledger technology and blockchain in Switzerland: An overview with a focus on the financial sector*. Federal Council Report.

The Tokenist. (2018). *Security tokens explained*. Retrieved from https://thetokenist.io/security-tokens-explained/

Tokenization Standards Association. (2019). *Tokenization standards*. Retrieved from https://bettertokens.org/pdf/Tokenization%20Standards.pdf

Wood, G. (2014). *Ethereum: A secure decentralized generalized transaction ledger*. Retrieved from https://gavwood.com/paper.pdf

World Economic Forum. (2015). *Deep Shift. Technology tipping points and societal impact*. Survey Report.

Zeng, S., & Ni, X. (2018). *A Bibliometric Analysis of Blockchain Research. Intelligent Vehicles Symposium (IV)*, Changshu, China.

ADDITIONAL READING

Abadi, J., & Brunnermeier, M. (2018). *Blockchain Economics*. NBER Working Paper No. 25407.

American Bar Association. (2019). *Digital and Digitized Assets: Federal and State Jurisdictional Issues*. Retrieved from https://www.americanbar.org/content/dam/aba/administrative/ business_law/buslaw/committees/CL620000pub/digital_assets.pdf

Antonopoulos, A., & Wood, G. (2018). Mastering Ethereum, CA: O'Reilly Media.

Au, S., & Power, T. (2018). *Tokenomics*. Birmingham: Packt Publishing.

Davidson, S., De Filippi, P., & Potts, J. (2016) *Economics of Blockchain*. Retrieved from SSRN: https://ssrn.com/abstract=2744751 or doi:10.2139srn.2744751

De Filippi, P., & Wright, A. (2018). *Blockchain and the Law: The Rule of Code*. London: Harvard University Press. doi:10.2307/j.ctv2867sp

Kops, M. (2019). *Assets on blockchain*. Tallin: Blockerix OÜ.

Mougayar, W. (2016). *The business blockchain: Promise, practice, and application of the next internet technology*. Hoboken: John Wiley & Sons.

Swan, M., Potts, J., Takagi, S., Witte, F., & Tasca, P. (Eds.). (2019). *Blockchain economics: Implications of distributed ledgers*. London: World Scientific. doi:10.1142/q0190

Tapscott, D., & Tapscott, A. (2016). *Blockchain revolution*. NY: Portfolio Penguin.

Voshmgir, S. (2019). *Token economy*. Berlin: Blockchain Hub.

KEY TERMS AND DEFINITIONS

Asset Tokens: Tokens that have its own intrinsic and stand-alone value and, therefore, can be considered products.

Cryptocurrency: Tokens whose function resembles legal tender coins or means of payment, but in a blockchain environment.

Initial Coin Offering (ICO): Public and decentralized issuance of tokens.

Initial Exchange Offering (IEO): ICO released through a exchange, introducing KYC and AML considerations.

Market Challenge: All legal challenges derived from the way of issuing, distributing, and trading tokens in a decentralized platform.

Product Challenge: All legal challenges derived from representing new assets or any kind of value, good or service in a decentralized platform.

Representative Tokens: Tokens that reflect, refer to or symbolize (tokenize) in a DLT environment an existing good or right in the physical world.

Security Token Offering (STO): The issuance of tokens representing securities and following regulatory standards for traditional securities issuance.

Token: A fragment of code that represents value in digital form, that is, an asset created or represented within a blockchain or DLT network.

Tokenization: The creation of a token representing either a good or a right over an underlying asset whose properties are verified by blockchain. Tokenization is, in consequence, the process of converting the value of an asset, tangible or intangible, into tokens that can be recorded, exchanged and stored in a blockchain system.

Chapter 3

The Financial Function in Era 4.0:
Challenges of Digital Transformation in SMEs

José Pablo Abeal Vázquez
Universidade da Coruña, Spain

ABSTRACT

The global system evolves at high speed. Megatrends emerge, and they develop, interact, multiply, and transform into a continuous and increasingly crazy movement. Companies have to dance this rhythm. It's not just about adapting, but about doing it the right way. SMEs also share these similarities even if they have their own casuistry. Due to the important weight that SMEs have in the globalized global economy, there is a growing interest in studying them and the way they create value. In this context, the figure of the financial director has acquired great relevance. The last major financial crisis has confirmed its important work in SMEs and also that his role is evolving to become an essential key to increase the value of the company. In this chapter, the authors discuss the role of the financial director and the challenges they have to take on in the new technological context.

INTRODUCTION

The world of today moves quickly under the influence of several trends. Among some of the most outstanding trends, there is the change at territorial level that is taking place in the global economic power and the consequent demographic and social

DOI: 10.4018/978-1-7998-2440-4.ch003

Copyright © 2020, IGI Global. Copying or distributing in print or electronic forms without written permission of IGI Global is prohibited.

changes. The rapid urbanization of some areas is one of its principal consequences. Likewise, the increasing competition for resources and climate change are two issues of special relevance and with a high degree of penetration in society. In addition, the constant technological revolution is another of the pillars on which present and future depend on. In this environment is where professionals dedicated to finance and accounting develop their activity and play a fundamental role facing the challenges in areas such as strategy, organization, governance or IT process (IFAC, 2018a).

This is why the appropriate use of technology by companies is a differential factor of great value. Companies that integrate successful disruptive technologies are more valued in market than those that have not yet taken this step or have done it without the determination to implement it successfully. This issue is particularly sensitive in the case of the category of small and medium enterprises (SMEs). Their lower financial capacity makes digital transformation an essential tool to maintain and increase their competitiveness in an increasingly competitive market.

The constant technological innovation is generating a new ecosystem where the functions usually attributed to the financial department are evolving to ensure their alignment with the whole organization. This new technological context requires avant-garde technological tools. Foremost among some of the most representative are blockchain, robotics, artificial intelligence, learning machine, or data mining. Likewise, it should not be forgotten resources such as social networks and new digital platforms.

Within this reality, the functions assigned to the financial manager extend their scope and are not just limited to traditional tasks such as internal control, treasury management, or negotiation with financial institutions. Nowadays the mission of financial manager has been extended to functions more typical of the general management of companies. Digitization creates value and financial management has the challenge of focusing the different decisions towards the same objectives, from both a strategic and operational perspective. The financial information usually used needs to be complemented with new variables that help define the value added by technology in the new digital business models. In light of the considerations mentioned above, the main objective of this chapter is to analyse the financial function in the era of digitalization and the main functions and challenges faced by the financial department and the chief financial officer (CFO).

Given the multidisciplinary nature of financial management, CFO and the whole financial department need to acquire and deepen their skills and competences outside the strictly financial sphere. In this vein, technological innovation is one of the essential elements that CFO will have to internalize, both directly and transversally, as one of his main functions.

Technological knowledge must be internalized as one of the keys factors to increase efficiency and add value to both shareholders and stakeholders. Thus, both

SMEs and large corporations require a new approach for the financial function. This approach will have to strengthen the resolution capacity and the interconnection between internal and external elements to the financial department, together with a greater strategic vision.

Therefore, one of the pillars of the transformation will start from the implementation of a vision 4.0 and the necessary skills to take advantage of the opportunities that the environment offers. The CFO of every SME should ask himself about the consequences that digital revolution supposse for his organization, how his team can support this transformation and what all of them need to successfully complete this task.

Taking into account the above, this chapter is structured as follows. It starts by showing the overall trends that shape the current economic reality and the challenges faced by companies and specifically by SMEs. Then, the chapter refers to the role played by SMEs in the disruptive paradigm configured by the increasing penetration of Information and Communications Technology (ICT) and Industry 4.0. After this previous contextualization, the financial management and the figure of CFO are analyzed, with particular attention being paid to the challenge of generating value in a digital economy. Finally, the main conclusions are stated.

THE SMES WITHIN THE GLOBAL TRENDS OF THE ENVIRONMENT

The irruption of the Internet at the end of the 20th century was one of the milestones that are irreversibly transformed society. In this sense, technological innovation is an important lever to promote modifications at all levels in the company. New models are born, consumer perceptions evolve or the influence of economic powers is rebalanced. The revolution can crystallize into diverse, interconnected factors, such as the appearance of cryptocurrencies, interest in the ecosystem, or artificial intelligence.

However, this process covers multiple aspects that not only adhere to technological issues. The set of trends that are presumed to generate large repercussions is numerous. Time has become an essential and scarce commodity. The collaborative economy grows strongly and individuals value not only the possession of goods and services that the economy offers, but also their ability to access them. For example, this allows consumers to buy and sell almost everything through simple apps. From a sociological perspective, the role of women is radically changing traditional values and helps to establish new family styles.

The concentration of wealth generates the demand for new products and personal brands are consolidated. The use of mobile phones in business relationships grows at unstoppable rates and services displace products in this area. The purchase experience is no longer limited only to one of its phases, but the value proposition occurs before, during, and after the specific act of the transaction. Likewise, consumers are increasingly inclined towards organic products, linked to the local economy and based on trust.

Technological innovations are incorporated into the value chain at an exponential rate, significantly increasing the weight of technology companies in the economy as a whole. For long years, the most prominent companies had an industrial approach, linked to mass production and natural resources. Subsequently, financial companies or companies linked to telecommunications were imposed in this ranking. However, today information has become the transcendental element, displacing the real economy.

Major economic trends tend to be the large increase in global debt and the exponential growth of the Chinese economy. The Chinese case is especially striking both for the speed with which its economy has become a world reference and its ability to innovate. One noteworthy example is the flourishing in this country of numerous megacities dedicated to the manufacture or production of technologies linked to the digital economy. The recent commercial tensions between the United States and China could mean the decline or slowdown of the global commercial expansion cycle.

Another of these global waves, and that not only affects China, is the growth of megacities throughout the world geography. Demographic projections indicate that Western countries and China will stabilize their population. On the contrary, the African continent and the rest of Asia are likely to show remarkable growth that will lead to accelerated urbanization. In this sense, the concept of smart cities and smart homes is growing rapidly. Thus, the weight of the urban population will increase rapidly and cities will be configured as greener and more technological spaces that will enjoy a network based on artificial intelligence and other technologies related to the digital era.

Let's not forget also how the greater use of renewable energies is making them a standard for the economy. Wind and solar energy will probably share much of the world's electricity production. Constant technological innovations will increasingly provide more efficient solutions in the use of these energies. Likewise, environmental awareness favors the nascent circular economy, where everything is reused in a continuous circular flow. However, the concept of recycling is only the spearhead of this perspective. Companies will have to integrate the concept of the three Rs, based on reducing, reusing and recycling throughout their entire production chain.

SMES IN THE NEW CONTEXT OF ICT AND INDUSTRY 4.0

Characterizing SMEs is not an easy task. Our interest is to provide the reader with some relevant ingredients that allow sketching their most obvious contours and then be able to contextualize SMEs with a greater perspective from the financial function. As the first relevant ingredient, it emerges that SMEs' investment capacity is reduced and both capital and external financing sources focus almost exclusively on their main business. Thus, the period of recovery of the investment should be as short as possible so that they do not drown financially. Their organic structure is simple, horizontal and has a reduced workforce. Ownership and management are often confused. The decisions are usually executed quickly and the operating mechanisms are usually quite flexible. They are also especially influenced by the environment and have a greater sensitivity to the risks that arise in their day to day. In this sense, IFAC (2018a) has recently made a comparison of the general characteristics of small, mid-sized and large enterprises.

Financial management is mainly considered through an internal perspective and its effectiveness is vital for the survival of the business. However, due to the scarce resources they have, SMEs tend to taclke with significant credit restrictions, reduced own resources, and greater impact on the weight of financial costs. Limited training in financial management leads in many cases to decisions without in-depth analysis. Also, the internal control and information technology used frequently presents structural weaknesses. Therefore, the strategies applied in SMEs go through building a model of qualified personnel, exhaustive internal control, and effective use of information technology that support corporate decisions at every moment.

Companies are always subject to transformations of all kinds, especially the technological ones. In fact, they survive by their adaptability to the changes that occur in the global environment caused by megatrends (Figure 1). Currently, the speed and repercussions of the changes are much greater than in the past and have a virulent impact on both the company and its surroundings. Therefore, it is not a question that can be dealt with from a traditional perspective, since the possible scenarios are very diverse and uncertain. The CFO has usually dealt with volatility scenarios, but in the present and in the future he is going to face a context closer to the concept of uncertainty. The report by the Association of Chartered Certified Accountants (2016) identified the main drivers for change in the accountant profession. One of the most relevant are the digital technologies.

If we were to make a historical analogy, the business models of the industrial revolution were based on simple processes and technology was mainly used to improve their productivity. Instead, in the current context it serves to create and analyze information. It is conceived as an essential complement based on innovation.

Figure 1. Characterization of the new context in SMEs
Source: Prepared by the author

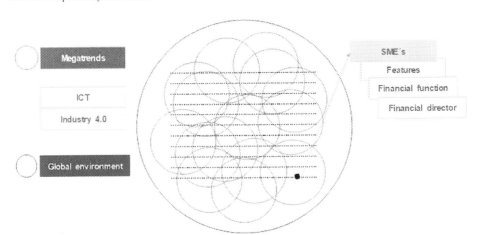

The digital era integrates technology as an intrinsic part of the core of the business, making it disruptive.

The Disruptive Paradigm of Information and Communications Technology

Creating a framework that measures the ability to integrate ICT is a difficult but very important issue for companies. It should be included in the business plan and fully integrated with the company's strategy, in order to enable the firm to realize its full potential. SMEs that invest in ICT with determination increase their capacity to increase their yield. Nevertheless, ICT generally have a low penetration in SMEs, so they are less able to take advantage of their capabilities than larger companies. They have limited resources and their technology is usually lower. However, they have more flexible and versatile structures which allow them to have greater adaptability.

There are a number of factors that do not favor investment in ICT. For example, the high initial investment and credit restrictions (from a financial point of view), the shortage of properly trained personnel and the absence of a compatible corporate strategy (from an organizational point of view) or the absence of a continuous training plan that goes ahead of events. In addition, the benefits of ICT begin to be perceived after a while, not always short, and the intensity of its effects depends on elements such as the business area in which it is located, the internal changes that occur within the company and its interaction with stakeholders. In this regard, Slusarczyk et al. (2015) concluded that the positive effect of ICT on productivity is seen more clearly in the long term.

Therefore, to improve the performance of its implementation, it is necessary to jointly analyze investments in ICT and the skills, resources and processes involved. In addition, other determining variables arise, such as the geographical situation of the company or the interest of clients or suppliers in implementing that same technology. Likewise, the support of state policies is vital to stimulate investment in ICT because it can reduce the existing gap, boost Internet access and bet on the accelerated training of the main users.

Companies invest in new information systems for issues related to specific operational reasons, such as working with a non-functional management software or insufficient information integration. However, there are also companies that support the implementation of ICT for strategic reasons. According to Kanchana and Sri Ranjini (2018), diverse variables limit the implementation of Enterprise Resource Planning (ERP), so case studies are necessary to focus on specific issues. They conclude that the adoption of these systems has different justifications in SMEs and in larger companies, since the former usually have lower levels of digitization. From a market approach, the results provided by Hangsten and Kotnik (2017) justify a positive relationship between ITC and the SMEs' export activity. They also found evidence that export energy is more linked to ICT capabilities than to the export decision itself.

The financial perspective was addressed by Pellegrina et al. (2017). In the area of SMEs, they verified that the most representative correspondence between the rates of credit growth and the use of ICT referred to the companies that used the technology to improve their communications, especially with respect to the financial system, customers and suppliers. Mbuyisa and Leonard (2017) conclude that using ICT increases productivity and revenue in SMEs. In addition, Qosasi et al. (2019) investigated how having ICT generated competitive advantage in small businesses. They found that the option of adopting ICT is adequate when the objective is to develop the supply chains and customer management.

Mixing The Ingredients Through Industry 4.0

The concept of Industry 4.0 was a proposal of the German government at the beginning of the 21st century as a measure to promote the competitiveness of the industry. It is about organizing production processes based on the use of technology and communication between devices in the value chain, beyond the company itself, and creating an inter-company technological cosmos. Its objectives were to improve both efficiency and productivity, and automation. Authors such as Lu (2017) and Stock and Selinger (2016) have schematized respectively the interoperability framework and the micro perspective of Industry 4.0.

Industry 4.0 is such a radical change that it has been labelled as the fourth industrial revolution. The functions between people and machines are blurred. In addition, systems, connected and autonomously, can relate and adapt themselves. Thus, the linking of physical elements with digital systems is established and an intelligent industry is created, which adapts to the variations that can occur in real time.

Most of the studies in this field take large companies as a reference, while SMEs occupy a secondary place. However, it is necessary to take into account the interrelationship between them all. Large companies usually act as suppliers and customers of SMEs and their activities condition their attitude towards the integrated technologies in Industry 4.0. Therefore, it is absolutely necessary to know in detail how they implement it and how it has an impact on the generation of value.

Industry 4.0 is not limited exclusively to the traditional manufacturing industry. It is also related to nanotechnology or biotechnology. The technologies integrated in Industry 4.0 are being used in industrial companies, although often without interconnection between them. The objective is the transformation towards an integrated, automated and optimized system of value chains. Thus, while in the past new technologies and machines served as a complement to human activity, it is currently machines that participate in decisions.

Business models tell us how companies offer value to their customers. Industry 4.0 has facilitated the creation and development of new business models. According to Müller et al (2018), this makes it possible for the business models of manufacturing SMEs to evolve and it shows that it is essential for the people who manage them understand in depth the variety of possible perspectives when using this new approach. In the Industry 4.0, companies generalize the use of real-time information and thereby they improve the decision making and the procedures of management. Industry 4.0 is based on several technologies. Among them, some that have special relevance on the financial function are: blockchain, robotics, artificial intelligence, machine learning, process mining, big data and analytics, the cloud, cybersecurity or the internet of things (IoT). They are not isolated, but they form a set that interact in unison with the company.

Blockchain technology allows the so-called data structure to serve as a non-relational public database and integrate a historical sequence of irrefutable information. This technology makes a varied type of transactions more secure, traceable and economical. For example, companies use it in bank transactions and payment systems. Big data and analytics aim to analyze large volumes of data that exceed the normally installed capacity. In the field of Industry 4.0, the analysis of large volumes of data helps in the decision making process. Also, robots have evolved rapidly towards greater flexibility and cooperation. Therefore, there will be many more tasks in which the replacement of labor by robots is profitable. The business ecosystem will be intertwined through computer systems, achieving automated value chains in every way. And the same will happen between the departments of a company. This issue will directly affect the financial function, both strategically and operatively.

With respect to the so-called internet of things, this allows field devices to communicate and interact with each other and with the central devices. It also helps to decentralize the analysis and decision-making, and to allow responses in real time. The increase in connectivity sharply emphasizes the need for cybersecurity to protect these systems and the requirement to safeguard both intellectual property and personal information. The generalization of the use of the cloud is another relevant issue. Production tasks increasingly require more information exchange and these technologies have to offer an immediate response capability.

Industry 4.0 is synonymous with challenges. Its implementation will be completely effective if the standardization of protocols and systems is achieved, tasks are adapted from the labor point of view, security and knowledge protection are increased, and workers can train and update their knowledge regularly. From the perspective of SMEs, it is not uncommon to observe how technological advances initially go unnoticed and there is no clear perception about the real effects they will have on market. In addition, SMEs usually have less access to financing, especially banking, and find it more difficult to undertake the investments required by the digital transformation. Likewise, the means of production have an inflexibility that makes it difficult to adapt and often also have little autonomy. Because of this, the public sector will be a relevant actor to create an environment that supports evolution towards this end. From the institutional perspective, the inconveniences may arise from the regulatory environment, which is who must configure the game board and its initial rules.

FINANCIAL MANAGEMENT AND THE CHIEF FINANCIAL OFFICER

The generation of value is the first objective of all companies. This is why it is very important to know and understand the intensity with which it occurs and how the features of the financial function and CFO contribute to the generation of value. From the perspective of large companies, it is important to highlight the efforts of the International Federation of Accountants (IFAC, 2002) to outline a definition of the ideal CFO. In this sense, the IBM Institute for Business Values, in its CFO Global Survey 2010 qualifies these CFOs as those that integrate value.

A series of investigations that aim to show the complexity faced by CFOs and the importance of not only knowing the necessary instruments but also of having the appropriate experience are discussed below. In CIMA (2016) the competencies of the CFO are based on five guiding principles: organizational leader, business partner and steward, integrator and navigator, finance and accounting leader, and professional.

Santero Sánchez et al. (2016) conclude that the last major financial crisis has modified the mix of financial products, increasing the weight of those used for treasury needs. They indicate that the effects have a greater intensity when the company is smaller and with more history. Likewise, Florackis and Sanainani (2018) study the ability of CFOs to influence cash policies and conclude that, ceteris paribus and from the proposed index, those companies that have CFOs defined as strong, are notoriously less effective than those with CFOs defined as weak.

Concerning the size, Briozzo et al. (2016) show that larger companies borrow more intensely. This relationship opens the door to underlining the need to develop segmented policies. On the other hand, the work of Guercio et al. (2017) shows that technological intensity is the variable with the greatest impact on the probability of resorting to the banking sector for financing. Likewise, integration in the high-tech sector reduces the expected probability of resorting to this type of financing.

There is a large literature that investigates different aspects of Chief Executive Officers (CEOs) and CFOs. However, investigations within the context of SMEs are scarcer. In this sense, Carrera (2017) compiles, from the perspective of family businesses, a wide range of previous studies on the role of the accounting. According to Van den Heuvel et al. (2006), the general managers of family SMEs consider that the role of service is more important than that one of control. However, the study of CFOs and CEOs from the perspective of a larger company provides interesting elements that should also be taken into account, although with certain precautions, within the context of SMEs. Thus, Chava and Purnanandam (2010) conclude that the CEO´s stimulus to reduce risk is related to lower leverage and higher treasury levels. Likewise, CFO incentives to reduce risk are related, among others, to safer debt maturities. On the operational level, Hiebl et al (2017) found that companies with CFOs from other companies adopt ERP systems more frequently than those with CFOs that had been developed in the company itself.

Zoni and Pippo (2019) concluded that, regardless of their roles, the influence of CFOs is positively related to their age and their background in business and industry. They verified that part of this predominance was justified by the fact that those who were members of the Board of Directors and enjoyed a closer relationship with shareholders were more influential. In turn, Habib and Houssain (2013) analyzed the relevance of considering the characteristics of CEOs and CFOs as an essential element in the results provided by the financial information. Zorn (2004) concluded that financial managers had an outstanding performance in most of the most important companies in the United States and that CFO positions were consolidated in the organization chart at a relevant level.

From the perspective of SMEs, the CFO also becomes a leading figure, although traditionally he did not have a clear projection out of the company. He was assigned a place in the backoffice, more focused on properly controlling the activity developed than the action. According to CIMA (2011) management accountants continue to profile themselves with a bias towards activities traditionally attributed to their function. SMEs that begin their activity initially focus on producing and selling, ensuring that their services or products are competitive. As they reach maturity and grow in size, these criteria strengthen and make subsequent changes difficult. The financial function, although considered very relevant, is often eclipsed by the above.

Hielb et al. (2013) demonstrated several relevant issues in the case of Germany. They found that in medium-sized companies a smaller proportion of CFOs held a University degree. They also found that the size of the company was not an element serving to differentiate the participation of CFOs in the strategic planning of the company.

The organizational structure of the companies is in a process of transformation. Due to their physiognomy, this especially affects SMEs, both for their survival and for their growth and profitability. The classic vertical structure, in which the decision-making capacity is at the top and the execution at the lower levels, is being adapted to the current circumstances. A substantial part of the executive tasks will leave room for the growing decision-making nodes. The CFO will have to make an effort to update his skills, the tools he employs and the skills of the team he leads.

Specific training is generally very segmented in this area. The way to access knowledge has been based mainly on experience, with the high risks and costs that this approach has. The professional and formative evolution of CFO in the future cannot be linear, but he must assume leadership in certain aspects in order to create value with the design and implementation of the strategy. It is important that the CFO's career becomes enriched through experiences in other departments, giving him a more accurate vision of the business as a whole. From the ability perspective, the person who will direct the financial function in the future must provide a solid financial experience, know the value chain and the departmental profiles, and actively participate in the design of the direction of the company. To that end, it is necessary to add flexibility and negotiation capacity, both inside and outside the organization.

The evolution of the financial function has led to the expansion of its smaller initial scope of action. CFO was traditionally assigned the function of accounting, negotiating and controlling the operations funded by credit institutions. Thus, he was responsible for the evolution of financial expenses. However, this was no his own responsibility, but shared with the company as a whole. It also prepared the budgets and the different reports on the financial situation. At the same time, it assessed the risks and applied the strategy defined from the general management, transferring the minimum necessary information to the rest of the society.

In his new role, his contribution has focused on value and profitability. The normative evolution has led to the achievement of objectives such as the maximization of value for the stakeholders, the design of the functional structure or the improvement of the efficiency of the processes. Together with the traditional areas of responsibility, the current role includes new skills and establishes new relationships (Figure 2). CFO becomes the manager of the resources used in the development of the business activity and the organizer of the company as a whole to achieve the objective of minimizing the burden of a suffocating financial dependence. Regarding his projection outside the company, he should not only be connected with the financial agents, but also with the different stakeholders.

The difficulty in financing the exploitation cycle helped raise it to a relevant position within the organization chart. However, his functions should not be limited solely to financing. The difficulty of obtaining external financing redirected his attention to other areas involved in the exploitation cycle. Thus, he has extended its functions to the development of operations and all that this implies. In this way, while demanding financial resources difficult to obtain the different areas of the company, is actively involved in all of them. Thus, his relevance has been set at the same level as other key departments for the business.

Unlike the classic model, the new CFO has the responsibility of being a facilitator of information and a coordinator of the financial needs of each department and business unit. In addition, he becomes an observer of the activity to anticipate the problems that arise. The scope of his functions are enlarged and integrated into the team that designs the corporate strategy. Likewise, he becomes a financial trainer of the company as a whole and promoter of the culture and financial values throughout the company.

Based on the CFOs' experience, it is possible to identify two possible typologies. On the one hand, those who developed their professional career in the company itself. On the other hand, those that have had to change companies in their professional growth process. The suitability of both profiles depends on the objectives to be achieved. In addition to the most genuine aspects of financial management, a constant relationship with the business and stakeholders is necessary. The more in-depth knowledge of the activity developed by the company, the more global the perception of reality will be, so the analysis performed will be better grounded and will have a more reliable perspective on the essential business variables.

The Challenge of Generating Value In A Digital Economy

Generating value requires setting a course focused on its management and linking strategy with action. This entails overcoming excessively bureaucratic approaches

Figure 2. Areas of responsibility of the CFO
Source: Prepared by the author

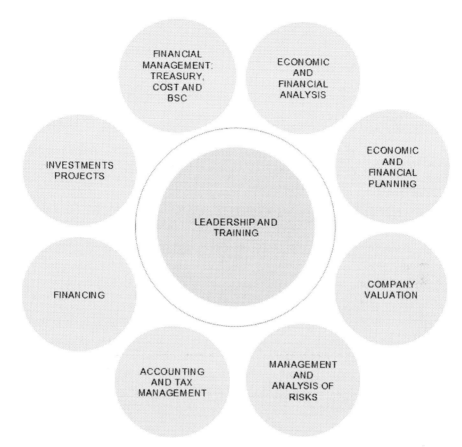

that can also arise in SMEs. In addition, modifying essential aspects of the business model also entails transforming the existing financing model. We start from the affirmation that CFOs are one of the organizational pillars that must underpin the growth of companies. This has become the today's business world, in which stakeholders are corporate co-designers and observers of the degree of compliance with the objectives set by the company's management. Likewise, the most important function of CFO is to build the value map and relate the value generated by each element of the value chain to the necessary investment to achieve it.

The financial hardships suffered recently have forced profound transformations both in companies and the sectors in which they are integrated. To survive, they have had to minimize their costs as much as possible. However, even while considering this process of cost reduction, they have taken steps to trace a further evolution towards control. In this process, the financial management must go one step further and focus on supporting decisions and promoting commitment to the implementation of the strategy, without losing the perspective of control.

With respect to the concept of value and its creation, it is necessary to define it, measure it and develop the appropriate actions to generate it. Each case will require a different mix and the financial officer will have to create it ad hoc. The accounting criteria are insufficient for this task, with notable differences between countries and open spaces to subjectivity that make it difficult to determine the mix accurately. Likewise, other variables, such as liquidity, have a direct relationship. Therefore, CFOs use concepts such as cash flow for their valuations. In addition to the above, value-based management is based on the development and implementation of a genuine and own scorecard. It is essential to have relevant information for its construction and subsequent elaboration of conclusions.

Investment decisions have a great impact on operations. Likewise, the financial processes most linked to the operational field can be integrated into purchases or sales, thus reducing fixed expenses. These interrelationships favor the existence of flatter organizations. The increasing proximity of CFO to the business and his global perspective will contribute to the development of a map of risks and priorities based on a joint analysis of the global risks that affect the company.

Likewise, CFO should never lose the objective of achieving sustainable profitability and liquidity. However, he should avoid risky policies that may cause liquidity problems in exchange for expectations of increases in profitability. These would raise the risk of presenting treasury tensions in the operating cycle and the company's own viability. In this sense, the CFO establishes a relationship of trust with the partners and the board of directors, although he is under the responsibility of the managing director. This fact gives the managing director a high power over financiers. This reality can serve to promote objectives that favor the partners or as a lever to coerce CFOs in an attempt of partisan manipulation of the information.

A corporate strategy that integrates the financial strategy must be designed. The search for value needs the strategy to be based on concrete actions at the operational level. Both CFO and managing director have to be clear about those activities that generate value. This identification must be objective and based on the numbers obtained from the information systems. It is essential to act on those elements that increase the value of the company and promote both profitable businesses and good growth prospects. The essence of this process is based on a robust infrastructure, starting with the organizational structure and skills of the human team, and following by having efficient information systems that are capable of providing the required information. It is also essential to have the channels to assess the different risks and know in detail the legal responsibilities, both directly and indirectly affecting the department.

In order to ensure that CFOs and their department can cover the needs of the companies in the current environment, it is convenient to develop changes both within their own function and in the other departments that configure the company. They all form a set that needs to be interconnected. The constant innovation has developed a virtual ecosystem in which the classic profiles of the financial function have to take on new challenges to achieve a solid and well aligned organization. These innovations are those that have been mentioned throughout the chapter and that represent a complex universe marked by the growing uncertainty that companies have to deal with.

The use only of financial figures and variables shows obvious limitations to depict the value of the models in the digital age. It is essential to refine them with the information, in many cases in real time, provided by the company as a whole and ranging from operations with customers to warehouse or human resources policy. Digital technologies allow centralized surveillance of actions and are a means to deal with problems arising from uncertainty. In short, they contribute to respond more effectively to the changes raised by the market. Likewise, they contribute to increase the financial function capacity for analysis and planning. The added value created by digital models needs to be measured from the development of new indicators that complete the current scorecard. IFAC (2018b) details the opportunities for accountants in the digital age and the concerns that emanate for the accountancy profession. Among the latter, the cybersecurity, outdated accounting systems, the change in the role of accountants and labor mobility are the most relevant.

Thus, blockchain technology has direct applications in matters related to payments, billing or accounting operations. Its application enables better security, lower costs or higher transparency. Robotics-based technology is applicable to continuous administrative procedures, in which one or more interconnected systems coexist. Artificial intelligence and machine learning will contribute to autonomy in tasks and value chains, while reducing costs and increasing efficiency. The process mining provides information from the real analysis of processes and promotes the deepening of control tasks that result in greater efficiency. However, the digital tools that are having a strong impact on the financial function are not limited only to the previous ones. The cloud, the internet of things, cybersecurity or fintech are other relevant tools with a broad implementation path (Figure 3).

The management of large databases, their mining and subsequent analysis may be used for the forecast of results, treasury, etc. Likewise, the use of big data and analytics can facilitate the exploitation and accessibility of data, with the objective of support the decision-making process. These tend to be somewhere within the information systems, but the ability to transform them into information is a task that so far many SMEs have failed to achieve successfully. These digital tools allow, for example, the financial function to perform simulations of results based

Figure 3. Incorporation of new digital tools to the financial function
Source: Prepared by the author

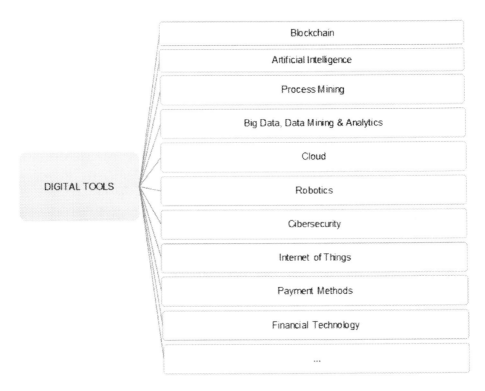

on information obtained in real time and the financial department to make all kind of predictions based on real demand, instead of using only historical data that not always reflect future trends.

CONCLUSIONS

The current megatrends envision transformations that are predicted to affect the whole system in a very significant way in the long term. This will be the habitat in which our society will be developed in the coming years and in which ICTs have a very important role. The process of incorporating ICTs in firms is complex and is greatly influenced by issues such as the management commitment, the existing organizational structure, the way of managing or the staff characteristics. Understanding the variables involved in the adoption of ICTs and their impact are essential to develop actions that promote SMEs to make investments in disruptive technologies and thus acquire or maintain the competitive advantages that ensure their survival.

It is increasingly common to observe how companies seek the adoption of sustainability initiatives and strive hard to meet the changing consumer preferences. In the search for an innovative environment, they are adopting multiple digital technologies. The recent introduction of these concepts greatly influenced industrial systems. These technologies, as well as Industry 4.0, are assuming a radical change in supply chain management at the individual and collective levels.

The financial function is transformed to respond to the new approaches that the environment demands. The study of this topic requires the conjunction of a professional and academic perspective. With a more effervescent and complex world economy, all kinds of risks increase. The financial function will aim to create value while defining the needs and tools to achieve this purpose. The financial information should flow to all corners of the company and will serve to improve all the functions. This will entail changing the time taken to develop each task. The concept of value can be applied to both clients and shareholders. The generation of shareholder value gives companies meaning and has been the driving force of such important trends as outsourcing or leasing. It is about achieving the highest economic profitability from the lowest possible investment. The activity of SMEs should be focused on orienting its scarce resources towards the main business.

In this context, the role of the CFO encompasses new perspectives and has as primary objective the generation of value. For this reason, CFO needs to know the necessary resources of the business model and position himself as an advisor to the general management. This is why, his profile is going to be more ecliptic and multidisciplinary. With the growing regulatory complexity, he will have to make a constant update effort. The great challenge that lies ahead is to demonstrate his ability to implement the company's strategy, acquire a technological profile and consolidate a philosophy of constant adaptation to the changes that occur. The proper use of technology will be an essential element to take advantage of innovations and contribute to the business, by identifying new opportunities, calibrating risks and monitoring the strategic approach. In short, it is about serving the company to increase its efficiency and value.

REFERENCES

Association of Chartered Certified Accountants. (2016). Professional accountants – the future: Drivers of change and future skills. Retrieved October 7, 2019, from https://www.accaglobal.com/content/dam/ members-beta/docs/ea-patf-drivers-of-change-and-future-skills.pdf

Briozzo, A., Vigier, H., Castillo, N., Pesce, G., & Speroni, M. C. (2016). Decisiones de financiamiento en pymes: ¿existen diferencias en función del tamaño y la forma legal? Estudios Gerenciales, 32(138), 71–81. doi:10.1016/j.estger.2015.11.003

Carrera, N. (2017). What Do We Know about Accounting in Family Firms? *Journal of Evolutionary Studies in Business*, 2(2), 97–159. doi:10.1344/jesb2017.2.j032

Chartered Institute of Management Accountants – CIMA. (2011). Finance Transformation a Missed Opportunity for SMEs? Retrieved May 5, 2019, from https://www.cimaglobal.com/Research--Insight/Finance-transformation-a-missed-opportunity-for-SMEs

Chartered Institute of Management Accountants - CIMA. (2016). A CFO's Key Competencies for the Future. Retrieved October 15, 2019, from https://www.ifac.org/system/files/publications/files/Role%20of %20the%20CFO.pdf

Chava, S., & Purnanandam, A. (2010). CEOs versus CFOs: Incentives and corporate policies. *Journal of Financial Economics*, 97(2), 263–278. doi:10.1016/j.jfineco.2010.03.018

Florackis, C., & Sainani, S. (2018). How do chief financial officers influence corporate cash policies? *Journal of Corporate Finance*, 52, 168–191. doi:10.1016/j.jcorpfin.2018.08.001

Guercio, M. B., Martinez, L. B., & Vigier, H. (2017). Las limitaciones al financiamiento bancario de las pymes de alta tecnología. Estudios Gerenciales, 33(142), 3-12. DOI: . 2017.02.001 doi:10.1016/j.estger

Habib, A., & Hossain, M. (2013). CEO/CFO characteristics and financial reporting quality: A review. *Research in Accounting Regulation*, 25(1), 88–100. doi:10.1016/j.racreg.2012.11.002

Hagsten, E., & Kotnik, P. (2017). ICT as facilitator of internationalisation in small- and medium-sized firms. *Small Business Economics*, 48(2), 431–446. doi:10.1007/s11187-016-9781-2

Hiebl, M., Gärtner, B., & Duller, C. (2017). Chief financial officer (CFO) characteristics and ERP system adoption: An upper-echelons perspective. *Journal of Accounting & Organizational Change*, 13(1), 85–111. doi:10.1108/JAOC-10-2015-0078

Hiebl, M., Neubauer, H., & Duller, C. (2013). The Chief Financial Officer's Role in Medium-Sized Firms: Exploratory Evidence from Germany. *Journal of International Business & Economics*, 13(2), 83–92. doi:10.18374/JIBE-13-2.8

IBM Institute for Business Values. (2010), APQC Webinar: Chief Financial Officer Global Study 2010. Retrieved May 7, 2019, from https://www.apqc.org/sites/default/files/files/WebinarPDFs/IBMCFOStudy 2010APQCJuly13Webinar.pdf

International Federation of Accountants. (2002). The Role of the Chief Financial Officer in 2010. IFAC. Retrieved May 9, 2019, from https://www.icjce.es/images/pdfs/TECNICA/C01%20-%20IFAC/C.01.073%20-%20PAIB%20-%20Other/PAIB-CFO_2010.pdf

International Federation of Accountants - IFAC. (2013). The Role and Expectations of a CFO. A Global Debate on Preparing Accountants for Finance Leadership. Retrieved May 9, 2019, from https://www.ifac.org/system/files/publications/files/Role%20of%20the%20CFO.pdf

International Federation of Accountants - IFAC. (2018a). The Crucial Roles of Professional Accountants in Business in Mid-Sized Enterprises. Retrieved Octuber 12, 2019, from https://www.ifac.org/system /files/publications /files/the-crucial-roles-of-pro.pdf

International Federation of Accountants – IFAC. (2018b). Information and Communications Technology Literature Review. Retrieved October 4, 2019, from https://www.ifac.org/system/files/publications /files/IAESB-Information-Communications-Technology-Literature-Review.pdf

Kanchana, V., & Sri Ranjini, S. (2018). Investigation and Study of Vital Factors in Selection, Implementation and Satisfaction of ERP in Small and Medium Scale Industries. *Iranian Journal of Electrical and Computer Engineering*, *81*(2), 1150–1155. doi:10.11591/ijece.v8i2.pp1150-1155

Lu, Y. (2017). Industry 4.0: A survey on technologies, applications and open research issues. *Journal of Industrial Information Integration*, *6*, 1–10. doi:10.1016/j.jii.2017.04.005

Mbuyisa, B., & Leonard, A. (2017). The Role of ICT Use in SMEs Towards Poverty Reduction: A Systematic Literature Review. *Journal of International Development*, *29*(2), 159–197. doi:10.1002/jid.3258

Müller, J. M., Buliga, O., & Voigt, K. (2018). Fortune favors the prepared: How SMEs approach business model innovations in industry 4.0. *Technological Forecasting and Social Change*, *132*, 2–17. doi:10.1016/j.techfore.2017.12.019

Pellegrina, L. D., Frazzoni, S., Rotondi, Z., & Vezulli, A. (2017). Does ICT adoption improve access to credit for small enterprises? *Small Business Economics*, *48*(3), 657–679. doi:10.1007/s11187-016-9794-x

Qosasi, A., Permana, E., Muftiadi, A., Purnomo, M., & Maulina, E. (2019). Building SMEs' Competitive Advantage and the Organizational Agility of Apparel Retailers in Indonesia: The role of ICT as an Initial Trigger, Gadjah Mada International. *The Journal of Business*, *21*(1), 69–90.

Santero Sánchez, R., De la Fuente-Cabrero, C., & Laguna Sánchez, P. (2016). Efectos de la crisis sobre la financiación bancaria del emprendimiento. Un análisis de las microempresas españolas desde el sector de las Sociedades de Garantía Recíproca. *European Research on Management and Business Economics*, *22*(2), 88–93. doi:10.1016/j.iedee.2015.10.006

Slusarczyk, M., Pozo, J.M., & Perurena, L. (2015). Estudio de aplicación de las TIC en las pymes. 3C Empresa, 4(1), 69-87.

Stock, T., & Seliger, G. (2016). Opportunities of sustainable manufacturing in industry 4.0. Procedia CIRP, 40, 536–541. doi:10.1016/j.procir.2016.01.129

Van den Heuvel, J., Van Gils, A., & Voordeckers, W. (2006). Board roles in small and medium-sized family businesses: Performance and importance. *Corporate Governance*, *14*(5), 467–485. doi:10.1111/j.1467-8683.2006.00519.x

Zoni, L., & Pippo, F. (2017). CFO and finance function: What matters in value creation. *Journal of Accounting & Organizational Change*, *13*(2), 216–238. doi:10.1108/JAOC-12-2014-0059

Zorn, D. M. (2004). Here a Chief, There a Chief: The Rise of the CFO in the American Firm. *American Sociological Review*, *69*(3), 345–364. doi:10.1177/000312240406900302

ADDITIONAL READING

Accenture. (2018). *The CFO Reimagined: from driving value to building the digital enterprise*. Retrieved Octuber 10, 2019, from https://www.accenture.com/_acnmedia/PDF-85/Accenture-CFO-ResearchGlobal. pdf#zoom=50

Brealey, R. A., Myers, S. C., & Allen, F. (2014). *Principles of Corporate Finance* (11th ed.). New York, United States: Mc GrawHill.

HMSC. (2017). *The Future of Cash Management*. Retrieved April 17, 2019, from https://www.slg.co.at/wp-content/uploads/2017/09/HSBC-Pr%C3%A4sentation-The-Future-of-Cash-Management.pdf

International Federation of Accountants. (2013). *The Role and Expectations of a CFO. A Global Debate on Preparing Accountants for Finance Leadership*. Retrieved Octuber 9, 2019, from https://www.ifac.org /about-ifac/professional-accountants-business/publications-resources/role-and-expectations-cfo-global

International Federation of Accountants. (2018). A Vision for the Finance Professional and the Finance Function. Retrieved Octuber 16, 2019, from https://www.ifac.org/system/files/publications/files/A-Vision-for-the-Finance-Professional-and-Finance-Function.pdf

KPMG. (2008). *Finance of the future – looking forward to 2020*. Retrieved May 12, 2019, from https://home.kpmg/content/dam/kpmg/pdf/2016/07/finance-of-the-future.pdf.

Leadind Treausry Professionals and The Institute of Chartered Accounts in Australia. (2012). *20 issues on the increasing significance of corporate treasury*. Retrieved May 25, 2019, from https://www.treasurers.org /ACTmedia/20_issues.pdf

Oracle (2013). *El director financiero como catalizador del cambio*. Retrieved May 17, 2019, from http://www.oracle.com/us/products/cfo-catalyst-of-change-es-2002720.pdf

The Economist Intelligence Unit. (2018). *How ready is treasury?* Retrieved April 22, 2019, from https://perspectives.eiu.com/sites/default/files/Final%20Briefing%20paper%2004_09_2018.pdf

Van Horne, C. J., & Wachowicz, J. M. (2010). *Fundamentals of financial Management* (13th ed.). Harlow, England: Prentice Hall.

World Economic Forum. (2018). *The Global Competitiveness Report 2018*. Retrieved June 3, from https://www.weforum.org/events/world-economic-forum-annual-meeting-2016/partners

KEY TERMS AND DEFINITIONS

Digitalization: Incorporation, in a broad sense, of digital technologies to the company in order to improve their capabilities and performance.
Disruptive Technology: Technology that facilitates the appearance of new products or services through a sudden break with the previous model.
Financial Function: Within the company, and with a classical and partial perspective, it is responsible for the management and control of financial resources.

Megatrend: It is a set of social and individual variables, such as beliefs and values, that transform society at all levels.

Strategic Thinking: A way of thinking that is characterized by setting a goal, analyzing how to achieve it and organizing the means to achieve it.

Uncertainity: Based on the concept of radical uncertainty, the future is unpredictable and cannot be known, so the confidence of the decision maker is important.

Value Chain: This is a theoretical model that analyzes the activities that an organization, mainly a business, develops to detect where value is generated.

Volatility: Usually applied in the economic and financial field to the frequency and intensity of changes in the prices of an asset.

Section 2
Financial Management, Funding, and Economic Cycle

Chapter 4
Effect of Venture Capital on the Growth of Information and Communication Technology University Spin-Offs:
Venture Capital Effect on the Growth of ICT-USOs

María Jesús Rodríguez-Gulías
Universidade da Coruña, Spain

Sara Fernández-López
Universidade de Santiago de Compostela, Spain

David Rodeiro-Pazos
https://orcid.org/0000-0002-5272-2676
Universidade de Santiago de Compostela, Spain

Ana Paula Faria
Universidade do Minho, Portugal

Natalia Barbosa
Universidade do Minho, Portugal

ABSTRACT

The creation of university spin-off firms (USOs) to commercialize the academic research outputs contributes to the economic development of the regions. These firms are often resource-constrained, which may hamper their growth. However, the involvement of venture capital (VC) partners in their management can partly counterbalance their traditional lack of resources. Within the USOs created in

DOI: 10.4018/978-1-7998-2440-4.ch004

Portugal and Spain, around one-third operate in the information and communication technology industry (ICT-USOs). This chapter aims to explore the effect of VC partners on the ICT-USOs' growth by using a sample of 127 Spanish and 176 Portuguese ICT-USOs over the period 2007–2013. The results show that the effect of VC on the ICT-USOs' growth depends not only on the country, but also on how firm growth is measured; whereas a weak positive effect on the sales growth is found, a negative one is obtained in the case of the employment growth.

INTRODUCTION

In recent decades, the creation of university spin-off firms (USOs) is one of mechanisms used by universities to transfer technology to society and contribute to the regions' economic development. The USO concept does not have a single and consensually accepted definition (Pirnay et al., 2003), but rather several proposals that are not always convergent. In a literature survey, Djokovic and Souitaris (2008) indicate that definition must contain two main issues: the agents involved and the elements to be transferred. Regarding the first one, the parent organization has to be a university or academic institution but there is no consensus on the need for participation of a university member in the company.

Regarding the second one, the new entity has to exploit knowledge produced from academic activities or academic pursuits. In this respect, whereas some authors use a very narrow definition, requiring that the rights transferred being of an exclusively technological nature (O'Shea et al., 2008), other ones argue that these rights may include both codified knowledge (for example, in the form of patents or copyrights) and tacit knowledge (technical know-how) (Hindle & Yencken, 2004). The output of these combinations has to be a separate legal entity to be considered a university spin-off.

In this paper, we follow the definition by Red OTRI, which considers USOs as start-ups exploiting university knowledge but not necessarily founded by university staff (Red OTRI, 2011). This definition of USO also appears to be one of the most widely employed among researchers (Zhang, 2009). Using this definition in the Spanish and Portuguese academic entrepreneurship contexts means to consider a mix of both technology and service-based spin-offs.

USOs are an important mechanism of transferring knowledge from Universities to society. In so doing, USOs contribute to create new high quality employment and accelerate the productivity of regional economies (Hayter, 2016; Shane, 2004). Therefore, policy-makers are increasingly investing in universities to foster the creation of innovative start-ups (Autio et al., 2014). However, several studies have suggested that USOs are not the best way to transfer knowledge from universities to industry as these firms tend to remain relatively small (Zhang, 2009).

USOs usually face certain problems, namely financial constraints and founder teams lacked of basic managerial skills. In this respect, the presence of venture capital (VC) partners may help USOs to gain access to the lacking resources, exerting a positive impact on their performance. Venture capitalists are a type of financial intermediary with three main functions (Metrick & Yasuda, 2010, p. 19); "screening potential investments and deciding on companies to invest in, monitoring these companies and providing value-added services for them, and exiting their investments in these companies by selling their stake to public markets or to another buyer". The object of VC capital investors is to contribute to the expansion and development of the company and, therefore, increases their value. Later, when the company has generated the expected value it is listed to be reversed, and, therefore shareholders, including venture capitalists, can obtain a recompense on the capital invested. The injection of VC funds is complemented by an added value with services like: advice, credibility with third parties, professionalization of management teams, openness to new business approaches, experience in other sectors or markets, etc.

A non-negligible share of created USOs operate in the information and communication technology (ICT) sector, those are ICT-USOs. Within ICT firms, asymmetrical information problems are frequently present due to the fact that the underlying business model is often not readily transparent for outsiders, unless technically well-versed, and the entrepreneurs may not reveal all risks resulting from it (Schröder, 2013). However, as venture capitalists are usually specialized in certain industries, such as ICT sector, their experience allows them to appropriately assess existing risks. Moreover, VC partners provide additional managerial experience (know-how) and networks that can allow ICT firms grow faster, as Schröder (2013) found in his study of German ICT firms. In this context, it can be expected that ICT-USOs also benefit from VC funding, which can mitigate financial constraints. In spite of this evidence, to the date, no work has addressed whether the presence of VC influences the ICT-USOs' performance.

The aim of this chapter is to analyse the effect of the involvement of VC on the growth of the ICT-USOs. More specifically, a dataset of 127 Spanish and 176 Portuguese ICT-USOs is used to explore how venture capitalists influence their employment growth and sales growth over the period 2007-2013. Obtaining empirical evidence on this issue becomes especially relevant since a huge amount of public funds has been spent on fostering USOs, and a significant share of these firms is created in the ICT sector -as we will see bellow, around one USO out of three in the case of Spain and Portugal. This public financial support only makes sense if these firms grow.

Effect of Venture Capital on the Growth of Information and Communication Technology

This chapter makes several contributions to the literature on the effect of VC on both USO firms and ICT industry. First, a sample of 303 ICT-USOs over the period 2007-2013 is used. In so doing, this chapter contributes to a better knowledge of firm growth in the ICT sector, which still remains limited (Lasch et al., 2007; Schröder, 2013). Second, given that the dataset comprises ICT-USOs from Portugal and Spain, it allows comparative analysis across two different national environments over a non-negligible period of study. Thus, this chapter provides the necessary regional perspective to design effective regional and national programs aimed at promoting the ICT-USOs' growth. Finally, the ICT-USOs' growth is measured through sales growth and employment growth, which allows obtaining a more complete picture of the growth dynamics in the sector.

THEORETICAL BACKGROUND

In the last two decades, literature on USOs has paid attention to firm growth as a measure of the USOs' success. In so doing, the resource-based view (RBV) of the firm (Penrose, 1959) has been the most widely used theoretical framework (Rodríguez-Gulías et al., 2017). From this approach, the firm's ability to collect and deploy valuable and non-substitutable resources (Barney, 1991) becomes the main driver of its success. In parallel, a reduced number of studies have adopted the knowledge-based theory of firm as main theoretical approach, given that USOs can be considered as firms that transform knowledge into products/services through the dynamic interaction between tacit and explicit knowledge at both individual and group-levels (Zahra et al., 2007). Moreover, drawing on the studies on top management teams (TMT), another stream of the literature has emphasized the characteristics of founders' firms as main drivers on the USOs' growth. In any case, the RBV of the serves as a "umbrella" theoretical framework since it explicitly and/or implicitly takes into account the resources highlighted by the other strand of the literature (i.e. knowledge and human capital of founders). Moreover, The RBV is also an appropriate framework for studying the effect of VC partners on the USOs' growth (Rodríguez-Gulías et al., 2018), given that venture capitalists provide firms with a richer set of valuable resources compared to non venture- backed USOs (Bertoni et al., 2011).

Stemming from this theoretical framework, there are five arguments that may explain why venture-backed USOs can gain a competitive advantage from VC endorsement (Figure 1).

First, VC partners are highly involved in the firm's day-to-day management (Colombo & Grilli, 2010; Bertoni et al., 2011). Such "monitoring" role ("coach" role) becomes especially relevant in the case of USOs, in order to mitigate the lack

Figure 1. Roles of VC in venture-backed firms
Source: Elaborated by the authors

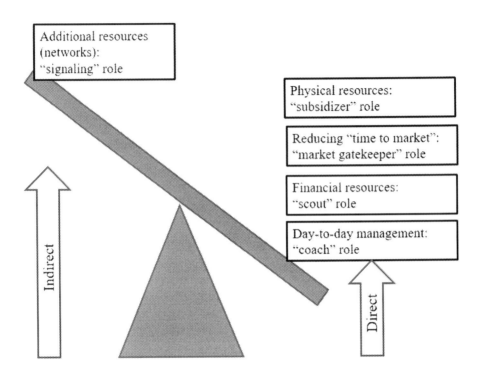

of managerial skills (Cantner & Goethner, 2011; Ortín & Vendrell, 2010; Ortín et al., 2007, 2008) and experience in the industry (Wennberg et al., 2011; Zahra et al., 2007) of the USOs' founders.

Second, VC investors provide venture-backed firms with financial resources, which are an important source of competitive advantages, especially for financially constrained firms such as USOs (Colombo & Grilli, 2010; Wright et al., 2006). It is not so obvious, however, that often they are the only investors who "dare" to finance this type of companies. Thus, USOs in general, and ICT-USOs in particular, have a large share of intangible assets that are difficult to value for outsiders. As mentioned, asymmetrical information problems frequently arise in the ICT firms because the underlying knowledge base is tacit and not readily transparent for external stakeholders, and the internal ones may not reveal all risks resulting from it (Schröder, 2013). Given that, compared to traditional investors, different venture capitalists specialize in different industries and types of investments (Hellman & Puri, 2002; Schröder, 2013), they are in a better position to appropriately assess the firms' underlying knowledge base (Bertoni et al., 2011; Colombo & Grilli,

2010). In other words, venture capitalists may be the most cost-efficient path of obtaining financial resources for ICT-USOs. In fact, to reduce the asymmetric information, venture capitalists subject the firms to strong scrutiny before being venture-backed ("explorer" or "scout" role), and, later, they play also the above-mentioned "monitoring" role.

Third, VC investors may exert an important impact on firm growth by reducing the time to bring new products to market. Moreover, Gompers and Lerner (2001) and Denis (2004) acknowledge that this "market gatekeeper" role of VC is especially relevant for innovative firms. In this respect, USOs could be frequently considered early-early deals (i.e., early-stage companies with early-stage products) (Klausner, 2005) and, consequently, they need professional support in transforming the research outputs into valuable product and service market outcomes.

Fourth, VC endorsement might be a source of competitive advantage by providing venture-backed firms with other physical resources (Gompers & Lerner, 2001; Denis, 2004). Thus, VC investors may offer incubation space at reduced rent. This "subsidizer" role of VC investors is even more important for early-stage firms, since it reduces their fixed costs and allows them to allocate the limited financial resources to the development of marketable outcomes.

The above-mentioned roles of venture capitalists (e.g., the coach, scout, market gatekeeper, and subsidizer) could be considered the direct pathways through which they can enhance the USOs' growth. Additionally, there is an indirect pathway through which the VC endorsement may leverage firm performance. Thus, given that venture-backed firms have successfully faced the necessary scrutiny of VC investors (Lockett et al., 2005; Bertoni et al., 2011), they are to some extent viewed as potentially valuable companies by the remaining stakeholders ("signalling" effect). In other words, VC involvement provides USOs with "entrepreneurial legitimation", which helps them in gaining access to additional resources. Thus, in fifth place, this "signalling" role of VC may be a positive sign for other investors (i.e., the next round of backing), as well as for other stakeholders (e.g., business partners, customers, or suppliers, among others).

In view of previous arguments, the following research hypothesis is established:

Hypothesis: The presence of VC partners positively affects the growth of ICT-USOs.

Although from a theoretical approach the involvement of VC partners is considered critical for the USOs' growth, the empirical evidence still remains scarce and inconclusive. Thus, Zhang (2009) found that the amount of funds raised in the first round of VC positive influences the employment growth in a sample of 704 USOs and 5,655 independent American companies over the period 1992 - 2001. Similarly, Rodríguez-Gulías et al. (2016) presented empirical evidence of the positive effect of

VC involvement on the sales growth of 212 Spanish USOs over the period 2001 - 2010. However, no significant relationship between VC and the USOs' growth was found by Yagüe-Perales and March-Chordà (2011) in the biotechnological industry. Similar results were obtained by Rodríguez-Gulías et al. (2018) in a sample of 904 Italian USOs during the period 2005 - 2013.

Two main conclusions can be deduced from previous studies. First, the need of focusing on one sector at a time. Indeed, the result concerning the effect of VC on the USOs' growth differs depending on whether a specific sector is considered (e.g. the biotechnological industry) or there are no distinctions of selected sectors. In this respect, not only each sector has its specificities, but also different venture capitalists specialize in different industries (Hellman & Puri, 2002; Schröder, 2013). In this chapter, the ICT industry has been selected. It not only represents a significant share of the firms created by universities, but also few empirical evidence is available on the growth conditions of this sector (Lasch et al., 2007). To the best of our knowledge, this chapter is the first to analyse the effect of VC involvement in the ICT-USOs. Second the need of considering the differences between the environments in which USOs and VC investors interact when cross-national datasets are used. Then two different subsamples are distinguished in the empirical analysis.

METHODOLOGY

Sample

To test the proposed hypothesis, a longitudinal dataset of 127 Spanish and 176 Portuguese ICT-USOs referred to the period 2007 – 2013 is used. This final sample was obtained from two previous originally constructed datasets used in Rodríguez-Gulías et al. (2015) and Conceição et al. (2017), both of them formed with data about firm-specific characteristics and financial performance from SABI database, provided by Bureau Van Dijk. Those initial datasets included 531 Spanish and 580 Portuguese USOs, respectively, created in 2010 or before (Table 1). Then, it was identified which of these 1,111 USOs were ICT firms following the second definition of the ICT sector stablished by the Spanish National Statistics Institute (INE) and which is classified according to the ISIC Rev.4 and the NACE Rev. 2 (see Annex 1 for details). The result was 312 ICT-USOs, 132 Spanish and 180 Portuguese firms. Finally, in order to avoid observations with missing data in the dependent variables the study period was established between 2007 and 2013. As a result, the final sample consisted of 127 Spanish and 176 Portuguese ICT-USOs.

Table 1. Summary of the sample (by country)

	Spain	Portugal	Total
USOs	531	580	1,111
Discarded NON ICT-USOs	-399	-400	-799
ICT-USOs	132	180	312
Discarded observations before 2007	-5	-4	-9
FINALLY STUDIED ICT-USOs	127	176	303

Source: Elaborated by the authors

Dependent, Independent and Control Variables

In new created firms, growth has been used as the most common indicator of performance (Wennberg et al., 2011). In this sense, the sales growth shows the market acceptance of the firm's goods/ services and it is therefore a good indicator of its success. However, this variable also presents certain limitations, as it could be the possibility of a company to grow with a low level of sales, a frequent case in high-technology companies, as ICT-USOs usually are. The employment growth is also considered a good indicator of the firm's success since it shows the necessity of additional resources to meet customer demands (Cantner & Goethner, 2011). Then it could reduce the limitations of sales growth indicator. Hence, in this chapter both sales growth and employment growth are used as dependent variables to obtain a more complete picture of the growth dynamics in the ICT-USOs. They were calculated as the natural logarithm of the difference in the size (sales or employment) of the firm following Wennberg et al. (2011):

$$GROWTH_{i,t} = \ln\left(\frac{Size_{i,t}}{Size_{i,t-1}}\right)$$

In order to contrast the stablished hypothesis, the main independent variable (VC) was constructed as a time-invariant dummy that takes the value 1 if the ICT-USO had at least one VC partner in its ownership structure, and 0 otherwise, as in the works of Bonardo et al. (2009), Yagüe-Perales and March-Chordà (2011) and Rodríguez-Gulías et al. (2018).

Finally, to approximate firm-specific characteristics a set of control variables was incorporated. Those control variables were the firm's age (LNAGE) and the firm size (LNTA), both of them previously used in Rodríguez-Gulías et al. (2016)

Table 2. Measures of variables and predictions

	VARIABLE		MEASURES
DEPENDENT	Sales growth[1]	GSALES	Natural logarithm of the difference in the sales
	Employment growth	GEMP	Natural logarithm of the difference in the number of employees
INDEPENDENT	Venture capital	VC	1 if the firm had VC funding, and 0 otherwise
	Age	LNAGE	Natural logarithm of the firm's age
	Size	LNTA	Natural logarithm of the total assets

Source: Elaborated by the authors

and Rodríguez-Gulías et al. (2018). Table 2 shows the measures of dependent, independent and control variables.

Model Specification

Due to the fact that the decision to incorporate VC partners in the shareholding is very closely linked to the firm's characteristics, the effect of being a venture-backed firm on the ICT-USOs' growth is also strongly related to the specificity of each firm. Hence, similarly to the works of Rodríguez-Gulías et al. (2016), Rodríguez-Gulías et al. (2018) and Yagüe-Perales and March-Chordà (2011), panel data methodology, which allows controlling for this individual heterogeneity by modelling it as an individual effect (α_i), was the methodology chosen to investigate the existence of an effect of the VC endorsement on the growth of the Spanish and Portuguese ICT-USOs. Particularly, as in Rodríguez-Gulías et al. (2018), the random effects GLS (Generalised Least Squares) model was applied due to the fact that the main independent variable (VC) is time-invariant. The random effects estimator assumes that the individual effects (α_i) are independent (uncorrelated) from the explanatory variables (x_{it}). Therefore, the basic specification of the model is as follows:

$$GROWTH_{it} = \alpha_i + \beta_1 VC_i + \beta_2 LNAGE_{it} + \beta_3 LNTA_{it} + \lambda_t + \varepsilon_{it}$$

Where α_i is unobserved heterogeneity of each firm, λ_t measures the time-specific effect by time dummy variables in order to control for the effects of macroeconomic variables that are common to all firms but change over the time, and ε_{it} is the random disturbance.

To eliminate outliers, observations were discarded when the sales growth or employment growth were below the one percentile or above the ninety-nine percentile by country[2].

Table 3. Descriptive statistics by subsamples

	Variable	Obs.	Mean	Std. Dev.	Min.	Variable
Spain	SALES[ab]	543	810.873	2053.040	0.355	27921.000
	GSALES[ab]	543	0.452	1.494	-0.909	13.919
	EMP[a]	494	11.482	13.669	1	127
	GEMP[a]	494	0.197	0.555	-0.600	3.000
	VC	658	0.181	0.385	0	1
	AGE[a]	658	7.208	3.402	1	16
	TA[ab]	658	1239.431	3501.245	1.468	60327.570
Portugal	SALES[ab]	413	1802.289	5718.723	0.000	62614.400
	GSALES[ab]	413	0.333	1.529	-1.000	13.932
	EMP[ad]	897	23.013	60.912	0	918
	GEMP[ad]	897	0.119	0.458	-1.000	3.000
	VC	1041	0.070	0.255	0	1
	AGE[a]	1041	9.609	6.240	1	31
	TA[ab]	1041	1933.693	5459.946	0.213	59000.000

Note: [a] Variables are not in logs, [b] Variables are in thousands of euros

Source: Elaborated by the authors

Figure 2. Mean rates of sales growth in the Spanish and Portuguese ICT-USOs (2007–2013)
Source: Elaborated by the authors

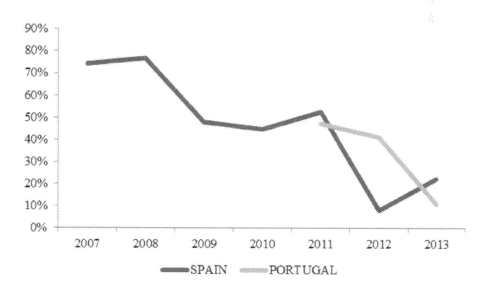

Figure 3. Mean rates of employment growth in the Spanish and Portuguese ICT-USOs (2007–2013)
Source: Elaborated by the authors

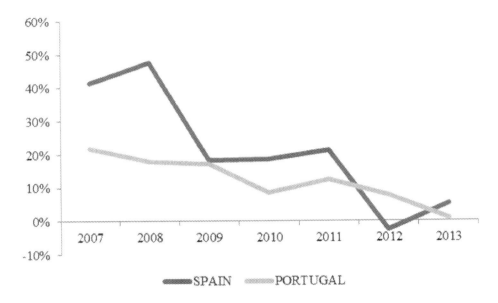

EMPIRICAL RESULTS

Descriptive Analysis

Table 3 displays the descriptive statistics for the dependent and independent variables by subsamples: Spain and Portugal.

The annual average sales growth rate, the first dependent variable, is 45.2% in the Spanish ICT-USOs and 33.3% in the Portuguese ones (Table 3). Figure 2 shows the mean sales growth rates by country and year[3].

Concerning the second dependent variable, the mean employment growth rate of the period is 19.7% in the Spanish ICT-USOs and 11.9% in the Portuguese ones (Table 2). Going into detail about it, Figure 3 shows the mean employment growth rates of the analysed period distinguishing between Spanish and Portuguese firms.

With regard to the main independent variable (VC), Table 3 shows that the percentage of the ICT-USOs with at least one VC partner in its ownership structure is higher in the Spanish case (18%) than in the Portuguese case (7%).

On average, the Portuguese ICT-USOs are older (9,6 years) than the Spanish ones (7,2 years) and also the former are larger in terms of total assets (1,9 millions of euros on average) than the latter (1,2 millions of euros on average) (Table 3).

Table 4. Correlation matrix

	GSALES	GEMP	LNAGE	LNTA
GSALES	1			
GEMP	0.2392*	1		
LNAGE	-0.2021*	-0.2394*	1	
LNTA	0.0688*	0.0668*	0.4469*	1

Notes: Table shows the Pearson correlation coefficients for the continuous variables considered in the empirical analysis. *p< 0.05; **p<0.01; ***p<0.001.

Source: Elaborated by the authors

Finally, Table 4 shows the correlation matrix of the dependent variable and the independent continuous variables.

Multivariate Analysis

The results for random effects GLS models (RE) on the sales growth and employment growth of the Spanish and Portuguese ICT-USOs are presented in Table 5. Additionally, the models were estimated under the alternative fixed effects estimator (FE) and Hausman tests were conducted. The results for Hausman tests (Table 5) indicated that FE model is preferred over RE model in the employment growth model for the Spanish ICT-USOs and in the sales growth and employment growth models for Portuguese ICT-USOs. However, FE models have an important drawback, they do not allow estimating the effect of any time-invariant variable (Baltagi, 2008) such as venture capital, our main independent variable. For this reason, RE models were chosen. In addition, the results obtained for the non-time-invariant variables in the FE models were in the same line than in RE models.

The obtained results partly confirm the proposed hypothesis when the ICT-USOs' growth is measured through the sales growth, since a positive relationship between the presence of VC partners and sales growth was found in the Portuguese UCT-USOs. In this respect, these firms could be taking advantages of the different roles (e.g. the coach, scout, market gatekeeper, subsidizer, and signalling) played by venture capitalists in venture-backed firms. In contrast, the estimated coefficients also show a negative relationship between the VC endorsement and the employment growth, which is highly significant in the case of the Spanish ICT-USOs, suggesting that the presence of VC negatively impacts the employment growth in these firms.

Taking together, previous results indicate that the impact of VC on the ICT-USOs' growth can differ across countries depending on the differences in the environments in which firms and VC investors interact. Moreover, they highlight that the effect

Table 5. Panel regressions for random effects GLS models on sales growth and employment growth: Spain and Portugal

	SPAIN		PORTUGAL	
	GSALES[4]	GEMP	GSALES	GEMP
VC	-0.069	-0.122**	0.295*	-0.017
	(0.069)	(0.043)	(0.138)	(0.051)
LNAGE	-0.314***	-0.260***	-0.223**	-0.156***
	(0.064)	(0.039)	(0.081)	(0.024)
LNTA	0.078***	0.049***	0.039*	0.036***
	(0.020)	(0.011)	(0.019)	(0.007)
yr2007c	0.074	0.127+		0.118*
	(0.111)	(0.066)		(0.047)
yr2008c	0.089	0.175*		0.063
	(0.112)	(0.069)		(0.045)
yr2009c	-0.058	0.015		0.084+
	(0.102)	(0.058)		(0.045)
yr2010c	-0.034	0.038		0.007
	(0.088)	(0.056)		(0.041)
yr2011c	0.021	0.044	0.160+	0.080+
	(0.089)	(0.059)	(0.087)	(0.042)
yr2012c	-0.191*	-0.084*	0.121	0.059
	(0.094)	(0.040)	(0.084)	(0.040)
CONS	0.283	0.295*	0.191	0.132*
	(0.177)	(0.115)	(0.180)	(0.059)
Observations	543	494	407	882
Firms	113	113	147	165
Wald X^2	58.49***	99.39***		60.19***
TEST OF HAUSMAN				
Chi^2	14.83	19.58	17.32	64.08
$Pr > Chi^2$	0.0625	0.0121	0.0017	0.0000

Notes: Robust standard errors are in parenthesis. * $p < 0.05$; ** $p < 0.01$; *** $p < 0.001$

Source: Elaborated by the authors

of VC involvement on the ICT-USOs' growth also depends on how firm growth is measured; whereas a weak positive effect is found in the case of sales growth, a negative one is obtained in the case of employment growth. This result is not necessary contradictory. Venture capitalists search a return on their investment. Moreover, in the ICT sector, VC investment is an investment in a product, rather than in a firm (Vinig et al., 1998). Thus, the selection of venture capitalists relies on the market potential of the product developed by the new ICT firms (Vinig et al., 1998). This specificity of the ICT sector could lead them to prioritize strategies for enhancing the sales growth and containing the job creation in the venture –backed firms as long as these strategies allow them to obtain a faster a return on their investment.

Finally, regardless of the measure of growth used or the country studied, firm age negatively impacts on the ICT-USOs' growth, whereas firm size positively influences on it.

SOLUTIONS AND RECOMMENDATIONS

In view of previous findings, meaningful scientific, managerial, and policy implications are discussed in this section. Hence, from a scientific perspective, the empirical results outline the need of adopting a "cross-national approach" in future studies since the effect of VC investors on the ICT-USOs' growth may differ across countries. Similarly, the findings speak in favour of differentiating between employment growth and sales growth when analysing this issue, because venture capitalists might sacrifice the former to obtain high sales growth rates and a faster return on their investment.

From a managerial perspective, the findings underline a potential conflict of interest between firm's founders and VC investors. This potential conflict of interest should be already addressed when negotiating the contract terms. Thus, on the one hand, entrepreneurs must be willing to give up employment growth to obtain a better financial performance. On the other hand, VC investors should be clear about their objectives from the beginning by establishing their milestones.

From a policy approach, the decision-makers cannot be oblivious to the role played by venture capitalists in supporting the creation of the ICT-USOs. Often, these stakeholders are the only "willing and qualified" investors to finance this type of companies. Then, policies aimed at reinforcing the VC endorsement in the ICT-USOs should be designed. At the same time, governments must be aware that this VC involvement can improve the sales growth of firms at the cost of damaging job creation. Hence, governments must keep this in mind when designing the incentives, chiefly tax advantages, geared towards encouraging the support of venture capitalists to the ICT-USOs. Moreover, the findings showed that the percentage of venture-backed ICT-USOs significantly differs between countries; 18% in Spain and 7% in Portugal. In other words, in Portugal, the presence of venture-backed ICT-USOs is quite limited, maybe because the Portuguese VC market is lesser developed than the Spanish one. In this respect, the Portuguese decision-makers should choose to promote VC investors as a way to support ICT-USOs or simply design other alternative mechanisms.

Finally, we propose a series of policies that can be applied to improve the supply of VC by policy-makers, including measures to improve the regulatory context:

- The investment policy; venture capital funds must have an investment policy and establish a mechanism to manage it. Successful funds choose investments in accordance with their criteria, but in a manner consistent with the general objectives of public policy.
- The way out; there must be an exit mechanism depending on the success of the investment. The most successful investments would be the object of selling shares in the company, however, it is possible that the fund will keep a few company shares or transferred to an independent entity at the end of the life of the fund and managed for the benefit of the region in question.
- The guarantees; instead of providing the financing itself some public authorities provide a guarantee to ensure financing in shares. Even the high risk to public authorities of the guarantee this mechanism has a very positive impact.

FUTURE RESEARCH DIRECTIONS

Previous evidence provides some novel insights into the effectiveness of venture capitalists in fostering firm growth in both the university spin-offs firms and ICT sector. However, this chapter also presents some limitations that pave the way for future research. First, the available data were conditioned by the information gathered by SABI database. More specifically, the main problem was that SABI database does not provide dynamic information on the ownership structure of the firms. In this respect, data referred to the specific date of entry of VC partners, as well as the amount of funds provided by them would yield more robust results.

Second, as mentioned different venture capitalists specialize in different industries and types of investments. In this respect, it would be interesting to analyse whether the specialization of the VC partners conditions their influence on firm growth. In other words, given that there are VC investors specialized in the ICT industry, as well as those ones specialized in USOS, future work could address whether the effect of VC endorsement on firm growth depends on the involvement of different types of venture capitalists.

Third, this chapter provides evidence of the effects of the VC investors on the growth of the ICT-USOs, however these effect could not be specifically associated to the different roles that the literature on VC traditionally attributes to this kind of investors (i.e. "coach," "scout," "market gatekeeper," "subsidiser," and "signalling" roles). Then, future research would benefit from going in-depth into what role/s venture capitalists are playing. Facing this challenge probably requires conduct interviews to the VC investors, which are frequently reluctant to publicly share their selection and investment strategies.

Fourthly, literature on success factor of new firms often highlights the role played by the human capital of the entrepreneurs. This aspect is especially relevant for the ICT-USOs, where the knowledge base is tacit and usually embedded in their founders. Addressing this issue would also require conduct interviews to the founders of the ICT-USOs.

Finally, cross-country factors affecting both venture capitalists' strategies and the dynamics of the ICT-USOs' growth should also be taken into account in future works. In other words, it is necessary to consider the differing country-specific environments in which both agents operate. In so doing, country-level variables referred to the macroeconomic and institutional environments in which VC investors and USOs develop their activities should be included.

CONCLUSION

In the last two decades, the creation of USOs has become an important way to transfer the research knowledge to society, at the same time that it contributes to the economic development of the regions. These firms are typically resource-constrained, especially in aspects as funding and managerial experience of their founders, which may hamper their growth. Around one third of the USOs created in Portugal and Spain operates in the ICT industry and shares this lack of managerial skills and financial resources, even more sharply than the USOs operating in other industries. In this context, the VC involvement in the management of the ICT-USOs can partly mitigate their traditional lack of resources, enhancing their growth.

The objective of this chapter was to explore whether the presence of VC impacts the ICT-USOs' growth, considering two different countries with the same methodology. More specifically, using a sample of 127 Spanish and 176 Portuguese ICT-USOs over the period 2007–2013 the effect of VC investors was tested on both the employment growth and the sales growth.

The results indicate that the influence of VC on the ICT-USOs' growth slightly differs across countries, suggesting that the differences in the environments in which firms and VC investors interact may affect this influence. Additionally, the findings show that the VC endorsement may have a different effect on sales growth than it has on employment growth. Thus, a weak positive effect was shown on sales growth, whereas a negative one was found on employment growth. Taking together, previous results underline that venture capitalists might prioritize strategies for increasing the sales growth while containing the job creation in order to obtain a faster a return on their investment in the ICT-USOs.

To finish this chapter, we want to point that VC might induce knowledge, technological and R&D spillovers. Spillovers occur when an innovation or improvement implemented by an agent increases the performance of another without the latter having to pay compensation. In a recent study, Schnitzer and Watzinger (2017) show that per dollar of investment in venture-backed start-ups, the knowledge spillovers from VC are almost nine times greater than the spillovers from corporate R&D. Therefore, VC can leverage the innovation and growth not only of the venture-backed companies but also of other firms.

ACKNOWLEDGMENT

The authors gratefully acknowledge the IACOBUS Program from the European Strategic Group of Territorial Cooperation Galicia/North of Portugal for a research fellowship.

REFERENCES

Autio, E., Kenney, M., Mustar, P., Siegel, D., & Wright, M. (2014). Entrepreneurial innovation: The importance of context. *Research Policy*, *43*(7), 1097–1108. doi:10.1016/j.respol.2014.01.015

Baltagi, B. H. (2008). *Econometric analysis of panel data*. John Wiley & Sons.

Barney, J. B. (1991). Firm resources and sustained competitive advantage. *Journal of Management*, *17*(1), 99–120. doi:10.1177/014920639101700108

Bertoni, F., Colombo, M., & Grilli, L. (2011). Venture Capital and the Growth of High-tech Start-ups: Disentangling Treatment from Selection Effects. *Research Policy*, *40*(7), 1028–1043. doi:10.1016/j.respol.2011.03.008

Bonardo, D., Paleari, S., & Vismara, S. (2009). When academia comes to market: Does university affiliation reduce the uncertainty of IPOs? Working paper, Department of Economics and Technology Management, University of Bergam.

Cantner, U., & Goethner, M. (2011). Performance differences between academic spin-offs and non-academic star-ups: A comparative analysis using a non-parametric matching approach. *DIME Final Conference*.

Colombo, M., & Grilli, L. (2010). On Growth Drivers of High-tech Start-ups: Exploring the Role of Founders' Human Capital and Venture Capital. *Journal of Business Venturing, 25*(6), 610–626. doi:10.1016/j.jbusvent.2009.01.005

Conceição, O., Faria, A. P., & Fontes, M. (2017). Regional variation of academic spinoffs formation. *The Journal of Technology Transfer, 42*(3), 654–675. doi:10.1007/s10961-016-9508-1

Denis, D. J. (2004). Entrepreneurial finance: An overview of the issues and evidence. *Journal of Corporate Finance, 10*(2), 301–326. doi:10.1016/S0929-1199(03)00059-2

Djokovic, D., & Souitaris, V. (2008). Spinouts from academic institutions: A literature review with suggestions for further research. *The Journal of Technology Transfer, 33*(3), 225–247. doi:10.1007/s10961-006-9000-4

Gompers, P., & Lerner, J. (1999). *The Venture Capital Cycle*. Cambridge, MA: MIT Press.

Grossman, G. M., & Helpman, E. (1992). *Innovation and growth in the global economy*. Cambridge, MA: MIT Press.

Hayter, C. S. (2013). Conceptualizing knowledge-based entrepreneurship networks: Perspectives from the literature. *Small Business Economics, 41*(4), 899–911. doi:10.1007/s11187-013-9512-x

Hellmann, T., & Puri, M. (2002). On the fundamental role of venture capital. *Economic Review (Federal Reserve Bank of Atlanta), 87*(4), 19–24.

Hindle, K., & Yencken, J. (2004). Public Research Commercialisation, Entrepreneurship and New Technology Based Firms: An Integrated Model. *Technovation, 24*(10), 793–803. doi:10.1016/S0166-4972(03)00023-3

Klausner, A. (2005). Biotech venture capital—It's not too late to be early. *Nature Biotechnology, 23*(4), 417–418. doi:10.1038/nbt0405-417 PubMed

Lasch, F., Le Roy, F., & Yami, S. (2007). Critical growth factors of ICT start-ups. *Management Decision, 45*(1), 62–75. doi:10.1108/00251740710718962

Lockett, A., Siegel, D., Wright, M., & Ensley, M. D. (2005). The creation of spin-off firms at public research institutions: Managerial and policy implications. *Research Policy, 34*(7), 981–993. doi:10.1016/j.respol.2005.05.010

Metrick, A., & Yasuda, A. (2010). *Venture Capital and the Finance of Innovation* (2nd ed.). John Wiley and Sons, Inc.

O'Shea, R. P., Chugh, H., & Allen, T. J. (2008). Determinants and consequences of university spinoff activity: A conceptual framework. *International Journal of Technology Transfer, 33*(6), 653–666. doi:10.1007/s10961-007-9060-0

OECD. (2003). *A Proposed Classification of ICT Goods*. Paris: OECD Working Party on Indicators for the Information Society.

Ortín, P., Salas, V., Trujillo, M. V., & Vendrell, F. (2007). *El spin-off universitario en España como modelo de creación de empresas intensivas en tecnología, Estudio DGPYME, Ministerio de Industria Turismo y comercio*. Secretaría General de Industria, Dirección General de Política de la Pyme.

Ortín, P., Salas, V., Trujillo, M. V., & Vendrell, F. (2008). La creación de spin-off universitarios en España. Características, determinantes y resultados. *Economía Industrial, 368*, 79–95.

Ortín, P., & Vendrell, F. (2010). University spin-off vs. other NTBFs: Productivity Differences at the Outset and Evolution. Searle Center Working Paper.

Penrose, E. T. (1959). *The theory of the growth of the firm*. Oxford, UK: Basil Blackwell.

Pirnay, F., Surlemont, B., & Nlemvo, F. (2003). Toward a typology of spin-offs. *Small Business Economics, 21*(4), 355–369. doi:10.1023/A:1026167105153

Red OTRI. (2011). Informe Red OTRI de Universidades, 2011. Madrid: Conferencia de Rectores de las Universidades Españolas, CRUE.

Rodríguez-Gulías, M. J., Rodeiro-Pazos, D. & Fernández-López, S. (2015). The regional effect on the innovative performance of University spin-offs: a multilevel approach. Journal of the Knowledge Economy, 1-21.

Rodríguez-Gulías, M. J., Rodeiro-Pazos, D., & Fernández-López, S. (2016). Impact of venture capital on the growth of university spin-offs. In Multiple Helix Ecosystems for Sustainable Competitiveness (pp. 169–183). Springer International Publishing; doi:10.1007/978-3-319-29677-7_11.

Rodríguez-Gulías, M. J., Rodeiro-Pazos, D., & Fernández-López, S. (2017). The growth of university spin-offs: A dynamic panel data approach. *Technology Analysis and Strategic Management, 29*(10), 1181–1195. doi:10.1080/09537325.2016.1277580

Rodríguez-Gulías, M. J., Rodeiro-Pazos, D., Fernández-López, S., Corsi, C., & Prencipe, A. (2018). The role of venture capitalist to enhance the growth of Spanish and Italian university spin-offs. *The International Entrepreneurship and Management Journal, 14*(4), 1111–1130. doi:10.1007/s11365-017-0489-9

Schnitzer, M., & Watzinger, M. (2017). Measuring the spillovers of venture capital. CESifo Working Paper.

Schröder, C. (2013). Regional and company-specific factors for high growth dynamics of ICT companies in Germany with particular emphasis on knowledge spillovers. *Papers in Regional Science, 92*(4), 741–772. doi:10.1111/j.1435-5957.2012.00457.x

Shane, S. A. (2004). Academic Entrepreneurship: University Spinoffs and Wealth Creation. Edward Elgar Publishing. doi:10.4337/9781843769828

Steurs, G. (1994). Spillovers and Cooperation in Research and Development (Doctoral dissertation). KU Leuven.

United Nations. (2004). *UN Social Economic Council's Report of the International Telecommunication Union on information and communication technologies statistics*. United Nations, Economic and Social Council.

Vinig, T.; Blocq, R.; Braafhart, J. & Laufer, O. (1998). Developing a successful information and communication technology industry: the role of venture capital, knowledge, and the government. ICIS 1998 Proceedings. doi:10.1145/353053.353070

Wennberg, K., Wiklund, J., & Wright, M. (2011). The effectiveness of university knowledge spillovers: Performance differences between university spinoffs and corporate spinoffs. *Research Policy, 40*(8), 1128–1143. doi:10.1016/j.respol.2011.05.014

Wright, M., Lockett, A., Clarysse, B., & Binks, M. (2006). University spin-out companies and venture capital. *Research Policy, 35*(4), 481–501. doi:10.1016/j.respol.2006.01.005

Yagüe-Perales, R. M., & March.Chordà, I. (2011). Performance analysis of research spin-offs in the Spanish biotechnology industry. *Journal of Business Research, 65*(12), 1782–1789. doi:10.1016/j.jbusres.2011.10.038

Zahra, S. A., Van de Velde, E., & Larrañeta, B. (2007). Knowledge conversion capability and the performance of corporate and university spin-off. *Industrial and Corporate Change, 16*(4), 569–608. doi:10.1093/icc/dtm018

Zhang, J. (2009). The performance of university spin-offs: An exploratory analysis using venture capital data. *The Journal of Technology Transfer*, *34*(3), 255–285. doi:10.1007/s10961-008-9088-9

ADDITIONAL READING

Baldini, N. (2010). University spin-offs and their environment. *Technology Analysis and Strategic Management*, *22*(8), 859–876. doi:10.1080/09537325.2010.520470

Czarnitzki, D., Rammer, C., & Toole, A. A. (2014). University spin-offs and the "performance premium". *Small Business Economics*, *43*(2), 309–326. doi:10.100711187-013-9538-0

Knockaert, M., Spithoven, A., & Clarysse, B. (2010). The knowledge paradox explored: What is impeding the creation of ICT spin-offs? *Technology Analysis and Strategic Management*, *22*(4), 479–493. doi:10.1080/09537321003714535

Lasch, F., Le Roy, F., & Yami, S. (2007). Critical growth factors of ICT start-ups. *Management Decision*, *45*(1), 62–75. doi:10.1108/00251740710718962

Lockett, A., & Wright, M. (2005). Resources, capabilities, risk capital and the creation of university spin-out companies. *Research Policy*, *34*(7), 1043–1057. doi:10.1016/j.respol.2005.05.006

Mastroeni, M. (2011). Finance for high-tech sectors: State-led support for start-ups and spin-offs. *International Journal of Entrepreneurship and Innovation Management*, *14*(2-3), 176–189. doi:10.1504/IJEIM.2011.041730

Oliveira, M. A., Ferreira, J. J. P., Ye, Q., & Van Geenhuizen, M. (2013, September). Spin-up: A comprehensive program aimed to accelerate university spin-off growth. In *Proceedings of the 8th European Conference on Innovation and Entrepreneurship (ECIE 2013)* (Vol. 1, pp. 34-44).

Ortín-Ángel, P., & Vendrell-Herrero, F. (2010). Why do university spin-offs attract more venture capitalists? *Venture Capital*, *12*(4), 285–306. doi:10.1080/13691066.2010.486166

KEY TERMS AND DEFINITIONS

Information and Communication Technologies (ICT): Technologies that provide access to information through telecommunications, including Internet, wireless networks, cell phones, and other communication mediums.

Information and Communication Technology (ICT) Industry or Sector: Combination of manufacturing and services industries that capture, transmit and display data and information electronically (OECD, 2003). ICT sector refers to equipment and services related to broadcasting, computing and telecommunications, all of which capture and display information electronically (United Nations, 2004).

Start-Up: A new and independent company or project initiated by an entrepreneur to develop a scalable business model.

University Spinoff: Start-ups exploiting university knowledge but not necessarily founded by university staff (Red OTRI 2011).

Venture Capital: Activity developed by specialized entities consisting in the contribution of financial resources of a temporary form (3-10 years) participating in the capital of companies with high growth and/or in the early stages of development.

ENDNOTES

[1] Sales of Portuguese ICT-USOs are only available from 2010, then sales growth only could be calculated from 2011.

[2] The authors also investigate the robustness of their results to the potential impact of outliers by re-estimating the models keeping the outliers. These results with outliers (unreported) are qualitatively similar to those reported in Table 5 (without outliers).

[3] In the case of the Portuguese ICT-USOs, data on sales are available only for the period 2010-2013.

[4] Unreported results excluding observations of years before 2010 for Spanish ICT-USOs show qualitatively similar results.

APPENDIX 1: SECOND DEFINITION OF THE ICT SECTOR (YEAR 2007)

Table 6.

ICT manufacturing industries		
ISIC (Rev.4)	NACE Rev.2	ACTIVITIES
2610	26.11	Manufacture of electronic components
	26.12	Manufacture of loaded electronic boards
2620	26.20	Manufacture of computers and peripheral equipment
2630	26.30	Manufacture of communication equipment
2640	26.40	Manufacture of consumer electronics
2680	26.80	Manufacture of magnetic and optical media

ICT trade industries

ISIC (Rev.4)	NACE Rev.2	ACTIVITIES
4651	46.51	Wholesale of computers, computer peripheral equipment and software
4652	46.52	Wholesale of electronic and telecommunications equipment and parts

ICT services industries
Software publishing

ISIC (Rev.4)	NACE Rev.2	ACTIVITIES
5820	58.21	Publishing of computer games
	58.29	Other software publishing

Telecomunications

ISIC (Rev.4)	NACE Rev.2	ACTIVITIES
6110	61.10	Wired telecommunications activities
6120	61.20	Wireless telecommunications activities
6130	61.30	Satellite telecommunications activities
6190	61.90	Other telecommunications activities

Information technology service activities

ISIC (Rev.4)	NACE Rev.2	ACTIVITIES
6201	62.01	Computer programming activities
6202	62.02	Information technology consultancy activities
	62.03	Computer facilities management activities
6209	62.09	Other information technology service activities

Web portals, data processing, hosting and related activities

ISIC (Rev.4)	NACE Rev.2	ACTIVITIES
6311	63.11	Data processing, hosting and related activities
6312	63.12	Web portals

continued on following page

Table 6. Continued

ICT manufacturing industries		
ISIC (Rev.4)	NACE Rev.2	ACTIVITIES
Repair of computers and communication equipment		
ISIC (Rev.4)	NACE Rev.2	ACTIVITIES
9511	95.11	Repair of computers and peripheral equipment
9512	95.12	Repair of communication equipment

Source: Spanish National Statistics Institute (INE) based on ISIC Rev4, NACE Rev.2.

Chapter 5
Are the New Sources for Financing SMEs a Reality or a Chimera?
The Spanish Case Study

José Pablo Abeal Vázquez
Universidade da Coruña, Spain

Begoña Alvarez García
https://orcid.org/0000-0001-7918-3986
Universidade da Coruña, Spain

Lucía Boedo Vilabella
Universidade da Coruña, Spain

ABSTRACT

Small and medium-sized enterprises (SMEs) are a key pillar of the European economy because they play an important role in generating growth, employment, and value added. However, SMEs cannot access funding from sources such as issuing securities because they do not meet the listing requirements of official markets. This is why these firms are forced to cover their financial needs by borrowing from banks and reinvesting profits. For this reason, several alternative markets have been launched in Europe. In the Spanish case, two alternative markets have been created (one equity trading market and one debt market). In this chapter, these markets are presented for the purpose of analyzing to what extent they are a real solution to the financing problems faced by Spanish SMEs. This research shows that these two markets follow different paths, although for the time being, they are not capable of reaching a large number of companies.

DOI: 10.4018/978-1-7998-2440-4.ch005

Copyright © 2020, IGI Global. Copying or distributing in print or electronic forms without written permission of IGI Global is prohibited.

INTRODUCTION

Small and medium enterprises (SMEs) are one of the major drivers of employment and wealth in the European economy due to their high relative weight in the fabric of the business world (DeWit & de Kok, 2014). In fact, SMEs represent 99% of all businesses in the European Union (EU), they are the backbone of its economy and generate two out of every three jobs (Muller et al., 2018). The contribution of SMEs is also essential in terms of the volume of transactions, added value and capacity to adapt to cyclical fluctuations (Audretsch et al., 2006; Coluzzi et al., 2015). The same is true in the Spanish case, where SMEs are of considerable importance because they account for more than half of the registered workforce and generate two-thirds of the gross domestic product (GDP). However, these companies face an increasing competition, arising from the process of market globalization and the technological evolution, which has altered the critical success factors and, consequently, has led to severe threats to their survival.

In addition to the pressure on these companies in terms of competitiveness, there are also financing problems (Hernández-Cánovas & Martínez-Solano, 2010; Beck et al., 2011; Infelise, 2014; Andrieu et al., 2018). SMEs find it more difficult to obtain financing through the market than large companies, so they try more to cover their financial needs by reinvesting profits or borrowing from banks (Kaousar Nassr & Wehinger, 2016). However, the use of such sources of finance can cause them problems, especially in periods of expansion, because these sources do not provide them with sufficient funding to take advantage of the investment opportunities available. In order to mitigate these problems, several alternative markets have been launched in Europe over the last two decades for opening up new funding channels for SMEs and help them gain publicity, reputation, and transparency.

Two new alternative markets have also been launched in Spain: one is an equity trading market (the Spanish Alternative Equity Market, also known in Spanish as Mercado Alternativo Bursátil or MAB), and the other is a debt market (the Alternative Fixed-Income Market, also known in Spanish as Mercado Alternativo de Renta Fija or MARF). These markets, like the others existing in Europe, are positioned as alternative possibilities for SMEs to obtain financing and open up to financial markets, because deliberate regulation, costs and requirements are adapted to the specific needs of SMEs. However, it is necessary to study whether in practice these alternative markets serve the purpose for which they were created (to help SMEs obtain financing) and to what extent they are a viable option for companies. For this reason, this chapter presents and analyses in detail the two new markets launched in Spain in order to draw some conclusions about their evolution and how effective they have been in achieving those initial goals which justified the creation of these markets.

To do this, the chapter is structured as follows. The Background section shows the reasons why SMEs have problems obtaining finance, with special reference to Spain, and the reasons why alternative markets have been launched. The section entitled Main Focus of the Chapter presents the evolution of the two Spanish alternative markets since their launch, and their operating characteristics. The companies listed in these markets are also analyzed on the basis of criteria such as sector distribution, capitalization, size or frequency of security issues. Finally, the section entitled Solutions and recommendations shows several possible answers to the problems presented.

BACKGROUND

Companies can use several funding sources, which are usually structured in two large groups: equity (mainly coming from shareholder contributions or self-funding) and debt (mainly coming from bank lending or debt issues). Despite the variety of possibilities, bank financing is the most widely used in Europe (Mercieca et al., 2009; Degg, 2009; Hernández-Cánovas & Martínez-Solano, 2010) and some authors, such as Lamothe Fernández & Monjas Barroso (2013) or Peña Cuenca (2015), indicate that in Europe there is an almost complete dependence on bank financing. This fact becomes more evident when comparing Europe and USA. In fact, as shown on table 1, the level of bank credit to the private non-financial sector (as a percentage of the GDP) in the Euro area almost doubles the level in the United States. From table 1 it can also be seen that there are important differences among the European countries, and Spain it is one of the countries with the greatest dependence on bank credit, although there has been a change in recent years towards the search for alternative sources of financing.

The difference between USA and Europe has not always been the case. It is explained by an extraordinary growth of the banking system in Europe since 1990 (Langfield and Pagano, 2016), which has led over the years to a bank bias in the European countries. This bank bias is one of the main reasons why the crisis has been so severe in Europe (although there were differences in behavior between the European countries) and that the recovery has been slower and later than in the USA. The mistrust and volatility spread through the markets from the very beginning of the crisis resulted in the inability of financial institutions to obtain financing in international financial centers and, as a consequence, the credit for companies dried up (Álvarez García and Abeal Vázquez, 2019). All the companies suffered the consequences of the lack of credit, but there is no doubt that the SMEs were the most affected. It is generally acknowledged that a SME is a small or medium enterprise in terms of income volume, equity value, and number of workers. More

Table 1. Bank credit to the private non-financial sector (% of GDP)

	2013	2014	2015	2016	2017	2018
Belgium	55.3	58.9	62	64	65.1	68.3
France	92.6	91	92.4	94.4	96.9	99.9
Germany	80.5	77.7	77	76.5	76.5	77.4
Greece	116.8	115.2	111.1	106.4	98.4	88.9
Italy	88.5	86.7	85.8	83.1	78.7	74.6
Spain	135.8	124.6	114.4	107.1	100.9	95
United Kingdom	92.4	88.9	88.5	88.9	87.3	88.2
United States	**48.7**	**49.1**	**50.4**	**51.6**	**51.6**	**51.2**
Euro area	**97.9**	**95**	**92.7**	**91.7**	**90**	**89.3**

Source: Prepared by the authors based on data from the Bank for International Settlements (https://stats.bis.org/statx/srs/table/f2.4)

specifically, by following the European Commission Regulation (EU) No 651/2014, it is considered that: (i) the category of micro, small and medium-sized enterprises is made up of enterprises which employ fewer than 250 persons and which have an annual turnover not exceeding EUR 50 million and/or an annual balance sheet total not exceeding EUR 43 million; (ii) within the SME category, a small enterprise is defined as an enterprise which employs fewer than 50 persons and whose annual turnover and/or balance sheet total does not exceed EUR 10 million; and (iii) within the SME category, a micro-enterprise is defined as an enterprise which employs fewer than 10 persons and whose annual turnover and/or balance sheet total does not exceed EUR 2 million.

SMEs are the companies that have suffered the most from the crisis for several reasons. Firstly, they face greater difficulties in accessing bank finance (Coshetal, 2009; Andrieu et al, 2017) because they do not usually offer as many guarantees as large companies, so in an environment of credit shortage they are the first to be left out of financing. Secondly, when they are able to access bank finance they bear a proportionally higher cost for their debt because the fixed costs of lending (such as administrative costs) are not proportional to the size of the loan (Ayadi, 2009; Beck et al., 2011; Hernández-Cánovas, 2010). Thirdly, they cannot access funding from sources such as those issuing securities because they do not meet the stringent listing requirements of debt and equity markets.

For all these reasons, alternative markets have been created in recent years in several European countries. These alternative markets are especially designed to help SMEs and overcome impediments to growth and opening up to the outside world because of financial problems. The same has happened in Spain, where all the difficulties arising from the crisis were particularly hard (Maudos, 2012; Calvo Bernardino & Martín de Vidales Carrasco, 2014; Bank of Spain, 2017). During the crisis, Spanish banks suffered a large undercapitalization (due to the loss of value of their most problematic assets, mainly those related to the real estate sector) and faced serious difficulties in obtaining international financing. The gravity of the situation went as far as to push the Spanish government to request external financial assistance in the year 2012 (by signing the Memorandum of Understanding between the Spanish and the European authorities). At that time a restructuring process of the banking system began in Spain, which figured among the most momentous in Europe (Berges & Ontiveros, 2013; Fernández de Lis & Rubio, 2013; Tajadura Garrido, 2015). In fact, the first signs of economic recovery did not start to emerge in Spain until the year 2014, while other European countries such as Germany or France were on a path to recovery much earlier. As a consequence, the financing from banking to companies was very slow in Spain until the year 2014 and many companies, especially SMEs, had to cease their activity in those years. In order to try to relieve these problems and seek solutions for SMEs, Spain also tried to make bids for alternative markets. Two alternative markets were launched: one equity trading market and one designed for the issuance of debt. The next section will present these markets in detail for the purpose of analyzing to what extent these new markets are a real solution to the financing problems faced in Spain by SMEs.

MAIN FOCUS OF THE CHAPTER

SMEs obtain financial resources mainly through bank financing and reinvestment of profits. As mentioned above, these companies find it very difficult, and in many cases impossible, to themselves obtain financing, and this can be very harmful for their potential development and their expansion into other countries or sectors (Infelise, 2014; Montañez Núñez, 2015). This is why several alternative markets have been launched aiming at facilitating SMEs access to finance. Likewise, new financing channels have emerged, such as venture capital entities, crowdfunding and crowdlending platforms, and blockchain-based financing platforms, (García-Vaquero and Roibás, 2018).

Alternative markets (whether designed for debt trading or equity trading) are unofficial markets which have been launched to facilitate SMEs' access to non-bank funding channels. In addition to helping in terms of financing, the access of these companies to markets also brings other important advantages. Thus, according to Pérez López and Palacín Sánchez (2009) and Carro Meana (2012), participating in a market increases the visibility and prestige of companies, improves transparency (because they are obliged to report periodically on their activities) and provides an objective assessment of the firm.

Alternative markets are attractive to companies for several reasons: they are more flexible than official markets in terms of regulation and the ability to adapt themselves to the needs of SMEs, they are swifter with regard to deadlines and also they mean lower costs for the companies listed on them.

In Europe there are several alternative markets: some of them are stock markets and the other have been designed for the issuance of corporate debt.

Concerning the alternative equity markets, the first and most successful one in Europe is the Alternative Investment Market (AIM). This growth market for SMEs came into operation in June 1995, as part of the London Stock Exchange, and since then it has been a reference market for the other European countries. Since its beginnings (with just 10 companies and a market capitalization of £82 million) it has been continuously expanding and more than 3,500 companies have joined AIM so far to raise more than £90 million in funds (London Stock Exchange, 2015). Other important alternative markets for stocks in Europe are Euronext Access and Euronext Growth. These markets are two pan-European alternative markets because they are part of Euronext, which is a big stock exchange founded initially by the merger between the stock exchanges of Paris, Amsterdam, and Brussels, and later joined in Europe by the Lisbon and Porto shares market, the London International Financial Futures and Options Exchange, the Irish Stock Exchange, and Oslo Bors. Euronext Access and Euronext Growth are appropriate platforms for startups and high-growth SMEs that do not have the critical mass to be quoted in the official market. More examples of alternative equity markets in Europe are, among others, the Athex Alternative Market (created in 2007 and depending on the Athens Exchange Group), the Deutsche Börse segment for SMEs that is called Scale for equities, and the market First North which is part of the Nasdaq Nordic Exchanges.

Concerning the European alternative debt markets, it should be noted that the first one came into operation in Norway in June 2005. It is the Nordic ABM market, which depends on the Oslo Bors. This market has two segments: one for the general public (Nordic ABM Retail) and one for professional investors (Nordic ABM Professional). Later, in July 2011, the German market BONDm was created also with the idea of targeting retailers and professionals. The alternative bond trading segment of the pan-European EuroNext market was launched in January 2012. In February 2013, a new professional market segment of the ExtraMOT market came into operation in Italy to issue bonds and commercial papers. This new segment is regulated by the Borsa Italiana.

All these alternative markets have some common characteristics. They are non-regulated markets, although their management depends on an official market (Lamothe Fernández & Monjas Barroso, 2013). They focus their activity on enhancing SMEs and are therefore adapted to the particularities of these companies. The companies listed on these markets have to designate a registered adviser who offers them specialized assistance.

In the case of Spain, two alternative markets have also been created with the aim of fostering the SMEs' access to financing: one is an equity trading market and the other is a debt market. These markets are presented below, by making reference to their most important characteristics, such as structure, participants, fees, sector distribution, and evolution.

The Spanish Alternative Markets

The Spanish Alternative Equity Market

The Spanish Alternative Equity Market (in Spanish, Mercado Aternativo Bursátil or MAB) was created in the year 2006 to facilitate the access of SMEs to financial markets. It is an unofficial stock trading market, which is organized as a Multilateral Trading Facility. It is a more flexible market than the official one, so access requirements for companies are simpler, and it has regulations and costs adapted to the particularities of SMEs. This market is managed and regulated by the company Bolsas y Mercados Españoles (BME), which is the operator of all the securities markets and financial systems in Spain, and is supervised by the National Securities Market Commission (CNMV).

This market is structured in six segments in order to include different kinds of companies, such as SICAVs (open-ended investment schemes), SOCIMIs or REITs (real estate investment trusts), VCFs (venture capital firms), hedge funds, investment funds, and growth companies. This research is focused on the segment of growth companies (henceforth, MAB-growth) because the other segments pertain to very specific activities.

The segment of growing companies was designed to facilitate the access to the market to SMEs wishing to expand their business. It came into operation in the year 2009 with the entry of the company Zinkia and currently it includes 41 companies.

Two relevant figures in MAB, and in the segment of growth companies, are the registered advisors and the liquidity providers, because when a firm seeks admission it needs to designate a registered advisor and to sign a contract with a liquidity provider.

The registered advisor is a legal person who guides the companies who are attempting to access the market and helps them during the process of listing. In addition, the registered advisor monitors whether companies comply with legal requirements at every moment. The role of the registered advisor is carried out by professionals specialized in security markets. They need to be independent and with no potential conflicts of interest with the company. It is necessary to nominate two individuals at least to fulfill the function of registered advisor. If the company does not appoint a registered advisor it could be excluded from the market. The first task of the registered advisor is to assist the company in preparing the information required for listing on MAB. After entering the market, the registered advisor also has the task of reviewing all the financial information presented by the company. The registered advisor should ensure regular contact with the company and present to the market a schedule of the meetings held with the company. This schedule should also include the names of the participants in the meetings.

The liquidity provider is important to guarantee that transactions are liquid and ensure sufficient trading frequency. This function is normally carried out by an investment service company or a credit entity that has to be independent of the company. The liquidity provider must maintain supply and demand positions for a minimum cash amount during the trading session for ensure constant liquidity for the stock.

Apart from having a registered advisor and a liquidity provider, candidates for listing on MAB (and specifically on MAB-growth) must meet several requirements. They must take the form of public limited companies, so their shares are freely transferable. In addition, their share capital has to be completely subscribed to and paid out. Likewise, companies listed on MAB has to maintain a correct degree of transparency, report information to the market, and maintain an adequate shareholder diffusion.

Concerning the information, the companies must report it half-yearly (an interim financial statement that at least includes a limited audit report issued by a qualified auditor) and annual information (the audited financial statements). Furthermore, the companies must report relevant information of interest to investors and significant holdings. Concerning the shareholder distribution, companies need to have at least 20 shareholders independent of the core shareholder or shareholders with stakes of less than 5% of the share capital. Likewise, the shares held by shareholders holding less than 5% of the share capital must have an estimated value of more than EUR 2 million.

The fees supported by companies listed on MAB-growth are lower than in the official stock exchange. They are shown in table 2.

At present, 41 companies are listed on the MAB-growth segment. They are companies from various sectors (figure 1), although the electronic and software sector (with 10 companies), the pharmaceutical and biotechnology sector (with 9 companies) and the engineering sector (with 6 companies) stand out over the others in terms of the number of companies. In fact, these three sectors together account for 61% of total MAB growth. These are sectors with great growth and whose companies have a clear technological profile.

Table 2. Main fees supported by companies listed on MAB-growth

MAB-growth companies	Min	Max
REGISTRATION		
Processing the listing application: €1,500		
Market listing: €6,000 + 0.05 ‰ on the capitalization of the securities to be listed		
Capital increases: €6,000 + 0.05 ‰ on the capitalization of the securities to be listed		
MAINTENANCE SERVICES: €6,000		
DEREGISTRATION: 0.5 ‰ on the market value	€1,500	€6,000

Source: Prepared by the authors based on the Circular 5/2017.

The capitalization of all the firms listed on MAB-growth is EUR 1,711 million. If we look at how this figure is spread out among the different sectors, it can be seen (figure 2) that there are 4 sectors which have greater weighting than the others. They are, ranked by order of importance, the renewable energy sector, other services, the electronic and software sector, and the pharmaceutical products and biotechnology sector. It draws the attention the disparity between the number of firms and the capitalization in the sectors of other services and renewable energies. The other services sector only includes one company, Proeduca Group. This company, which provides online higher education in eight different countries, has the higher capitalization in

Figure 1. Sector distribution in MAB-growth
Source: Data from https://www.bolsasymercados.es/mab/esp/Home.aspx

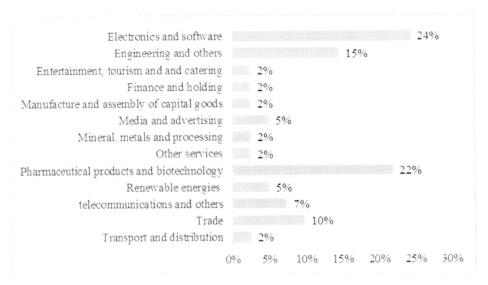

Are the New Sources for Financing SMEs a Reality or a Chimera?

Figure 2. Capitalization by sector in MAB-growth
Source: Data from https://www.bolsasymercados.es/mab/esp/Home.aspx

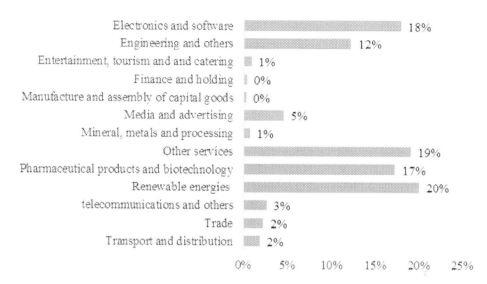

the MAB-growth (EUR 325 million), and this is why it accounts 19% of the total capitalization. This firm has entered the MAB-growth in the year 2019.

The renewable energy sector includes two companies: Greenalia Group and Grenery Renovables. Greenalia Group is an independent power producer, which started its activity in the area of renewable energy in the year 2006. The company works in several business lines and it entered the MAB-growth in the year 2017. Its current capitalization is EUR 148 million. Grenergy renovables is also a Spanish independent power producer that designs, develops, and executes renewable energy plants on a large scale. The company was founded in the year 2007 and in the year 2012 it was embarked upon a process of expansion to Latin America. The company decided to enter the MAB in the year 2015 and its current capitalization is EUR 193 million.

In MAB-growth the securities can be traded on two different modalities, on the continuous market or on the fixing system. The choice between them depends on the size and trading volume of the securities. In the continuous market modality, it is possible to buy and sell securities during all the session. In the fixing system, securities remain under auction during the session with two closing periods (at 12:00 and 16:00 pm). At this moment, 42% of the companies are traded in the continuous market while the other 68% remain in the fixing system. This is logical given the low liquidity of most listed companies.

Table 3. Access of companies to MAB-growth

2009	2010	2011	2012	2013	2014	2015	2016	2017	2018	2019
1	6	4	1	2	5	8	6	3	3	2

Source: Data from http://www.bmerf.es

Concerning the evolution of the access of the companies currently listed on MAB-growth over time, it can be seen in table 3 that the trend is not increasing. In fact, since 2016 the market has less appeal to companies than in previous years. This progress does not seem to be very positive and it seems that this market has not really been consolidated.

We are going to present the alternative debt market before identifying analyzing the main causes of the poor performance of MAB-growth.

The Spanish Alternative Fixed-Income Market

In the same way that it was considered necessary in Spain to create an alternative equity market to enable SMEs to issue shares, it was also considered necessary to create an alternative market that would allow medium-sized solvent companies to issue fixed income assets. Therefore, the Alternative Fixed-Income Market (in Spanish, Mercado Alternativo de Renta Fija or MARF) came into operation in October 2013 to offer a new way of financing to SMEs so that they could have access to liquidity in the short and medium term through the issue of fixed-income securities.

In the Spanish case, the unofficial debt market (MARF) is operated by the management board of the Spanish Corporate Debt Market (AIAF). Both markets (unofficial and official) are integrated in the holding Bolsas y Mercados Españoles (BME) and are supervised by the CNMV. However, due to the fact that MARF is an alternative market, it is easier for firms to have access to it and issue debt than in the official market and also the costs faced by firms are lower.

The main protagonists of MARF are companies seeking for funds through the issue of fixed income securities, but these need, in turn, other participants to carry out the issuance process. These other participants are: market members, brokers, registered advisors and rating agencies.

- The market members are entities that are authorized to launch buy and sell orders of the securities traded on MARF. The market members are credit institutions and investment companies registered in the CNMV. Currently there are 21 entities playing the role of market members in MARF.

- The market members may act through brokers. Therefore, the brokers' activity is the intermediation between the market members and the qualified investors. Currently, there are 5 entities playing the role of brokers in MARF. All market members and brokers are subject to the same rights.
- Companies need to be supported at any time by a registered advisor. The registered advisor is a legal entity with extensive knowledge of capital markets and experience in advising companies on the issuance of securities. It is the registered advisor who informs the companies about market regulations and the requirements to be listed on MARF. Once the company is part of the MARF, the registered advisor should coordinate both the documentation of every issue and the regular reporting that the company has to do.
- Rating agencies are independent companies who assess the risks and creditworthiness of issuers and issues. Currently, the agencies rating MARF companies are: Moody´s, Standard & Poor´s, Fitch, Axesor, Creditreform and Scope.

Any company with no legal or statutory restrictions that prevent it from issuing or trading fixed income securities may be listed on MARF. The application form can be made by the company itself, by a market member or, in the case of securitizations, by the manager of the securitization fund. In order to apply for the securities listing on MARF, the company needs to meet several requirements. These requirements include having a credit rating of the issue or the issuer granted by a rating agency recognized by ESMA (European Securities and Market Authority) and presenting the annual audited accounts of the last years, filed with the mercantile register. Recently (as a result of the publication of the Circular 2/2018, of 4 December) the requirement of credit rating has been relaxed. In fact, it should only be presented if such credit rating was requested by the issuing firm or by the investors. After receiving the application form to be listed on MARF, an evaluation is made as to whether the securities meet the listing requirements and the application is submitted to the Board of Directors of MARF, which will issue a decision within a period of less than one month (Peña Cuenca, 2015). In total, the issuance process can last between 6 and 8 weeks, which means a significant acceleration with respect to the official listing markets. Furthermore, the fees supported by firms operating in the MARF (table 4) are lower than in the market AIAF. In fact, the firms operating in AIAF pay more and for more services.

The fixed income securities that can be issued in MARF are: bonds, notes, commercial papers, assetbacked securities and other securities that recognize a debt according to the laws of the financial market. An important detail to bear in mind is that securities will have a minimum nominal value of €100,000 per unit. This

Table 4. Main fees supported by companies in MARF

MARF	Min	Max
Annual fee	€6,000	€6,000
Securities listing study		
If maturing < 12 months: 0.025‰ on the max. outstanding balance	€2,000	€20,000
If maturing > 12 months: 0.025‰ on the face amount of the securities	€3,000	€20,000
Securities listing		
If maturing < 12 months: 0.005‰ on the face amount of the securities	€1,000	€20,000
If maturing < 12 months: 0.025‰ on the face amount of the securities	€2,000	€20,000
Securities delisting		
0.025‰ on the face amount of the securities	€1,250	€20,000
Securities maintenance		
0.005‰ on the face amount of the securities	€2,000	€27,500

Source: Prepared by the authors based on the Circular 9/2013, of 18 December.

minimum value is quite high, so MARF is mainly oriented towards professional and qualified investors.

The first bond issue in MARF was launched by the firm "Sociedad Anónima de Obras y Servicios Copasa" in December of the year 2013. This firm issued 5-year bonds with a coupon of 7.50%. Many things have happened since then. The issued capital (figure 3) has increased year by year (with the exception of the year 2017), from a capital of EUR 50 million in the year 2013 up to EUR 413 million in the year 2019 (until July). From the beginnings of MARF to today, bonds and notes have been issued for a total of EUR 2,197 million and the current outstanding balance of commercial papers reaches a total value of EUR 4,405 million. The number of

Figure 3. Total capital issued
Source: Prepared by the authors based on data from http://www.bmerf.es

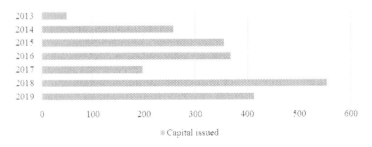

Figure 4. Number of issues and firms issuing
Source: Prepared by the authors based on data from http://www.bmerf.es

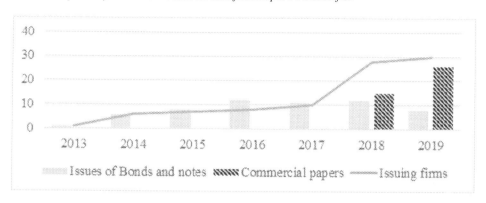

companies and issues has also gradually increased over the years (figure 4), reaching a total of 70 companies. The trend followed so far is growing and gives us insight into the consolidation of MARF, especially considering that this market has only been operating for 6 years.

MARF has attracted companies from 13 different sectors (figure 5), although the firms from the energy and water sector account for the highest number (11 firms), followed closely by the finance providers sector (10 firms).

Figure 5. Sector distribution in the MARF
Source: Prepared by the authors based on data from http://www.bmerf.es

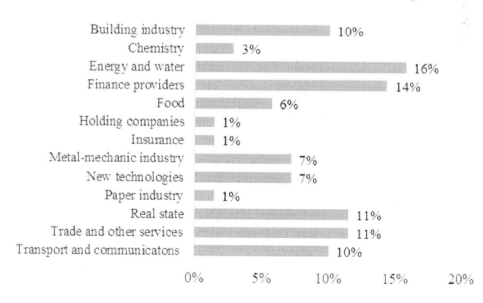

Table 5. Average annual coupon of bonds and notes issued in MARF

	2013	2014	2015	2016	2017	2018	2019
Average coupon (in percentage)	7.5	6.325	4.74	4.41	4.05	5.32	4.58

Source: Prepared by the authors based on data from http://www.bmerf.es

Concerning the bonds and notes, the average amount issued by companies is around EUR 47 million. The largest issue (EUR 199.5 million) was launched by Magdalena SME Securitization Fund and the smallest one by Saint Croix Holding Immobilier, SOCIMI (EUR 2 million).

It should be noted that companies listed on MARF have been able to sell their securities at a decreasing cost (table 5). In fact, the coupon offered for bonds and notes has been progressively reduced until 2018, when it rose slightly, although always above the coupons paid in the official market. This decline in coupons is explained by the general fall in interest rates that has taken place in recent years in the European scene and also because MARF is an increasingly known market gaining more and more trust from investors. The average interest rate is 5%, being 7.50% the highest rate offered in the first issue of Copasa and 2.50% the lowest offered by the company Saint Croix Holding Immobilier, SOCIMI, in 2016.

Regarding the frequency of coupon payments, 61% of companies establish an annual coupon, 13% a half-yearly coupon, 15% a quarterly coupon, and 11% a monthly coupon. As can be seen in figure 4, more securities have been issued in the years in which the coupons cost less.

Concerning the commercial papers, it should be noted that they are the most prevalent debt instruments in MARF. At present, 29 companies have outstanding commercial papers. Most of these companies have made more than one issue. For example, Tubacex has the highest number of outstanding issues (24 in total). Many companies issue several types of securities (bonds, notes, and commercial paper). This is the case of Jorge Pork Meat, Grupon Pikolín or Sacyr. However, there are companies such as El Corte Inglés or Barceló Corporación Empresarial that prefer to finance themselves only by issuing commercial papers.

The value of commercial papers issues vary greatly. It is possible to find an issue of €100,000 made available by the company Sociedad Anónima de Obras y Servicios COPASA; and also an issue of EUR 81million launched by El Corte Inglés.

Analysis of the Spanish Alternative Markets

In this section a comparative analysis is carried out among the Spanish alternative markets and other markets in order to understand to what extent they are helping SMEs in the process of finding sources of funding.

The segment of MAB for growing companies (MAB-growth) has been running for 10 years and this is not yet consolidated. Only 41 companies are listed on MAB-growth and the evolution has been subject to various ups and downs. In order to understand the current market status it is necessary to refer to important problems of transparency and reliability that have taken place in MAB-growth. One of the companies listed on market (the company Let's Gowex) became involved in a scandal in the year 2014 that brought into question the future of the market.

The company Let's Gowex, from the communications sector, was listed on MAB-growth in the year 2010. Initially this company was quoted at a price of 3. 5 euros, although the share price did not stop rising until it reached an all-time high of €26.34 in 2014. At that time, the company had the largest market capitalization and was considered the jewel of MAB-growth. However, those figures were dishonest. In the summer of the year 2014 the firm Gotham City Research LLC, a firm from USA that is focused on due diligence-based investing, published a report in which it valued the shares of Let's Gowex at €0 and said that 90% of the company's income did not exist. Initially Let's Gowex managers denied the published information, although the value of the company fell by 60% in two days and the trading was suspended.

The most disturbing issue was that the company's accounts had been manipulated for several years and the market, the registered advisor, and the CNMV did not notice these irregularities. This is why this scandal significantly affected MAB, leading to important disinvestments in the companies listed at the time.

Unfortunately, this was not the only case that has contributed to widespread distrust in the companies listed on MAB-growth. The company Carbures, from the aerospace industry also raised serious concerns in the year 2014. This company, that started quoting in the year 2012, was suspended from trading for 3 months for alleged false accounts. During an audit process, the auditing company observed some irregularities in the information reported by Carbures up to that time. Finally, the problems of Carbures were solved and it returned to the market 3 months later, although on the day of its return to market the value of the company fell by 66%.

All these facts have done a great deal of damage to the reputation of MAB-growth. The disinformation of investors, the lack of transparency of the companies and above all the lack of control on the part of the supervisory bodies of the market, have placed MAB between the closing and the renewal. Although MAB has since made significant efforts to overcome difficulties and ensure transparency, the market has not grown as expected and has not been able to attract foreign companies. In fact, all the companies listed on MAB-growth are Spanish with the exception of the firm Ebioss Energy. This company, located in Bulgaria and devoted to engineering, have been listed on MAB since the year 2013. The head office of Ebioss Energy is based at Bulgaria due to business preferences and the strategic assets hold by the firm in that country. However it may be said that it is "de facto" a Spanish company, whose board members and directors are mainly from Spain. In the past there were some issues regarding the lack of transparency and reliable accounting of this company, so this is another example of wrongdoing in the MAB.

Notwithstanding the above, it should be noted that MAB-growth is made up of companies of all sizes (large, medium, small and even micro-enterprises), so it does play a role as an alternative for financing small companies, at least for the companies listed on it. In fact, the size distribution of the companies listed on MAB-growth is the following: 13% are large-sized companies, 27% are medium-sized companies, 55% are small-size and 5% are micro-enterprises. It is therefore important to highlight the importance that could have this market in a country where bank financing is the most prevalent source of funding.

Even if MAB- growth has not had the expected growth, the other segments of this market are more dynamic. In fact, 58 of the 100 companies listed on MAB are SOCIMIs (this is, real estate investment trusts).

When comparing the European alternative markets with each other (table 6), it is possible to see that AIM is the most important in terms of capitalization and number of companies. This market is a long way from everyone else. In fact, if the capitalization of all the other markets were added, it would only represent 56% of the capitalization of AIM. However, this ratio is not maintained in the number of companies. Currently, 1,036 companies are listed on AIM and 1,389 in the alternative markets of the other countries, therefore it is possible to drawn the conclusion that the companies on the other markets have, on average, a lower capitalization than those listed on AIM. It is important to note that the MAB data shown in table 6 refers to the six segments of MAB and not just to MAB-growth. As can be seen in table 6, MAB is the sixth largest market in Europe by number of companies, although it ranks 15th out of 17by capitalization, so it is at the end of the queue.

Concerning the MARF, it may be said that it is a young market, because it has only been in operation for 7 years. Nevertheless, it has managed to attract more companies each year until reaching a total of 70 and also that the number of issues has increased little by little. The trend followed so far by MARF is much more regular and positive than that followed by MAB-growth, so one would expect it to continue to grow at a good pace in the future. When comparing the number and amount of admissions that have taken place in MARF since its launch to the present moment with what has happened in AIAF (which is the official market), it is possible to gain an idea of the operational capacity and impact of MARF. As can be seen in table

Are the New Sources for Financing SMEs a Reality or a Chimera?

Table 6. SME markets in Europe

		Year 2018	
Exchange	**Name of the market**	**Capitalization (in USD million)**	**Number of companies**
Athens Stock Exchange	*ATHEX Alternative Market (EN.A)*	123.306	12
BME Spanish Exchanges	*MAB*	13,403.113	105
Budapest Stock Exchange	*Xtend*	10.811	1
Cyprus Stock Exchange	*Emerging Companies Market - Cyprus*	1,104.040	34
Deutsche Börse AG	*Scale*	7,641.123	64
Euronext	*Euronext Growth*	11,696.234	206
Irish Stock Exchange	*Enterprise Securities Market*	5,991.988	24
Kazakhstan Stock Exchange	*Alternative Market*	1,660.935	51
LSE Group	*AIM*	124,109.456	1,036
Luxembourg Stock Exchange	*Euro MTF*	1,735.493	125
Malta Stock Exchange	*Alternative Companies List*	2.747	1
Luxembourg Stock Exchange	*Growth Sector*	171.090	3
Moscow Exchange	*Innovations and Investments Market*	5,196.872	10
Nasdaq Nordic Exchanges	*First North*	17,826.485	348
Oslo Stock Exchange	*Oslo Axess*	631.287	17
Warsaw Stock Exchange	*NEWCONNECT*	1,968.661	387
Zagreb Stock Exchange	*CE Enter Market*	16.500	1

Source: Prepared by the authors based on data from the World Federation of Exchanges members

7, the MARF figures are very far from AIAF although they bring to light the effort made in this alternative market and that the trend is very positive.

Nevertheless, it should not be forgotten that the amount of the debt issuing usually made in MARF is large and therefore not very accessible to small companies. MARF is a market more oriented towards medium-sized enterprises, so that in practice it does not contribute to opening up new financing channels for micro-enterprises or small-sized enterprises. Therefore, at the present time it is not a real alternative source of funding for small companies.

As a result of the foregoing, it is clear that MAB-growth and MARF ARE two small markets that follow two different trends. MAB-growth actually offers services to small businesses, although unfortunately it is not having the expected success but seems to have stalled. In contrast, MARF is working better but offering services to medium and not small companies.

Table 7. Comparative analysis of admission in MARF and AIAF

	2013	2014	2015	2016	2017	2018	2019
Transactions of admissions							
MARF	1	6	8	12	11	27	34
AIAF	9,221	3,396	2,446	2,201	1,343	791	358
Amounts of admissions (in EUR million)							
MARF	50	258	355,5	368,6	197,6	553,8	413,5
AIAF	130,491.82	115,009.32	145,891.43	130,138.13	151,710.91	86,423.19	78,987.94

Source: Prepared by the authors based on data from http://www.bmerf.es

SOLUTIONS AND RECOMMENDATIONS

The two main problems observed when analyzing the existing alternative markets in Spain (MAB-growth and MARF) are that they are not capable of reaching a large number of companies (especially in the case of MAB-growth) and that they mainly offer their services to medium-sized companies, without really reaching small companies.

Concerning the first problem, it should be noted that despite the fact that both markets have been operating for more than 5 years, they are still quite unknown to the general public and that is worse for many companies. A study by Duréndez Gómez-Guillamón et al. (2014) on the possibility of listing the Spanish family firms on MAB showed that only 40% of these firms knew the MAB and among those that knew it there was scarce knowledge of listing requirements. It would therefore be highly recommendable to take action to further publicize alternative markets so that many potential candidates to be listed on them consider at least the possibility of attempting it. The responsibility for publicity rests primarily on the authorities and those responsible for the markets, but other actors such as researchers or companies themselves can also help to raise awareness about these markets and the opportunities they offer. All of them should try to help as much as possible so that companies are aware of the financing options available to them.

Tax incentives are also an important element in promoting market access. In this regard, it should be noted that some Autonomous Communities have taken a step forward to attract SMEs to the MAB-growth by applying tax incentives to investors. The number of Communities offering incentives is still small, 4 out of 19, which are Catalonia, Aragon, Madrid and Galicia. However, if we analyze the geographic distribution of companies in the MAB-growth, we can see that these communities have an important representation in the market. In particular, 33% of the MAB-growth companies have their headquarters in the Community of Madrid, 27% in Catalonia and 8% in Galicia. Therefore, tax incentives maintained over time and extended to more Communities could really help to boost these markets.

It is also very important that both markets, but especially the MAB because of the bad experiences in which it has been involved, work hard to ensure transparency and the maximum protection of investors, who are ultimately the ones who determine the future of the markets. Transparency and trust are the most valuable assets in the financial arena and their guarantee is essential to attract companies and investors.

Concerning the second problem, it is observed that at the present time these markets fail to reach small companies, especially the MARF. The recommendation in this respect would be to further relax and simplify the market requirements and regulations in order to make the process of listing simpler for small firms.

FUTURE RESEARCH DIRECTIONS

As a continuation of this work we would like to analyze the financial characteristics of companies listed on MAB-growth and MARF in order to know the growth strategy they propose after accessing these markets and to what extent they are expanding to other countries.

CONCLUSION

Over the last two decades several alternative markets have been created in Europe to allow the quotation of companies unable to meet the listing requirements of official markets. The first one of them was AIM, the alternative market launched by the London Stock Exchange. This market is an example of success that has inspired many other countries to promote similar experiences. In the case of Spain, it was considered necessary to create two alternative markets (one alternative debt market and one alternative stock market) to try to counteract the sharp decline in bank credit that followed the outbreak of the crisis. Thus in 2009 the MAB-growth was created and in the year 2013 MARF was created. These markets are still young, although it already seems clear that they are on separate paths. While MAB-growth is a market with reduced growth (due to the bad experiences of some companies listed on this market that distorted their accounts without the authorities noticing), MARF is a market that seems to be in an expansion phase. However, while MAB-growth is a market able to reach small companies, MARF is primarily geared towards medium-sized companies.

It is evident that both markets are necessary and can play an important role in the financing of Spanish SMEs. However, strong and consistent support from the authorities is needed to reach many more companies, together with a firm commitment to transparency, control and investor protection.

REFERENCES

Alvarez García, B., & Abeal Vázquez, J. P. (2019). Fragility of the Spanish Banking System and Financial Exclusion. Lessons Learned from the Global Crisis and New Challenges for the 21th Century Banking Sector. In S. Nayak & A. Behl (Eds.), *Maintaining Financial Stability in Times of Risk and Uncertainty* (pp. 69–91). Hershey, PA: IGI Global. doi:10.4018/978-1-5225-7208-4.ch004

Andrieu, G., Stalianò, R., & van der Zwan, P. W. (2018). Bank debt and trade credit for SMEs in Europe: Firm-, industry-, and country-level determinants. *Small Business Economics*, *51*(1), 245–264. doi:10.100711187-017-9926-y

Audretsch, D. B., Heger, D., & Veith, T. (2015). Infrastructure and entrepreneurship. *Small Business Economics*, *44*(2), 219–230. doi:10.100711187-014-9600-6

Audretsch, D. B., Keilbach, M. C., & Lehmann, E. E. (2006). *Entrepreneurship and economic growth*. Oxford, UK: Oxford University Press. doi:10.1093/acprof:oso/9780195183511.001.0001

Ayadi, R. (2009). SME financing in Europe: Measures to improve the rating culture under the new banking rules. In M. Balling, B. Bernet, & E. Gnan (Eds.), *Financing SMEs in Europe*. SUERF – The European Money and Finance Forum.

Bank of Spain. (2017). *Informe sobre la Crisis Financiera y Bancaria en España, 2008-2014*. Retrieved from https://www.bde.es/f/webbde/Secciones/Publicaciones/OtrasPublicaciones/Fich/InformeCrisis_Completo_web.pdf

Beck, T., Demirguc-Kunt, A., & Martinez Peria, M. S. (2011). Bank financing for SMEs: Evidence across countries and bank ownership types. *Journal of Financial Services Research*, *39*(2), 35–54. doi:10.100710693-010-0085-4

Berges, A., & Ontiveros, E. (2013). Sistema bancario español: Una transformación sin precedentes. *Harvard Deusto Business Review*, *229*, 16–28.

Bustos, E., & Martínez, I. (2012). El MAB EE. In *El mercado alternativo bursátil* (pp. 35–60). Pamplona: Thomson Reuters.

Calvo Bernardino, A., & Martín de Vidales Carrasco, I. (2014). Crisis y cambios estructurales en el sector bancario español: Una comparación con otros sistemas financieros. *Estudios de Economía Aplicada*, *32*(2), 535–566.

Carro Meana, D. (2012). La Pyme ante el reto de la cotización en los mercados. In *Pequeña y mediana empresa: impacto y retos de la crisis en su financiación* (pp. 215–234). Madrid: Fundación de Estudios Financieros.

Circular 2/2018, of 4 December, on admission and removal of securities in the Alternative Fixed Income Market (MARF). (n.d.). Retrieved from: http://www.bmerf.es/docs/ing/normativa/circulares/2018/Circular_2_2018_de_4_December,_on_admision_and_removal_of_securities_i.pdf

Circular 5/2017, rates applicable to the Alternative Equity Market. (n.d.). Retrieved from: https://www.bolsasymercados.es/mab/docs/normativa/ing/circulares/2017/Tarifas_MAB_Circular_5-2017_eng.pdf

Circular 9/2013, of 18 December, on Alternative Fixed Income Market fees. (n.d.). Retrieved from: http://www.bmerf.es/docs/ing/normativa/circulares/2013/Circular%209-2013.pdf

Coluzzi, Ch., Ferrando, A., & Martinez-Carrascal, C. (2015). Financing obstacles and growth: An analysis for Euro area non-financial firms. *European Journal of Finance*, 21(10-11), 773–790. doi:10.1080/1351847X.2012.664154

Deeg, R. (2009). The rise of internal capitalist diversity? Changing patterns of finance and corporate governance in Europe. *Economy and Society*, 38(4), 552–579. doi:10.1080/03085140903190359

Demary, M., Hornik, J., & Watfe, G. (2016). *SME Financing in the EU: Moving beyond one-size-fits-all*. Bruges European Economic Policy Briefings 40/2016.

DeWit, G., & de Kok, J. (2014). Do small businesses create more jobs? New evidence for Europe. *Small Business Economics*, 42(2), 283–295. doi:10.100711187-013-9480-1

Duréndez Gómez-Guillamón, A., García Pérez de Lema, D., & Mariño Garrido, T. (2014). El Mercado Alternativo Bursátil: Una novedosa oportunidad para las empresas familiares. *Revista de Empresa Familiar*, 4(2), 37–46.

Fernández de Lis, S., & Rubio, A. (2013). *Tendencias a medio plazo en la banca española* (BBVA Working Paper No. 13/33). Retrieved from BBVA website: https://www.bbvaresearch.com/publicaciones/tendencias-a-medio-plazo-en-la-banca-espanola/

Ferrando, A., & Griesshaber, N. (2011). *Financing obstacles among Euro area firms. Who suffers the most?* European Central Bank. Working Paper Series n° 1293. Retrieved from https://www.ecb.europa.eu/pub/pdf/scpwps/ecbwp1293.pdf

García-Vaquero, V., & Roibás, I. (2018). *Recent developments in non-bank financing of Spanish firms*. Economic Bulletin, 4/2018, Banco de España. Retrieved from https://www.bde.es/f/webbde/SES/Secciones/Publicaciones/InformesBoletinesRevistas/ArticulosAnaliticos/2018/T4/descargar/Files/beaa1804-art32e.pdf

Giralt, A., & González Nieto, J. (2012). Financiación de la Pyme en el mercado financiero español. La experiencia y proyección del MAB. In *Pequeña y mediana empresa: impacto y retos de la crisis en su financiación* (pp. 235–258). Madrid: Fundación de Estudios Financieros.

Hernández-Cánovas, G., & Martínez-Solano, P. (2010). Relationship lending and SME financing in the continental European bank-based system. *Small Business Economics*, *34*(4), 465–482. doi:10.100711187-008-9129-7

Infelise, F. (2014). *Supporting Access to Finance by SMEs: Mapping the Initiatives in Five EU Countries*. ECMI Research Report No. 9. Retrieved from https://ssrn.com/abstract=2430116

Kaousar Nassr, I., & Wehinger, G. (2016). Opportunities and limitations of public equity markets for SMEs. *OECD Journal: Financial Market Trends*, *2015*(1). doi:10.1787/fmt-2015-5jrs051fvnjk

Langfield, S., & Pagano, M. (2016). Bank bias in Europe: Effects on systemic risk and growth. *Economic Policy*, *31*(85), 51–106. doi:10.1093/epolic/eiv019

London Stock Exchange. (2015). *A guide to AIM*. Retrieved from https://www.londonstockexchange.com/companies-and-advisors/aim/for-companies/companies.htm

Maudos, J. (2012). El impacto de la crisis en el sector bancario español. *Cuadernos de Información Económica*, *226*, 155–163.

Mercieca, S., Schaeck, K., & Wolfe, S. (2009). Bank Market Structure, Competition, and SME Financing Relationships in European Regions. *Journal of Financial Services Research*, *36*(2-3), 137–155. doi:10.100710693-009-0060-0

Montañez Núñez, M., Rubio González, A., Ruesta Baselga, M., & Ulloa Ariza, C. (2015). La financiación de las pymes españolas. *ICE*, *885*, 133–149.

Muller, P., Mattes, A., Klitou, D., Lonkeu, O-K., Ramada, P., Aranda Ruiz, F., … Steigertahl, L. (2018). *Annual report on European SMEs 2017/2018*. European Commission.

Peña Cuenca, I. (2015). Situación y futuro de la renta fija y la financiación alternativa en España y Europa. *Anuario sobre renta fija y financiación alternativa IEB-Axesor*, 20-58. Retrieved from: https://www.axesor.es/docs/default-source/estudios/anuario_axesor_ieb_2018.pdf

Regulation of the Mercado Alternativo de Renta Fija. (2018). Retrieved from: http://www.bmerf.es/docs/esp/Documentos/REGLAMENTO_ES_MARF.pdf

Revest, V., & Sapio, A. (2013). Does the alternative investment market nurture firm growth? A comparison between listed and private companie. *Industrial and Corporate Change*, 22(4), 953–979. doi:10.1093/icc/dtt021

Tajadura Garrido, C. (2015). El sistema financiero español tras la crisis: Menor en tamaño, más seguro y menos rentable. *Análisis Financiero*, 127, 1–19.

ADDITIONAL READING

AECA. (2011). *Potencialidad del Mercado Alternativo Bursátil (MAB) en España*. Madrid: Estudios Empíricos AECA.

Casey, E., & O'Toole, C. M. (2014). Bank-lending constraints, trade credit and alternative financing during the financial crisis: Evidence from European SMEs. *Journal of Corporate Finance*, 27, 173–193. doi:10.1016/j.jcorpfin.2014.05.001

Parsa, S., & Kouhy, R. (2008). Social Reporting by Companies Listed on the Alternative Investment Market. *Journal of Business Ethics*, 79(3), 345–360. doi:10.100710551-007-9402-8

Rupeika-Apoga, R. (2014). Alternative financing of SMEs in the Baltic States: Myth or reality? *Procedia: Social and Behavioral Sciences*, 156, 513–517. doi:10.1016/j.sbspro.2014.11.231

KEY TERMS AND DEFINITIONS

Bank Financing: It is the process by which a bank offers financial services to a firm, such as lending money, issuing of current or saving accounts, facilitation of monetary transactions, etc.

Debt Market: A market that is involved in the trading of debt instruments. This market may also be called as bond market or credit market.

Equity Market: A market in which shares/stocks are issued and trade. This market may also be called as stock market or stock exchange.

Official Market: It is the marketplace and/or the collection of exchanges of securities which operate under a defined set of regulations specified by the authorities.

Sources of Finance: They are the different ways a company can obtain financial resources. Some examples of sources of finance are issuing shares, issuing bonds, retaining earnings, or borrowing.

Chapter 6
Shadow Banking:
A Practical Approach

Antonio Javier Grandío Dopico
Universidade da Coruña, Spain

José Álvarez Cobelas
ANJOCA, Spain

ABSTRACT

Shadow banking has gained prominence in recent years, and especially after the world financial and economic crisis because, on the one hand, it favours the funding of firms that have difficulty accessing the tradicional banking system, and, on the other hand, it offers to investors alternatives to the traditional bank deposits. However, shadow banking involves risks because it is subject to a lower level of regulation than the traditional system and it is clearly pro-cyclical, contributing to worsening the economic climate in times of recession. The chapter shows in detail how the shadow banking works and what the advantages and disadvantages of this alternative system are. In addition, reference is made to the debate about the possibility of reinforcing the regulation of this sector, although so far, the supervisory authorities prefer maintaining a vigilant attitude while not imposing strict requirements, which would lead to limit the role played by shadow banking.

INTRODUCTION

The Financial Stability Board (FSB) defines shadow banking as "a credit intermediation system made up of entities and activities that are outside the traditional banking system" (FSB, 2018). In other words, it is a banking system parallel to the traditional system in which financial intermediaries perform the same activities of liquidity, maturity, and credit transformation than in the traditional system but in a different way (Bakk-Simon et al., 2011; Kessler & Wilhelm, 2013; Parramón Jiménez, 2014; Guttmann, 2016; Adrian & Ashcraft, 2016). While in banks everything arises from bank deposits, here everything arises from the issuance of financial assets. It is important to highlight that these entities and activities can be totally or partially outside the traditional banking circuit, that is, shadow banking is not a world independent of traditional banking, but the border between them is not clearly defined and is absolutely permeable, both in activities and in actors (Bengtsson, 2013; Harutyunyan et al., 2015; Plantin, 2015; Judge, 2017).

The growth of shadow banking over the last decade has been spectacular (Pozsar et al., 2010; Nersisyan & Wray, 2010; Ordóñez, 2018). According to data from the EU Shadow Banking Monitor (European Systemic Risk Board, 2018), shadow banking represented 40% of the total European financial system at the end of 2017, with a business volume of 42.3 trillion euros, that is very similar to the one reported at the end of 2016. This report is part of a periodic series that analyzes the risk that shadow banking can pose on the financial system as a whole. In these series risks are classified into four groups:

1. Liquidity risk and risks associated with indebtedness in some types of investment funds.
2. Interconnectivity and risk of contagion between sectors and within the shadow financial system itself.
3. Procyclicality, indebtedness and liquidity risk created by using derivatives.
4. Vulnerabilities in some parts of the financial system due to the scarcity of information about the transactions carried out.

Before entering into an analysis of the different types of risks generated by the shadow banking activity, it is necessary to deepen the concept of shadow banking and its way of acting.

BACKGROUND

Shadow banking is a credit intermediation system made up of entities and activities that are outside the traditional banking system.

In the traditional system, banks receive deposits from clients and they use these deposits to give loans. Banks receive a liquid asset, usually in the short term and without risk, and they transform it into a long-term asset, illiquid until maturity and with risk of default. In shadow banking, agents receive liquidity by issuing financial assets, which they use to finance new financial assets that may have the same or different maturity, degree of credit risk, and liquidity (Pozsar, 2014; Sunderam, 2015). Therefore, the functions are the same. Only the starting point differs. Nevertheless, it is a fundamental difference, because as we will see throughout the chapter, while in traditional banking the volume of credit granted is limited according to the deposits that entities have, in the case of shadow banking the financing granted can reach practically infinite amounts, that is, entities can "create" money in an unlimited way. The lack of regulation allows this flexibility that the traditional system does not have, which prevents exhaustive monitoring by the monetary authorities of a risk that, as seen in the recent economic crisis, has systemic character (Ricks, 2010; Stein, 2010; Plantin, 2015). Hence the FSB concern to control the volume of the shadow financial system and identify the types of assets and risks over the whole economy generated by an uncontrolled growth of this financial system. This is why FSB has created a special office for monitoring the shadow financial system permanently and reporting periodically its conclusions.

Generation of Money in The Shade

Let's take an example of shadow creation of money. We start from a traditional bank that provides finance to individuals, both in the form of mortgages and consumer loans. This bank builds a diversified portfolio with this type of assets (because there are many debtors with very different casuistry) and sells them to a shadow financial institution. This institution becomes the owner of a portfolio that entitles it to receive a series of future cash flows and on this portfolio the institution creates securities that entitle it to receive a portion of that future cash flow. This process is known as securitization. In order to give greater security to these securities, the institution ensures the issuance with some insurance companies that cover possible defaults in highly unlikely scenarios, but that allow to attribute to the issue a very high rating. This high rating leads to an increase in the demand for these securities and reduces their cost, because of the reduction of the profitability required by investors for their acquisition. With the money generated with this operation, the institution can buy a new portfolio of loans that will be securitized in order to obtain new financing and so on (Figure 1).

The operation described is very basic, but the activity of shadow banking is not as simple as the one described, in which, after all, there is a limit in the capacity to generate money.

A new variable is added when the entities carry out repurchase agreements – also known as repo's. The entity that has issued the securities places them in the market, not at their maturity but with a repurchase agreement in a relatively shorter period of time, and obviously at a higher price. This operation is a deposit with guarantee

Figure 1. Shadow banking operating scheme. Basic securitization
Source: Prepared by the authors

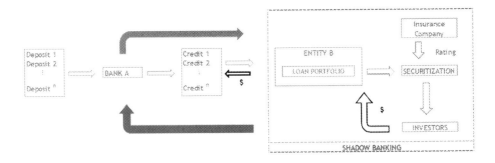

of the assets that form the portfolio for cases of default. In this case, not only the issuer has received liquidity to undertake new investments; also who has received collateral for lending money to the issuer, can again make a repo with those assets to get liquidity and buy, with resale agreements, new portfolios. In this way, with an initial bank deposit, the traditional bank has lent money and transferred that asset to the shadow banking to get additional financing with which to undertake new investments. And with the guarantee of that same asset, the shadow banking has generated "new money" in practically unlimited amounts (Figure 2).

Figures 1 and 2 show, in a very simple way, the shadow banking process of creation of money. It should be noted that even though the traditional banking world and

Figure 2. Shadow banking operating scheme. Use of repo´s
Source: Prepared by the authors

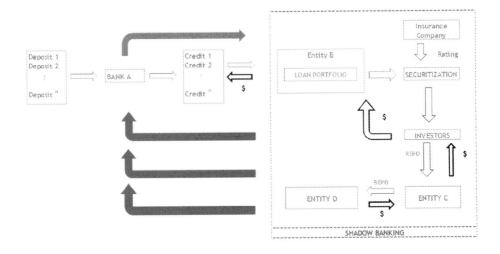

shadow banking appear to be two different worlds, the interrelation between them is permanent and very deep (Luck, 2015). This is why the separation between them is represented with a broken line. In addtion, even whether in figure 3 there are three entities (in particular, entities B, C, and D), the number of entities participating in this operation could be practically infinite, as well as the number of transactions made between them using the same initial assets.

The variants that can be though of in this shadow system grow when derivative instruments are introduced, especially derivatives on credit risks, since with small amounts of money it is possible to bet on important volumes of assets.

These operations, based on the lack of a risk control regulation similar to the one applied in the traditional banking, can generate significant liquidity, credit, and interconnectivity risks, which can exponentially multiply the risk of "collapse" of the system if they are not kept under control (Stein, 2010; Fiaschi et al., 2014).

The Example of Subprime Mortgages

During the seventies, an idea emerged in USA that revolutionized the financial market at that time (Ashcraft & Schuermann, 2008). The vast majority of loans granted by banks were used to finance the acquisition of housing. Since the last thing that normally people stop paying is the mortgage, this kind of mortgage loans traditionally had a percentage of defaults practically zero. Then, the idea of creating collateralized debt obligations (CDO) or mortgaged securities arose. A bank issues securities that anyone can buy. These securities have a reduced nominal value and investors will receive a periodic interest that will be guaranteed by the flows of interest paid by the mortgaged people and, ultimately, by the property itself. At firt glance, these instruments seemed safe, because historically no one stopped paying their mortgage. In addition, due to the money paid in from these bonds, the bank has liquidity again to deal with other investments.

From the nineties, financial entities began to relax the lending requirements and more changes occurred. Mortgage loans were extended to people with precarious jobs, the mortgage share represented an increasing percentage of household's income, a higher percentage of the mortgage was granted on the value of the asset reaching even more than 100% of the real property that guaranteed the operation. This is why bonds issued by the bank no longer had the same credit quality as the first ones. However, bonds continued to be rated as AAA (Cintra & Farhi, 2008; Covitz et al., 2012; Lysandrou & Nesveitailova, 2015).

In addition, synthetic CDOs or CDO squared began to be created and traded. A synthetic CDO is a securitiy whose underlying asset is no longer the real property, but other CDO. Therefore, the holder of a synthetic bond depended on the fact that the person who initially bought his house made the morgage payments and that, in

Figure 3. Primary and synthetic CDO´s
Source: Prepared by the authors

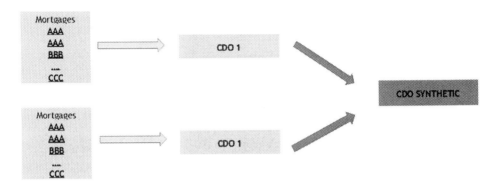

turn, the holders of the primary CDOs also made their payments, and the same for the holders of secondary CDOs, tertiary CDOs, etc. With this structure, mortgages for an amount of EUR 1,000 million could support CDOs for an amount of EUR 100,000 million (Figure 3).

All this scheme remained until the beginning of the 21st century, when defaults on mortgages began to increase. The holders of subprime mortgages - those with lower credit quality - no only stopped supporting the periodic interest and amortization payments, but they even saw how the value of the assets underlying the loans fell below the nominal value of the mortgages.

At that time the credit default swaps (CDS) started to emerge. They are credit insurance that covers the holder of the credit against an eventual default of the debtor in exchange for the payment of a premium. The CDO issuers began buying CDS to cover the first defaults. The problem arises when in the years 2007-2008 the defaults of the subprime mortgages grew exponentially, reason why the issuers of CDS could not face their commitments and, consequently, the CDO lost much of their value and the investors registered millionaires loses. Lehman Brothers was the first entity to fall and a liquidity crisis started and gave rise to a serious economic crisis. What happened? The system collapsed like a house of cards when the value of the last assets that were giving guarantee to the whole system was reduced. When the value of the house falls below the amount of the loan granted with the guarantee of the house itself, the system becomes unstable since in each of the phases the assets are worth less than the loans and the system ends up collapsing. Obviously, the fall is transferred to entities which belong to the traditional banking system precisely because of the interconnectivity between the traditional banking system and the entities that make up the shadow system.

In other words, the financial system was "separated" from the real economy. The issues had a rating higher than the one granted to the assets acquired as collateral (Cintra &Farhi, 2008; Lysandrou &Nesvetailova, 2015). Each asset served as the basis for several linked operations, so if one of them failed all the others were affected, the customers of shadow banking entities were also affected and ultimately the effect could also arrive to the client that had make the bank deposit in the traditional bank. An asset with little value was sold several times as a virtually certain asset, generating a multiplier effect in the financial environment when the value falls in the real economy.

It is not the object of this article to analyze the consequences of the aforementioned crisis on the traditional financial system, but we do draw attention to the permeability that exists between both worlds and how, once a failure is triggered, it quickly moves to the financial system as a whole.

Hence the vigilant attitude of the European Systemic Risk Board (ESRB) to avoid, as far as possible, that situations like the one described can be repeated again.

MAIN FOCUS OF THE CHAPTER

Pros and Cons of Shadow Banking Activity

One of the fundamental aspects of shadow banking is that it is seen as an additional source of financing for companies, which is especially important at a time when banks have tightened in an important way the requirements for granting financing (Pozsar, 2014; Parramón Jiménez, 2014).

Additionally shadow banking offers to investors alternatives to the traditional bank deposits. This activity is of special relevance when the interest rates set by the monetary authorities and therefore, those determined in the money and debt markets, are practically null in most parts of the world and with expectations of staying at these levels for quite some time.

Thereby, the entities that operate outside the traditional financial system find niche markets to which they can additionally contribute in order to optimizing the portfolio management. Likewise, these entities can reach business activities that for different reasons would have great difficulty to access to traditional financing sources (Ghosh et al., 2012; Chernenko & Sunderam, 2014; Lu et al., 2015). A recent example, that is becoming more and more popular, is crowdfunding (Mollick, 2014; Belleflamme et al., 2014). Crowdfunding can support innovative activities that have difficulties to access traditional financing, either because of the risk profile of the project or the risk profile of the entrepreneur (Sorenson et al., 2016; Stanko & Henard, 2017). Other example is private equity activities, especially venture capital, which are committed to projects that would not see the light otherwise due to their high levels of credit risk (Kortum & Lerner, 2000).

Concerning the problems related to shadow banking, it is possible to allude to the risk analysis carried out by the ESRB and that can be summarized in the following points (Financial Stability Board, 2018).:

1. Procyclicity
2. Liquidity tensions
3. Interconnectivity with the traditional financial system
4. Lack of information and transparency in certain cases

Shadow banking is clearly pro-cyclical (Thiemann et al., 2018). It generates beneficial effects in the cycle's upturn times because of its contribution to the financing of business projects, but also it generaltes a chain-down effect in times of recession when the final asset, on which the entire shadow banking system has been built, is devalued. Shadow banking institutions deploy their activity especially in the early phases of the expansive cycle, where the traditional banking system still has restrictive financing conditions both in risk analysis and price. Thereby, these entities contribute to achieve high economic growth with some speed and later they transfer the prominent role to banks and credit institutions.

Liquidity tensions are caused precisely by the number of times the same asset is used to finance and refinance, which has come to be called "over-leverage". Thus, any liquidity problem in an operation triggers tensions in the rest of the links of the chain of operations, and may generate a situation of lack of global liquidity that acts as a trigger or amplifier of the economic crisis.

Traditional banking and shadow banking are intimately related. Even though in our operating scheme of the shadow banking there is a clear separation between both "worlds", the reality is that the permeability between them is extensive and permanent (Huang, 2018). Traditional banking itself acts by performing operations categorized as shadow banking, so interconnectivity is even born in its own balance sheets, regardless of receiving funding from this type of entities. Therefore, what happens in one world quickly moves to the other, in a one-to-one relationship.

Finally, the lack of transparency in certain operations means that the final investor does not know exactly the risks that he is running. Without a correct assessment of risks, it is not possible to design an adequate coverage of them and the vulnerability of the entities to crisis scenarios is multiplied. To this fact it must be added that half of the shadow banking operations in the European Union are carried out by non-financial entities that do not publish complete information about their activities, thereby generating a niche of unquantified and potentially high risk (Bakk-Simon et al., 2011).

Next section will briefly review the opinions that the ESRB makes about each of these risks and the current situation of them. However, previously it is necessary to conceptualize the lack of regulation of this type of operations: Is it a virtue of the system or can it be framed as one of its weaknesses? Without a doubt, the answer is that it is possible to classify it in both categories. The lack of regulations allows the financing of investment operations that have no place within the traditional financial system, since the hedges and the own resources requirements needed would make the operation unviable. This would affect new activities, entrepreneurs without experience and other types of projects that have importance within the GDP of any country and that presumably will have even more in the future as a result of the 4.0 revolution. But on the other hand, it is precisely this lack of regulation, which leads to get the maximum value from these practices, leaving the comfort zones and assuming pyramid risks that can lead to the bankruptcy of the entity and, by contagion, a good part of the system (Gorton et al., 2010; Risks, 2010; Guttmann, 2016; Judge, 2017).

Is it then possible to regulate the system in depth or maintain the current situation? We understand that the regulation of shadow banking should not be deepened. The fundamental reason is that we understand that the benefits it brings to the system are very important, however excessive regulation would liquidate these additional sources of funding and would not contribute to curtailing the systemic risk of this type of practices. A vigilant attitude, such as the one that is currently being carried out by the financial authorities, is the way to avoid repeating cases such as the latest financial crisis (precisely caused by this king of practices) and to allow them to continue contributing to the GDP growth by financing business projects that would be excluded from traditional financing.

Shadow Banking Today. Data from the European Systemic Risk Board

According to the data published by ESRB (2018), the shadow banking system represented 40% of the financial system of the European Union (EU). The total volume reaches 42.3 trillion euros for the whole of the EU and 33.8 trillion in the euro area, having fallen by 0.1% in the EU while the whole financial system grew by 0.9% and having fallen by 1.2% in the Eurozone while this area grew by 2.8%. This behavior contrasts sharply with that experienced in the 2012-2015 period with an annual growth of 8.6%, much higher than that of the traditional banking sector. This fact reinforces our theory that the contribution of shadow banking is much more important in the early phases of the upward cycle, and becomes more moderate once the economy has reached the cruising speed and the traditional system fully deploys its battery of financial instruments.

Figure 4. Types of entities that operate in shadow banking, degree of activity, and risks in European Union and Euro Zone)
Source: Prepared by the authors

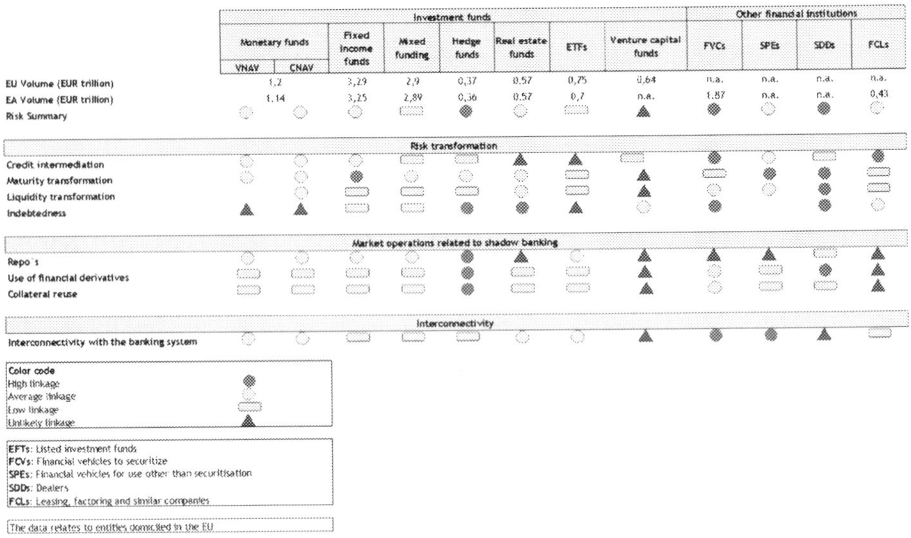

So far we have exemplified shadow banking by describing briefly some of its activities. However, who are the actors in the shadow banking system? Figure 4 shows who are the actors involved in shadow banking, their degree of involvement in the different activities that make up this system, and the interrelation with the traditional banking system. The level of linkage is established by ESRB (2018).

Figure 4 summarizes perfectly who the actors are, how they act, how their degree of involvement in the financial intermediation activity is, how the interrelation between the traditional banking system and shadow banking is and how the degree of use of the activity's amplifying elements (repos, collaterals and derivatives) is. This figure is also useful to deduce the potential risks faced by actors and that may end up moving to the system. It is possible to say that figure 4 represents the shadow banking scorecard that includes the indicators that have to be constantly monitored to foresee possible risk situations and define appropriate corrective measures to avoid their transfer to the whole system.

Conclusion of the Conceptual Framework

The term shadow banking is not the most fortunate to define the set of financial intermediation activities that are totally or partially carried out from the traditional banking system. The term "shadow" refers to the lack of exhaustive regulation similar to that which is applyed to the traditional banking system and, in certain cases, to the lack of reliable information on the volume and detail of the operations carried out.

However, shadow banking should not be seen as something negative, as a world of speculation, with agents without scruples and with a destabilizing character (Parramón Jiménez, 2014; Harutyunyan, et al., 2015).

Shadow banking encompasses activities that have an important impact from the point of view of business financing (Ghosh et al., 2012; Fiaschi et al., 2014). Likewise, shadow banking contributes to economic growth because it allows executing investment operations that otherwise would never see the light thanks to the lower regulation and requirements of own resources demanded in comparison to the traditional banking system. This is, in turn, its greatest risk: lower requirements and the need to permanently offer high returns can lead to make again and again operations with different actors but with the same assets as guarantee, which exponentially increases the risk of contagion to the system as a whole in the event that a few operations do not have the expected returns.

The crisis of subprime mortgages taught us that there is a systemic risk that was not controlled (Fox Gotham, 2009; Demyanyk & Van Hemert, 2011). For this reason, the authorities have responded by suggesting to apply a prudential surveillance but no regulation that could reduce the operational agility that is considered to have more advantages than disadvantages (such as, risks). Currently the collateralized loan obligations (CLOs) have replaced the CDOs. These are similar instruments but based on corporate debt issues instead of mortgage loans (Lucas et al., 2007; Tavakoli, 2008). In fact, the volume of CLOs issued is similar to that registered by the CDOs in the years prior to the crisis, so they are being followed closely by the supervisory authorities, although the probability of generating a new systemic crisis is in this case remote.

Therefore, in our opinion the set of activities that take place outside the traditional financial circuits is positive and an in-depth regulation of them would only stop this kind of funding operations, with the consequent drop in creation of wealth, employment ... In short, innovative investment projects from not yet consolidated entrepreneurs and pioneers would not be launched due to lack of funding. In addition, investors who invest in this type of securitized assets would be left without products with high returns, amplifying the poverty factor. Likewise, the traditional financial system itself would suffer as it would stop entering a significant amount in fees for collaborating in the design and placement of much of these operations. And, in an environment of interest rates close to zero or even negative, this would be a terrible news for banks and, therefore, for the economy as a whole. In this sense, a more "statistical" approach, analyzing magnitudes and warning of potential risks is much more effective than legislation in this regard.

Some Practical Example

Private Equity Funds

Private equity funds invest in the acquisition and / or concession of external financing. This financing is usually debt with some kind of subordination in companies that have difficult access to traditional financing, because either they present high levels of risk, or they do not have sufficient size to go directly to the fixed income markets through the issuance of fixed income securities. It is in this market segment where the operations of what is generally called as venture capital are focused. Venture capital looks for companies with a business project that can generate very high growth in short periods of time. These are business projects with a higher risk profile than those developed in consolidated sectors or by consolidated entrepreneurs, but in return they offer more attractive returns in relatively short periods of time.

The investments that venture capital companies make can combine the participation in the company's own resources and the granting of financing, generally subordinated - which means that in case of bankruptcy the company would be the penultimate creditor in collecting, only ahead of the shareholders. The venture capital contributions reinforce the company's own resources, which in many cases makes it feasible for banks to provide financing with certain limits.

One of the characteristics of venture capital investments is that venture capital negotiates exit conditions at the moment of entering the company (Kortum & Lerner, 2000; Engel & Keilbach, 2007). That is, it is already agreed with the entrepreneur when he buys back the participation from the venture capital company and amortizes the subordinated credit. Likewise, it is also agreed the price at which the entrepreneur will do both operations. Obviously, it is also agreed a "payment on account" in the form of periodic interest or dividends, but the key is exit conditions.

In this way, there is an entrepreneur who has created a company to undertake a business project with a fast amortization capacity, say in 5 years. He has needed to go to venture capital with which he pacts an entry into the company's capital and a participative loan with an interest of 8%. An exit value of the capital of 150% is agreed, with annual dividends of 15%. This means that during the five years, the average return that venture capital achieves (assuming 50% of entry into the capial and 50% equity loan) is 15% in terms of IRR.

The idea is to achieve a diversified portfolio of investments in business projects so that they reach a volume and diversification by sector that minimizes the risk of default. And from this point, the idea is to securitize this portfolio offering very attractive returns compared to other traditional financial products and place it in the market. These securities generally have an expiration date that coincides with

Shadow Banking

the average maturity of the portfolio of loans and participations provided, although it is also possible to make them indefinitely.

Securitization can be of two types: 1) homogeneous securities, where all securities have the same rights and obligations over the entire investment portfolio and 2) securities that offer different returns and that start from a heterogeneous division of risks. In this case, senior debt is considered as the one which has the safest investments as collateral, while the rest will offer greater profitability in exchange for bearing greater risks. A prudent securitization will maintain a safety margin to prevent possible investments that become insolvent from being transferred to the final investors who buy these assets (Figure 5).

Figure 5. Private equity and financing business projects
Source: Prepared by the authors

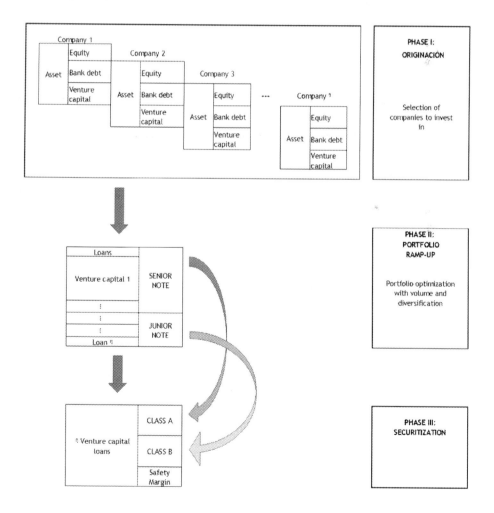

A large number of entities participate in an operation of this type: the analysts who select the companies to invest in, law firms, audit firms, banks, etc., which means that the costs of starting up an operation of this type are elevated. If the fund is also listed on any market, commissions will be paid to provide liquidity to these securities. All this implies that this type of operations requires projects with large returns to be able to pay all the agents involved in the process as well as an attractive return to the final investor.

Company Financing Vehicle. Structure Project finance

In contrast to the previous example, where the venture capital fund creates a portfolio with many investments in a multitude of medium or even small-size companies, it is possible to propose an operation for a large multinational of sufficient size to bear all the transaction costs related to this kind of operation. The company is considering a new investment project and seeks financing for it. If the volume of the finance needed is very large, there are two main alternatives: the first one, looking for a broad banking pool that will cover the financing needs of this new project within the treasury scheme of the entire business group, and the second one, creating a specific company to launch the aforementioned project (a "vehicle" society). In this second case, all the cash-flows of the company will come from the new project for which the operation is structured and the project itself is the only guarantee of the financing.

Initially, the project to be financed is analyzed, by estimating both the necessary investments and the cash flows that will be generated in the future (Yescombe, 2002; Gatti, 2013). Based on these analyses, the structure of own resources and external financing is estimated, so that the cash flows could adequately pay the external financing. In this way, the shareholder and promoter of the investment should contribute his share of own resources while the entity in charge of structuring the operation will be in charge of finding the investors that contribute the sufficient foreign resources. Generally, two categories of own resources are established: equity - which will be borne by the investor - and subordinated debt, which is usually financed in the market in a differentiated debt tranche, with greater profitability due to the greater risk involved.

Any Project Finance (Figure 6) has two main characteristics:

1. Investors have full control over the project finances through the figure of the agent or manager of the Project Finance. An account is opened for the service of the pledged debt that the entrepreneur can not dispose of. The resources generated by the project go to this account until they reach enough volume to meet the financial commitments of interest of the following periods (6 months or even one year). Only from that moment, the initial investor can release

Shadow Banking

Figure 6. Project Finance Vehicle Company
Source: Prepared by the authors

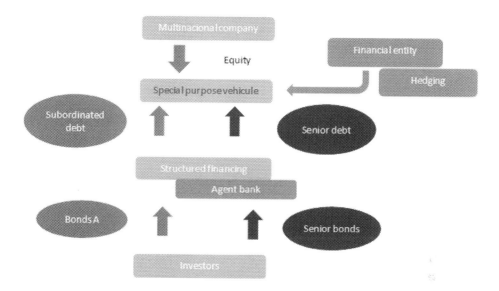

resources and always with restrictions. This is one of the elements that give greater security to the probability of payment of interest and principal on the debt.

2. Derivatives can be introduced to eliminate any kind of risk different from the main one of the investment. This would involve applying derivative instruments to eliminate risks due to changes in interest rates, currency exchange, etc., in order to get the project to function in real life as it would do in a laboratory and then meeting the base scenario of investment and the expected results of the entire process.

Once analyzed the project, tested by auditors and consultants, both senior and subordinated bonds are issued and placed on the market among final investors who know that in this case they concentrate all the probability of success or default in a single project and not in a multitude. of projects as is the first example seen.

A variation of this kind of financing has been applied many times to the public-private collaboration schemes (Grimsey & Lewis, 2004). These represent the union of interests between private companies and the public sector to develop investments for which the public sector does not have financial capacity. The investment is carried out by the private sector who is going to recover it from the public sector in the long term. In most cases also the maintenance of the investment is also supported by the private sector, being the maintenance subject to compliance with a series of previously fixed indicators. It should be noted that this kind of financing is highly demanded by the final investors, since they implicitly count on the guarantee of the public sector which significantly reduces the risk of default.

FUTURE RESEARCH DIRECTIONS

It would be very interesting to continue this line of research by comparing the development of the shadow banking system in several European countries and by studying shadow banking in USA (where the shadow banking sector is almost the same size as the traditional banking system), and in non-European countries. In so doing, it could be shown if the evolution has been different among countries and what the main characteristic features in each country are.

Another line for future development could be to analyse how shadow banking affects some important macroeconomic variables and what is the impact it has on the savings and investments of households and public and private companies.

CONCLUSION

Several important ideas that shape the main conclusion of this chapter are the following:

1. Shadow banking plays a fundamental role in the financial world. On the one hand, it made it possible to finance projects that would be left out of the traditional banking system because of their risk profile (risk coming from either the entrepreneur or the project). On the other hand, it enables investors who are willing to assume certain risks to get yields well above those obtained by traditional bank deposits.
2. The interrelation between the traditional banking system and shadow banking is total. There is a permeable line between these two worlds that is bidirectional.
3. The shadow banking plays an important role in the economic growth but, in turn, it involves risks that must be constantly evaluated by the supervisory authorities to avoid a new liquidity crisis and, consequently, an economic crisis such as the one caused by the subprime mortgages.
4. The surveillance scheme carried out by the ESRB is adequate. This international body identifies risks, analyzes possibilities of contagion and deploys a continuous monitoring on them.
5. Greater regulation would not be beneficial for economic growth.

6. The type of operations carried out by shadow banking is practically infinite, so it is essential to know at any time all the characteristics of the products in which investment are being made. Transparency and information are key elements.

The term shadow banking is not the most adequate to define a financial world complementary to the traditional banking system and that, with its risks, contributes decisively to economic growth and the generation of wealth.

REFERENCES

Adrian, T., & Ashcraft, A. B. (2016). Shadow banking: a review of the literature. In G. Jones (Ed.), *Banking Crises* (pp. 282–315). London: Palgrave Macmillan.

Ashcraft, A. B., & Schuermann, T. (2008). Understanding the Securitisation of Subprime Mortgage Credit. Foundations and Trends in Finance, 2(3), 191–309. doi:10.1561/0500000024

Bakk-Simon, K., Borgioli, S., Giron, C., Hempell, H. S., Maddaloni, A., Recine, F., & Rosati, S. (2011). Shadow Banking in the Euro Area: An Overview. ECB Occasional Paper No. 133. Retrieved from https://ssrn.com/abstract=1932063

Belleflamme, P., Lambert, Th., & Schwienbacher, A. (2014). Crowdfunding: Tapping the right crowd. *Journal of Business Venturing*, 29(5), 585–609. doi:10.1016/j.jbusvent.2013.07.003

Bengtsson, E. (2013). Shadow banking and financial stability: European money market funds in the global financial crisis. *Journal of International Money and Finance*, 32, 579–594. doi:10.1016/j.jimonfin.2012.05.027

Chernenko, S., & Sunderam, A. (2014). Frictions in Shadow Banking: Evidence from the Lending Behavior of Money Market Mutual Funds. *Review of Financial Studies*, 27(6), 1717–1750. doi:10.1093/rfs/hhu025

Cintra, M. A. M., & Farhi, M. (2008). A crise financeira e o global shadow banking system. Novos Estudos CEBRAP, (82): 35–55. doi:10.1590/S0101-33002008000300002

Covitz, D., Liang, N., & Suarez, G. (2012). The Evolution of a Financial Crisis: Collapse of the Asset-Backed Commercial Paper Market. *The Journal of Finance*, 68(3), 815–848. doi:10.1111/jofi.12023

Demyanyk, Y., & Van Hemert, O. (2011). Understanding the Subprime Mortgage Crisis. *Review of Financial Studies, 24*(6), 1848–1880. doi:10.1093/rfs/hhp033

Engel, D., & Keilbach, M. (2007). Firm-level implications of early stage venture capital investment— An empirical investigation. *Journal of Empirical Finance, 14*(2), 150–167. doi:10.1016/j.jempfin.2006.03.004

European Systemic Risk Board. (2018). EU Shadow Banking Monitor, No 3, September 2018. Retrieved from https://www.esrb.europa.eu/pub/pdf/reports/esrb.report180910_shadow_banking.en.pdf

Fiaschi, D., Kondor, I., Marsili, M., & Volpati, V. (2014). The Interrupted Power Law and the Size of Shadow Banking. *PLoS One, 9*(4), e94237. doi:10.1371/journal.pone.0094237 PubMed

Financial Stability Board. (2018). Global shadow banking monitoring report 2017. Retrieved from https://www.fsb.org/wp-content/uploads/P050318-1.pdf

Fox Gotham, K. (2009). Creating Liquidity out of Spatial Fixity: The Secondary Circuit of Capital and the Subprime Mortgage Crisis. *International Journal of Urban and Regional Research, 33*(2), 355–371. doi:10.1111/j.1468-2427.2009.00874.x

Gatti, S. (2013). *Project finance in theory and practice. Designin, structuring, and financing private and public proyect* (2nd ed.). San Diego, CA: Academic Press.

Ghosh, S., González del Mazo, I., & Ötker-Robe, İ. (2012). *Chasing the Shadows: How Significant is Shadow Banking in Emerging Markets? Economic Premise, No. 88.* Washington, DC: World Bank; Retrieved from https://openknowledge.worldbank.org/handle/10986/17088

Gorton, G., Metrick, A., Shleifer, A., & Tarullo, D. K. (2010). Regulating the Shadow Banking System. Brookings Papers on Economic Activity, 2010(Fall), 261–312. doi:10.1353/eca.2010.0016

Grimsey, D., & Lewis, M. K. (2004). *Public private partnerships. The worldwide revolution in infrastructure provision and project finance.* Edward Elgar Publishing, Inc.

Guttmann, R. (2016). Finance-Led Capitalism: shadow banking, re-regulation, and the future of global markets. Hampshire, UK: Palgrave MacMillan; doi:10.1057/9781137529893.

Harutyunyan, A., Massara, A., Ugazio, G., Amidzic, G., & Richard Walton, R. (2015). Shedding Light on Shadow Banking. IMF Working Paper, WP/15/1. Retrieved from https://www.imf.org/external/pubs/ft/wp/2015/wp1501.pdf

Huang, J. (2018). Banking and shadow banking. *Journal of Economic Theory*, *178*, 124–152. doi:10.1016/j.jet.2018.09.003

Judge, K. (2017). Information gaps and shadow banking. *Virginia Law Review*, *103*(3), 411–480.

Kessler, O., & Wilhelm, B. (2013). Financialization and the Three Utopias of Shadow Banking. *Competition & Change*, *17*(3), 248–264. doi:10.1179/1024529 413Z.00000000036

Kortum, S., & Lerner, J. (2000). Assessing the contribution of venture capital to innovation. *The Rand Journal of Economics*, *31*(4), 674–692. doi:10.2307/2696354

Lu, Y., Guo, H., Kao, E. H., & Fung, H. G. (2015). Shadow banking and firm financing in China. *International Review of Economics & Finance*, *36*, 40–53. doi:10.1016/j.iref.2014.11.006

Lucas, D. J., Goodman, L. S., & Fabozzi, F. J. (2007). Collateralized Debt Obligations and Credit Risk Transfer. Yale ICF Working Paper No. 0706. Retrieved from SSRN http://depot.som.yale.edu/icf/papers/fileuploads/2503/original/07-06.pdf

Luck, S., & Schempp, P. (2015). Banks, Shadow Banking, and Fragility. ECB Working Paper No. 1726. Retrieved from https://ssrn.com/abstract=2479948

Lysandrou, Ph., & Nesvetailova, A. (2015). The role of shadow banking entities in the financial crisis: A disaggregated view. *Review of International Political Economy*, *22*(2), 257–279. doi:10.1080/09692290.2014.896269

Mollick, E. (2014). The dynamics of crowdfunding: An exploratory study. *Journal of Business Venturing*, *29*(1), 1–16. doi:10.1016/j.jbusvent.2013.06.005

Nersisyan, Y., & Wray, L. R. (2010). The Global Financial Crisis and the Shift to Shadow Banking. Levy Economics Institute Working Paper No. 587. Retrieved from https://ssrn.com/abstract=1559383 or doi:10.2139srn.1559383

Ordóñez, G. (2018). Sustainable Shadow Banking. American Economic Journal. Macroeconomics, *10*(1), 33–56. doi:10.1257/mac.20150346

Parramón Jimenez, E. (2014). Claves para entender la banca en la sombra: Shadow Banking. *Análisis Financiero*, *125*, 67–76.

Plantin, G. (2015). Shadow Banking and Bank Capital Regulation. *Review of Financial Studies*, *28*(1), 146–175. doi:10.1093/rfs/hhu055

Pozsar, Z. (2014). Shadow Banking: The Money View. Office of Financial Research Working Paper. Retrieved from https://ssrn.com/abstract=2476415

Pozsar, Z., Adrian, T., Ashcraft, A., & Boesky, H. (2010). *Shadow banking, Staff Report, No. 458*. New York, NY: Federal Reserve Bank of New York.

Quinn, S., & Roberds, W. (2015). Responding to a Shadow Banking Crisis: The Lessons of 1763. *Journal of Money, Credit and Banking*, *47*(6), 1149–1176. doi:10.1111/jmcb.12240

Ricks, M. (2010). Shadow Banking and Financial Regulation. Columbia Law and Economics Working Paper No. 370. Retrieved from https://ssrn.com/abstract=1571290

Sorenson, O., Assenova, V., Li, G. C., Boada, J., & Fleming, L. (2016). Expand innovation finance via crowdfunding. *Science*, *35*(6319), 1526–1528. doi:10.1126/science.aaf6989 PubMed

Stanko, M. A., & Henard, D. H. (2017). Toward a better understanding of crowdfunding, openness and the consequences for innovation. *Research Policy*, *46*(4), 784–798. doi:10.1016/j.respol.2017.02.003

Stein, J. (2010). Securitisation, Shadow Banking, and Financial Fragility. *Daedalus*, *139*(4), 41–51. doi:10.1162/DAED_a_00041

Sunderam, A. (2015). Money Creation and the Shadow Banking System. *Review of Financial Studies*, *28*(4), 939–977. doi:10.1093/rfs/hhu083

Tavakoli, J. M. (2008). Structured finance and collateralized debt obligations. New developments in cash and synthetic securitization (2nd ed.). Jon Wiley & Sons, Inc.; doi:10.1002/9781118268230.

Thiemann, M., Birk, M., & Friedrich, J. (2018). Much Ado About Nothing? Macro-Prudential Ideas and the Post-Crisis Regulation of Shadow Banking. KZfSS Kölner Zeitschrift für Soziologie und Sozialpsychologie, 70(S1), 259–286. doi:10.100711577-018-0546-6

Yescombe, E. R. (2002). *Principles of project finance*. San Diego, CA: Academic Press.

ADDITIONAL READING

Gabor, D. (2016). A step too far? The European financial transactions tax on shadow banking. *Journal of European Public Policy*, *23*(6), 925–945. doi:10.1080/13501763.2015.1070894

Guillaume Plantin, G. (2015). Shadow Banking and Bank Capital Regulation. *Review of Financial Studies*, 28(1), 146–175. doi:10.1093/rfs/hhu055

Moreira, A., & Savov, A. (2017). The Macroeconomics of Shadow Banking. *The Journal of Finance*, 72(6), 2381–2432. doi:10.1111/jofi.12540

KEY TERMS AND DEFINITIONS

European Systemic Risk Board (ESRB): It is a Union-level body established in the year 2010 to oversee the financial system of the European Union (EU) and prevent and mitigate systemic risk. The ESRB is responsible for the macroprudential oversight of the EU financial system.

Financial Stability Board (FSB): It is an international body that monitors and makes recommendations about the global financial system.

Project Finance: It is a way of funding used to provide funds to large projects that require a very important initial investment and the period to make it profitable is very long. The debt and equity used to finance the project are paid back from the cash flows generated by the project.

Securitization: Conversion of an asset into marketable securitites.

Shadow Banking: Is a credit intermediation system made up of entities and activities that are outside the traditional banking system.

Chapter 7
Recent Developments in Mortgage Loans in Spain and the Effects of the Subsequent Legislative Reforms

Lucía Boedo Vilabella
Universidade da Coruña, Spain

Begoña Alvarez García
https://orcid.org/0000-0001-7918-3986
Universidade da Coruña, Spain

ABSTRACT

This chapter analyses the evolution of the mortgage loan in Spain during the present century. The economic development of Spain is described with its great connection to mortgages. The text centres on the new conditions incorporated in the loans in the years before the crisis, which were subsequently demonstrated to be unfair terms and caused serious problems for consumers and a lack of confidence in the financial sector. This provoked the reaction of legislators. This chapter studies the effectiveness of the subsequent mortgage laws in their intention to minimize the asymmetrical positions that the lender and the borrower occupy in the contractual relationship. Among the conclusions of the chapter, the authors highlight how each law is more precise but its effectiveness is lacking if the banking culture is not changed in terms of the relationship between to clients.

DOI: 10.4018/978-1-7998-2440-4.ch007

Recent Developments in Mortgage Loans in Spain and the Effects

INTRODUCTION

The financial system of a country is a very important element in the functioning of any economy and this importance is increased in the case of Spain by a strong tendency for companies to be financed with bank loans. The growing volume of banking business, together with regulation that gave the sector a great freedom of action, contributed to the growth of the Spanish banking sector throughout the 20th century, making it one of the sectors with the greatest profits and strongest representation in the Ibex 35.

With the arrival of the 21st century, the financial system brings to light a set of problems that had been brewing for years and that causes this more or less amicable relationship between banking and society to end, giving way to a climate of confrontation that does not benefit either of the parties. These problems are a consequence of the serious asymmetry of information between the knowledge base of the bank and the client (company or individual).

To this we must add, on the one hand, the investment policy focused on the real estate sector that banks have followed since the nineties and, on the other hand, the design and massive sale of new financial products, as well as the incorporation of new contractual conditions to the mortgage loans (ML) that turned out to be enormously unfavourable to citizens.

With the outbreak of the crisis in 2008, society reacted and began to file lawsuits against banks. The number of consumers who initiate legal proceedings would gradually increase until a flood of cases was brought to court. This makes the abuse that the bank had been committing a major issue in the media and on the street, but it also represents a first step toward balancing the power of the bank and the client.

The situation becomes so evident and complicated that successive governments in Spain during the last ten years have been forced to act. With the aim of protecting the consumer, and trying to reestablish a relationship of trust between banks and citizens, new laws, in number and importance not seen until now, have been passed that regulate banking activity. These new rules mean important changes for the consumer and also have great implications for banking.

The main objective of this chapter is to analyse the conditions that were incorporated in the mortgages in Spain, the serious risks and damages that such conditions implied and the effectiveness of the legislative changes promulgated to resolve the problem.

This chapter addresses these issues by structuring the topic as follows:

The Background section describes the recent economic development of Spain and its connection to financial activity. Economic growth is based on the real estate sector and for its development the role of banking is fundamental, both by lending to construction companies and to home buyers. It shows the huge growth of the mortgage market in a short time, and in addition, great transformation of banking business as a whole, so that new contracts are increasingly complex and with new conditions.

The Main Focus of the Chapter analyses the new conditions that have been incorporated into mortgage contracts and their serious subsequent consequences. Next, we describe normative and legislative changes that successive governments have carried out with the aim of protection and we discuss their effectiveness.

Finally, the Solutions and Recommendations section proposes new procedures and ways of acting that we believe may reduce the climate of distrust in Spanish society regarding financial institutions. These recommendations mainly encourage a greater uniformity in the manner of the presentation of the same type of product by financial institutions, a clarity of intention in the drafting of contracts and a constant and rigorous financial training of bank employees. The new way of acting is essentially a change in the banking culture as a whole.

BACKGROUND

Spain has had an economic development similar to the rest of the countries in our zone in some aspects, but very different in others. This development is briefly explained in order to analyse the role played by the Spanish financial system.

If we go back to the beginning of the 20th century, the starting point is very different: in Spain there is a great economic and social backwardness with respect to other European countries such as France, Italy or Germany. In the year 1936 the outbreak of the civil war took place and later a long period of self-sufficiency that ended with the "Stabilization plan of 1959". Really, the Spanish economy does not open to the outside until almost the sixties and seventies and that is when the entry of foreign investment and the tourist phenomenon begins. To this is added the still important inflow of remittances that were generated by the enormous Spanish emigration abroad.

However, the international crisis of the mid-seventies also affects Spain and with a greater impact as a consequence of the still fragile and young economic development of our country. Spain is a country with a great weight to its agricultural sector, with an industrial sector focused on large companies with great state intervention and thus uncompetitive, a situation inherited from the Franco regime. Inflation exceeds 26% in 1977, companies begin to close and unemployment to increase. This generates an emergency situation that causes all the political parties to reach an agreement and sign the so-called "Moncloa pacts", from which institutional, fiscal and industrial restructuring reforms are carried out, which allow orderly and consistent improvements to begin.

The crisis continued until practically 1984 and a long period of growth then began until 2008, with the exception of the short but intense crisis of the years 1992-94. Spain joined the European Community, opened to the outside and began to develop a welfare system based mainly on health and education (García Delgado, 2013).

However, this stage of growth also has its spectre, since the engine of economic development, mainly from the nineties, is real estate investment, a sector that does not allow sustained and lasting growth, does not generate investment in sectors that facilitate innovation nor does it demand the training needs of the labour involved and, in addition, it caused significant damage to the environment and the landscape of many cities and towns, especially the coast.

The expanding cycle based on construction produces a drag on the whole economy, creating a very high internal demand that translates into very high growth rates and very low unemployment rates. Although in its beginnings this activity does not depend in excess on debt, with the arrival of the new century the ratio between bank loans and total share assets of the different companies start to increase notably, with companies in the construction sector companies at the top of the list.

The global financial crisis of 2008, unites in Spain with the abrupt end of the development model: the real estate bubble explodes and reveals that the creation of the giant was made with feet of clay. This finally translates into the need for Spain to ask for bank bailout amounting to 60,000 million euros and the beginning of a long and intense recession with an economic and social impact of enormous magnitude.

Throughout this expansive process, banking plays a key role: on the one hand, it grants large loans to the construction sector, that is, it allows the growth of supply and, on the other hand, it grants significant numbers of mortgage loans of significant size and without the rigor or the desirable evaluation of the solvency of the client, that is to say, allows a great growth of demand.

This is observed in figures number 1 and 2. The first shows the number of mortgages signed within the period 1993-2002 and the second figure shows the number of mortgages signed within the period 2003-2018. This is due to a methodological change made by the Institute of National Statistics in 2003 (so the data is not exactly the same). In these figures we observe a continued growth in the number of mortgages which is more pronounced from 2001 and reaches its peak in 2006 with 1,900,000 mortgages signed. From this point the decline begins, the number of mortgages in the year 2014 (the minimum value of the figure) is 315,535 and last year (2018) the number was 477,425 mortgage loans.

The financial sector at a national level undergoes a very important transformation during all the years of economic growth. Financial products advance towards a greater level of complexity and risk. In the case of mortgages, traditional mortgages give way to more complex loans. For the North American market, this process has been the object of numerous studies (Amromin et al, 2018; Agarwal et al, 2014; Carlin & Manson, 2011, Bond et al, 2009).

In Spain there have also been published articles and studies on the growth of the mortgage and its consequences (Roldán, 2015; Rodríguez Fernández, 2017; Dominguez Martínez, 2019). But, in the case of Spain, the main problem was not changes in financial calculations, but rather, the incorporation of unfair terms in the traditional mortgage contracts. The development of this whole process is the central theme of this current work.

Figure 1: Number of Mortgages in Spain during 1995-2002
Source: Institute of National Statistics

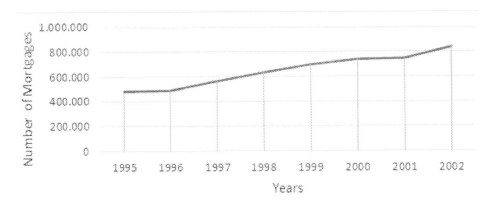

Figure 2: Number of Mortgages in Spain during 2003-2018
Source: Institute of National Statistics

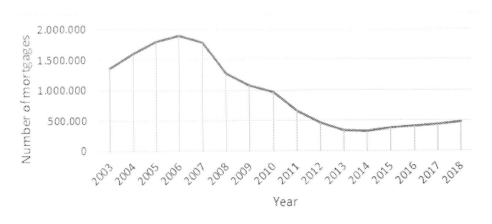

MAIN FOCUS OF THE CHAPTER

Financial business during the nineties suffers a very important process of transformation at an international level. But this global transformation of the sector is intertwined with the economic development of each country and, in the case of Spain, as the construction sector is the engine of growth, the relevance of the mortgage loan is enormous.

This growth of mortgages has been accompanied by an increasing complexity in these contracts, with clauses and new conditions apparently of great attractiveness and interest for the client but that subsequently proved clearly harmful. These conditions had such a degree of implementation and its social and economic consequences were so serious for society that it generated a substantial climate of discontent and distrust among the population towards its financial system.

In effect, Spanish society understands banking as the provider of financial services. For this reason, it constitutes an indispensable role, which could be classified as a basic service, similar to the health system or the education system. In fact, practically all of the population has to have contact with the financial world and financial exclusion also causes social exclusion (Álvarez García & Abeal Vázquez, 2018). But this basic service, unlike others, has to negotiate with companies that do not trust it: The clientele considers the financial institution as an unreliable counterpart to be wary of.

The great platform that these new conditions constitute is only possible due to the asymmetrical position that the lender and the borrower occupy in the contractual relationship. In effect, the asymmetry of information, and how that advantage has been used by banks, is the key of the problem. This is because Finances has its own terms and its own mathematical calculations. This difficulty in understanding finances has increased in recent years due to the growing complexity of financial products in general and of the clauses of mortgages loans in particular.

ABUSIVE CLAUSES INCORPORATED INTO MORTGAGES. CHARACTERISTICS AND CONSEQUENCES

The most common abusive clauses in mortgage loan contracts in Spain have been the following: the floor clause, the expiry clause, the default interest clause, the multi-currency clause, the Mortgage loan Reference Index (*Indice de referencia de los Préstamos Hipotecarios, IRPH*) clause and the initial mortgage fees. Below, they are described briefly:

- The floor-ceiling clause establishes a maximum interest rate for adjustable rate mortgages that the client will not take on, even if the interest rate of the loan reached such a figure and a minimum interest rate that the client should pay, although the interest rate is inferior.
    - Before the economic crisis, when Euribor was rising, the financial entities incorporated this clause in their mortgage loans. The clause itself was not against the law since, in essence, it was a coverage clause for both the client and the bank. Its purpose was to cover, in exceptional situations, damages that, eventually, either party could suffer and was marketed with this justification: in exceptional situations, the client would not be "surprised or harmed" by excessive rates, nor would the bank be "surprised or hurt" by exceptionally low rates. However, as the later reality showed, this clause was not really a protection mechanism for both signatories, but an instrument of additional profit for the bank.
    - However, again the asymmetry of information was exploited in bad faith. Firstly, in the years of massive signing of loans with this condition, the beginning of a period of low interest rates was already expected and, in fact, the high rates prior to the crisis responded to a policy of the European Central Bank (ECB) to curb private indebtedness and soften the expected change in the economic cycle. This was known by experts and, of course, by banking but not by the average citizen. Secondly, the limits set as floor and ceiling were not at all reasonable: the ceiling clause was never put into effect and since 2009, the floor clause has been active.
- The multi-currency clause implies the denomination of the loan in a currency other than the euro, mainly the dollar, the yen and the Swiss franc. It is a high-risk product as the debt, and the loan payments, changes according to the exchange rate.
    - Multi-currency clauses were inserted in many mortgages at a time when reference currencies tended to depreciate against the euro, since in this way the mortgage was cheaper for the consumer. However, later, the economic crisis and the depreciation of the euro against the yen or the Swiss franc, made the mortgage debt of these consumers soar in many cases.
- The expiry clause can be inserted in any type of contract causing the relationship to end before the date agreed by the parties due to the breach by one of them of any of their obligations. Therefore, a mortgage loan implies that, if the customer stopped paying the loan, the entity reserved the right to dissolve the contract and demand the repayment of the entire outstanding loan.

- At a time when an economic crisis causes high unemployment rates, it is quite common to find families that could not afford the payment of mortgages. Therefore, the usual practice of the Banks was to apply the said clause.
- Default interest will be generated when the debtor does not make the payment on time. It supposes a percentage that is applied to the unpaid amount.
  - The unfairness of the clause is that, in some contracts, this interest rate on arrears was disproportionately high.
- The acronym IRPH refers to *"Indice de referencia de los Préstamos Hipotecarios"*. In English, Reference Index of Mortgage Loans. It is a reference index of the adjustable-rate mortgages in Spain and is calculated by the simple mathematical average of the interest rates on mortgage loans of over three years that the banks have set up or renewed during the month.
  - The reality is that the IRPH is a higher index than the Euribor (normally with a difference between 1.5% and 3%). Furthermore, the variation of the IRPH, mainly in the descent, is slower than the Euribor. Precisely the loans that include the clauses are sold with an emphasis on its stability and the maintenance of the mortgage payments. In consequence, the consumer understood that it was an index without risk. Another problem, which was demonstrated a posteriori is that the banks can manipulate this index. When the building bubble burst and Euribor was at a minimum, this index went up. And many debtors couldn't afford mortgage repayments.
- In the clauses of mortgage costs, the contract establishes that it is the client who has to pay them.
  - The initial mortgage cost clause was accepted practice until the avalanche of lawsuits in respect to the other above described unfair terms.

In the years before the crisis, the consumers begin to file lawsuits against banks. This grew into an avalanche with the outbreak of the crisis. These lawsuits centre on the floor clause along with the rest of the explained unfair terms. This generated a general national climate of distrust towards the Spanish financial system, which provoked the reaction of the governments. New laws were promulgated which stood out not only for their transition towards a more wary vigilance of banking but also because they constituted the beginning of a period of important changes to the rules that the banks must comply with.

The Evolution of Regulations of Mortgage Loans in Spain

In Spain, the Minister of Economy and Finance is authorized to issue informative and contractual obligations to financial institutions since the enactment of Law 26/1988, of July 29 (*Ley 26/1988 de 29 de julio*). The result of this authorization is the order of December 12, 1989 (*Orden del 12 de diciembre de 1989*) that was the subject of development in Bank of Spain Circular 8/1990 of September 7 (*Circular 8/1990 de 7 de septiembre del Banco de España*).

This first regulation addresses issues that were already problematic in the seventies and eighties. With regard to the information to be provided to the client, simple and general rules were established such as how the entities had to have in their offices a permanent bulletin board in clearly visible place in which data such as the preferential interest rate, a brochure with a list of fees and references to the claims service of the bank of Spain.

In 1994 the order of May 5, 1994 (*Orden de 5 de mayo de 1994*) was promulgated "with the purpose of guaranteeing the adequate information and protection of those who apply for mortgage loans" and the mandatory delivery of a prospectus being required in which the financial conditions of the loans are clearly laid out for the prospective client. This ruling is developed in Circular 5/1994 of the Bank of Spain (*Circular 5/1994 del Banco de España*). These regulations emphasize that the bank must "facilitate the perfect understanding of the financial implications of the mortgage loan contract" and also, for the first time, specify the information this mentioned prospectus must include.

The previous regulations became obsolete as a consequence of the great growth of the mortgage loan that took place from the end of the nineties until the beginning of the crisis in 2008 and due to the greater complexity of its conditions.

In this sense, Law 2/2011 of March 4 is enacted (*Ley 2/2011 de 4 de marzo*), whose importance lies in the fact that, for the first time, reference is made to the responsibility of banks in the process of granting of loans. The objective is a greater responsibility in concessions and for this the law establishes that the bank must carry out a rigorous evaluation of the client. As a consequence of this law, there was issued the ruling EHA/2899/2011, of October 28, (*Orden EHA/2899/2011*) in which the concept of "responsible loan" is introduced. The precise rules of this order are developed in Circular 5/2012, of June 27, of the Bank of Spain (Circulars 5/2012 del Banco de España) and in Chapter V the policies and procedures of the "responsible loan" are described and in particular it is established that " when the entities offer and grant loans or credit to their clients, they must be honest, impartial and professional, taking into account the personal and financial situation and the preferences and objectives of their clients, and must highlight any condition or characteristic of the contracts that does not answer to said objective".

Table 1: Pre-contractual information form

1	Data of credit institution
2	Loan characteristics
3	Interest rate
4	Tying practices and initial costs
5	Annual Percentage Rate (APR)
6	Early repayment

Source: Appendix 1 of the Ministerial order EHA/2899/2011

The importance of this order is that for the first time the actual wording of the rules allows the conclusion that the bank lacked the required honesty and professionalism.

This new law also precisely establishes what should be the necessary information provided in a mortgage loan and these guidelines are set out in two documents: the FIPRE (*Ficha de Información Precontractual*), Pre-contractual Information Sheet, and the FIPER (*Ficha de Información Personalizada*), Personal Information Sheet. This supposes a great improvement in the information that the client must have at his disposal on each one of the types of mortgage loans that the bank offers, since the information is to be the same for all the banks and there is a high level of precision to this information.

With respect to FIPRE, the information must necessarily be set out in 6 sections that are summarized in table 1. The regulation also indicates the information of each section. In addition, article 11 of this order states that "the information, documentation and communications addressed to customers of banking services ... shall be written in easily understandable terms".

The FIPER is the personalized information sheet, it is therefore a document adapted to the specific needs of the user and their particular financial characteristics. It has no cost and it is a non-binding document. Its content is shown in table 2.

The previous regulation soon became obsolete with the Directive 2014/17/EU (*Directiva 2014/17/UE*). Member states were obligated to incorporate this into their national regulations within two years. In Spain it took five years to incorporate this law into its legal framework and finally in the year 2019 the Law 5/2019 (so-called "New Mortgage Law") is enacted (*Ley 5/2019*). This law not only transposes this directive into national legislation, but also introduces additional provisions with the objective of strengthening the guarantees of the borrowers.

The primary objectives of Directive 2014/17 /EU were: to create a uniform market for mortgage credit in Europe and guarantee consumer protection through accurate information that is adequate and not misleading (Arroyo Amayuelas, 2017). To do this, it designs a series of measures based precisely on what was mentioned

Table 2: Personalized information sheet

1	Data of credit institution
2	Loan characteristics
3	Interest rate
4	Periodicity and number of payments
5	Amount of each mortgage payment
6	Amortization table, showing the amount that has to be paid in each period
7	Tying practices and initial costs
8	Early repayment
9	Right of subrogation
10	Customer service department
11	Bank of Spain claims service
12	Breaches of tying commitments and their consequences for the client.
13	Additional Information
14	Risks and warnings

Source: Appendix 2 of the Ministerial order EHA/2899/2011

at the beginning of this chapter and which the directive expresses impeccably in the following way: "The financial crisis has shown that irresponsible behaviour by market participants can undermine the foundations of the financial system, leading to a lack of confidence among all parties, in particular consumers, and potentially severe social and economic consequences. Many consumers have lost confidence in the financial sector and borrowers have found their loans increasingly unaffordable, resulting in defaults and forced sales rising. As a result, the G20 has commissioned work from the Financial Stability Board to establish principles on sound underwriting standards in relation to residential immovable property" (article 3).

Among the outstanding aspects of this directive we point out a change in the information provided to the client set out in a document called European Standardised Information Sheet (ESIS) *(Ficha Europea de Información Normalizada, FEIN)* whose main difference with the FIPER is that it is binding and that it strongly specifies more precise information to be supplied and above all focuses on the clarity of this information. The calculation of the APR (annual percentage rate) is also subject to maximum harmonization, but the problem, as pointed out by Arrollo Amayuelas, 2017 and as we have shown throughout the work in several occasions, is that the average consumer will not always understand certain information that, due to the to the very nature of the product, have a technical nature. To show the problem, it would be enough to refer to the APR and its calculation, which sometimes includes a real APR and an illustrative APR, in addition to running the risk that the consumer confuses it with the interest rate applicable to the contract.

The reading of the directive already allowed a prediction of the general lines of the new mortgage law, since this directive is rich in recommendations and obligations of both information, calculation and determination of variables. Also it incorporates for the first time the requirement for a specific financial training for the personnel that sell these mortgages and for the managers who design them: "It is appropriate to ensure that the relevant staff of creditors, credit intermediaries and appointed representatives possess an adequate level of knowledge and competence in order to achieve a high level of professionalism. This Directive should, therefore, require relevant knowledge and competence to be proven at the level of the company, based on the minimum knowledge and competence requirements set out in this Directive" (article 32).

This directive lays down rules for the remuneration of staff in order to limit the bad sales practices. It aims to ensure that the form of remuneration of staff does not interfere with the obligation to take into account the interests of the consumer.

The law 5/2019 that transposes this directive contains changes of great importance in the Spanish regulations on the mortgage loan. Without pretensions to be exhaustive, for the enormous amount of aspects that this new law incorporates, indicated below are the most important and most pertinent to the reduction of information asymmetry.

- The information that is to be supplied to the client is increased. In addition to the European Standardised Information Sheet (ESIS) *(Ficha Europea de Información Normalizada, FEIN in spanish)*, a Standardized disclaimer sheet must be provided (*Ficha de advertencies estandarizadas, FiAE in spanish*), in which is explained which are the clauses or elements relevant and, if the mortgage is variable, a separate document with the payments in various scenarios.
- Clauses that violate the regulations established by the new mortgage law will be declared null and void. This means that there is no time limit to be able to report their abuse.
- Complaints and claims related to mortgage loans will be processed through new institution litigation in the financial sector. But nevertheless, this agency has not yet started to work, so until then the Claims Service of the Bank of Spain is responsible for these efforts.
- It is also specified that the remuneration policy of banks to their employees cannot link the salary with the number of mortgage loans granted.
- An important element of the new Law is that it makes it mandatory that the borrower go to the notary before the signing of the contract where a reading of the contract will be made and they will explain, free of charge, all the

clauses that comprise it. At the end of the reading, a series of questions is asked where the borrower must show that he has understood the content of the contract. The notary must certify that the borrower has understood the mortgage loan.
- One of the aspects included in the new law is the requirement for an officially accredited financial training in how to design and sell a mortgage loan. In its article 32 it specifies a body of knowledge that must be acquired through training. Some of the points of this article are already included in an economics or administration degree. Other knowledge corresponding to the points of this article will have to be obtained in complementary studies. In any case, continuous training will be required. For this training gives a period of adaptation until 2020 so that the staff can acquire the knowledge and competence to which the indicated article refers. Until then, it may provide services under supervision.

This regulation also clarifies the following aspects:

- Finally, the initial expenses that the client must take on and those that must be taken on by the bank are clearly stated by law. As expected, the bank will take on all the costs except the property valuation.
- The application of a minimum interest on adjustable rate mortgages is specifically prohibited. Therefore, the banks cannot incorporate the well-known floor clauses anymore. Nor are they allowed to consider a 0% Euribor when this rate is negative.
- Multi-currency mortgages are regulated. The customer has the right to convert them to euros whenever they want. In addition, banks must periodically report the increases in debt that occur due to the increases due to the exchange rate.
- It lowers the commission or compensation for early repayment, either partially or totally. In addition, it can only be charged if the bank incurs a financial loss.
- The maximum default interest rate is also established (3 points above the interest rate of the mortgage itself).
- Stricter requirements are established to activate the anticipated expiry clause, with specific limits so that the bank can initiate the end of the mortgage.
- The regulation prohibits the obligation to purchase of products linked to the mortgage, such as life insurance, pension plans, credit cards, etc. However, it does allow the combination the entity to offers reduced interest in exchange for subscribing to its services.

ANALYSIS OF THE EFFECTIVENESS OF THE SPANISH REGULATIONS ON MORTGAGE LOANS

As can be deduced from the previous section, already from the order of 1994 until the last one in 2019, the goal of the legislature is to reduce the problem of financial contracts: the asymmetrical positions of the lender and borrower. But this is not easy and, in fact, the loan contracts have been incorporating new clauses and have grown in technical complexity so the information asymmetry has increased. Therefore, reality has shown that the standards developed so far have not decreased the problem. This is why the latest law passed has an accuracy not previously seen: It contains specific figures in relation to fees and penalties that can be applied and it details the information that the bank must incorporate in the different documents. Also, it expressly prohibits certain practices and oblige banks to ensure that all the agents involved in the mortgage loans, from the sales person to the creator of the product, have a suitable financial education.

Since this law has just entered into force in June 2019, it is still not possible to make an assessment of its degree of effectiveness and its implications. However, this section will deal with this by gathering the first assessments of this law. After a reading of the first impressions that this law causes in institutions such as banking, user protection associations, specialized law firms and the first articles about the issue, we note that the criticisms of this law are quite unanimous and focus on the following points:

The arrangement fee is not eliminated. Its maintenance is now even less reasonable when the Bank is forced to evaluate the solvency of the prospective borrower, task that this law states are to be free. This evaluation was the justification to charge this fee.

One of the most controversial aspects is related to linked products because although the law expressly forbids them, in fact, their maintenance is allowed in a subterfuge, since the bank can market an added or reduced nominal interest rate applied to the loan. However, their inclusion in the calculation of the APR is not always simple and may even involve increases in the loan.

New documents are created that are the ESIS (FEIN in Spanish) and the FiAE. However, the starting information which the client has available to compare alternative offers continues to be the FIPRE whose content has not changed.

We have carried out a review of the FIPRE of the main banks before and after the entry into force of the law (since it is the public document available to the client). The document has changed slightly after the approval of the law and the conclusions are discouraging:

- As a first conclusion it can be said that reading these documents is difficult and its information is unclear.

- In general, language is too technical in many aspects, including issues such as equivalence of interest rates, the process of interest calculation, aspect related to expenses or to the APR.
- There is an excess of information in scarcely relevant points. This density of information makes it difficult reading and distracting from the main information.
- In general, FIPRE are very visually unattractive documents. With the current design trends in new media, it is surprising that the format of this document is so arid.
- With regard to the homogeneity between the FIPRE, the conclusion is that, although all must follow the points as dictated by the order EHA / 2899/2011, brought together in table 1 of this work, the reality is that the information that each entity includes in each of these 6 points is very different.

Another measure that tries to ensure the client's understanding of what he signs is the obligation of going to the notary. But this can actually have a negative effect because the notary may not have the necessary training to understand the contract. In addition, this action may protect the bank from any future claim by hiding behind the notary's signature.

The training and skills of the personnel that sells the loans are important aspects, but we must bear in mind that nowadays the majority of the employees in charge of the mortgages have already graduated in Business administration and they already know the characteristics of the product that is offered.

One of the points that modifies the regulations are the deadlines to be able to carry out the mortgage, which implies a greater risk for banks. This could imply an excessive prudence in the concession of loans. If to this is added how the new law attributes most of the initial costs of the mortgage, this could produce a rise in its cost, as has been pointed out by the Bank of Spain in its Bulletin of March 2019.

SOLUTIONS AND RECOMMENDATIONS

The contractual relationship between bank and client will always be an asymmetrical relationship. For the great majority of the population, including that with higher educated, financial terms and calculations are not easy to understand. But this should not prevent the relationship from occurring within the fair play required for any negotiation. With this objective, the essential element is a cultural change that affects the way in which the entities have been acting so far.

One of the main aspects is a shift in the strategy from the ivory towers of decision making to a more personable face to face partnership of the banks with the people and bid for a responsible, honest and transparent bank. The product and the cost must be adjusted to the client profile. As indicated by Uria (2017) the most important impact of the regulations that steer the performance of the bank, is not the obligation of compliance, but that it insists on a deep and strategic reflection on their business model and the way they lend and market their products.

From our point of view, the mortgage loan's complexity is not justified. From a strictly financial angle, it has to be understanding of the client, for which the essential issues are the honesty, professionalism, transparency and responsibility of the lender. These are, in essence, the ideals which all laws aim at, but that no law can achieve without the deep conviction of the banks themselves.

Indeed, financial institutions can invest a large amount of funds in the proper training of the staff, but while that helps make their explanations more didactic and effective, the important thing is the adaptation of the mortgage to the specific profile of the client, in which the sales person has guidelines in this regard and not only in accordance with what is convenient for the entity according to the expected evolution of the economy and markets. It is a change of philosophy, but without being unappreciative of the monetary investment in and also the renunciation of staff's working hours to achieve the required expertise. From our point of view, this new training regulation is an excellent opportunity for collaboration between University and banking in training and advice.

Another important aspect is that the contracts must be written to be open to easy comprehension. One's attention is drawn to the contrast between the simplicity of advertising and the confusion of precontractual information. We have carried out a review of the FIPRE of the main banks after the entry into force of the law and note that it continues to be an unclear document, with excessive information in many aspects, with unnecessary technicalities and moreover, visually unattractive. These characteristics impede understanding of the basic issues of the loan and its comparison with those of the other banks. As expressed in the law, it is a free document in the nature of guidance but this bid is no longer effective if its degree of difficulty is not reduced.

The whole country has the maximum interest in a solvent, safe and profitable bank and therefore if this is the path that banks take, society will perceive this change in attitude, helping us towards the final objective that the relationship between bank and client is a relationship of trust and not suspicion.

FUTURE RESEARCH DIRECTIONS

As future lines of research we propose the following:

- Analysis of the degree of effectiveness of the new mortgage law, highlighting those points which are effective and those that need to be reconsidered.
- It is necessary to write more about the change of culture within financial institutions as regarding the relationship with the client, since this is the basis of contractual relationships between them and within the framework of a fair play.
- Compare the information requirements of the new Spanish mortgage law with that of other countries
- It is necessary to investigate the consequences of information asymmetry in digital banking: What will happen when the personal contact has almost disappeared?
- Extend the study to personal loans, loans by credit cards and any other type of loan offered by banks.
- We are talking about financial institutions, but not only banks grant loans. This is a great challenge and we must not neglect control and guidance.
- The great implementation of so-called fast loans is worrying. It is necessary to study its implementation, characteristics and consequences.

CONCLUSION

The global financial crisis of 2008 sees in Spain the abrupt completion of a model of development based on the construction sector. In all this expansive process the bank has a role that is key when granting mortgage loans in great numbers and of significant figures. To this we must add the increasing complexity of mortgage loans, with new and seemingly great conditions attractive and interesting to clients. However, these new conditions were actually abusive clauses with very serious economic and social consequences.

The great power that these new conditions had was only possible because of the asymmetrical position in the contractual relationship between the lender and the borrower and for the fraudulent use that financial institutions have made this inequality both in financial knowledge and in developments in the economy.

All the rules and laws issued so far and analysed in this current work have demanded clarity and transparency by banks and the latest laws even incorporate professionalism and honesty, showing that the bank lacks these values.

However, the problem has not been resolved, so the solution does not lie only in complete and effective legislation, but also in a cultural change within the bank entities themselves.

ACKNOWLEDGMENT

The research was supported by the Universidade da Coruña.

REFERENCES

Agarwal, S. A.-D., Amromin, G., Ben-David, I., Chomsisengphet, S., & Evanoff, D. D. (2014). Predatory lending and the subprime crisis. *Journal of Financial Economics*, *113*(1), 29–52. doi:10.1016/j.jfineco.2014.02.008

Álvarez García, B., & Abeal Vázquez, J. P. (2018). *Fragility of the Spanish banking System and Financial Exclusion. Lessons learned from the golbal crisis and new challenges for the Century Balnking Sector*. Hershey, PA: IGI Global.

Amromin, G., Huang, J., Sialm, C., & Zhong, E. (2018). Complex Mortgages. *Review of Finance*, *22*(6), 1975–2007. doi:10.1093/rof/rfy016

Arroyo Amayuelas, E. (2017). La directiva 2014/17/UE sobre los contratos de crédito con consumidores para bienes inmuebles de uso residencial. *Revista para el análisis del derecho InDret*. Retrieved from www.indret.com

Bank of Spain. (2019). *Boletín económico 1/2019. Informe trimestral de la Economía española*. Retrieved from www.bde.es/secciones/publicaciones

Bond, P. M., Musto, D. K., & Yilmaz, B. (2009). Predatory mortgage lending. *Journal of Financial Economics*, *94*(3), 412–427. doi:10.1016/j.jfineco.2008.09.011

Bueno Campos, E. (2001). *Evolución y Perspectivas de la banca española*. Madrid: Civitas.

Carlin, B. I., & Manso, G. (2011). Obfuscation, learning, and the evolution of investor sophistication. *Review of Financial Studies*, *24*(3), 754–785. doi:10.1093/rfs/hhq070

Circular 13/1993 del Banco de España: Circular 13/1993 de 21 de diciembre, a Entidades de crédito, sobre modificación de la circular 8/1990, sobre transparencia de las operaciones y protección a la clientela. Published in the Boletín Oficial del Estado (BOE), No. 313, 31 December 1993.

(1994, August). Circular 5/1994 del Banco de España: Circular 5/1994, de 22 de julio, a entidades de crédito, sobre modificación de la circular 8/1990 sobre transparencia de las operaciones y protección de la clientela. [BOE]. *Published in the Boletín Oficial del Estado*, *3*(184), 25106–2511.

Circular 5/2012 del Banco de España: Circular 5/2012, de 27 de junio, del Banco de España, a entidades de crédito y proveedores de servicios de pago, sobre transparencia de los servicios bancarios y responsabilidad en la concesión de préstamos. Published in the Boletín Oficial del Estado (BOE), No. 161, 6 July 2012.

(1990, September). Circular 8/1990 del Banco de España: Circular 8/1990 de 7 de septiembre a entidades de crédito sobre transparencia de las operaciones y protección de la clientela, del Banco de España [BOE]. *Published in the Boletín Oficial del Estado*, 20(226), 27498–27508.

Directive 2014/17/EU of the European Parliament and of the Council of 4 February 2014 on credit agreements for consumers relating to residential immovable property and amending Directives 2008/48/EC and 2013/36/EU and Regulation (EU), No. 1093/2010 Text with EEA relevance. (n.d.). Retrieved from http://data.europa.eu/eli/dir/2014/17/oj

Domínguez Martínez, J. (2019). *El sistema bancario en España: evolución reciente, situación actual, y problemas y retos planteados.* Madrid: Instituto Universitario de Análisis económico y social, Universidad de Alcalá.

García Delgado, J. M. (2013). *Lecciones de Economía española.* Thomson- Civitas.

Ley 2/2011: Ley 2/201 de 4 de marzo, de Economía sostenible. *Published in the Boletín Oficial del Estado, No.*, 55, 5.

Ley 26/1988: Ley 26/1988 de 29 de julio, sobre Disciplina e Intervención de las entidades de crédito, published in the Boletín Oficial del Estado, No. 182, 30 July 1988, 23524-23534.

Ley 5/2019: Ley 5/2019, de 15 de marzo, reguladora de los contratos de crédito inmobiliario. *Published in the Boletín Oficial del Estado*, 16(65), 26319–26399.

Orden de 5 de mayo de 1994: Orden de 5 de mayo de 1994, sobre transparencia de las condiciones financieras de los préstamos hipotecarios. Published in the Boletín Oficial del Estado (BOE), No. 112, 11 May 1994.

Orden del 12 de diciembre de 1989: Orden del 12 de diciembre de 1989, sobre información de tipos de interés y comisiones, normas de actuación, información a clientes y publicidad de las entidades de crédito. Published in the Boletín Oficial del Esado (BOE), No. 303, 19 December 1989.

Orden EHA/2899/2011: Orden EHA/2899/2011, de 28 de octubre, de transparencia y protección del cliente de servicios bancarios. Published in the Boletín Oficial del Estado (BOE), No. 261, 29 October 2011.

Real Decreto 309/2019: Real Decreto 309/2019, de 26 de abril, por el que se desarrolla parcialmente la Ley 5/2019, de 15 de marzo, reguladora de los contratos de crédito inmobiliario y se adoptan otras medidas en materia financiera. *Published in the Boletín Oficial del Estado*, *29*(102), 43114–43128.

Rodríguez Fernández, F. (2017). El sector bancario español. Foto de una reestructuración en movimiento. *Mediterráneo Económico*, *29*, 35–47.

Roldán, J. Y. (2015). *Las entidades financieras en España. Un sistema en evolución al servicio de la sociedad*. Madrid: Fundación de Estudios Financieros.

Uría, F. (2017). La regulación financiera y su efecto sobre el negocio bancario. *Mediterráneo económico*, 101-122.

ADDITIONAL READING

Aguado, J. (2019): Comentarios al Real Decreto 309/2019, de 26 de abril, por el que se desarrolla parcialmente la Ley 5/2019, de 15 de marzo, reguladora de los contratos de crédito inmobiliario y se adoptan otras medidas en materia financiera, *Inmueble. Revista del sector inmobiliario*, 192, 5-12.

Berges Lobera, A., & Ontiveros Baeza, E. (2019). La reestructuración del sistema bancario: Gestación, gestión y digestión, *Información Comercial Española, ICE. Revista de economía*, *906*, 45–56.

Bucks, B. K., & Pence, K. (2008). Do borrowers know their mortgage terms? *Journal of Urban Economics*, *64*(2), 218–233. doi:10.1016/j.jue.2008.07.005

Gibson, D., Luis, J., & Saugar, R. (2019). Diez años desde la crisis financiera, *Información Comercial Española, ICE. Revista de economía*, *906*, 57–71.

Zunzunegui, F. (2019). *Asesoramiento en la Ley de crédito inmobiliario (Advisory Services in Law Regulating Credit Agreements Relating to Residential Immovable Property)*. Available at SSRN: https://ssrn.com/abstract=3410936 or doi:10.2139srn.3410936

KEY TERMS AND DEFINITIONS

Annual Percentage Rate (APR): Is the annual rate charged for borrowing. It includes any fees or additional costs associated with the loan (except the valuation of the residential property) and not only the amortization and the interest.

Default Interest: Interest generated when the debtor does not make the payment on time. It supposes a percentage that is applied to the unpaid amount.

European Standardised Information Sheet (ESIS): Pre-contractual information with a standardized format. The bank has the obligation to provide this document to the client and it is binding.

FEIN: *Ficha europea de Información estandarizada*. Is the acronym of ESIS in Spanish.

FiAE: Acronym of *Ficha de advertencias estandarizadas*. Additional mandatory document that the law 5/2019 incorporate. The bank has the obligation redact and give this document to the client. In it the relevant elements of the loan are explained.

FIPRE (Ficha de Información Precontractual): Pre contractual Information Sheet of each Mortgage loan of a bank. In Spain, the banks have to draft and facilitate this document to the clients. It serves as a guide and to compare the offers of the different banks

Floor-Ceiling Clause: Clause that establishes a maximum interest rate for adjustable rate mortgages that the client will not take on, even if the interest rate of the loan reached such a figure and a minimum interest rate that the client should pay, although the interest rate is inferior.

Foreign Currency Loan: Loan in a currency other than the euro (in the eurozone), mainly the dollar, the yen, and the Swiss franc.

IRPH: Is the acronym IRPH of "*Indice de referencia de los Préstmos Hipotecarios*". In English, Reference Index of Mortgage Loans. It is a reference index of the adjustable-rate mortgages in Spain and is calculated by the simple mathematical average of the interest rates on mortgage loans of over three years that the banks have set up or renewed during the month.

Unfair Terms: Term in a contract that causes a significant imbalance in the parties' rights and obligations under the contract, to the detriment of the consumer.

Chapter 8

Financial Contagion and Shock Transmission During the Global Financial Crisis:
A Review of the Literature

Thomas J. Flavin
https://orcid.org/0000-0002-9469-5063
Maynooth University, Ireland

Dolores Lagoa-Varela
Universidade da Coruña, Spain

ABSTRACT

After the recent financial crisis, the analysis of shock transmission across the financial system has received a great deal of attention. In particular, the role of financial contagion as a shock propagation mechanism has been studied in detail. The globalisation of financial and banking markets has increased the connections and relationship between them. Hence, recent crises have spread all around the world. The stability of linkages between financial assets across different market conditions cast doubt upon the benefits of portfolio diversification. This chapter reviews the extant literature on financial contagion during the global financial crisis and thus provides information for both portfolio managers (when optimizing their investment portfolios) and policymakers (when designing their strategies in order to mitigate spillover effects during crisis periods).

DOI: 10.4018/978-1-7998-2440-4.ch008

INTRODUCTION

The credit crisis that began to unfold in U.S. markets in August 2007 heralded a period of financial turbulence that, firstly, spread across the U.S. financial system and, later, across global financial markets. The crisis was prolonged and persistent and impacted greatly on the real economies of many countries, especially in the large developed markets and later in the Eurozone periphery. The propagation of the crisis and the channels through which it spread have been studied extensively in its aftermath, as academics, governments, participants in the financial markets and policy makers all strive for a better and deeper understanding of the transmission of the crisis. Only when this transmission is fully identified can these agents design policies and regulations to make the global financial system more resilient and better prepared to absorb financial shocks.

Defining contagion has proven to be a contentious issue in the literature and an excellent overview of the various definitions employed in the literature to that point is provided by Pericoli and Sbracia (2003). Early studies, like King and Wadhwani (1990), labelled any significant increase in correlation during a crisis period as contagion but Forbes and Rigobon (2002) showed the importance of differentiating between contagion and interdependence, by accounting for changes in the volatility of asset / market volatilities between normal and crisis periods. They showed that failure to account for changes in volatility could lead to an erroneous finding of contagion, simply due to correlation changes induced by the increase in asset volatilities during the crisis. Although there is a considerable debate about the definition and characteristics of financial contagion, a consensus has begun to emerge that contagion is an excess comovement of asset markets during a crisis episode, i.e. the comovement is greater than could be predicted from the interdependence that prevails during normal market conditions.

BACKGROUND

It is now generally accepted that the origins of the U.S. credit crisis lay in the market for securitized products, such as Collateralized Debt Obligations and other complex credit derivatives whose underlying pool of income-generating assets were becoming increasingly concentrated in the U.S. real estate sector, and in particular, on subprime mortgages, see Brunnermeier (2008), Gorton (2009) and Dungey et al. (2013) among others. The spectacular growth of this sector in the early 2000s and its subsequent decline led to widespread financial turbulence for the banking industry. It's interesting to note that this sector of the financial system was relatively small. Dywer and Tkac (2009) estimate that as of December 2006, this market segment accounted for only about 1% of global bond values, stock values and bank deposits. Yet, the sudden decline of this market triggered the most widespread financial market decline since 1929. Consequently, the question of how such a small sector created such a global financial crisis and economic recession has spawned a burgeoning literature. The extant literature has already shown that banking crisis often have severe repercussions for the real economy. Bernanke (1983) shows that banking crashes have the potential to trigger recessionary periods in the real economy and this is backed up by empirical evidence presented in Reinhart and Rogoff (2009), even though Dwyer et al. (2013) report examples of where banking crisis did not translate into economic recessions. Tong and Wei (2009) identify two channels through which the banking crisis may be transmitted to the real economy; the finance channel and the demand channel. The former refers to the reduction in credit availability for non-financial firms and the latter refers to the reduced demand for goods and services by consumers.

This is the literature that we review here, and in particular we examine the role of contagion in the transmission of the shock. Specifically, we propose to structure the work in the following sections:

- Contagion within the US Financial System.
- Contagion in international bank markets.
- Contagion between Financials and Non-Financials.
- Contagion in international stock markets.
- Contagion in international bond markets (mainly within the Eurozone).
- Contagion between bank markets and sovereign debt markets.

This structure is motivated by an approximate timeline of the crisis. As already stated, it began within the U.S. subprime-mortgage sector and initially was contained within the U.S. financial system. Its global transmission was, initially, through other banks as funding markets became impaired and interbank lending was curtailed. The market for short-term funding was reduced dramatically, causing a global banking crisis and associated negative consequences for non-financial firms and international stock markets. Aït-Sahalia et al. (2009) attribute the internationalisation, at least in part, to the collapse and bankruptcy of Lehman Brothers in September 2008. The globalization of the crisis led to severe difficulties in the banking sectors of the Eurozone periphery and subsequently in the sovereign bond markets of these countries.

MAIN FOCUS OF THE CHAPTER

Contagion within the US Financial System

Given that the credit crunch of 2007-08 originated in the U.S., we first examine contagion within the U.S. financial system. Longstaff (2010) was the first paper to examine this phenomenon and concluded that there was significant contagion running from the relatively small mortgage-backed securities market to U.S. equity markets, sovereign and corporate bond spreads and money markets. The timing of the crisis appears somewhat arbitrary in the analysis and this is addressed by Flavin and Sheenan (2015). Allowing the crisis regime to be endogenously determined, they conclude that there is limited evidence of contagion during the crisis period and rather that the transmission of the crisis can be explained by the high level of interdependence between the different sectors of the U.S. financial system. Guo et al. (2011) report mixed evidence of contagion within stock markets, the real estate market, the credit default market and energy markets. They find that shocks emanating from equity and oil markets are stronger driving forces for changes in financial markets, while finding no evidence of contagion from credit markets to the real estate sector. More recent evidence from both Guidolin et al. (2019) and Hippler et al. (2019) points to contagious effects within the U.S. financial system and from the financial system to the real economy respectively.

Contagion in International Bank Markets

International banking integration is a very important contagion channel in financial crises. The financial markets have recently become much more integrated providing important advantages in terms of gains in efficiency and diversification, but it also offers potential pitfalls, such as transmitting the effects of a crisis to the whole world faster and more intense. Ahrend et al. (2015) indicate that when financial turmoil arises in some part of the global financial system, high levels of international banking activity pose serious risks to global financial stability. Acemoglu et al. (2015) indicate that the highly interconnected nature of financial system contributes to its fragility, as it facilitates the spread of financial distress and solvency problems from institutions to the rest in an epidemic-like fashion.

The health of the banking sector plays a very important role and must be considered by policy makers as the banking problems have contributed significantly to the financial and economic downturns in many countries, particularly, those regions where economic activity is influenced economic activity is influenced by their reliance on bank financing. Accordingly, central banks should ensure a high level of liquidity in order to mitigate spillover effects during crisis periods. The financial crisis has highlighted the need of delving into the development of financial regulation and supervision of credit and liquidity activities. Recently, International Monetary Fund and the World Bank have emphasized the importance of maintaining a healthy banking system and regulating the banking operations as bank failures may involve significant macroeconomic costs. Ashcraft (2005) provides evidence that healthy-bank failures have significant and apparently permanent effects on real economic activity. Dungey et al. (2018) analyze the consequences in the wider economic and financial environments. Because doubts about the existence of an operative credit channel, most empirical studies have examined whether banking shocks are propagated through linkages between countries, such as a financial channel. Cicarelli et al. (2013), in a study focused on the Euro area, evidence the importance of transmitting a monetary policy shock to the real economy via the bank lending channel. Recently, Balluck (2015) describes how interconnections between investment banks and other financial institutions can act as a channel for the transmission of losses throughout the system while the complexity of some of their activities also contributes significantly to risks in the global financial system. In this line, some papers document that the propagated losses vary across the national banking sectors depending not only on their sizes but also on their interconnectivity. Paltalidis et al. (2015) find that the cross-border transmission of systematic shocks depends on the size and the degree of exposure of the banking sector. Particularly, the more exposed domestic banks are to the foreign banking systems, the greater are the systematic risks and the spillover effects from foreign financial shocks to the domestic banking sector. However, other authors have argued that monetary policy shocks might not affect bank lending as long as banks insulate their portfolios from these shocks, while others have argued that firms can access alternative credit sources if bank loan supply does tighten.

An interesting issue in this context of banking contagion is to analyse, to what extent, all the banks exert some influence in this global contagion as well as both large and small banks seem sensible in relation to spillover effects. Ahrend and Goujard (2015) provide strong evidence that global banks are an important and general driver of the spread of banking crises, with shocks towards foreign creditor banks being amplified by exposure to borrowing from global banks. These results are consistent with those of Cetorelli and Goldberg (2011) for the 2007-2009 global financial crises. Basset et al. (2014) states the explanation of the increased interconnection of global banking markets is largely attributable to the systematic component. Huang, Zhou and Zhu (2012) provide an interesting way of measuring the systematic risk of a financial system using a portfolio of 22 major banks from eight economies in Asia and the Pacific during the recent financial crisis. The elevated systematic risk is initially driven by the rising risk aversion and a decomposition analysis shows that the marginal contribution of individual banks to the systematic risk is mostly determined by its size, or the "too big to fail" doctrine. Gropp et al. (2009) find evidence of cross-border contagion for large European banks while there is no evidence for smaller banks.

Fry and Hsiao (2015) define a new test for financial market contagion based on changes co-kurtosis and co-volatility. They find an increase in the correlation between the US banking sector and the returns for eight countries from four regions (Asia, Europe, Latin America and North America) during the crisis 2008-2009. With the new approach applied during the crisis 2008-2009, they find significant contagion from the US banking sector to the banking markets in the four regions through extremal dependence test while they show significant contagion effects from US banking to the volatility of banking sectors in Korea, France, Germany and Chile with asymmetric dependence test.

Contagion Between Financials and Non-Financials

In general, financial crises often generate losses in economic activity, with effects on employment rate, investment or consumption. One of the main channels transmitting crisis to the real economy is the financial channel although not all studies support this hypothesis. Claessens et al. (2011b) found the euro crisis affected non-financial firms more through a financial channel versus a trade channel. On the other hand, Claessens et al. (2011a) consider the role of financial linkages to be relatively weak during the global financial crisis while Grant (2016) finds credit disruption is the primary contagion driver. The financial channel is largely explained by credit constraints based on gradual tightening of lending rules as well as credit rationing by financial intermediaries to companies. This fact can exert a multiplier effect on original crisis and this influence is a key determinant of the relationship between credit market and real economy.

In some cases, these credit constraints may adversely affect non-financial companies as they find difficulties for getting external finance, especially firms that are dependent on bank credit. Some papers evidence these credit restrictions affect with greater intensity those non- financial companies unable to replace bank credits by other sources of funding (Laeven and Valencia, 2013). In the same line, Klein (2014) found that a negative credit supply shock applied to SMEs (small and medium companies) during the global financial crisis has an adverse effect on economic activity, and this impact is greater in countries that have a high share of SMEs, concluding that the performance of industries that are heavily reliant on external financing is generally weaker than others when financial conditions are tight.

Non-banking sources have become significantly more important since the onset the global financial crisis and some firms, particularly larger companies, were able to access to these sources for meeting their financing needs during the recent crisis.

Casey and Toole (2014) indicate that while larger companies were able to substitute bank credit with direct loans, smaller and medium sized companies were unable to access these markets. These SME companies relied on trade credit for finding the funds. Tong and Wei (2009) construct portfolios with non-financial return stocks according to its degree of liquidity constraint and to its sensitivity to a consumer demand contraction during the 2007-2008 crisis finding for both regressors a negative coefficient statistically significant. Tong and Wei (2009) define financial constraint based on an index proposed and used by Whited and Wu (2006), who employ this index to study whether financial constraints represent a source of priced risk finding evidence that firm-level external finance constraints do indeed represent a source of undiversifiable risk that is priced in financial markets. With a different approach, Lin and Paravisini (2012) demonstrate how the systematic risk of returns reacts increasing to exogenously imposed financing constraint, results in line with the findings from Lidvan, Sapriza and Zhang (2009).

An interesting issue is to investigate if negative shocks to the financial sector can be offset by holdings of non-financial stocks. Dungey et al. (2018), in a study with eleven Eurozone countries (where many suffered large negative shocks in their banking systems) during the period 2004-2015, found non-financial sectors suffered little contagion from external and domestic banking shocks. However, non-financial companies became more sensitive to domestic banking shocks in relation to global shocks. This decoupling may be explained by the fact that the companies of the study are large firms and probably they could find alternative sources of finance. Adrian et. al (2012) document both bank and bond financing are quantitatively important in providing credit to nonfinancial corporations and evidence an increase in bond financing in USA during the global financial crisis in order to compensate the credit tighteting. Becker and Ivanshina (2014) indicate that in the most recent financial crisis, there was a considerable shift from loans to bonds in US firms, starting in late 2007 and being particularly pronounced during 2009.

Contagion In International Stock Markets

The global financial crisis caused large financial losses in the U.S. stock market, sending a great deal of uncertainty to markets in both developed and emerging economics. Many countries began to experience turbulence in their financial markets leaving the global financial system on the verge of meltdown. The leader role of the U.S. market in the financial world is visible throughout all causality tests and in all time periods so the international transmission of shocks, contagion and spillover effects from stock markets in the U.S. to other regions during the global crisis of 2007-2010 has attracted much attention in recent years. However, the transmission of shocks reduces the potential benefits of international portfolio diversification, which is traditionally viewed as an effective way to achieve a higher risk-return relative to a portfolio only holding domestic assets (Grubel, 1968 and De Santis and Gerard, 1997, among others). Chian et al. (2007) and Mollah et al. (2014) do not support this hypothesis as they show that during crisis periods the gains from international diversification decline.

Bekaert et al. (2014) perform an analysis of the transmission channels of the global financial crisis and while they find evidence of contagion from the U.S. to the global financial sector, the effects are small. The paper also finds that those portfolios in countries with weak economic fundamentals, poor policies and bad institutions experienced more contagion. Mollah et al. (2014) analyse contagion effects during global financial crisis across a wide range of markets. They confirm the presence of contagion in most of the markets analysed (except for Sweden) and show the global financial crisis spreads through a financial channel. Other studies, such as Morales et al. (2014) emphasize the differences between contagion and spillover effects. They indicate the markets suffered spillover effects with origin in the U.S. and were transmitted by several key regions around the world such as Singapore, Asia, UK and Europe.

However, many studies about the contagion from the U.S. stock market during the global financial crisis focus on the effects on specific regions in order to identify the areas that suffered most during this period.

Dungey and Gajurel (2014) test for the existence of equity market contagion originating from the US to advanced and emerging markets during the crisis period and they find large contagion effects in equity markets. The results also suggest that contagion effects are not strongly related to the level of global integration. Focusing in the Euro Area, Dees et. al (2007) find the equity markets are highly synchronous as they observe financial spillovers and external equity market shocks from USA to Europe are transmitted rapidly. Galesi and Sgherri (2009) find that equity markets in Europe are more synchronous than banking systems, indicating that asset prices are the main channel through which financial shocks are transmitted globally.

Samarakoon (2011) analyses the propagation of return stocks from the US to emerging and frontier markets. In the case of emerging markets, no contagion is observed (except for Latin America) while in frontier markets there is evidence of interdependence and contagion, although small in magnitude. However, Kenourgios and Padhi (2012), in a study focused on 9 emerging countries from various regions around the world, show contagion effects of the subprime crisis in all regions, being Asian emerging countries those suffering hardly the spillover effects. Both studies evidence a similar finding for Latin America, as this area displays the lower vulnerability to the crisis subprime.

Some papers document that contagion exists not only from the US market to the developed equity markets of Europe and Asia, but also to the BRIC economies

(Brazil, Russia, India and China). Bekiros (2014) examine the transmission of the U.S. subprime crisis to the fastest growing economies exhibiting spillover effects from the U.S. market to BRIC economies and, more specifically, highly significant spillover feedback effects between them in the post-crisis period. A contagion effect and increasing comovement among USA and BRICS is also observed by Dimitrou et al. (2013) from early 2009 onwards, implying that their dependence with the U.S. is larger in bullish markets. In this line, Mensi et al. (2016) provide evidence of an increase in the linkages between the U.S. and the BRICS (with the exception of Russian stock markets) after Lehman Brothers collapse. Both Bekiros (2014) and Dimitrou et al. (2013) evidence that the crisis accelerates the integration process as the BRICS become more internationally integrated after the U.S. financial crisis.

Luchtenberg and Viet (2015) analyse financial contagion in equity markets during global financial crisis at both the regional and country level in the most dynamic economic regions of the world, employing the Forbes and Rigobon (2002) definition of contagion. They find that the U.S., Germany and Japan are the biggest sources of contagion followed by China, Hong Kong and the UK. They also find that the U.S. only receives financial shocks from the global crisis while it is quite immune from receiving contagion from individual regions. Hong Kong and the UK are the most affected by contagion from the U.S., while there is no evidence of contagion to China, Japan or Germany.

Gamba-Santamaria et al. (2017) observe that the U.S. is a net volatility transmitter of spillover effects to Latin American countries, with Brazil, Chile, Colombia and Mexico encountering substantially higher spillovers between 2008 and 2012, a period of intense volatility in financial markets. They also provide evidence that shock transmission from the U.S. to those countries increases significantly around the Lehman Brother´s episode.

Jiang et al. (2017) examine six major stock markets (US, UK, China, Hong Kong, Japan and Germany) and observe that co-movements increased significantly when the global financial crisis emerged in August 2007 and the effect of a shock in the U.S. stock market is higher during the financial crisis relative to post-crisis period.

Contagion In International Bond Markets

As the U.S. credit crisis developed into a liquidity crisis, more international markets became embroiled in the turmoil. The weaknesses that were inherent in the Euro zone area were exposed and many sovereigns found it increasingly difficult to borrow on international markets. The Eurozone periphery countries of Greece, Ireland, Italy, Portugal and Spain – the so-called GIIPS – were all subject to more intense monitoring and lenders began to seek higher yields to compensate for the risk that they faced. This reversed a trend during the tranquil years when the bonds of all Eurozone countries were perceived to be roughly the same, leading to investors to short the lower-yielding bonds of the core countries and taking long positions in the higher-yielding sovereign bonds of the periphery countries. This phenomenon was labelled 'the greatest carry trade ever' by Acharya and Steffen (2015). The result was that many investors were holding the sovereign bonds of the GIIPS countries in the run up to the crisis and began to unwind these positions as the crisis began. This reversal in investor behaviour coupled with deteriorating public finances in many countries saw many of the GIIPS struggling to borrow on international markets. Greece, Ireland and Portugal all needed bailouts from the EU, ECB and IMF troika. Spain and Italy avoided such a bailout as the EU launched a bond buyback programme that created a demand for their sovereign bonds and thus, alleviated the upward pressure on their yields.

Many studies have focused on this period to analyse the role of contagion in propagating the sovereign bond crisis across the member states of the Eurozone. Most focus on the GIIPS as the source of the shock, with most attention being afforded to the role of Greek bonds as a source of contagion. The results are mixed. Most studies find some evidence that contagion played a role in the transmission of the crisis, but the source of the shock and the timing of the contagion remains contentious. Metiu (2012) finds strong evidence of contagion in the Eurozone in the early part of the crisis, with the contagion emanating from all the GIIPS. A similar finding is due to Arghyrou and Kontonikas (2012) who report extensive evidence of contagion. They find that Greece was the main source of contagion in the early stages of the crisis, while the later stages of the crisis were characterised by multiple sources of contagion. Mink and de Haan (2013) concentrate on Greece as source of the shock and find that sovereign bond prices in other distress countries (Ireland, Portugal and Spain) all react to news about Greece. Other studies that find widespread evidence of contagion during the early stages of the Eurozone debt crisis include Arezki et al. (2011), Alfonso et al. (2011), De Santis (2012) and Muratori (2014).

In contrast, a number of studies find a more limited role for contagion. Both Beirne and Fratzscher (2013) and Claeys and Vasicek (2014) document very short periods during which contagion played a role in the propagation of the Eurozone sovereign bond crisis and conclude that contagion is limited in time and markets. Caporin et al. (2013) attribute the propagation of shocks in Eurozone bond markets to integration (or interdependencies) rather than contagion, while neither Philippas and Siriopoulos (2013) nor Pragidis et al. (2015) find any support for the hypothesis that Greece acted as the source of contagious shocks for the other Eurozone member states. Blatt et al. (2015) distinguish between contemporaneous contagion and dynamic spillovers. Interestingly, they find that Greece does not generate immediate contagion for its fellow member states but rather its shocks are transmitted through a change in dynamics. On the other hand, Italy, Spain and Portugal are found to be potentially contagious (with immediate effects) to other Eurozone countries. In a similar vein, Conefrey and Cronin (2015) find a marked increase in spillovers between Eurozone bond markets during the crisis and find that Greece becomes increasingly detached from the other markets after its second bailout in March 2012. The decoupling of Greece and its reducing influence on other markets is also documented by Dungey et al. (2019). Cronin et al. (2016) also find a limited role for contagion in the transmission of the crisis but show that the crisis should not be treated as a single homogeneous period (see also Bird et al., 2017). Modelling the crisis as two distinct phases – the bad and the ugly – they show that contagion increased during the latter period and the source of the contagious effects was not limited to the periphery countries.

Pentecost et al. (2019) examine the drivers of contagion in the Eurozone sovereign bond markets and find that Ireland generated a different pattern of contagion than Greece, Portugal and Spain. Furthermore, they show that financial linkages are relatively more important than trade linkages in explaining a country's vulnerability to contagion.

The cross-market linkages between stocks and sovereign bonds is another relationship that appears to have suffered from contagion during the recent turmoil, especially for the Eurozone peripheral countries. Even though it has been shown that the correlation between stock and sovereign bond returns has exhibited significant time variation over a long period (see Baele et al., 2010), the pre-crisis evidence was consistent in that stock and bond returns generally exhibited negative correlation during crisis periods. Evidence consistent with this for the U.S. market is provided by Connolly et al. (2005), Guidolin and Timmermann (2006), Anderson et al. (2008), Yang et al. (2009) and Flavin et al. (2014) among others, while a similar relationship is documented for international markets by Baur and Lucey (2009) and Chang and Hsueh (2013). The explanation for this negative correlation was that sovereign bond markets acted as a safe haven for equity investors during stock market turmoil. Investors would sell off stocks and invest the proceeds in safe assets. This type of behaviour has been dubbed a 'flight to safety'. In this sense, sovereign bonds acted as an effective hedging instrument against stock market shocks.

However, a number of studies show that the safe haven properties of sovereign bonds for equity investors did not hold up during the Eurozone sovereign debt crisis. This change fits our definition of contagion, whereby cross-market linkages are significantly different during a crisis from those that prevail in normal times. From the onset of this crisis period – late 2009 – Jammazi et al. (2015) find the stock-bond relationship turned positive and remained so until the end of their sample in Spain, Greece, Ireland, Portugal and Belgium. Acosta-González et al. (2016) reach a similar conclusion for Spain and Italy. Flavin (2019) confirms this result for Greece, Ireland, Italy, Spain and Portugal (GIIPS) but shows that the negative correlation between stock and bond returns continued in the larger, developed markets of Germany, France and the UK. Flavin and Lagoa-Varela (2019) analyse the stock-bond relationship for the GIIPS at a finer level of disaggregation by focusing on sectoral indices of the stock market. They conclude that a common driving force across all of these countries was the relationship between financials and the domestic sovereign bond. Even though, there is a great deal of heterogeneity across countries for the other sectors, the relationship between the return on financial stocks and the bond return is consistently positive across countries. In the next section, we analyse the relationship between financials (banks) and sovereign bonds in greater detail.

Contagion Between Bank Markets and Sovereign Debt Markets

One of the key features of the Eurozone sovereign debt crisis was the strong links that developed between the domestic banks and the domestic sovereign bonds of the GIIPS during the financial turmoil. These links arose during the crisis, disrupting existing linkages and thus fitting with our definition of contagion. Such was the severity of the (near-) simultaneous decline in these markets that the relationship between banks and sovereigns has been labelled as a 'deadly embrace' by Fahri and Tirole (2018) and a 'diabolical loop' by Brunnermeier et al. (2016).

Studies such as Acharya et al. (2014) and Mody and Sandri (2012) model an 'Irish-style' crisis where the domestic banking sector becomes severely impaired and is bailed out by the domestic government, resulting in a transfer of private losses to the sovereign. As the banking sector becomes more distressed, the government guarantee becomes less credible and reduces the sovereign's ability to access international bond markets. The two become inextricably linked with any financial weakness in either, producing an adverse reaction from investors for both. Other studies, such as Bocola (2016) and Sosa-Padilla (2018), focus on the reverse causality for the crisis – a 'Greek-style' crisis. In these models, the trigger for the crisis is the deteriorating public finances. They impact adversely upon the domestic banking sector through the banks holdings of domestic sovereign bonds. As they lose value or cannot be sold on the secondary market without a substantial discount, the balance sheets of domestic banks weakens, meaning that the likelihood of they requiring a bailout increases. Again, the two sectors become 'joined at the hip' as suggested by Mody and Sandri. A number of other studies, such as Acharya and Rajan (2013), Albertazzi et al. (2014) and Gennaioli et al. (2014), show the potential impacts of downturns in the domestic sovereign bonds for the domestic banking sector. Feedback loops between the two sectors are analysed in Fahri and Tirole (2018) and Cooper and Nikolov (2018).

Merton et al. (2013) summarise the dynamics that lead to such a connection between sovereign bonds and the financial sector. The contingent liability created by government guarantees, either implicit or explicit, to the domestic banking sector may be valued as a put option on the value of the banking sector's assets. The value of the put option increases as the asset values decline and / or the volatility of the asset values increase. Furthermore, the sensitivity of the option value increases in a non-linear fashion implying that consecutive declines in the value of banks' assets will have increasingly large negative repercussions for the government (option writer) and this impairs the valuation of its sovereign debt and its ability to issue new bonds. The 'doom loop' of banks and sovereign debt is exacerbated by banks holding large amounts of sovereign debt which again can be valued as a put option, this time written by banks on the value of government debt. Declines in the value of sovereign debt lead to losses for banks, which reinforces the adverse loop between the two entities.

The issue of contagion is directly addressed in a number of studies. De Bruyckere et al. (2013) find evidence of excess correlation between the two sectors during the crisis, while Allegret et al. (2017) find evidence of contagious effects from sovereign bonds to the European banking sector. Georgoutsos and Moratis (2017) present evidence of contagion between banks and sovereigns but suggest that the nature of this contagion changed between the global banking crisis of 2007-09 and the post-2010 Eurozone sovereign debt crisis. Dungey et al. (2019) show that there was significant bidirectional contagion between the sectors, which intensified as the crisis unfolded for many of the GIIPS.

SOLUTIONS AND RECOMMENDATIONS

Financial contagion and the transmission of shocks is a topic of great interest to different groups of financial market participants, mainly, investors and policy makers.

For investors, contagion threatens the effectiveness of the portfolio diversification strategies when they are most needed to deliver. Empirical evidence has shown that diversification benefits can be reduced during market downturns (Butler and Joaquin, 2002). It is important for asset allocation and risk management strategies to take into account the empirical properties of contagion effects as well as common movements in high volatility regime. Decreased diversification benefits due to financial contagion during a crisis need to be better understood and, in particular, investors need to disentangle the contagious effects in common shocks (which investors are endeavouring to diversify away) from those arising from previously idiosyncratic shocks (which reduce the diversification potential). This would be useful for the formulation and implementation of investors´ asset allocation and risk management strategies.

Policy makers need to formulate policies to curb the spread of contagion during a crisis period. The extent literature suggests that, in general, small and medium sized companies face difficulties during credit crunch contexts in accessing some markets such as bonds. Therefore, there is a clear need of alternative sources as well as policies for making easier to access these markets. It is crucial to encourage and promote policies in order to facilitate the access to bond markets, which would be really an important support for those companies suffering contagion effects by the bank credit channel. In addition to all financial regulations (many of which were undertaken during the global financial crises), this should be an interesting political measure for mitigating contagion and spillover effects on credit constrained companies, and consequently, on real economy.

FUTURE RESEARCH DIRECTIONS

In general, one of the main strategies to reduce risk without sacrificing return is diversification. The optimal strategy will be to manage portfolios with assets whose returns are uncorrelated or with assets being exposed to different risks.

However, during economic downturns these diversification benefits can be reduced, mainly for national portfolio managers. For this reason, fund managers should formulate and implement new management strategies in order to deal in this new scenario.

Although there are many studies about contagion and shock transmission between different markets and countries, not many providing a useful information for helping investors in their portfolio decisions during periods of financial distress. It would be really interesting to undertake more studies focused on the stability market linkages between assets in different market conditions in order to identify safe haven assets in non-normal market conditions.

CONCLUSION

The recent history of financial markets has been determined by the global financial crisis, which originated in the U.S. and spread across global financial markets, leading to the greatest financial crisis since the Great Depression and one of the more tumultuous events of recent history.

Academic research has provided evidence of the existence of contagion within the U.S, within the Eurozone and internationally for the 2007-2009 global financial crisis and the ensuing Eurozone sovereign debt crisis. This chapter provides an extensive review of the literature on the topic of contagion, analysing the transmission of the crisis.

Firstly, we concentrate on the crucial role of the U.S. and the transmission of shocks within its financial system. Many authors highlight the role of contagion in transmitting the original shock to the U.S. subprime-mortgage sector to other assets and markets.

Secondly, we emphasize the importance of the banking sector when transmitting the spillover effects of the global financial crisis. Section 2 focuses on shocks across the banking sector. The high degree of international banking integration contributed to the spread of the crisis internationally and to the the real economic activity, particularly in regions where economic activity is reliant on bank financing. Banking sectors of the Eurozone periphery experienced serious difficulties which lead to interventions of the governments in order to mitigate spillover effects of the crisis. Section 3 discusses the extent of the contagion suffered by the non-financial companies. Most of the studies provide evidence that the financial channel (largely explained by credit constraints) is the primary contagion driver for the non-financial sector. A number of studies show that negative effects were stronger for those companies (primarily small and medium companies) that were not able to replace banking sources for alternative funds, such as trade credit or bond markets.

The fourth section focuses on contagion across international stock markets. The literature documents that most regions experienced spillover effects from the U.S, although the intensity of the contagion effects for different markets are mixed. In general, developed equity markets in Europe and Asia are shown to have suffered the strongest contagious effects. Several studies also document the contagion effect from the U.S to BRIC countries.

Section 5 reviews the transmission of shocks across the Eurozone sovereign bond markets and shows that there is strong evidence of contagion. Interestingly, there is little consensus on the direction of contagion or on the source of the most contagious effects. We also document the changing relationship between stock and bond markets, especially in the Eurozone periphery countries. Finally, section 6 shows that the main driver of the changing stock-bond relationship is the banking sector shocks.

Overall there is strong evidence of contagion. The global financial crisis appears to have generated contagious effects across different sectors and shows that investors and policy makers need to build this into their models in formulating asset allocation strategies and policies to increase the resilience of the global economy.

REFERENCES

Acemoglu, D., Ozdaglar, A., & Tahbaz-Salehi, A. (2015). Systematic risk and stability in financial networks. *The American Economic Review*, *105*(2), 564–608. doi:10.1257/aer.20130456 PMID:29543414

Acharya, V., Drechsler, I., & Schnabl, P. (2014). A pyrrhic victory? Bank bailouts and sovereign credit risk. *The Journal of Finance*, *69*(6), 2689–2739. doi:10.1111/jofi.12206

Acharya, V., & Rajan, R. (2013). Sovereign debt, government myopia and the financial crisis. *Review of Financial Studies*, *26*(6), 1526–1560. doi:10.1093/rfs/hht011

Acharya, V., & Steffen, S. (2015). The "greatest" carry trade ever? Understanding Eurozone bank risks. *Journal of Financial Economics*, *115*(2), 215–236. doi:10.1016/j.jfineco.2014.11.004

Acosta-González, E., Andrada-Félix, J., & Fernández-Rodríguez, F. (2016). Stock-bond decoupling before and after the 2008 crisis. *Applied Economics Letters*, *23*(7), 465–470. doi:10.1080/13504851.2015.1083072

Adrian, T., Colla, P., & Shin, H. S. (2012). Which financial frictions? Parsing the evidence from the financial crisis of 2007 to 2009. Working paper no.18335. National Bureau of Economic Research.

Ahrend, R., & Goujard, A. (2015). Global banking, global crises? The role of bank balance-sheet channel for transmission of financial crises. *European Economic Review*, *80*, 253–279.

Aït-Sahalia, Y., Andritzky, J., Jobst, A., Nowak, S., & Tamirisa, N. (2009). *How to stop a herd of running bears. Market response to policy initiatives during the global financial crisis*. IMF Working Paper, No. WP/09/204.

Akhtaruzzamn, M., & Shamsuddin, A. (2016). International contagion through financial versus non-financial firms. *Economic Modelling*, *59*, 143–163. doi:10.1016/j.econmod.2016.07.003

Albertazzi, U., Ropele, T., Sene, G., & Signoretti, F. (2014). The impact of the sovereign debt crisis on the activity of Italian banks. *Journal of Banking & Finance*, *46*, 387–402. doi:10.1016/j.jbankfin.2014.05.005

Alfonso, A., Furceri, D., & Gomes, P. (2011). Sovereign credit ratings and financial markets linkages: Application to European data. *Journal of International Money and Finance*, *31*(3), 606–638. doi:10.1016/j.jimonfin.2012.01.016

Allegret, J. P., Raymond, H., & Rharrabti, H. (2017). The impact of the European sovereign debt crisis on banks stocks. Some evidence of shift contagion in Europe. *Journal of Banking & Finance, 74*, 24–37. doi:10.1016/j.jbankfin.2016.10.004

Andersson, M., Krylova, E., & Vähämaa, S. (2008). Why does the correlation between stock and bond returns vary over time? *Applied Financial Economics, 18*(2), 139–151. doi:10.1080/09603100601057854

Arezki, R., Candelon, B., & Sy, A. (2011). *Sovereign Rating News and Financial Market Spillovers: Evidence from the European DebtCrisis*. Working paper No. 11/68. International Monetary Fund.

Arghyrou, M., & Kontonikas, G. (2012). The EMU-sovereign debt crisis: Fundamentals, expectations and contagion. *Journal of International Financial Markets, Institutions and Money, 22*(4), 658–677. doi:10.1016/j.intfin.2012.03.003

Ashcraft, A. (2005). Are banks really sepecial? New evidence from the FDIC-Induced failure of healthy banks. *The American Economic Review, 94*(5), 1712–1730. doi:10.1257/000282805775014326

Baele, L., Bekaert, G., & Inghelbrecht, K. (2010). The determinants of stock and bond return comovements. *Review of Financial Studies, 23*(6), 2374–2428. doi:10.1093/rfs/hhq014

Balluck, K. (2015). Investment banking: linkages to the real economy and the financial system. *Bank of England Quarterly Bulletin*.

Basset, W. F., Chosak, M. B., Driscoll, J. C., & Zakrajsek, E. (2014). Changes in bank lending standards and the macroeconomy. *Journal of Money, Credit and Banking, 62*, 23–40.

Baur, D., & Lucey, B. (2009). Flights and contagion – An empirical analysis of stock-bond correlations. *Journal of Financial Stability, 5*(4), 339–352. doi:10.1016/j.jfs.2008.08.001

Baur, D. G. (2012). Financial contagion and the real economy. *Journal of Banking & Finance, 36*(10), 2680–2692. doi:10.1016/j.jbankfin.2011.05.019

Becker, B., & Ivashina, V. (2014). Cyclicality of credit supply: Firm level evidence. *Journal of Monetary Economics, 62*, 76–93. doi:10.1016/j.jmoneco.2013.10.002

Beirne, J., & Fratzscher, M. (2013). The pricing of sovereign risk and contagion during the European sovereign debt crisis. *Journal of International Money and Finance, 34*, 60–82. doi:10.1016/j.jimonfin.2012.11.004

Bekaert, G., Ehrman, M., Fratzscher, F., & Mehl, A. (2014). The global crisis and equity market contagion. *The Journal of Finance, 69*(6), 2597–2649. doi:10.1111/jofi.12203

Bekiros, S. D. (2014). Contagion, decoupling and spillover effects of the US financial crisis: Evidence from the BRIC markets. *International Review of Financial Analysis, 33*, 58–69. doi:10.1016/j.irfa.2013.07.007

Bernanke, B. (1983). Non-monetary effects of the financial crisis in the propagation of the Great Depression. *The American Economic Review, 73*(3), 257–276.

Bird, G., Du, W., Pentecost, E. J., & Willett, T. (2017). Was it different the second time? An empirical analysis of contagion during the crises in Greece, 2009-2015. *World Economy, 40*(12), 1–14. doi:10.1111/twec.12553

Blatt, D., Candelon, B., & Manner, H. (2015). Detecting contagion in a multivariate time series system: An application to sovereign bond markets in Europe. *Journal of Banking & Finance, 59*, 1–13. doi:10.1016/j.jbankfin.2015.06.003

Bocola, L. (2016). The Pass-Through of Sovereign Risk. *Journal of Political Economy, 124*(4), 879–926. doi:10.1086/686734

Brunnermeier, M. K. (2008). *Deciphering – The liquidity and credit crunch 2007–2008*. National Bureau of Economic Research (NBER), Working Paper No. 14612.

Brunnermeier, M. K., Garciano, L., Lane, P., Pagano, M., Reis, R., Santos, T., ... Vayanos, D. (2016). The sovereign-banking diabolical loop and ESBies. *The American Economic Review, 106*(5), 508–512. doi:10.1257/aer.p20161107

Butler, K. C., & Joaquin, D. C. (2002). Are the gains from international portfolio diversification exaggerated? The influence of downside risk in bear markets. *Journal of International Money and Finance, 21*(7), 981–1011. doi:10.1016/S0261-5606(02)00048-7

Campelo, M., Graham, J., & Harvey, C. R. (2009). *The real effects on financial constraints: evidence from a financial crisis.* Working paper no. 15552. National Bureau of Economic Research.

Caporin, M., Pelizzon, L., Ravazzolo, F., & Rigobon, R. (2013). *Measuring Sovereign Contagion in Europe.* NBER Working paper 18741.

Casey, E., & O'Toole, C. M. (2014). Bank lending constraints, trade credit and alternative financing during the financial crisis: Evidence from European SMEs. *Journal of Corporate Finance, 27*, 173–193. doi:10.1016/j.jcorpfin.2014.05.001

Cetorelli, N., & Goldberg, G. (2011). *Global banks and international shock transmission: evidence from the crisis*. Working paper no 15974. National Bureau of Economic Research.

Chang, C. L., & Hsueh, P. L. (2013). An investigation of the flight-to-quality effect: Evidence from Asia-Pacific countries. *Emerging Markets Finance & Trade*, *49*(sup4), 53–69. doi:10.2753/REE1540-496X4905S404

Chian, T. C., Nam, B., & Li, H. (2007). Dynamic correlation analysis of financial contagion: Evidence from Asian markets. *Journal of International Money and Finance*, *26*(7), 1206–1228. doi:10.1016/j.jimonfin.2007.06.005

Cicarelli, M., Maddaloni, A., & Peidró, J. L. (2013). *Heterogeneous transmisión mechanism monetary policy and financial regulity in the euro area*. Working paper no. 1527. European Central Bank.

Claessens, S., Tong, H., & Wei, S. (2011a). From the financial crisis to the real economy: Using firm-level data to identify transmission channels. *Journal of International Economics*, *88*(2), 375–387. doi:10.1016/j.jinteco.2012.02.015

Claessens, S., Tong, H., & Zuccardi, I. (2011b). *Did the Euro crisis affect non-financial firm stock prices through a financial or trade channel?* Working paper no. 11/227. International Monetary Fund.

Claeys, P., & Vasicek, B. (2014). Measuring bilateral spillover and testing contagion on sovereign bond markets in Europe. *Journal of Banking & Finance*, *46*, 151–165. doi:10.1016/j.jbankfin.2014.05.011

Conefrey, T., & Cronin, D. (2015). Spillover in Euro area sovereign bond markets. *The Economic and Social Review*, *46*(2), 197–231.

Connolly, R., Stivers, C., & Sun, L. (2005). Stock market uncertainty and the relation between stocks and bond returns. *Journal of Financial and Quantitative Analysis*, *40*, 161–194. doi:10.1017/S0022109000001782

Cooper, R., & Nikolov, K. (2018). Government debt and banking fragility: The spreading of strategic uncertainty. *International Economic Review*, *59*(4), 1905–1925. doi:10.1111/iere.12323

Coval, J., Jurek, J., & Stafford, E. (2009). The economics of structured finance. *The Journal of Economic Perspectives*, *23*(1), 3–25. doi:10.1257/jep.23.1.3

Cronin, D., Flavin, T. J., & Sheenan, L. (2016). Contagion in Eurozone sovereign bond markets? The good, the bad and the ugly. *Economics Letters*, *143*, 5–8. doi:10.1016/j.econlet.2016.02.031

De Bruyckere, V., Gerhardt, M., Schepens, G., & Vander Vennet, R. (2013). Bank/sovereign risk spillovers in the European debt crisis. *Journal of Banking & Finance*, *37*(12), 4793–4809. doi:10.1016/j.jbankfin.2013.08.012

De Santis, G., & Gerard, B. (1997). International asset pricing and portfolio diversification with time-varying risk. *The Journal of Finance*, *52*(5), 1881–1912. doi:10.1111/j.1540-6261.1997.tb02745.x

De Santis, R. (2012). *The Euro Area Sovereign Debt Crisis: Safe Haven, Credit Rating Agencies and the Spread of the Fever from Greece, Ireland and Portugal*. Working paper No. 1419. European Central Bank.

Dees, S., Mauro, F., Pesaran, M., & Smith, V. (2007). Exploring the international linkages of the euro area: A global VAR analysis. *Journal of Applied Econometrics*, *22*(1), 1–38. doi:10.1002/jae.932

Dimitrou, D., Kenourgios, D., & Simos, T. (2013). Global financial crisis and emerging stock market contagion: A multivariate FIAPARCH-DCC approach. *International Review of Financial Analysis*, *30*, 46–56. doi:10.1016/j.irfa.2013.05.008

Dungey, M., Dwyer, G., & Flavin, T. (2013). Systematic and liquidity risk in suprime-mortgage backed securities. *Open Economies Review*, *24*(1), 5–32. doi:10.100711079-012-9254-4

Dungey, M., Flavin, T., & Lagoa-Varela, D. (2018). Are banking shocks contagious? Evidence from the Eurozone. *Journal of Banking & Finance*, 105386. doi:10.1016/j.jbankfin.2018.07.010

Dungey, M., Flavin, T. J., & Sheenan, L. (2019). *Banks and sovereigns: Did adversity bring them closer?* (Unpublished manuscript). Maynooth University.

Dungey, M., & Gajurel, D. (2014). Equity market contagion during the global financial crisis: Evidence from the world's eight largest economies. *Economic Systems*, *38*(2), 161–177. doi:10.1016/j.ecosys.2013.10.003

Dwyer, G., & Tkac, P. (2009). The financial crisis of 2008 in fixed-income markets. *Journal of International Money and Finance*, *28*(8), 1293–1316. doi:10.1016/j.jimonfin.2009.08.007

Dwyer, G. P., Devereux, J., Baier, S., & Tamura, R. (2013). Recessions, growth and banking crises. *Journal of International Money and Finance*, *38*, 18–40. doi:10.1016/j.jimonfin.2013.05.009

Fahri, E., & Tirole, J. (2018). Deadly embrace: Sovereign and financial balance sheets doom loops. *The Review of Economic Studies*, *85*(3), 1781–1823. doi:10.1093/restud/rdx059

Flavin, T. J. (2019). From bulls to bears: Analysing the stock-bond relationship of European countries across different market regimes. In S. Boubaker & D. K. Nguyen (Eds.), *Handbook of Global Financial Markets: Transformations, Dependence, and Risk Spillovers*. World Scientific Publishing. doi:10.1142/9789813236653_0002

Flavin, T. J., & Lagoa-Varela, D. (2019). On the stability of Stock-bond comovements across market conditions in the Eurozone periphery. *Global Finance Journal*, 100491. doi:10.1016/j.gfj.2019.100491

Flavin, T. J., Morley, C. E., & Panopoulou, E. (2014). Identifying safe haven assets for equity investors through an analysis of the stability of shock transmission. *Journal of International Financial Markets and Money*, *33*, 137–154. doi:10.1016/j.intfin.2014.08.001

Flavin, T. J., & Sheenan, L. (2015). The role of U.S. subprime mortgage-backed assets in propagating the crisis: Contagion or interdependence? *The North American Journal of Economics and Finance*, *34*, 167–186. doi:10.1016/j.najef.2015.09.001

Fleming, J., Kirby, C., & Ostdiek, B. (1998). Information and volatility linkages in the stock, bond, and money markets. *Journal of Financial Economics*, *49*(1), 111–137. doi:10.1016/S0304-405X(98)00019-1

Forbes, K. J., & Rigobon, R. J. (2002). No contagion, only interdependence: Measuring stock market comovements. *The Journal of Finance*, *57*(5), 2223–2261. doi:10.1111/0022-1082.00494

Fry-McKibben, R. A., & Hsiao, C. Y. (2015). *Extremal dependence tests for contagion*. CAMA Working paper 40/2015. Australian National University.

Galesi, A., & Sgherri, S. (2009). *Regional financial spillovers across Europe: A global VAR analysis*. Working paper no 09/23. International Monetary Fund.

Gamba-Santamaria, S., Gomez-Gonzalez, J. E., Hurtado Guarin, J. L., & Melo-Velandia, L. F. (2017). Stock market volatility spillovers: Evidence for Latin America. *Finance Research Letters*, *20*, 207–216. doi:10.1016/j.frl.2016.10.001

Gennaioli, N., Martin, A., & Rossi, S. (2014). Sovereign defaults, domestic banks, and financial institutions. *The Journal of Finance*, *69*(2), 819–866. doi:10.1111/jofi.12124

Georgoutsos, D., & Moratis, G. (2017). Bank-sovereign contagion in the Eurozone: A panel VAR approach. *Journal of International Financial Markets, Institutions and Money, 48*, 146–159. doi:10.1016/j.intfin.2017.01.004

Gorton, G. (2009). Information, liquidity and the (ongoing) panic of 2007. *The American Economic Review, 99*(2), 567–572. doi:10.1257/aer.99.2.567

Grammatikos, T., & Vermeulen, R. (2012). Transmission of the financial and sovereign debt crises to the EMU: Stock prices, CDS spreads and exchange rates. *Journal of International Money and Finance, 31*(3), 517–533. doi:10.1016/j.jimonfin.2011.10.004

Grant, E. (2016). *Exposure to international crises: trade versus financial contagion*. Working Paper no 30/2016. European Systematic Risk Board.

Gropp, R., Lo Duca, M., & Vesala, J. (2009). Cross-border bank contagion in Europe. *International Journal of Central Banking, 5*(1), 97–139.

Guidolin, M., Hansen, E., & Pedio, M. (2019). Cross-asset contagion in the financial crisis: A Bayesian time-varying parameter approach. *Journal of Financial Markets, 45*, 83–114. doi:10.1016/j.finmar.2019.04.001

Guidolin, M., & Timmermann, A. (2006). An econometric model of nonlinear dynamics in the joint distribution of stock and bond returns. *Journal of Applied Econometrics, 21*(1), 1–22. doi:10.1002/jae.824

Guo, F., Chen, C., & Huang, Y. S. (2011). Markets contagion during financial crisis: A regime switching approach. *International Review of Economics & Finance, 20*(1), 95–109. doi:10.1016/j.iref.2010.07.009

Hippler, W. J. III, Hossain, S., & Hassan, M. K. (2019). Financial crisis spillover from Wall Street to Main Street: Further evidence. *Empirical Economics, 56*(6), 1893–1938. doi:10.100700181-018-1513-9

Huang, X., Zhou, H., & Zhu, H. (2012). Assessing the systematic risk of heterogeneous portfolio of banks during the recent financial crisis. *Journal of Financial Stability, 8*(3), 193–205. doi:10.1016/j.jfs.2011.10.004

Jammazi, R., Tiwari, A., Ferrer, R., & Moya, P. (2015). Time-varying dependence between stock and government bond returns: International evidence with dynamic copulas. *The North American Journal of Economics and Finance, 33*, 74–93. doi:10.1016/j.najef.2015.03.005

Jiang, Y., Yu, M., & Mohsin, S. (2017). The financial crisis and co-movement of global stock markets-a case of six major economics. *Sustainability*, *9*(2), 1–19. doi:10.3390u9020260

Kenourgios, D., & Padhi, P. (2012). Emerging markets and financial crises: Regional, global or isolated shocks? *Journal of Multinational Financial Management*, *22*(1-2), 24–38. doi:10.1016/j.mulfin.2012.01.002

King, M., & Wadhawani, S. (1990). Transmission of volatility between Stock Markets. *Review of Financial Studies*, *3*(1), 5–33. doi:10.1093/rfs/3.1.5

Klein, N. (2014). *Small and medium size enterprises, credit supply shocks and economic recovery in Europe*. Working Paper no 14/98. International Monetary Fund.

Laeven, L., & Valencia, F. (2013). The real effects of financial sector interventions during crises. *Journal of Money, Credit and Banking*, *45*(1), 147–177. doi:10.1111/j.1538-4616.2012.00565.x

Lin, H., & Paravisini, D. (2012). The effect of financial constraints on risk. *Review of Finance*, *17*(1), 229–259. doi:10.1093/rof/rfr038

Livdan, D., Sapriza, H., & Zhang, L. (2009). Financially constrained stock returns. *The Journal of Finance*, *64*(4), 1827–1862. doi:10.1111/j.1540-6261.2009.01481.x

Longstaff, F. (2010). The subprime credit crisis and contagion in financial markets. *Journal of Financial Economics*, *97*(3), 436–450. doi:10.1016/j.jfineco.2010.01.002

Luchtenberg, K., & Viet, Q. (2015). The 2008 financial crisis: Stock market contagion and its determinants. *Research in International Business and Finance*, *33*, 178–203. doi:10.1016/j.ribaf.2014.09.007

Mensi, Q., Hammoudeh, S., Nguyen, D., & Hoon, S. (2016). Global financial crises and spillover effects among the U.S. and BRIC stock markets. *International Review of Economics & Finance*, *42*, 257–276. doi:10.1016/j.iref.2015.11.005

Merton, R. C., Billio, M., Getmansky, M., Gray, D., Lo, A. W., & Pelizzon, L. (2013). On a new approach for analyzing and managing macrofinancial risks. *Financial Analysts Journal*, *69*(2), 22–33. doi:10.2469/faj.v69.n2.5

Metiu, N. (2012). Sovereign risk contagion in the Eurozone. *Economics Letters*, *117*(1), 35–38. doi:10.1016/j.econlet.2012.04.074

Mink, M., & de Haan, J. (2013). Contagion during the Greek sovereign debt crisis. *Journal of International Money and Finance*, *34*, 102–113. doi:10.1016/j.jimonfin.2012.11.006

Mody, A., & Sandri, D. (2012). The Eurozone crisis: How banks and sovereigns came to be joined at the hip. *Economic Policy, 27*(70), 199–230. doi:10.1111/j.1468-0327.2012.00281.x

Mollah, S., Zafifov, G., & Shahiduzzama, A. (2014). *Financial market contagion during the Global Financial Crisis*. Working Paper, no 2014/5. Center for Innovation and Technology Research.

Morales, L., & Afreosso-O'Callaghan, B. (2014). The global financial crisis: World market or regional contagion effects? *International Review of Economics & Finance, 29*, 108–131. doi:10.1016/j.iref.2013.05.010

Muratori, U. (2014). Contagion in the Euro Area Sovereign Bond Market. *Social Sciences, 4*(1), 66–82. doi:10.3390ocsci4010066

Paltalidis, N., Gounopoulos, D., Kizys, R., & Koutelidakis, Y. (2015). Transmission of systematic risk and contagion in Europe. *Journal of Banking & Finance, 61*, 536–552. doi:10.1016/j.jbankfin.2015.03.021

Pentecost, E. J., Du, W., Bird, G., & Willett, T. (2019). Contagion from the crises in the Euro-zone: Where, when and why? *European Journal of Finance, 25*(14), 1309–1327. doi:10.1080/1351847X.2019.1589552

Pericoli, M., & Sbracia, M. (2003). A Primer on Financial Contagion. *Journal of Economic Surveys, 17*(4), 571–608. doi:10.1111/1467-6419.00205

Philippas, D., & Siriopoulos, C. (2013). Putting the 'C' Into Crisis: Contagion, Correlations and Copulas on EMU Bond Markets. *Journal of International Financial Markets, Institutions and Money, 27*, 161–176. doi:10.1016/j.intfin.2013.09.008

Pragidis, I. C., Aielli, G. P., Chionis, D., & Schizas, P. (2015). Contagion effects during financial crisis: Evidence from the Greek sovereign bonds market. *Journal of Financial Stability, 18*, 127–138. doi:10.1016/j.jfs.2015.04.001

Reinhart, C. M., & Rogoff, K. S. (2009). The aftermath of financial crises. *The American Economic Review, 99*(2), 466–472. doi:10.1257/aer.99.2.466

Samarakoon, L. (2011). Stock market interdependence, contagion and the US financial crisis: The case of emerging frontier markets. *Journal of International Financial Markets, Institutions and Money, 21*(5), 724–742. doi:10.1016/j.intfin.2011.05.001

Sawyer, S., & Tapia, A. (2005). The sociotechnical nature of mobile computing work: Evidence from a study of policing in the United States. *International Journal of Technology and Human Interaction, 1*(3), 1–14. doi:10.4018/jthi.2005070101

Sosa-Padilla, C. (2018). Sovereign defaults and banking crises. *Journal of Monetary Economics*, *99*, 88–105. doi:10.1016/j.jmoneco.2018.07.004

Tong, H., & Wei, S.-J. (2009). *The misfortune of non-financial firms in a financial crisis: Disentangling finance and demand shocks.* CEPR Discussion paper no. 7208. National Bureau of Economic Research.

Whited, I. M., & Wu, G. (2006). Financial constraints risk. *Review of Financial Studies*, *19*(2), 531–559. doi:10.1093/rfs/hhj012

Yang, J., Zhou, Y., & Wang, Z. (2009). The stock-bond correlation and macroeconomic conditions: One and a half centuries of evidence. *Journal of Banking & Finance*, *33*(4), 670–680. doi:10.1016/j.jbankfin.2008.11.010

KEY TERMS AND DEFINITIONS

Credit Constraints: Gradual tightening of lending rules as well as credit rationing by financial intermediaries to companies.

De-Coupling: When the transmission mechanism is dampened in the crisis regime or the response is statistically significantly lower than expected given market interdependence.

Economic Downturns: A period of an economic contraction, sometimes limited in scope or duration

Financial Contagion: A situation where sudden large losses in one country, one sector or one particular asset spread out across the economy and increase the risk of subsequent large losses in the same as well as in other countries, sectors or assets.

Flight to Safety: Investors buy bonds (safer investments) when they sell stocks (higher-risk investments) in order to reduce the losses that investors suffer in crises periods.

Global Financial Crisis: Period of extreme stress in global financial markets and banking systems between mid-2007 and early 2009.

Safe Haven Asset: An investment with low market risk and high liquidity that is sought by investors to limit their exposure to losses during market downturns.

Spillover Effects: Secondary effects or collateral effects.

Section 3
Financial Education and Inclusion

Chapter 9
The Economic and Social Value of Financial Literacy

José Manuel Sánchez Santos
https://orcid.org/0000-0003-2678-3755
Universidade da Coruña, Spain

ABSTRACT

The main objective of this chapter is to provide new insights into the economic and social value that financial literacy has for individuals and societies. Financial literacy has implications that are relevant both at a micro (especially for households) and macro-level (for the financial system and for the national economy as a whole). On the one hand, a lack of financial literacy put households a risk from making sub-optimal financial decisions and prevent them to maximize their wellbeing. On the other hand, financial literacy favors a better allocation of resources, reduces the risks associated with episodes of financial instability, and therefore, contributes to the increase of social welfare. The analysis and the empirical evidence showing the benefits (costs) of financial literacy (illiteracy) allows to conclude that policymakers have a key role to play implementing initiatives aiming to improve financial literacy of the population at all stages of life.

INTRODUCTION

Financial literacy is an important life skill with significant implications at both, micro (for individuals) and macro (for society as a whole) level. On the one hand, financial literacy lacks usually has effects on individuals' finance management and on their ability to save for long-term goals such as financing retirement, buying a house etc. In particular, financial illiteracy is behind ineffective financial planning and has costs

DOI: 10.4018/978-1-7998-2440-4.ch009

in terms of saving and investment returns, and also in terms of consumers' debt management (Campbell, 2006; Lusardi, 2019). Moreover, money mismanagement may lead to a higher vulnerability of consumers to financial crisis in the event of a negative economic shock such as a job loss or a long-lasting illness. On the other hand, at a macro level, informed buyers of financial products contribute to create both more competitive and more efficient financial markets, increasing the market discipline and forcing the financial institutions to operate more efficiently. More efficient financial markets, ultimately, contributes to allocate capital efficiently and, in turn, to promote economic growth.

More specifically, in retail financial markets, there are a number of circumstances that make consumers of financial products and services particularly vulnerable. Behavioral economics offers a perspective that identifies some of the main biases inherent in the demand for financial products. These biases, in turn, are at the root of some anomalies in financial products demand and, ultimately, constitute an objective justification for the need to increase consumer financial knowledge (Loerwald & Stemmann, 2016). The approach to savers and investors behaviors in retail financial markets using behavioral economics perspective allow not only assess the extent to which financial literacy can contribute to eliminating or at least correcting apparently irrational or anomalous behavior of financial products consumers, but also raise regulatory issues.

As far as the implications of financial literacy at a macro-level, economic theory has demonstrated the importance of both financial intermediaries and financial markets as drivers of economic growth (King & Levine, 1993; Levine, 1997). Financial literacy has the potential to impact the economic growth to the extent that it contributes both to personal saving and to the development of the financial sector. In particular, the scope of the financial system contribution is mainly linked to their role as a channel of savings towards productive investment and as a driver to the efficient allocation of capital. However, the optimal performance of these functions requires, among other things, that participants in financial markets (i.e. buyers of financial products) make informed decisions and, to this end, it is essential that they have a certain financial literacy.

Financial knowledge becomes an issue particularly important at a time characterized by the availability of a wide range of increasingly complex financial products in the retail financial markets. Moreover, in the wake of the last global financial crisis, the costs of financial illiteracy and its distributional effects has emerged as one of the main concerns for policymakers. Given that financial literacy is low not only in less developed countries but also advanced economies with well-developed financial markets (Lusardi, 2019), and taking into account the substantial changes both in the economic and financial environment, improvement in population's financial literacy levels has become a social priority. In this context, policymakers, financial regulators, supervisors, and financial institutions have a key role to play in the task of providing financial education with the aim that people can make informed financial decisions.

In short, the analysis developed in this chapter is intended to emphasize how financial education and financial literacy can contribute to mitigating the possible negative effects for the consumer resulting from the existence of market failures (i.e. imperfect and asymmetric information) in retail financial markets. The most relevant aspect of this approach is that, ultimately, the progress made in this area will result in an improvement in consumer welfare.

Overall, the contents of this chapter emphasize that citizens need a better understanding of financial concepts, financial products and of how the financial system works so that they can better manage their investments, their mortgage or consumer debts or save effectively for retirement. In this sense, a growing number of governments have recognized that they must help people in this task, putting financial education on the public agenda.

The main topics covered in the chapter can be summarized as follows. The background section deals with the concept of financial literacy, the metrics most used in the literature to operationalize this concept and the main determining factors. The main focus of the chapter section outlines how financial knowledge can contribute to enhancing the results of personal financial management, and how, ultimately, results in more consistent savers and more responsible investors and debtors. Furthermore, in this section is summarized the empirical evidence available about the role played by financial literacy in promoting saving, wealth accumulating, financial inclusion and financial stability. Taking as a reference this empirical evidence, the solutions and recommendations section discusses the main challenges faced by policymakers when implementing initiatives aiming to improve financial literacy. Finally, some conclusions and future avenues of research are presented.

BACKGROUND

According to the OECD definition, financial literacy is "a combination of awareness, knowledge, skill, attitude, and behavior necessary to make sound financial decisions and ultimately achieve individual financial well-being." (OECD INFE, 2011, p.3). The S&P's Global Financial Literacy Survey defines financial literacy in a similar way as "the ability to understand essential financial concepts in making informed decisions about saving, investing and borrowing" (Klapper, Lusardi & van Oudheusden, 2015, p.4). In other words, following authors as Vitt, Anderson, Kent, Lyter, Siegenthaler and Ward (2000), financial literacy reflects an individual's ability to understand, analyze, manage, and communicate affairs related to personal finance. To summarize, Hastings, Madrian and Skimmyhorn (2013) noted that any definition of financial literacy, ultimately, encompass several sorts of knowledge (i.e of financial concepts and financial products), abilities (i.e. having the numeracy required for making optimal financial decisions), and attitudes (i.e. engagement financial planning).

Beyond any agreement on the definition, authors such us Calvet, Campbell, and Sodini (2009) reveal that the best way to measure financial literacy in practice is subject to some controversy. On the one hand, the most traditional metrics try to test financial knowledge using a battery of standard questions about some economic and financial concepts. On the other hand, other kinds of measures focus on measuring participation in a course, curriculum, or seminar developed to provide financial education.

In practice, most of the studies dealing with financial literacy often measure this concept taking as a starting point several multiple-choice questions that evaluate respondents' knowledge about basic concepts such as knowledge of numeracy, interest rates, inflation, and risk diversification. In Appendix 1, the researchers provide an example of one of the standard set of questions most widely used in the academic literature that investigated issues related to financial literacy. This set includes the three questions chosen by Lusardi and Mitchell (2011). Another example of metric used to measure financial literacy is the S&P's Global Financial Literacy Survey that includes four questions that measure as many essential concepts for making financial decisions. In this case, a respondent is considered financially literate if she responds correctly at least three out of the four questions. The answers to this kind of questions have become a conventional instrument to generate scores and indexes that allow assessing levels of financial literacy across countries around the world.

An overview of data relative to the population levels of financial literacy allows observing a wide range of variation in financial literacy among countries around the world (see table 1). Based on the S&P's Global Financial Literacy Survey (2014 data), about 33 percent of the world's adult's population can be considered as financially literate. Thus, the rest of the adult population, around 3.5 billion, would have very limited financial capabilities. In a context characterized by the growing availability and complexity of financial products, the population financial literacy has become a matter of special concern for policymakers.

Most of the adults showing a lack of an understanding of basic financial concepts live in developing countries. For instance, only in one country in Africa (no country in South America) more than half of the people are considered financially literate. By contrast, advanced economies exhibit the highest levels of financial literacy.

Europe shows the highest wide-ranging differences in financial literacy. There are countries in Scandinavia, particularly Norway and Sweden with the highest scores. Within the European Union, Denmark, Germany, the Netherlands, and Sweden have the highest literacy rates. Conversely, rates of financial literacy are

The Economic and Social Value of Financial Literacy

Table 1. Adults financially Literate (%)

ECONOMY	ADULTS FINANCIALLY LITERATE	ECONOMY	ADULTS FINANCIALLY LITERATE	ECONOMY	ADULTS FINANCIALLY LITERATE
Denmark	71	Tanzania	40	Argentina	28
Norway	71	Ukraine	40	China	28
Sweden	71	Zambia	40	Peru	28
Canada	68	Lithuania	39	Bos & Herz	27
Israel	68	Mauritius	39	Egypt	27
U. Kingdom	67	Belarus	38	Iraq	27
Germany	66	Cameroon	38	Moldova	27
Netherlands	66	Kenya	38	Namibia	27
Australia	64	Madagascar	38	Panama	27
Finland	63	Russia	38	Thailand	27
New Zealand	61	Serbia	38	Chad	26
Singapore	59	Togo	38	Guatemala	26
Czech Repu	58	UAE	38	Nigeria	26
Switzerland	57	Benin	37	Pakistan	26
United States	57	Italy	37	Portugal	26
Belgium	55	Taiwan	37	Rwanda	26
Ireland	55	Azerbaijan	36	Philippines	25
Bhutan	54	Malaysia	36	Venezuela	25
Estonia	54	Brazil	35	W. B. & Gaza	25
Hungary	54	Bulgaria	35	Bolivia	24
Austria	53	Costa Rica	35	Burundi	24
Luxembourg	53	Cyprus	35	Jordan	24
Botswana	52	Côte d'Ivoire	35	Turkey	24
France	52	Dominican Re	35	Vietnam	24
Myanmar	52	Gabon	35	Honduras	23
Spain	49	Malawi	35	Romania	22
Latvia	48	Sri Lanka	35	El Salvador	21
Montenegro	48	Uganda	34	Macedonia	21
Slovak Republic	48	Algeria	33	Sierra Leone	21
Greece	45	Belize	33	Sudan	21
Tunisia	45	Burkina Faso	33	Uzbekistan	21
Uruguay	45	Jamaica	33	Iran	20
Croatia	44	Korea, Rep.	33	Kosovo	20
Kuwait	44	Mali	33	Nicaragua	20
Lebanon	44	Mauritania	33	Bangladesh	19
Malta	44	Colombia	32	Kyrgyz Rep	19
Slovenia	44	Congo	32	Armenia	18
HK, China	43	Ethiopia	32	Cambodia	18
Japan	43	Ghana	32	Haiti	18
Poland	42	Indonesia	32	Nepal	18
South Africa	42	Mexico	32	Tajikistan	17
Chile	41	Puerto Rico	32	Angola	15
Mongolia	41	Congo, Rep.	31	Somalia	15
Turkmenistan	41	Niger	31	Afghanistan	14

continued on following page

203

Table 1 continued

ECONOMY	ADULTS FINANCIALLY LITERATE	ECONOMY	ADULTS FINANCIALLY LITERATE	ECONOMY	ADULTS FINANCIALLY LITERATE
Zimbabwe	41	Saudi Arabia	31	Albania	14
Bahrain	40	Ecuador	30	Yemen	13
Kazakhstan	40	Georgia	30		
Senegal	40	Guinea	30		

Source: S&P's Global Financial Literacy Survey (2014 data)

considerably lower in economies of southern Europe. Countries as Greece, Spain, Italy, and Portugal have some of the lowest literacy rates.

According to quantitative evidence provided by OECD on knowledge, behavior, and attitudes, there is a wide scope for improving the levels of financial literacy across the G20 countries, because a substantial part of the population of this group of countries lacks basic financial knowledge (OECD, 2017).

With regard to the factors determining financial literacy, some authors such as Skagerlund, Lind, Strömbäck, Tinghög and Västfjäll (2018) have analysed the potential impact of cognitive and emotional factors in financial literacy. Furthermore, Mouna and Anis (2017) investigated the sociodemographic determinants and they found evidence showing that financial literacy level is affected by factors such as age, education level, and the annual income.

For instance, one of the most significant results are the differences between men and women. Particularly, according to the most recent OECD data for the G20 countries, the percentage of men and women who attain the minimum score required for financial literacy is 11 percentage points.

Overall, data reveal that women and the poor usually have lower financial literacy. In this sense, empirical evidence provided by Delavande, Rohwedder and Willis (2008) shows, on the one hand, that women score lower levels of financial literacy than men. On the other hand, these authors find that financial literacy increase with income and age. However, at an aggregate level, it is not possible to establish a close correlation between financial literacy and poverty. For instance, countries like Russia and China with very few extremely poor people also have extremely low financial literacy rates.

When analyzing aggregate data to deepen the relationship between income and financial literacy across countries, the most recent results drawn from the S&P's Global Financial Literacy Survey revealed that, in general, financial literacy tend to be higher in countries with higher GDP per capita levels. However, this relationship only holds in the case of the richest half of economies. For this group of countries, more than a third of the differences in financial literacy rates can be attributed to differences in income across countries. By contrast, for the poorest 50 percent of economies, there is no evidence of a correlation between income and financial literacy. This result can be interpreted as evidence that in these economies other factors such for instance national-level policies related to education and consumer protection are more relevant as a determinant of financial literacy levels.

MAIN FOCUS OF THE CHAPTER

The objective of this chapter is twofold. On the one hand, to analyze how financial literacy contributes to improve the economic outcomes of individuals' financial decisions and their well-being. On the other hand, to deal with the role played by financial literacy at a macro-level paying attention to its effects on saving, wealth inequality, financial inclusion and financial stability.

Behavioral Biases and Financial Decisions

Empirical evidence shows that financial literacy has a positive influence on saving, investment behavior, debt management and borrowing practices (Lusardi, 2019). This positive effect might be partially related to the fact that one of the main reasons by which individuals make sub-optimal decisions: behavioral biases.

From an analytical point of view, behavioral economics identifies several contexts in which individuals suffer from cognitive biases that lead them to make decisions that, according to the assumptions of rational choice theory, would be irrational. Cognitive biases have their origin in basic statistical, information-processing, or memory errors and they are, usually, consequence of a faulty reasoning. Although biases have an influence on consumer choices in a wide range of markets, cognitive biases are particularly likely to impact decisions in retail financial markets. Several reasons explain this especial incidence in this specific area (Campbell, Jackson, Madrian & Tufano, 2011; de Meza, Irlenbusch & Reyniers, 2008). For instance, most consumers find financial products complex (Benartzi & Thaler, 2001; Huberman & Jiang, 2006), many financial decisions require assessing risk and uncertainty and require making trade-offs between the present and the future. Additionally, many of this kind of decisions have an emotional suffer from emotional biases that stem from impulse or intuition.

The role played by economics and financial behavioral as analytical tools that allow identifying the above mentioned typical irrationalities is relevant to the extent they contribute to avoiding most common mistakes in financial decision making. Behavioral economics helps us to understand how these errors when choosing and using financial products rise, why they persist, and what can be done to avoid them. It is also important to know how firms benefit of to these consumers' mistakes because this allows the policymakers to focus on the key issue of consumer protection in retail financial markets, an environment in which participants are particularly exposed to biases. In this sense, it is worth noting that insurance is one of the sectors in which financial literacy may have a greater impact on insurers' well-being. Particularly, the development of insurance awareness allows consumers to avoid some of the anomalies that characterize the insurance demand (Kunreuther, Pauly & McMorrow, 2013).

Behavioral finance offers some explanations of how the most common biases, anomalies, and heuristics impact on the quality of the decisions made by consumers in retail financial markets. In this line, and in order to get a better understanding both of the nature and the scope of these problems, Loerwald and Stemmann (2016), systematize the main biases, anomalies, and heuristics taking as a reference, the phases of a decision-making process. Following the approach of these authors, three phases could be identified:

First, in the information perception phase, arise the framing bias or the phenomenon of selective perception. Second, in the information processing and evaluation phase, appear anchoring and adjustment heuristic, ambiguity aversion or overconfidence bias with the phenomenon of the illusion of control. Finally, in the phase of decision making, individuals are exposed to the reflection effect, hindsight bias, loss aversion, or the self-control bias.[1]

Within this framework, a key issue is to assess the influence of financial literacy and behavioral biases on investors' behavior. Authors as Altman (2012) argue that financial education can play a crucial role through the development of appropriate learning mechanisms aimed to teach to the students the relevant anomalies, biases, and heuristics. Furthermore, financial education can also teach strategies for preventing the above-mentioned biases. In the same line, de Meza et al. (2008) based on the results of research developed in the fields of psychology and behavioral economics describe some debiasing techniques which would enable individuals to recognize biases and to make optimal financial decisions. This is especially relevant for users of financial products because for most of them, is difficult to learn about them. Moreover, some financial decisions (i.e taking out a mortgage, subscribe to life insurance or retirement planning) are infrequent and the results (costs or returns) are known only after a long time. Additionally, the optimality of some decisions depends on macroeconomic circumstances that usually are beyond the knowledge of consumers. In addition to the above, it should be noted that as most people are reluctant to talk about personal financial affairs, the opportunities to learn from others are very limited

The Economic and Social Value of Financial Literacy

Financial Literacy and Personal Finance Management

A growing body of academic literature has reported many potential benefits for individuals derived from financial literacy. Overall, empirical evidence suggest that financial literacy appears to be linked to better personal financial decision making and, ultimately, with better financial outcomes. Therefore, the role of financial literacy as a determinant of individual well-being should not be under-estimated.

For instance, the findings of authors such as Lusardi and Mitchell (2007a, 2007b), Sekita (2011) or van Rooij, Lusardi and Alessie (2012) show that individuals endowed with higher levels of financial literacy have a better performance in retirement planning. People financially literate are also less likely to have excessive debt (Lusardi & Tufano, 2015) and are more likely to participate in financial markets (van Rooij, Lusardi & Alessie, 2011) having portfolios more diversified (Calvet et al, 2009; Abreu & Mendes, 2010; von Gaudecker, 2015). Moreover, Deuflhard, Georgarakos and Inderst (2018) found that financial literacy appears also associated to higher returns on deposit accounts and to a greater willingness to withdraw deposits from troubled banks (Brown, Henchoz & Spycher, 2018).

Regarding stock market participation, van Rooij et al., (2011), using different measures of financial literacy show that lack of financial knowledge is a significant deterrent to stock ownership and stock market participation. More specifically, Hastings et al (2013) found that individuals with higher levels of financial literacy paid lower fees for mutual funds. The negative impact of this kind of cost on the net return of such investments can be sizable. This evidence reveals that financial literacy boosts investors' net returns and, as Cocco, Gomes and Maenhout (2005) have made it clear, this has significant consequences for individuals because the welfare loss of not participating in the stock market can be substantial.

In a similar vein, authors such as von Gaudecker (2015), using Dutch data identifies portfolio under diversification as one of the main mistakes made by households with lower levels of financial knowledge because it is potentially costly for households. Particularly, this author shows that households with high scores on financial knowledge or those that rely on professionals or personal contacts for advice obtain reasonable returns on their investments. By contrast, households with relatively low levels of financial literacy that make the decisions for themselves achieve poorer outcomes on average. These findings are consistent with the evidence showing that financially savvy persons usually achieve greater wealth accumulation (Lusardi, Michaud, and Mitchell, 2017). This kind of findings is no negligible because these differences in net returns can cause sizable levels of inequality in wealth.

Another implication of financial literacy is that, in general, financial literacy and retirement planning are closely correlated. Indeed, high financial skills are associated with greater retirement planning and also with greater wealth accumulation at the retirement stage (Lusardi and Mitchell, 2014). This result has to do with the fact that people financially literate have more information about pension system rules, they also incur in lower investment fees when managing their retirement accounts, and they implement better strategies of diversification of their pension assets (Hastings et al, 2013).

Moving on to the household liability management, empirical evidence suggests several patterns in behaviour of people less informed and with low levels of financial literacy. For instance, Moore (2003) found evidence that people with low levels of financial literacy are more likely to take out costly mortgages. Moreover, Campbell (2006) noted that it is less likely that they refinance their mortgages when interest rates fall. This kind of findings was corroborated by Mottola (2013), who provided evidence suggesting that the least financially literate engage more frequently in high-cost credit card behaviour. More recently, Lusardi and Tufano (2015) showed that financial illiterate people also spend more on transaction costs, pay higher fees and use high-cost borrowing methods. These authors also show that a lack of understanding of basic financial concepts is behind a bigger debt burden and an inability to evaluate debt positions. In short, the most significant costs associated with financial ignorance include that consumers end up borrowing more, save less money and, ultimately, accumulate less wealth (Stango and Zinman, 2009).

An additional aspect to be taken into account has to do with the consequences of a lack of financial literacy on the demand for financial advice. The last global financial crisis has brought two clear consequences for financial advice: a loss of confidence in the traditional banking system and an increase in savers' requirements. These facts have led to the emergence of new figures dedicated to advising, which are only intermediaries, that is, independent financial advisory companies.

Although financial culture differs across countries, banks, savings banks or insurance companies still account for a high percentage of the advice. Within this context, the investor must understand that independent advice has an added value because if the advisor also sells financial products, as is the case with banks, there is a conflict of interest. That is, instead of offering the best financial product according to a profile, as an interested party will try to place its products. In this line, Calcagno and Monticone (2015) evaluated how investors' financial literacy affects their decision to demand professional advice. On the one hand, they found that investors with a low level of financial literacy are less likely to consult an advisor. Indeed, financial advisors provide more information to financially literate investors. To the extent that this latter kind of investors anticipates this, it is more likely that they demand financial advice when making decisions. On the other hand, those authors also concluded that to rely on non-independent advisors is not sufficient to mitigate the costs of low financial literacy.

Finally, to complement the aforementioned considerations, it should be noted that authors such as Agarwal, Driscoll, Gabaix and Laibson (2009) reported further evidence showing that mistakes in making financial decisions are more common among the young and elderly, the age segments that, in turn, have the lowest scores of financial literacy. However, increasing financial literacy has significant benefits for all citizens, current or potential users of financial products and services, regardless of age and income level. Life is full of financially important decisions (the formation of a family, the acquisition of a house, the purchase of a car, retirement) and it is important that all citizens, faced with these decisions, can be aware of their financial consequences and learn to evaluate them.

At this point, it should be noted that in spite of the abovementioned association between financial literacy and individual behaviour, it is difficult to establish a causal relationship, mainly because this correlation might be a result of the impact of other factors, such as individual cognitive ability (Skagerlund et al, 2018).

Financial Literacy, Saving, Wealth Accumulation and Inequality

Among the benefits of financial literacy at the aggregate level, its effects on savings deserve special mention. There is a growing body of literature dealing with the links between retirement planning, saving, and financial literacy. From a theoretical point of view, financial development promotes saving by raising the efficiency of financial intermediation and creating savings vehicles. In King and Levine (1993) and Levine (1997) can be found a complete analysis of this relationship, both from the theoretical and empirical point of view. The impact of financial development on savings and investment behaviour partially depends on people's financial literacy. Indeed, financial literacy would boost economic growth by promoting both savings and financial development (Bayar, Sezgin & Öztürk, 2017).

Evidence supporting the role of financial literacy as a driver of personal saving can be found in a wide range of works. Jappelli and Padula (2013) provide empirical evidence showing that economies with higher rates of financial literacy save more. Authors such Bernheim, Garrett and Maki (2001), Prusty (2011), Beckmann (2013) also provide evidence supporting a statistically and economically meaningful association between financial literacy and saving.

For instance, Bernheim and Garrett (2003) have verified that receiving financial education in high school and the workplace has a favourable influence on people's saving inclination. In the same line, Lusardi and Mitchell (2007a, 2007b) and Hilgert, Hogarth and Beverly (2003) demonstrated the existence of a direct link between financial knowledge levels and the likelihood to plan for retirement. As a consequence, people with low financial literacy accumulate less wealth. This relationship is corroborated by Stango and Zinman (2007), who argue that people who are not able to calculate interest rates from a flow of payments will end up accumulating higher levels of debt and lower levels of wealth.

The academic literature provides several explanations for the impact of financial literacy on wealth accumulation (Lusardi & Mitchell, 2014). For instance, as we have previously pointed out, there is evidence showing that people with higher financial knowledge are more prone to plan for retirement. One of the possible reasons that are behind this behaviour is that financially savvy people benefit from a better understanding the implications of interest compounding and, moreover, they are endowed with greater skills for doing calculations (Delavande et al, 2008). According to a model developed by Lusardi et al (2017), financial literacy allows individuals to optimize the allocation of their lifetime resources in contexts characterized by uncertainty and imperfect insurance. One of the main predictions derived from this model is that financial literacy emerges as a significant driver of wealth inequality. Thus, this relationship between financial literacy and wealth accumulation has implications in distributive terms.

In a similar vein, Lo Petre (2013) emphasizes how economic literacy mediates the relationship between finance and inequality. Particularly, empirical evidence provided by this author shows that income inequality growth is lower in countries where economic literacy is higher. Moreover, financial development only contributes to reduce inequality growth when it is accompanied by economic literacy. This is a consequence of the growing complexity of financial products that is associated with financial development. In such a context, the ability to take advantage from investment opportunities depends on economic literacy. This result is in line with Lusardi et al (2017), who concluded that a high proportion of wealth inequality might be explained by the fact that financial knowledge helps people to make investments more sophisticated and with higher returns.

Another relevant finding of the research is that some segments of the population, particularly, people with both low education and income levels exhibit different saving patterns, especially when compared to better educated and more affluent households. This finding is important because underlines the need for design specific programs adjusted to the needs of disadvantaged segments and that contribute to overcoming the barriers to saving they face. In this sense, authors such as Schreiner, Clancy and Sherraden, (2002) reported evidence of some targeted programs that have been implemented in practice and that have been relatively successful in promoting saving among the poor.

Despite the above-mentioned evidence supporting the existence of a positive relationship between financial literacy and saving, as Jappelli and Padula (2013) pointed out, it has not yet been possible to demonstrate that this relation is causal. Indeed, both variables depend on other factors such as preference parameters, households' resources, and the costs of literacy.

Financial Literacy and Financial Inclusion

The concept of financial inclusion refers to the possibility of individuals and firms to access to financial products that meet their needs (i.e. transactions, payments, savings, credit, and insurance). In many countries around the world, particularly, in developing economies, financial inclusion is a means of reducing poverty and strengthening the well-being and local economy. In some countries, lack of financial inclusion is a serious problem as can be seen from the data of the last available wave of The Global Findex according to which 1,7 billion adults in the world remained unbanked in 2017 (Demirgüç-Kunt, Klapper, Singer, Ansar, & Hess, 2018).

Existing evidence suggests that financial inclusion is closely related to economic growth and inequality (Demirgüç-Kunt, Klapper & Singer, 2017). More specifically, academic research dealing with financial inclusion reports works reported some positive effects derived from increasing financial inclusion. For instance, financial inclusion reduces poverty in rural environments and increases employment, expenditures, and savings (Burgess & Pande, 2005; Dupas & Robinson, 2013; Bruhn & Love, 2014; Brune, Giné, Goldberg & Yang (2016). Therefore, an improvement in financial inclusion can have important welfare effects on the economy.

Within this context, it becomes especially interesting to investigate if financial literacy has any influence in financial inclusion. Recently, Grohmann, Klühs and Menkhoff (2018) have conducted a very comprehensive empirical research dealing with the association between financial literacy and financial inclusion. These authors approach financial inclusion using four variables: (i) the percentage of the population in a country that has a bank account at a financial institution, (ii) the proportion of adults holding a debit card, (iii) the proportion of the population that use a bank account to save, and (iv) the percentage of the population that having a debit card made use of it during the last year. The first two variables just measure access to financial services, and the last two variables aim to measure the use of financial services.

The authors' justification for the choice of the aforementioned variables can be summarized as follows. First, a bank account facilitates the completion of financial transactions. Moreover, bank accounts enable individuals to hold and handle money more easily and safely. Hence, with this variable is possible to approach the most basic form of financial inclusion. Second, a debit card provides undoubted benefits to its holder. Indeed, it is both a more convenient and safer form of payment than cash. Third, the main benefits that bank customers obtain from saving at a financial institution have to do with safety reasons. Moreover, this saving method can contribute to impulse control to the extent that money immediately available. Finally, a condition for people to benefit from having debit cards is to use them.

Logically, the above mentioned proxies of financial inclusion are expected to be positively influenced by financial literacy, mainly because making complex financial decisions requires a reasonable level of financial knowledge. Grohmann et al (2018) provide direct evidence that confirms this relationship.

Furthermore, given that financial inclusion also depends on the financial infrastructure, Grohmann et al (2018) analyze the interaction between financial literacy and financial depth and how this interaction influence access to and use of financial services. Their results show that improving financial literacy would favor account ownership. This impact is more significant in economies where financial depth is very limited. In fact, in such a context, remarkable progress in financial education could compensate for low development of financial infrastructure. These results suggest that financial education could be a powerful instrument of financial development and it could be a good complement to the most traditional policy focused on developing financial infrastructure.

Financial Literacy, Financial Markets Efficiency and Financial Stability

In modern economies, financial markets are essential for promoting economic efficiency. Financial markets contribute to the efficient allocation of financial resources (capital), which in turn favors an increase in aggregate output and greater efficiency for the economy as a whole.

In practice, efficient, stable and sound financial markets provide financial services of quality. A necessary condition to make these benefits effective is that individual participants in financial markets must understand the most basic and relevant financial concepts and principles. For this reason, it is important to offer financial education and to ensure financial literacy for all financial market participants.

The task of properly managing and distributing the financial resources of individuals and households is increasingly complex and the skills and knowledge required are greater than in previous generations. Indeed, the last global financial crisis has caused severe losses that could have been prevented or at least mitigated if people were financially literate.

Furthermore, Šoškić (2011) argues that one of the main motives by which financial literacy and financial education are important has to do with the fact that these variables are key to build confidence, which is a prerequisite to financial stability. Moreover, financial education increases awareness of risk, thus contributing to financial stability, reducing non-performance rates and favoring more diversified and therefore safer savings and investment. So, people had a higher level of financial knowledge, the crisis would probably have been less-deep and less far-reaching.

Buch (2018) discusses the association between financial literacy and financial stability. This author notes that although financial literacy by itself may not guarantee financial stability, lack of it can be an important factor behind financial instabilities. Investors with low levels of financial knowledge may take on excessive risk and assume more risks than they could afford. This individual behavior may generate systemic problems, particularly under two kinds of circumstances. These problems may arise, first, when there are common exposures to the same risk factor and, second, when risks are concentrated in a particular group of financial intermediaries or financial market segments. So, all participants in financial markets may have adequate levels of financial knowledge, but at the same time, they likely neglect the effects of their behavior on the functioning and stability of the financial system as a whole. Moreover, financial knowledge does not prevent participants in financial markets to make mistakes in forecasting future market developments.

A clear example of a factor that is behind the generation of systemic risks to financial stability are housing market bubbles. Crowe, Dell'Ariccia, Deniz and Rabanal (2013) reported that on the one hand, housing market booms preceded most of the banking crises, and, on the other hand, most of the housing market collapses are followed by a financial crisis. Moreover, financial crises associated to unsustainable developments in housing markets were more damaging when the market inflation was financed by a large growth of credit that led to excessive levels of leverage of private households and other participants in housing markets (Jordà, Schularick & Taylor, 2015). In particular, for the US case, Gerardi, Goette and Meier (2013) argued that lack of borrowers' numeracy could explain partially the high rates of mortgages defaults observed in the last financial crisis. In this context, financial education and financial literacy could contribute to reducing the probability of mortgage defaults.

In short, although the origin and propagation of a financial crisis cannot be attributed to a single cause, the role played for financial illiteracy concerning credit and investment seems undeniable. Nevertheless, this does not mean to neglect that financial institutions, experts and regulators with their actions and decisions unquestionably must carry most of the responsibility as triggers of the most recent financial crisis.

Financial Literacy and Labor Markets

Financial literacy is not only important for financial markets functioning but also for labor markets. Several reasons explain such relevance. For instance, Michaud (2017) emphasizes three motives. First, workers without basic financial knowledge are more exposed to have financial problems. The stress produced by these problems may have potential negative impacts in terms of absenteeism and work productivity. Second, if workers cannot undertake complex economic calculations, they may be compelled to extend their working life to achieve the same level of retirement income. The reason for this is that they probably were unable to save for retirement or they have saved inefficiently, investing in low-return financial assets. Third, workers with high standards of financial knowledge are more enabled to grasp a company's financial position, something, particularly important in a vulnerable environment. This better understanding may contribute also to attain more reasonable outcomes for both companies and workers in the process of collective bargaining.

SOLUTIONS AND RECOMMENDATIONS

Given the large empirical evidence showing the limited financial capabilities of the general public across, policymakers should take into account that the initiatives aimed to increase the financial literacy may to contribute in a significant way to the individuals' wellbeing and also to the social welfare.

From the economic theory perspective, policy interventions would be justified when they contribute to correct market failures. Among the market failures that emerge in retail financial markets are externalities, information asymmetries or market power. In an environment characterized by those market failures, many consumers are in a disadvantaged situation and public interventions can help them to make optimal financial decisions and to attain better financial outcomes.

Particularly, the complexity of some of the financial products, the problems of imperfect and asymmetric information, cognitive and emotional biases with the consequent anomalies in demand are some of the elements that make up a scenario in which the treatment given to information, transparency, and advice occupies a prevalent place as issues to be addressed through financial regulation.

Financial education aims precisely to ensure the existence of a population endowed with the necessary knowledge and skills to make sound financial decisions throughout their lives and to know their rights and obligations as users of financial products. Financial literacy (e.g., as studied by Lusardi and Mitchell, 2014) is a necessary condition for effective financial disclosure, an aspect especially relevant for low-income households. With the aim of protecting consumers with low financial knowledge, the policymakers should implement more strict regulations in terms of transparency and the requirements to sell specific products.

Policy debates about the need for public intervention and its effectiveness have received especial attention of both academics and practitioners in the aftermath of the last global financial crisis. Within the framework of these discussions, financial education emerges as an indispensable tool for the authorities concerned with the protection of financial users. Furthermore, financial education complements the traditional regulation and supervision of the solvency and conducts of institutions, and ultimately contributes to financial stability.

Although one of the objectives of public interventions is address the problems associated with behavioral biases, authors as Lusardi et al (2017) developed a model that allows explaining why financial education programs may not work well as drivers of significant changes in individuals' behavior. Ineffectiveness of this kind of programs becomes particularly clear for individuals that find it suboptimal to invest in financial knowledge.

A specific field in which becomes especially relevant to improve the quality of households financial decisions is the buying and financing of a house. For a great number of households this is one of the most important financial decisions. Taking into account what previously mentioned in this chapter about the relationship between the housing market and financial instability, it becomes clear that the improvement of financial literacy related to financing a house can reduce the likelihood of financial crisis triggered by excessive indebtedness of households (Buch, 2018).

This is also a context that allows emphasizing some of the limitations of policy interventions aimed to enhance the population's financial literacy. Among this limitations it worth to note that even in the case that public intervention increase financial culture, this does not solve the problem of negative externalities that individual decisions generate for the financial system as a whole. That's why macroprudential policies focused on the housing market are thus required. No then, the effectiveness of this kind of regulations will depend on the levels of households' financial literacy. This rationale could be extended to any other markets in which excessive credit can be a troubling issue. Indeed, financial regulation and financial education should be considered as complements rather than substitutes.

The awareness of the importance of promoting final literacy has led to international organizations, governments, central banks or even private financial institutions to design and implement diverse strategies. However, a potential problem is that such interventions are often ineffective. In this sense, policymakers should promote the formulation of specific education programs and pay high attention to the monitoring and assessment of their effectiveness (Michaud, 2017). Moreover, financial education programs must be targeted taking into account the singularities that characterize the diverse segments of population (i.e. differences by genre, age, education or income).

Policymakers should also assume that financial inclusion is an important goal of economic and financial development. Under this premise, public policies that promote financial inclusion can contribute to attaining the Sustainable Development Goals (Klapper, El-Zoghbi & Hess, 2016). For that reason, policymakers should focus on factors that affect financial inclusion and, in particular, on how policies implemented to enhance financial literacy can affect those factors. In this sense, Grohmann el al (2018) provide solid evidence supporting the positive effect of increasing financial literacy on financial inclusion. According to the findings of these authors, for economies at early phases of financial development, the objective of increasing financial literacy can be an alternative to improve financial infrastructure. By contrast, in economies more financially developed, financial literacy contributes to making full use of available infrastructure.

High and growing levels of wealth inequality are a matter of concern for most of the today's societies, and financial knowledge plays a crucial role in shaping wealth inequality (Lusardi, Michaud & Mitchell, 2017). Hence, this is an additional reason that reinforces the recommendation of fostering financial education actively, starting at the earliest ages and being incorporated into educational plans. In particular, given that differences in financial literacy may exacerbate wealth inequality, early interventions may be an effective political tool to reduce wealth inequality.

FUTURE RESEARCH DIRECTIONS

Future research can be developed following several directions. First, further analytical research is needed to get a better understanding of the relationship between individual decision making and aggregate outcomes. Second, better research must be developed with the aim of informing the design of effective financial education interventions more tailored to target groups. Particularly, more empirical evidence is required in order get an optimal allocation of financial education resources. Third, further efforts are needed to obtain better metrics of both financial literacy and financial education. Four, additional experimental research focused on the nature of the causality between financial literacy and economic well-being would be also welcomed, because, although the empirical evidence available suggests that financial literacy impacts financial decision making, from a methodological point of view is difficult to verify the existence of a causal relationship between financial literacy and individuals' economic behavior. Five, future research should address the role of the new technologies and fintech industry in enhancing financial literacy and the bias caused by financial literacy in the use of fintech in the individuals' money management. Finally, the future lines of research should also contribute to extending the analysis of the role of financial literacy beyond households' behavior to small and medium-sized enterprises (SMEs). In particular, it should be especially interesting to investigate to what extent financial knowledge can contribute to enhancing the sustainability of SMEs.

CONCLUSION

The results of most of the studies addressing financial literacy reveal that financial illiteracy is a serious problem for a great number of countries and for specific segments of population. Indeed, the results serve to justify policy interventions and some particular policy recommendations. The analysis previously developed in this chapter has emphasized that lack of financial knowledge has negative consequences on both individual social levels. On the one hand, a low level of financial literacy put households a risk from making sub-optimal financial decisions and prevent them to maximize their well-being. On the other hand, as consumers of financial products, they will not exert the necessary pressure for promoting efficiency in financial markets. In this sense, financial literacy is becoming increasingly important, favoring a better allocation of resources, reducing the risks associated with episodes of financial instability and, therefore, contributing to the increase of social welfare. A solid financial literacy, therefore, helps individuals and households to take better advantage of opportunities, to achieve their goals and to contribute to the greater financial health of society as a whole.

To the extent that financial education contributes to reduce the probability of making mistakes when individuals choose and use financial products, it could be considered as a useful instrument to reduce the considerable losses associated with those mistakes. As a general conclusion regarding public intervention aimed to provide financial education to general public, it should be noted that it is necessary to analyze the effectiveness of the different initiatives based on accumulated experience to rationalize the use of the available resources, giving continuity to the most effective actions and proposing new strategies in the fields with the highest potential for improvement.

Finally, it should be noted that the debate about the role that should play financial regulation and financial education continues still open, but there is a certain degree of consensus about that financial regulation and financial education are complementary tools of consumer protection.

ACKNOWLEDGMENT

This research received no specific grant from any funding agency in the public, commercial, or not-for-profit sectors.

REFERENCES

Abreu, M., & Mendes, V. (2010). Financial Literacy and Portfolio Diversification. *Quantitative Finance, 10*(5), 515–528. doi:10.1080/14697680902878105

Agarwal, S., Driscoll, J., Gabaix, X., & Laibson, D. (2009). The age of reason: Financial decisions over the lifecycle. *Brookings Papers on Economic Activity, 2009*, 51–101. doi:10.1353/eca.0.0067

Altman, M. (2012). Implications of behavioural economics for financial literacy and public policy. *Journal of Behavioral and Experimental Economics, 41*(5), 677–690.

Bayar, M. Y., Sezgin, H. F., & Öztürk, O. F. (2017). Impact of Financial Literacy on Personal Savings: A Research on Usak University Staff. *Journal of Knowledge Management. Economics and Information Technology, 7*(6), 1–19.

Beckmann, E. (2013). Financial Literacy and Household Savings in Romania. *Numeracy, 6*(2), 1–22. doi:10.5038/1936-4660.6.2.9

Benartzi, S., & Thaler, R. H. (2001). Naive Diversification Strategies in Defined Contribution Savings Plans. *The American Economic Review, 91*(1), 79–98. doi:10.1257/aer.91.1.79

Bernheim, D., Garrett, D., & Maki, D. (2001). Education and saving: The long-term effects of high school financial curriculum mandates. *Journal of Public Economics, 85*(3), 435–565. doi:10.1016/S0047-2727(00)00120-1

Brown, M., Henchoz, C., & Spycher, T. (2018). Culture and Financial Literacy: Evidence from a within-country language border. *Journal of Economic Behavior & Organization, 150*(1), 62–85. doi:10.1016/j.jebo.2018.03.011

Bruhn, M., & Love, I. (2014). The Real Impact of Improved Access to Finance: Evidence from Mexico. *The Journal of Finance, 69*(3), 1347–1369. doi:10.1111/jofi.12091

Brune, L., Giné, X., Goldberg, J., & Yang, D. (2016). Facilitating Savings for Agriculture: Field Experimental Evidence from Malawi. *Economic Development and Cultural Change, 64*(2), 187–220. doi:10.1086/684014

Buch, C. M. (2018). *Financial Literacy and Financial Stability*. Speech prepared for the 5th OECD-GFLEC Global Policy Research Symposium to Advance Financial Literacy, Paris, France.

Burgess, R., & Pande, R. (2005). Do Rural Banks Matter? Evidence from the Indian Social Banking Experiment. *The American Economic Review*, *95*(3), 780–795. doi:10.1257/0002828054201242

Calcagno, R., & Monticone, C. (2015). Financial literacy and the demand for financial advice. *Journal of Banking & Finance*, *50*, 363–380. doi:10.1016/j.jbankfin.2014.03.013

Calvet, L. E., Campbell, J. Y., & Sodini, P. (2009). Measuring the financial sophistication of households. *The American Economic Review*, *99*(2), 393–398. doi:10.1257/aer.99.2.393 PMID:29504738

Campbell, J. Y. (2006). Household Finance. *The Journal of Finance*, *61*(4), 1553–1604. doi:10.1111/j.1540-6261.2006.00883.x

Campbell, J. Y., Jackson, H. E., Madrian, B. C., & Tufano, P. (2011). Consumer Financial Protection. *The Journal of Economic Perspectives*, *25*(1), 91–113. doi:10.1257/jep.25.1.91 PMID:24991083

Cocco, J., Gomes, F., & Maenhout, P. (2005). Consumption and portfolio choice over the lifecycle. *Review of Financial Studies*, *18*(2), 490–533. doi:10.1093/rfs/hhi017

Crowe, Ch., Dell'Ariccia, G., Deniz, I., & Rabanal, P. (2013). How to deal with real estate booms: Lessons from country experiences. *Journal of Financial Stability*, *9*(3), 300–319. doi:10.1016/j.jfs.2013.05.003

de Meza, D., Irlenbusch, B., & Reyniers, D. (2008). *Financial capability: a behavioural economics perspective*. FSA Consumer Research Paper 69.

Delavande, A., Rohwedder, S., & Willis, R. (2008). *Preparation for Retirement, Financial Literacy and Cognitive Resources*. University of Michigan Retirement Research Center Working Paper 2008-190.

Demirguc-Kunt, A., Klapper, L., & Singer, D. (2017). *Financial Inclusion and Inclusive Growth – A Review of Recent Empirical Evidence*. World Bank Policy Research Paper, No. 8040.

Demirgüç-Kunt, A., Klapper, L., Singer, D., Ansar, S., & Hess, J. (2018). *The Global Findex Database 2017: Measuring Financial Inclusion and the Fintech Revolution*. Washington, DC: World Bank. doi:10.1596/978-1-4648-1259-0

Deuflhard, F., Georgarakos, D., & Inderst, R. (2018). Financial literacy and savings account returns. *Journal of the European Economic Association*, *17*(1), 131–164. doi:10.1093/jeea/jvy003

Dupas, P., & Robinson, J. (2013). Savings Constraints and Microenterprise Development: Evidence from a Field Experiment in Kenya. *American Economic Journal. Applied Economics*, *5*(1), 163–192. doi:10.1257/app.5.1.163

Gerardi, K., Goette, L., & Meier, S. (2013). Numerical ability and mortgage default. *Proceedings of the National Academy of Sciences of the United States of America*, *110*(28), 11267–11271. doi:10.1073/pnas.1220568110 PMID:23798401

Grohmann, A., Klühs, T., & Menkhoff, L. (2018). Does financial literacy improve financial inclusion? Cross country evidence. *World Development*, *111*, 84–96. doi:10.1016/j.worlddev.2018.06.020

Hastings, J. S., Madrian, B. C., & Skimmyhorn, B. (2013). Financial Literacy, Financial Education, and Economic Outcomes. *Annual Review of Economics*, *5*(1), 347–373. doi:10.1146/annurev-economics-082312-125807 PMID:23991248

Hilgert, M., Hogarth, J., & Beverly, S. (2003). Household financial management: The connection between knowledge and behavior. *Federal Reserve Bulletin*, 309–322.

Huberman, G., & Jiang, W. (2006). Offering versus Choice in 401(k) Plans: Equity Exposure and Number of Funds. *The Journal of Finance*, *61*(2), 763–801. doi:10.1111/j.1540-6261.2006.00854.x

Jappelli, T., & Padula, M. (2013). Investment in Financial Literacy and Saving Decisions. *Journal of Banking & Finance*, *37*(8), 2779–2792. doi:10.1016/j.jbankfin.2013.03.019

Jordà, O., Schularick, M., & Taylor, A. M. (2015a). Leveraged bubbles. *Journal of Monetary Economics*, *76*(S), 1-20.

King, R. G., & Levine, R. (1993). Finance and growth: Schumpeter might be right. *The Quarterly Journal of Economics*, *108*(3), 717–737. doi:10.2307/2118406

Klapper, L., El-Zoghbi, M., & Hess, J. (2016). *Achieving the Sustainable Development Goals – The Role of Financial Inclusion*. CGAP Working Paper.

Klapper, L., Lusardi, A., & van Oudheusden, P. (2015). *Financial Literacy around the World. Insights from the Standard & Poors Ratings Services Global Financial Literacy Survey*. Retrieved from https://responsiblefinanceforum.org/wp-content/uploads/2015/12/2015-Finlit_paper_17_F3_SINGLES.pdf

Kunreuther, H., Pauly, M. V., & McMorrow, S. (2013). *Insurance and Behavioral Economics: Improving Decisions in the Most Misunderstood Industry*. Cambridge University Press.

Levine, R. (1997). Financial development and economic growth: Views and agenda. *Journal of Economic Literature*, *35*(2), 688–726.

Lo Petre, A. (2013). Economic literacy, inequality, and financial development. *Economics Letters*, *118*(1), 74–76. doi:10.1016/j.econlet.2012.09.029

Loerwald, D., & Stemmann, A. (2016). Behavioral Finance and Financial Literacy: Educational Implications of Biases in Financial Decision Making. In International Handbook of Financial Literacy. Springer Verlag. doi:10.1007/978-981-10-0360-8_3

Lusardi, A. (2019). Financial literacy and the need for financial education: Evidence and implications. *Schweizerische Zeitschrift für Volkswirtschaft und Statistik*, *155*(1).

Lusardi, A., Michaud, P. C., & Mitchell, O. S. (2017). Optimal Financial Knowledge and Wealth Inequality. *Journal of Political Economy*, *125*(2), 431–477. doi:10.1086/690950 PMID:28555088

Lusardi, A., & Mitchell, O. (2007a). Baby boomers retirement security: The role of planning, financial literacy and housing wealth. *Journal of Monetary Economics*, *54*(1), 205–224. doi:10.1016/j.jmoneco.2006.12.001

Lusardi, A., & Mitchell, O. (2007b). Financial literacy and retirement preparedness: Evidence and implications for financial education. *Business Economics (Cleveland, Ohio)*, *42*(1), 35–44. doi:10.2145/20070104

Lusardi, A., & Mitchell, O. (2011). Financial literacy around the world: An overview. *Journal of Pension Economics and Finance*, *10*(4), 497–508. doi:10.1017/S1474747211000448 PMID:28553190

Lusardi, A., & Mitchell, O. (2014). The Economic Importance of Financial Literacy: Theory and Evidence. *Journal of Economic Literature*, *52*(1), 5–44. doi:10.1257/jel.52.1.5 PMID:28579637

Lusardi, A., & Tufano, P. (2015). Debt Literacy, Financial Experiences, and Overindebtedness. *Journal of Pension Economics and Finance*, *14*(4), 332–368. doi:10.1017/S1474747215000232

Michaud, P. C. (2017). The value of financial literacy and financial education for workers. *IZA World of Labor*, *2017*, 400.

Moore, D. (2003). *Survey of Financial Literacy in Washington State: Knowledge, Behavior, Attitudes, and Experiences*. Washington State University Social and Economic Sciences Research Center Technical Report 03-39.

Mottola, G. R. (2013). In Our Best Interest: Women, Financial Literacy, and Credit Card Behavior. *Numeracy, 6*(2). Available at: http://scholarcommons.usf.edu/numeracy/vol6/iss2/art4

Mouna, A., & Anis, J. (2017). Financial literacy in Tunisia: Its determinants and its implications on investment behavior. *Research in International Business and Finance, 39*, 568–577. doi:10.1016/j.ribaf.2016.09.018

OECD. (2017). *G20/OECD INFE report on adult financial literacy in G20 countries*. Paris: OECD.

OECD INFE. (2011). *Measuring Financial Literacy: Core Questionnaire in Measuring Financial Literacy: Questionnaire and Guidance Notes for conducting an Internationally Comparable Survey of Financial literacy*. Paris: OECD.

Prusty, S. (2011). Household Saving Behaviour: Role of Financial Literacy and Saving Plans. *Journal of World Economic Review, 6*(1), 75–86.

Schreiner, M., Clancy, M., & Sherraden, M. (2002). *Saving Performance in the American Dream Demonstration: A National Demonstration of Individual Retirement Accounts," Final Report*. St. Louis, MO: Center for Social Development, University of Washington.

Sekita, S. (2011). Financial Literacy and Retirement Planning in Japan. *Journal of Pension Economics and Finance, 10*(4), 637–656. doi:10.1017/S1474747211000527

Skagerlund, K., Lind, T., Strömbäck, C., Tinghög, G., & Västfjäll, D. (2018). Financial literacy and the role of numeracy-How individuals' attitude and affinity with numbers influence financial literacy. *Journal of Behavioral and Experimental Economics, 74*, 18–25. doi:10.1016/j.socec.2018.03.004

Šoškić, D. (2011, September 15). *Financial literacy and financial stability*. Retrieved from https://www.bis.org/review/r110929e.pdf?ql=1

Stango, V., & Zinman, J. (2007). *Fuzzy math and red ink: When the opportunity cost of consumption is not what it seems*. Working Paper, Dartmouth College.

Stango, V., & Zinman, J. (2009). Exponential Growth Bias and Household Finance. *The Journal of Finance, 64*(6), 2807–2849. doi:10.1111/j.1540-6261.2009.01518.x

van Rooij, M., Lusardi, A., & Alessie, R. (2011). Financial literacy and stock market participation. *Journal of Financial Economics, 101*(2), 449–472. doi:10.1016/j.jfineco.2011.03.006

van Rooij, M., Lusardi, A., & Alessie, R. (2012). Financial Literacy, Retirement Planning, and Household Wealth. *Economic Journal (London)*, *122*(560), 449–478. doi:10.1111/j.1468-0297.2012.02501.x

Vitt, L. A., Anderson, C., Kent, J., Lyter, D. M., Siegenthaler, J. K., & Ward, J. (2000). *Personal finance and the rush to competence: Financial literacy education in the U.S.* Middleburg, VA: Institute for Socio-Financial Studies.

von Gaudecker, H. M. (2015). How Does Household Portfolio Diversification Vary with Financial Sophistication and Advice? *The Journal of Finance*, *70*(2), 489–507. doi:10.1111/jofi.12231

ADDITIONAL READING

Aprea, C., Wutke, C., Breuer, K., Koh, N. K., Davies, P., Greimel-Fuhrmann, B., & Lopus, J. S. (Eds.). (2016). International Handbook of Financial Literacy. Singapore: Springer Science+Business Media. doi:10.1007/978-981-10-0360-8

Erta, K., Hunt, S., Iscenko, Z., & Brambley, W. (2013). *Applying behavioural economics at the Financial Conduct Authority.* Fiancial Conduct Authority Occasional Paper No. 1.

Malatji, J.B. (2013). *Financial Literacy: The Basic Requirement for Financial Freedom.*

Morton, H. (2015). *Financial Literacy: A Primer for Policymakers.* National Conference of State Legislatures. Washington D.C.:CreateSpace Independent Publishing Platform.

OECD (2015). *National Strategies for Financial Education.* OECD/INFE Policy Handbook.

KEY TERMS AND DEFINITIONS

Behavioral Bias: Psychological deviations from rationality that affects individuals' behavior and perspective, based on predetermined mental notions and beliefs. There are conscious and unconscious biases.

Financial Inclusion: The process of ensuring access to appropriate financial products and services needed by vulnerable groups such as weaker sections and low-income groups at an affordable cost in a fair and transparent manner by mainstream Institutional players.

Financial Literacy: A combination of awareness, knowledge, skill, attitude, and behavior necessary to make sound financial decisions and ultimately achieve individual financial well-being.

Financial Regulation: A form of regulation or supervision which subjects financial institutions to certain requirements, restrictions or guidelines, aiming to maintain the integrity of the financial system.

Financial Stability: The absence of crises in the various groups of institutions and markets and the stable evolution of the main monetary and financial macro magnitudes (monetary supply, credit supply, interest rates, etc.).

Market Failure: A situation in which the allocation of goods and services by a free market in not Pareto efficient. The existence of market failures is often behind governments economic interventions.

Numeracy: The ability to reason and to apply simple numerical concepts. Basic numeracy skills consist of comprehending fundamental arithmetic like addition, subtraction, multiplication, and division.

Systemic Risk: The possibility that an event or decision at an individual level trigger instability or collapse an entire sector or economy.

ENDNOTE

[1] The meaning and the scope of the bias, anomalies and heuristics related to financial decisions can be found in Lowerwald and Stemmann (2016).

The Economic and Social Value of Financial Literacy

APPENDIX 1

Questions used by Lusardi and Michell (2011)
- Suppose you had $100 in a savings account and the interest rate was 2 percent per year. After 5 years, how much do you think you would have in the account if you left the money to grow: [**more than $102**; exactly $102; less than $102; do not know; refuse to answer.]
- Imagine that the interest rate on your savings account was 1 percent per year and inflation was 2 percent per year. After 1 year, would you be able to buy: [more than, exactly the same as, or **less than today** with the money in this account; do not know; refuse to answer.]
- Do you think that the following statement is true or false? "Buying a single company stock usually provides a safer return than a stock mutual fund." [true; **false**; do not know; refuse to answer.]

APPENDIX 2

Questions used in the S&P's Global Financial Literacy Survey
Risk diversification
Suppose you have some money. Is it safer to put your money into one business or investment, or to put your money into multiple businesses or investments?
[one business or investment; **multiple businesses or investments**; don't know; refused to answer]
Inflation
Suppose over the next 10 years the prices of the things you buy double. If your income also doubles, will you be able to buy less than you can buy today, the same as you can buy today, or more than you can buy today? [less; **the same**; more; don't know; refused to answer]
Numeracy (interest)
Suppose you need to borrow 100 US dollars. Which is the lower amount to pay back: 105 US dollars or 100 US dollars plus three percent? [105 US dollars; **100 US dollars plus three percent**; don't know; refused to answer]
Compound interest
Suppose you put money in the bank for two years and the bank agrees to add 15 percent per year to your account. Will the bank add more money to your account the second year than it did the first year, or will it add the same amount of money both years? [**more**; the same; don't know; refused to answer]

Suppose you had 100 US dollars in a savings account and the bank adds 10 percent per year to the account. How much money would you have in the account after five years if you did not remove any money from the account? [**more than 150 dollars**; exactly 150 dollars; less than 150 dollars; don't know; refused to answer]

Chapter 10
Tool for the Financial Inclusion of Informal Retailers in Colombia

Gustavo Adolfo Diaz
Universidad Santo Tomás, Colombia

Olga Marina García Norato
Universidad Santo Tomás, Colombia

Alvaro Andrés Vernazza Páez
Universidad Santo Tomás, Colombia

Oscar A. Arcos Palma
Universidad Santo Tomás, Colombia

ABSTRACT

One of the structural problems in Colombia is the informality of economic activities. Indeed, there is a high proportion of informal retailers in large cities of the country. This chapter propounds a tool, Credit Scoring, for the financial inclusion of this population. The tool is designed for obtaining resources at lower financial costs, and it aims at improving the commercial activities of these agents. In this way, informal financing, which increases poverty, is avoided. Also, in connection with this subject, surveys conducted among a thousand informal retailers in five Colombian cities—Bogotá, Cúcuta, Ibagué, Villavicencio and Arauca—were taken into account.

DOI: 10.4018/978-1-7998-2440-4.ch010

INTRODUCTION

In Colombia there is a big concern about how to achieve greater financial inclusion for low-income households and people employed in informal jobs, such as retailing. These agents face several limitations that stop them from conveniently and effectively gaining access to the resources of the formal financial system; these limitations include: the lack of previous banking history, low income, and high financial costs; and, from the point of view of the financial institutions, the risks incurred, especially when obtaining reliable information about the socioeconomic conditions of informal workers is difficult.

Some studies aimed at knowing how agents finance their economic activities in informal scenarios, point to the modality of informal credits. These are financial resources, to which no major restrictions are imposed, for example, regarding guarantees. Despite the high costs underlying this form of financing, the costs of informal credits are almost equal to, or higher than, the costs in the formal financial system. In Colombia, where the informality rate in the labor market is close to 50%, an estimate for the proportion of informal loans is close to half of that figure (DANE, 2019).

Among the population engaged in informal economic activities, there is a significant part working in informal trade in the public space of cities with relevant economic dynamics. In most cases, informal retailers act as intermediaries for the selling of industrial products, and, in other less significant cases, they sell goods manufactured by themselves, especially culinary products. Government policies and programs designed to promote financial inclusion in the country have focused essentially on productive activities involving the transformation of raw materials, which, to some extent, require the hiring of specialized workforce, thus the creation of formal jobs. Accordingly, informal retailers who are not engaged in activities dealing in industrial production, and work only as intermediaries in the retailing of goods, are excluded from these programmes.

Considering the rates of informality in developing economies, in which informal trade has a relative importance, we think that it is necessary, as a transitional strategy aimed at reducing poverty, and, simultaneously, as a way to create financial habits among this population, to take into account tools allowing the integration of the population engaged in informal commercial activities into the formal economy. In this way, a progressive improvement in the process of formalizing the economy could be achieved. Indeed, creating better financing practices, would allow these agents to engage in commercial and productive activities that generate profit, and, therefore, that could improve the quality of life of people and households.

Different alternatives that have been considered when defining and measuring labor informality and, based on technical criteria, employ the definitions related to the lack of lack of affiliation to social security schemes (healthcare and pensions) and that of DANE for measuring the intensity of informality in the twenty-three major Colombian cities. The results show that when defining informality as the lack of affiliation to social security, nearly six out of ten employees belong to the informal sector. Additionally, informal workers in Colombia are characterized by low educational and income levels, besides from working in smaller establishments, when compared to the formal workers (Galvis, 2012).

In this chapter, we propose to apply the Credit Scoring tool to the issue of integrating the informal retailers into the formal financial system. The application of this tool is based on a study on informal retailing from nearly one thousand surveys carried out in key sectors of the cities of Bogotá, Cúcuta, Ibagué Villavicencio, and Arauca. These five cities show informality rates, which, according to official figures, exceed the national average of 50%. In the aforementioned cities, information was obtained regarding the economic, social, and financial aspects of the people engaged in informal commercial activities in the public space. The study found that a significant proportion of the people interviewed feel excluded from the formal financial system due to its numerous restrictions. This is why informal retailers are forced into taking illegal informal loans known in Colombia as "drop by drop" (*gota a gota*) loans, that is, a form of onerous loans that exceed by far the conventional interest rates, and in which payments have to be made daily, and word assurances are constantly demanded, heightened sometimes by criminal intimidations.

Confronted with this unsustainable reality, we believe that implementing the Credit Scoring tool as a means of integrating the informal retailers into the formal financial system, would not only relieve the financial needs of this population, but also set the country about shifting from informality to formality, thus, reducing poverty. Indeed, this might be achieved, on the one hand, through measures aiming at preventing the negative effects of regulatory costs, for example, taxes and high interest rates, and, on the other hand, by developing educational programs and financial habits that could help integrating this population into the formal economic and social life of the country. Such considerations reveal, therefore, the need to design special programs in collaboration with Banks of Development and Opportunities, as observed in recent international experiences. The novelty, in our case, is that we think that not only should the financial inclusion of the general public and productive economic units be promoted, but also that of a population whose commercial activity consists mainly in the merchandise-money-merchandise intermediation.

Thus, in this chapter, we try to justify the relevance of applying the Credit Scoring tool to the question of integrating informal retailers into the formal economy. This chapter also includes some remarks on the current public policy for financial inclusion in Colombia; a description of informal retailers in five Colombian cities;

and a methodological framework designed to apply the aforementioned tool to the question at hand.

BACKGROUND

Some of the reasons that justify the application of the Credit Scoring tool to the question of informal retailing are: the absence of an inclusive financial system adjusted to the social and economic reality of this population in developing countries; high financial costs of intermediation rates –v. gr., the Colombian case, where intermediation rates (the difference between collection rates and placement rates) range between 10% and 15%, whereas in developed countries these do not exceed 5%; regulatory non-differentiated tax burdens; procedures; lack of information, and formal guarantees, to name a few. From the point of view of the financial market, reasons concern the problems of asymmetrical information and moral hazard, that is, high costs in obtaining financial information about informal retailers, and the risk of non-payment on credits.

Commercial banks are therefore reluctant to grant loans to "non-formal" individuals and economic units, especially if they are not frequent customers, or lack previous banking history, and some kind of long established business practice. And credit programs designed by public institutions extend actually to commercial banks, and, therefore, generally have a bias towards financially capable people who are already part of the formal labor market, and economic units that comply with the requirements of regulatory formality.

Thus, fragmentation within the financial market and negative discrimination against informal retailers are aspects that prevail, to a greater or lesser extent, in Latin American economies. If we add the use of differentials in the interest rates for the loans based on the size of the economic unit; the small percentage of SMEs that benefit from credits allocated by financial institutions; and the wide practice of self-financing for obtaining working capital or carrying out investments, it is clear that developing economies face great difficulties in helping informal workers gain access to credits; further, these restrictions point to increased inequalities in productive capabilities and market inclusion (Minzer, 2011).

Credit rationing can hinder investment to expand production or make innovations. Moreover, in extreme cases, it could lead to the closing of economic units. Therefore, the fact that SMEs benefit only from a small portion of the credits offered by financial institutions, can be mainly attributed to insufficient information, and to high risks linked to their financing. In addition, high costs of financing, demands of banks and other bureaucratic procedures, and insufficient guarantees (mortgages, personal savings or finances), result in banks being reluctant to grant loans. Problems within the functioning of credit markets are then an obstacle to the economic growth of countries. They affect particularly economic units in the informal sector.

Dealing with financial risks, especially credit and market risks, is essential when designing a proposal for inclusion. In this sense, the aim of the investigation carried out in the five cities that we mentioned above, apart from giving a description of the population employed in informal commercial activities, was to put in place a tool allowing financial institutions to allocate loans with a minimum risk for their assets. In turn, this could promote, in a real and effective way, the equitable inclusion of informal retailers into the formal system, mainly, by enabling the access to financial resources, and the building of mutual trust between economic agents. Finally, poverty could be reduced. Indeed, conditions could be created for a progressive transformation that reduces informality and increases formality. Assuredly, this requires also policies that would make the new relationship between the financial system and informal retailers a viable solution for increasing formality. These measures must include the development of capabilities and financial habits, as well as real opportunities for innovation, and personal and business realizations in market contexts. Increasing trust is then one of the central aspects that would be achieved by applying the Credit Scoring tool.

Moreover, the study shows that, in addition to the formal and positive normative conditions generating financial exclusion, it should also be included among these the phenomenon of self-exclusion. The results obtained from the surveys show that a portion of the targeted population has, as a matter of fact, the capacity, sustained by personal financial resources, to assume economic and financial commitments. Consequently, there is no reason why they could not meet the requirements imposed by the formal banking system.

In Colombia, informality within the credit market is a given fact, which, as we mentioned above, prevents people from acquiring financial habits that would allow them to manage their household and company finances. This is why we regard as an important task the promotion of policies designed to encourage the access to formal financial services for people living in conditions of general informality and poverty, and, in particular, for informal retailers and economic units. Thus, measures such as micro-savings, micro-insurances, and microcredits are all relevant for this purpose, and reinforce the advantages expected from the financial tool for which we advocate.

MAIN FOCUS OF THE CHAPTER

Public Policies for The Financial Inclusion In Colombia: Contextual Remarks

Financial inclusion is linked to economic growth and development, and contributes to poverty reduction. From this premise, public policies have been introduced to facilitate the access and use of financial services for people. Colombia has not been unaffected by this trend, and in recent years it has consolidated important efforts to generalize the use of financial products and services. In 2006, the Government introduced the Bank of Opportunities (*Banca de las Oportunidades*) financial inclusion policy. As a consequence of which, the "Bank of Opportunities (*Banca de las Oportunidades*)" Investment Program was created. Its object is to create the necessary conditions for promoting the access to credits and other financial services for the low-income population, medium and small businesses (SMEs), and entrepreneurs.

If we look at the guidelines set by the Inter-Sectorial Commission for the Financial Inclusion in Colombia (CIIFC in Spanish), it is clear that, based on international recommendations and standards, there is a National Strategy for the Financial Inclusion, with the following broad objective: "to prioritize the populations and products to be worked, to define goals, and to establish institutional structures for the coordination of actions" (CIIFC, 2016).

The joint work between the Colombian public and private institutions, under regulatory frameworks such as the one described above, has helped to overcome the most important restrictions regarding financial inclusion. Indeed, progress has been made, especially through the following strategies:

a) One of the main priorities for the Bank of Opportunities program, is to increase the geographical reach of the financial system. When *Conpes* 3424 was issued in 2006, the banking sector was present in 71% of the country's municipalities. However, if we exclude the Agrarian Bank, the proportion is only 25%. To reverse this situation, "credit institutions were authorized to enter into contracts with non-financial third parties, such as supermarkets and drug stores, so that they could provide financial services, and reach areas where the operation of traditional banking is expensive. This figure, known as 'Bank Correspondents' (BC), received an initial boost from the Government through an incentive programme aimed at the industry[1]" (CIIFC, 2016).

In Colombia, the BC model has been successful, and has shown great potential. Its implementation has allowed financial institutions to expand their operations to other regions. Since then, the amount of financial transactions has increased positively.

b) Colombia has made a great effort to increase the use of savings accounts, and simplified financial products, bringing financial services, at a lower cost, closer to the population. For example, by enacting Law 1735 of 2014. Indeed, this law introduced a new, clearer, financial license for Companies Specialized in Deposits and Electronic Payments (SEDPES in Spanish). SEDPES can only deal in savings, and financial services such as payments, transfers, and bank's orders.

Regarding SMEs, it is worth mentioning that only half of these companies resort to credits (ANIF, 2013)[2]. The reasons are: the standard procedures and requirements for application, and the extra costs when credits are allocated (Banca de las Oportunidades y Superintendencia Financiera de Colombia, 2014a).

c) As for the rural sector, it is considered as one of the most important economic sectors. Indeed, it is a central issue in the Colombian peace agreement of 2016, namely, the proposal for an integral rural reform. Here, financial inclusion is a key aspect for its implementation.

By December 2014, there were about 4.7 million savings accounts in municipalities classified as rural areas (Banca de las Oportunidades y Superintendencia Financiera de Colombia, 2014b), which means that only 39% of the adult population living in these regions have access to a savings account. This percentage is low both with respect to other Latin American countries (46%), and to larger cities and medium-size municipalities in Colombia (87%) (CIIFC, 2016).

Some studies suggest that this could be explained by the lack of regular supply of goods and services that would take into account the specific needs of the rural sector, as well as to incongruities introduced by public policies promoting agricultural financing that affect the operations of the Agrarian Bank, thus generating restrictions on access to, and use of rural financial services in general (Marulanda Consultores, 2013). But the Government has encouraged actions with the purpose of eliminating these restrictions.

In 2016, Finagro rediscount operations dealing with cooperatives supervised by the Superintendence of the Solidarity Economy were extended, thus supporting the Finagro Rural Microcredit line. In the same way, Law 1731 of 2014 established, and Decree 1449 of 2015 regulated, the Rural Microfinance Fund entrusted with financing, supporting, and developing rural microfinances in the country.

Table 1. Informality rates in Colombia (February-April 2016-2019)

City	2016	2017	2018	2019
Cúcuta	70.4	69.7	69.4	70.6
Ibagué	58.5	57.4	55.8	52.7
Villavicencio	56.4	57.8	56.3	56.8
Bogotá	47	47	47.5	46.5
Quibdó	62.4	62	57.6	59.1
23 cities	48.6	48.2	48.6	47.7

Source:https://www.dane.gov.co/index.php/estadisticas-por-tema/salud/informalidad-y-seguridad-social/empleo-informal-y-seguridad-social-historicos

d) Some studies show that financial habits in Colombia are rare. According to the latest World Bank survey carried out in 2013, only 37% of adults take part in financial planning. Although 87% are familiar with the concept of interest, only 35% know how to calculate simple interests, and 26% compound interests. These figures contrast negatively against levels observed in more developed countries, and other countries in the region such as Mexico (World Bank, 2013). In 2015, the CIIFC developed the strategy for the Financial and Economic Education (EEF), thus advancing the education in economic and financial management.

e) The Government has also designed financial inclusion strategies that follow international recommendations and standards. In particular, by encouraging initiatives making improvements in the areas of access, use, and quality of financial products as indicated by AFI (2013)[3]. These plans are part of a wider range of policies, the aims of which are poverty reduction, formalization of the economy, traceability of financial transactions, security, and improvement of the quality of life of citizens.

Socioeconomic Representation Of Informality In Five Colombian Cities: Bogotá, Cúcuta, Ibagué, Villavicencio, And Quibdó

Informality is widely present in many Colombian cities. Mainly, it originates from high levels of unemployment. Indeed, the rate of unemployment in April 2019 was about 12.1% in the 23 most important cities (table 2). Some of the underlying causes of informality in the targeted cities are: general unemployment linked to the need of resources to meet basic expenses; population displacements from rural areas, migration from Venezuela; and the absence, in some cases, of state institutions.

Table 2. *Unemployment rates in the cities with the highest informality rates in Colombia (February-April 2016-2019)*

City	2016	2017	2018	2019
Cúcuta	15.9	16.7	16.2	15.5
Ibagué	14.3	13.6	14.2	16.8
Villavicencio	13	12.5	12.2	13.9
Quibdó	19.7	18.2	17.6	20.8
Bogotá	8.5	10.7	10.5	11.9
23 cities	10.1	10.9	11.1	12.1

Source: https://www.dane.gov.co/index.php/estadisticas-por-tema/mercado-laboral/empleo-y-desempleo.

The cities with the highest rates of informality (table 1) are then: Cúcuta (70.6%), Quibdó (59.1%), Villavicencio (56.8%), and Ibagué (52.7%). These figures show that these cities significantly exceed the national average (DANE, 2019).

The highest unemployment rate is found in the city of Quibdó (table 2), the capital of the department of Choco located in the Pacific region (20.8%). This percentage, according to some analysts, is due to insufficient public policies that would otherwise encourage entrepreneurship in the region, or indeed to few collaborations between the public and private sectors. Quibdó is followed by Ibagué, capital of the department of Tolima (16.8%), and Cúcuta, on the border between Colombia and Venezuela (15.5%).

Bogotá, the capital of Colombia, records the largest number of informal population (table 3), that is, 29.5% out of a total of 23 cities (DANE, 2019). However, Cúcuta is the city with the largest number of informal retailers. In 2019, 237,000 people, out of a total of approximately 750,000 inhabitants, that is, 31% of the population,

Table 3. *Informal population rates in Colombia (February-April 2016-2019)*

	Informal population (by thousands)				Rates per city out of a total of 23 cities			
City	2016	2017	2018	2019	2016	2017	2018	2019
Cúcuta	249	238	234	237	4.3%	4.1%	4.1%	4.1%
Ibagué	143	140	138	123	2.5%	2.4%	2.4%	2.1%
Villavicencio	117	128	125	129	2.0%	2.2%	2.2%	2.2%
Bogotá	1,789	1,661	1,732	1,694	31.1%	28.9%	30.1%	29.5%
Quibdó	21	22	20	19	0.4%	0.4%	0.3%	0.3%
23 cities	5,747	5,694	5,763	5,635				

Source: https://www.dane.gov.co/index.php/estadisticas-por-tema/salud/informalidad-y-seguridad-social/empleo-informal-y-seguridad-social-históricos

Table 4. Survey distribution

City	Number of surveys	%
Cúcuta	180	36.81
Maicao	181	37.01
Arauca	128	26.18
Total	489	100

Source: Department of Economics of the Santo Tomás University (USTA), Bogotá-Colombia, 2018.

was found to be working in informal retailing. The percentage then is slightly higher than the corresponding rate in Bogotá, and with respect to the national average.

Reasons Referred by Informal Retailers For Using Informal Financing Resources

Informal retailers have to face many difficulties when applying for a loan from formal financial institutions. Some of the difficulties referred by them are: time lapses for the approval of applications, tedious procedures, insufficient information, to name a few. And if we add that informal retailers have no credit history, it is evident why, despite of the high interest rates and the continuous warnings for late payments, they turn to informal money lenders. Indeed, there is no need for them to comply with guarantees. Nevertheless, most of the people interviewed declare that it would be better if they could rely on formal financial institutions. For all that, the official requirements, as we have seen, together with the necessity for instantly having the money at their disposal, force them, as a last resource, to turn to informal loans as a way of financing their commercial activities.

Let's consider now the informal financing survey conducted by the Department of Economics of the Santo Tomás University (table 4). The survey was conducted among a representative group of 489 informal retailers living in cities located mainly on the border between Colombia and Venezuela.

The cities analyzed in this survey, just as in our targeted cities, show high levels of unemployment and informality. That said, the investigation sheds a light on what informal retailers expect from the financial system, thus showing how financial institutions could adapt to meet the financial needs of this population. In general, this is what they say: banks should help in the process of loans acquisition, they should engage in non-discriminatory practices, help to identify low-income populations that could benefit from their products and services, and give specialized advice (table 5).

On the whole, informal retailers confess their dissatisfaction with the excessively high interest rates set by informal lenders. But, in particular, they reveal their

Tool for the Financial Inclusion of Informal Retailers in Colombia

Table 5. Opinions of informal retailers on how to increase financial inclusion

What should banks do to stop you from turning to "drop by drop" loans?	Cúcuta	Arauca	Maicao
Help in the process of obtaining a loan	46.3%	38%	58%
Insurance against risk and uncertainty	14.8%	28%	44%
More offices and divisions	9.3%	17%	11%
Non-discriminatory practices	44.4%	48%	60%
Provide guidance	25.9%	32%	25%
Identification of key populations	27.8%	25%	15%
More effective public policies	18.5%	24%	6%
Information and advice services	16.7%	32%	42%
Identification of low-income populations	44.4%	48%	37%

Source: Department of Economics of the Santo Tomás University, Bogotá-Colombia. Table made by the authors based on the results of surveys carried out among 489 informal retailers in 2018.

preference for formal financial institutions. Indeed, they feel that these institutions could favor their commercial activities. We can then conclude from what has been said so far, that banks should play an important part in increasing the percentage of informal retailers that could benefit from their products and services.

Scoring Model for The Allocation Of Credits To Informal Retailers

Credit risk analysis is one of the control measures applied to supervised financial institutions. These measures, such as complying with the international regulations of the Basel Committee II, allow financial institutions to benefit from a solid portfolio. These regulations apply to all kinds of clients, from commercial to corporate and institutional banking. Nonetheless, risk models have not been adapted yet to the particularities of small businesses, despite the fact that Microfinance Institutions (MFI) have been recently implementing models measuring credit risks for small commercial units.

Moreover, these models have become a source of financial exclusion, because they fail to take into account what, precisely, defines individuals and economic units under informal conditions, namely, small financial assets, insufficient guarantees, and such characteristics as we have listed above. Thus, risks linked to an unbalanced microcredit portfolio within financial institutions have notably led to situations in which informal retailers, and vulnerable social groups, are excluded from the financial system and the benefits that in the end would improve their small economic activities.

Credit Scoring is a credit valuation method used to formally determine the likelihood of applicants fulfilling or not their payments obligations. Sometimes, the term "application score" is used to distinguish it from the "performance score", and whose object is to keep under observation and predict the rating of payments on a loan for a given costumer. The so-called "score cards" or "classifiers", besides some other tools used for estimating the probability of defaults on loans, use predictive variables based on the forms submitted by applicants to financial institutions (Hand & Henley, 1997).

Although there are rating models that have been designed for allocating loans to SMEs, our objective here is to propose a rating model that could be used by financial institutions, banks of opportunities or microfinance institutions, for allocating credits to informal retailers, thus complying with the requirement of a probabilistic evaluation on payments obligations.

The majority of work related to credit evaluation has been oriented to the micro entrepreneurs' segment. Bravo, Maldonado, and Weber (2010) consider that loans directed to micro entrepreneurs representing an important part of financing in Chile and other Latin American countries, because they have an important way to improve your economic activities. Therefore, it has been necessary to define risk models associated with the realities of these economic agents, they suggest a thorough review of variables such as income for the determination of payment or non-payment of credit or variables that show financial strength such as ownership of assets. It is also important to consider other aspects such as market volatility, being very sensitive to economic cycles, for this reason the design of financial tools must be adjusted to the needs of these users. (Bravo, Maldonado, & Weber, 2010)

Esquivel, León and Arley (2013) prepared a study that allowed generating the construction of the tool "Matrix Credit Scoring SMEs" whose purpose was to analyze the level of delinquency of an SME company in the initial process of a loan. It could be detected that there is no initial analysis to be carried out on a new SME company to measure the level of delinquency and possible payment behavior if a credit was granted by the financial institution. (Esquivel, León & Arley, 2013)

Schreiner (2002), credit scoring refers to the characteristics and performance related to loans from the past and thus predicts into the future. Among the benefits of this tool, this author mentions the following: it allows each client to be qualified, it is more efficient in time because it reduces costs, each credit has a score so that it is easy to follow up on each of the applicants, and this tool is expected to be objective and consistent (Schreiner 2002).

Scoring models for the evaluation of microfinances have been developed mainly in some Latin American countries, Africa, and Asia where there are high levels of unemployment, informality, inequality in income distribution, and where financial needs demand immediate solutions for people with low income. These models have been used mainly in connection with solidarity groups to which the applicant is affiliated. But it has been shown that the results are not valid for the evaluation of the entire credit allocation process.

This is the case in the study conducted by Sharma and Zeller in Bangladesh, which analyses the payment rates of 128 credit groups belonging to credit programs from the three groups: the Association for the Social Advancement (ASA), the Rural Advancement Committee of Bangladesh (RACB), and the Rural Service Rangpur Dinajpur (RSRD). The authors resort here to the TOBIT analysis, by means of which specific tests are carried out on determining variables, such as: group size, the amount of the loan, level of credit rationing, and the amount of companies within the groups, demographic characteristics, relations and social status, and frequency of idiosyncratic crises. Based on these actors, the authors conclude that if users follow the basic principles of prudential banking, regardless of their condition, whether they belong to poor and / or remote communities, the payment rates can be positive (Sharma & Zeller, 1997).

One way of reducing the risk of non-payment on loans, especially in the case of informal retailers, is by implementing a measurement or control tool known as "Credit Scoring". This model uses mathematical, statistical, econometric, and artificial intelligence techniques.

Further, the Credit Scoring model takes into account several credit scoring models, which can be divided into two main categories: parametric models, and non-parametric models. The former includes linear probability models, logit or probit model, based on discrimination analysis and neural networks, whereas the latter include mathematical programming, classifying trees, the neighboring model, and the Analytical Hierarchy Process model (AHP) (Saardchom, 2012).

Since the AHP model and intelligent system models in general, do not require historical data, the model could therefore be adopted by banks that do not possess enough data to run a standard credit rating model. Thus, the AHP model is capable of combining expert's assessments regarding the applicant's performance, and transform these evaluations into credit scores (Saardchom, 2012).

In order to apply this model to the problem that we have here set to go about, we can choose a dependent variable and a group of independent variables obtained from the survey mentioned above. Then, the variables can be formulated as follows:

- Dependent variable: binary variable establishing the probability of payment or non-payment.
- Independent variables: net value of profits, term, income, circulation of goods, duration of the economic activity… (Table 6).

Table 6. Independent variables for elaborating a Credit Scoring model

Group	Variables x_k	Expected result on payment probability
Qualitative Variables	Sex	Positive
	Education	Positive
	Location	Negative
	Sector (economic activity)	
	Contribution to social security	Positive
	Rent	Negative
	The person knows the requirements for taking part in the financial system	Positive
Quantitative Variables	Income	Positive
	Age	Positive: the younger the person, the bigger the probability
	Duration of the economic activity in which the person is employed.	Positive: the longer the duration, the more solid the activity.
	Circulation of goods	Positive: the faster the circulation, the bigger the probability
	Net utility	Positive
	Term	Negative: the longer the term, the bigger the risk of non-payment.
	Number of people who depend on the economic activity for their livelihood	Negative
	Supply (in days)	Positive: few days.
	Competition	Negative: the stronger the competition, the smaller the probability of improving sales.
	Informal credit	Negative

Source: Department of Economics of the Santo Tomás University, Bogotá-Colombia.

Since we are dealing here with two possibilities: whether the client pays or doesn't pay, we apply a binary logistic regression model (dichotomous or dummy variable).

The expected positive or negative signs from the groups of independent variables are very important when carrying out the credit evaluation process. For example, if the retailing business is located in a high-risk area, then the corresponding sign of the variable (location) is negative. In other words, it affects the probability of the payment on the loan. With respect to the other variables, if the sign is positive, such as in: income, age, duration of activity… then we can be sure that they will have a favorable influence on the payment rating. On the contrary, if the sign is negative, such as in: term, number of people, or informal loans... then the risk of non-payment is high (table 6).

A binary regression model determines a linear function with qualitative and quantitative independent variables. It allows knowing how the dependent binary variable is related to the independent variables. The mathematical equation for the model can be formulated thus:

$$Y = \beta_0 + \beta_1 x_1 + \beta_2 x_2 + \beta_3 x_3 + \beta_4 x_4 + \beta_5 x_5 + \beta_k x_k \qquad (1)$$

The dependent variable Y represents the probability ρ of the frequency of the event, that is, the default or not on loans. It takes values between zero and one.

Logistic regression is based on a logistic function that links the dependent variable to a series of independent variables, in which the binary dependent variable with probability p_i of default is represented in the equation:

$$p_i = \frac{1}{1+e^{-z}} + \mu_i \qquad (2)$$

Z represents the logistic score where

$$z_i = \beta + \beta_1 x_1 + \beta_2 x_2 + \beta_3 x_3 + \beta_k x_k \qquad (3)$$

and μ_i is a random variable (Fernández & Pérez, 2005, p. 106).

Thus, the aim of the model is to establish the probability of payment or non-payment based on the parameters of the logistic regression model (equations (2) and (3)), and on the results obtained from the explanatory variables (positive or negative) by means of their respective coefficients.

The probability of an applicant failing to pay its obligation must be estimated from the information submitted for the first time in the application form. Thus, the estimate serves as a basis for deciding whether the applicant is suitable for benefiting from a loan. The ratings therefore allow creditors and applicants alike to know if the operation is beneficial for both of them. For the former, it means higher profits or reduced losses, and for the latter, it means that they can avoid committing themselves on disproportionate loans (Hand & Henley, 1997).

That said, the procedure for evaluating the probability of non-payment takes into account the following aspects:

a) The analysis of the socioeconomic aspects, namely: duration of the economic activity; according to the type of business, whether they rely upon other

economic agents; quantity, quality, and type of goods being traded; rent payments; circulation of goods etc.
b) The analysis of the financial situation, in particular, income and previous loans (formal or informal).
c) The analysis of the macroeconomic situation, which includes variables such as: inflation, interest rates, and unemployment and informality rates.

Inflation rates make it possible to determine how prices influence the costs in the retailing of goods, affect sales or generate risks.

High unemployment rates, when social protections are weak, usually lead to an increase in the informality rate, and, consequently, to an increase on default rates.

Interest rates play an important part in the evaluation of credit allocations. Thus, in the case of informal retailers, microfinance-friendly institutions should apply low interest rates in order to avoid high credit costs that could increase the risk of default from costumers who rely mostly on income obtained through informal economic activities.

In addition to the above, it should be considered that credit scoring also implies that the risk is related to other aspects such as age, gender, the sector where the merchant lives, the economic activity that they develop in their venture, years of business performance if they are street vendors, occasional or stationary or if they pay any rent for the space they occupy despite being public. In this regard it is important to establish what proportion of risk is associated with these factors in order to be included in the rating criteria. In Colombia and Bolivia, scoring for microfinance has been implemented. (Schreiner, 2000).

Other aspects such as:

- Analysing what links they have with any financial institution if they have products such as savings, or credit cards, and if they have no connection.
- Analysing if they have any type of relationship with non-formal entities.
- When there is no credit life, evaluating whether they have had collective credits or solidarity credits with any NGO, Foundation or if they have had informal credits.
- Analysing if they have had extensive experience in the use of informal loans such as drop by drop, with pawnshops, or friends or chains and what have been their results regarding the payment of these commitments, especially for the value of the interest rate that is paid, the absence of guarantees, the term and the ease in granting these resources.
- Analysing the behaviour of credit from the productive unit; since most are informal traders, some of them have a productive project related to the

marketing activity. This aspect will allow scoring points to evaluate the productive project.

In general, informal merchants in many cases have not had the need to resort to formal banking to improve their ventures, but in some cases they use family, friends or loan sharks to cover working capital needs or have rarely had access to special programs of financing through non-governmental organizations. When they resort to microcredits they have been for small amounts and these do not cover their financing expectations, due to the small moments, requirements and especially the guarantees required to maintain the ventures (Zamora, 2017).

In short, if microcredits are to correspond to the financial needs of informal retailers, then it is necessary to adapt the Credit Scoring tool accordingly, especially if we bear in mind how important it is to replace informal loans with formal credits in developing countries. Financial institutions can thus contribute, by applying this tool, to the goal of achieving greater financial inclusion for this segment of the population.

SOLUTIONS AND RECOMMENDATIONS

Regarding the criteria for the approval of credits by risk analysts, we suggest applying the Analytical Hierarchy Process model (AHP). Indeed, since analysts cannot always obtain reliable information on the financial conditions of informal retailers, especially when they have never taken part in the formal financial system, the AHP model is particularly appropriate in this case: it only takes into account the results or estimates of the betas that the model finds each time, that is, the socioeconomically variables describing the commercial activities. Therefore, by applying this model, greater financial inclusion could be achieved, since the allocation of resources would foster, and improve the conditions underlying commercial activities. As a result, we can expect a reduction in the unemployment and informality rates.

In developing countries such as Colombia, the use of this financial tool could have a big impact, especially in reducing poverty. But, if this is to be accomplished, the financial tool for which we advocate here requires also a normative framework that would give it legitimacy. Only then, the advantages for the financial system and for the targeted population, and the economy in general, could be fully perceived.

The assessment of the risk of non-payment of those who are self-employed is a major challenge of microfinance. So far the innovations in microfinance have been the use of solidarity groups and detailed evaluations of individual credit applicants. In the credit evaluation, micro-lenders or financial entities committed to this segment, could establish ranges of classification of applications in order to facilitate the evaluation and link future credit beneficiaries with the lowest risks.

FUTURE RESEARCH DIRECTIONS

In future, we hope to continue in the research areas of social and organizations' economy. These are included in the institutional halfway line of economy and humanism, which pretends working towards the common good.

CONCLUSION

- First, credit evaluations carried out by MFIs and credit risk analysts should take into account the context in which retailers engage in their economic activities. In particular, they should take notice of variables such as: time spent on the commercial activity; type of activity (production or retailing); competition; rents; behavior of other economic actors...
- Second, the socio-economic characteristics of informal retailers should be taken into account, namely, among other variables: sex, age, education, social security contributions, income, and number of people who depend on that income, net profits...
- Third, only people who can provide some sort of guarantee – but not mortgages, since most of the people in informal situations do not have sufficient real guarantees – should be considered for a loan. Institutional guarantees, in the form of Guarantee Funds, could meet these requirements, because they would be specially conceived for the financial needs of informal retailers.
- Fourth, credit analysts in microfinance institutions should, under the above mentioned conditions, approve the credit.

REFERENCES

AFI. (2013). *Empoderamiento del consumidor y conducta del mercado*. Nota de orientación, 8.

Banca de las Oportunidades. (2015). *Reporte Trimestral de Inclusión Financiera: diciembre de 2015*. Author.

Banca de las Oportunidades y Superintendencia Financiera de Colombia. (2014a). *Inclusión Financiera en Colombia: Estudio desde la Demanda*. Author.

Banca de las Oportunidades y Superintendencia Financiera de Colombia. (2014b). *Reporte de Inclusión Financiera: 2014*. Author.

Better than Cash. (2015). *Development Results Focused Research Program. Country Diagnostic: Colombia*. Bankable Frontier. Retrieved from https://btca-prod.s3.amazonaws.com/documents/5/english_attachments/Colombia-Diagnostic-Long-ENG-Jan-2015.pdf?1431983488

Bravo, C., Maldonado, S., & Weber, R. (2010). Experiencias Prácticas en la medicion de riesgo crediticio de microempresarios utilizando modelos de Credit Scoring. *Revista Ingenieria de Sistemas*, 24(20), 69–88.

CGAP. (2013). *Incentivos para la Apertura de Corresponsales No Bancarios de la Banca de las Oportunidades en Colombia*. Retrieved from https://www.cgap.org/sites/default/files/colombia_agent_subsidy_program_spanish.pdf

CIIFC. (2016). *Estrategia Nacional de Inclusión Financiera en Colombia*. Bogotá: Comisión Intersectorial para la Inclusión Financiera. Retrieved from https://www.superfinanciera.gov.co/descargas/institucional/pubFile1030467/estrategia_nacional_inclusion_financiera.pdf

DANE. (2019). *Empleo informal y seguridad social*. Retrieved July 15, 2019, from https://www.dane.gov.co/index.php/estadisticas-por-tema/mercado-laboral/empleo-informal-y-seguridad-social. http://microdatos.dane.gov.co/index.php/catalog/599/get_microdata

Esquivel, G., León, R., & Arley, V. (2013). *Modelo CREDIT SCORING PYMES para la medición del riesgo de morosidad de pequeña y mediana empresa: Un caso de aplicación en Entidad financiera (Unpublished End-of- Degree Project)*. Instituto Técnico de Costa Rica, San José de Costa Rica.

Fernández, C., & Pérez, R. (2005). El modelo logístico: Una herramienta estadística para evaluar el riesgo de crédito. *Revista Ingenierías Universidad de Medellín*, 4(6), 1–22.

Galvis, L. (2012). *Informalidad Laboral en las áreas urbanas de Colombia*. Documentos de Trabajo sobre Economía Regional, 164, Banco de la República, Cartagena, Colombia. Retrieved from https://www.banrep.gov.co/sites/default/files/publicaciones/archivos/DTSER-164_0.pdf

Hand, D., & Henley, W. (1997). Statistical Classification Methods in Consumer Credit Scoring: a Review. *Journal of the Royal Statistical Society*, 160(3), 523-541.

Marulanda Consultores. (2013). *Propuestas de Reforma al Sistema de Financiamiento Agropecuario*. USAID - Programa de Políticas Públicas.

Minzer, R. (2011). *Las instituciones microfinancieras en América Latina: factores que explican su desempeño*. CEPAL, Serie Estudios y Perspectivas, 128. Retrieved from https://repositorio.cepal.org/bitstream/handle/11362/4910/1/S2011012_es.pdf

Saardchom, N. (2012). Expert Judgment Based Scoring Model. *Journal of Business and Economics*, 3(3), 164–175. doi:10.15341/jbe(2155-7950)/03.03.2012/002

Schereiner, M. (2000). A Scoring Model of the Risk Costly Arreals from Loans from Afiliates Womens World Banks in Colombia. Report to Women's World Banking, Bogotá, Colombia.

Schreiner, M. (2002). *Ventajas y desventajas del scoring estadistico para las microfinanzas*. Retrieved November 2, 2019, from http://www.microfinance.com/Castellano/Documentos/Scoring_Ventajas_Desventajas.pdf

Sharma, M., & Zeller, M. (1997). Repayment performance in group-based credit programs in Bangladesh: An empirical analysis. *World Development*, 25(10), 1731–1742. doi:10.1016/S0305-750X(97)00063-6

World Bank. (2013). *Capacidades financieras en Colombia: resultados de la encuesta nacional sobre comportamientos, actitudes y conocimientos financieros*. Author.

Zamora, D. (2017). *Guia para elaborar un scoring de credito para reinsertados del postconflicto colombiano* (Unpublished End-of-Degree Project). Universidad Autónoma de Occidente, Santiago de Cali, Colombia. Retrieved from http://red.uao.edu.co:8080/bitstream/10614/9780/1/T07448.pdf

KEY TERMS AND DEFINITIONS

Informal Economy: This concept is relatively recent and is associated with alternative forms of production caused by lack of opportunities, deficiencies in education and the productive apparatus, excluding regulations in the financial and labor system in favor of certain population groups and economic sectors. This issue arises mainly in the urban sphere of many poor or developing countries, due to the appearance of spontaneous activities in response to problems associated with unemployment, precarious employment and lack of opportunities in the labor market. However, there has been a conceptual change from the informal sector to the informal economy as explained by the ILO to support the statistical measurement of informal sector activities (http://www.ilo.org/wcmsp5/groups/public/---dgreports/----stat/documents/publication/wcms_501585.pdf).

Informal Retailers: The category informal retailers refer in general to those people who are engaged in various activities, such as the supply of goods or services on streets, sidewalks and other public spaces, which make up the area in which they are and perform informal work. However, there are three different types of people dedicated to informal sales that may be affected by the measures, policies or programs aimed at recovering the public space occupied by them, namely: a) stationary informal retailers, which they are installed together with the goods, implements and merchandise that apply to their work in a fixed way in a certain segment of the public space, excluding the use and enjoyment of the same by other people permanently, so that the occupation of the space subsists even in the hours in which the seller is absent from the place; b) sellers or semi-stationary informal sellers, who do not permanently occupy a certain area of public space, but nonetheless, due to the characteristics of the goods they use in their work and the merchandise they sell, must necessarily occupy transitory form a certain segment of the public space, such as people who sell hot dogs and hamburgers, or who push fruit or grocery cars through the streets; and c) informal retailers, who, without occupying public space as such, carry with them - that is, physically carrying - the goods and merchandise that apply to their work, do not obstruct the transit of people and vehicles beyond their personal physical presence.

ENDNOTES

[1] Banca de Oportunidades made three project calls between 2007 and 2010 to increase the use of bank correspondents in 187 municipalities.

[2] According to a survey carried out in 2015, demand for credits varies by sector: commerce represents the highest percentage (52%), followed by industry (48%) and services (37%). (http://anif.co/sites/default/files/uploads/GRAN%20ENCUESTA%20PYME%20II-2015_0.pdf)

[3] AFI is an institution formed by 104 financial institutions from 87 countries. Its purpose is to formulate policies aimed at bringing about financial inclusion.

Chapter 11
The Role of Financial Inclusion:
Does Financial Inclusion Matter?

Ulkem Basdas
https://orcid.org/0000-0002-7142-149X
Philip Morris International, Portugal

ABSTRACT

This chapter highlights the importance of financial education, its link with financial decision-making process, comparative status of different countries, and efforts to improve current situation. Unfortunately, there is no standard definition for neither financial education nor measures to quantify it. Therefore, this chapter first aims to provide a comprehensive definition in order to explain how financial knowledge affects the decision-making process. Then, financial literacy measures from previous studies over different countries would be discussed to show financial illiteracy problem is global. Lastly, solutions and recommendations would be discussed at three different levels: younger people, individuals, and national strategies.

INTRODUCTION

Recent financial crisis of 2007-8 triggered by the US housing bubble not only cost billions of dollars to the global economy, but also resulted in the collapse of large financial institutions such as Lehman Brothers, one of the biggest investment banks in the world. Some researchers considered this crisis as the worst one since the Great Depression. This is why several regulation changes together with preventive action plans were set into place in order not to experience such a crisis again. Only after a decade, things could get "normal". Unfortunately, in the other part of the world debt crises sparkled starting from 2010 European sovereign debt crisis: Greece, Portugal,

DOI: 10.4018/978-1-7998-2440-4.ch011

Copyright © 2020, IGI Global. Copying or distributing in print or electronic forms without written permission of IGI Global is prohibited.

Ireland, Spain and Cyprus experienced difficulties to finance the government debt. Now looking closer to today's economic and financial environment, it may be said that everything is fragile and constantly changing: a trade war is going on between the U.S. and China, interest rates and exchange rates are very volatile, once charmingly profitable cryptocurrencies are losing attention, and investment opportunities or safe options are born and fade away very fast. According to the 2019 April Equifax Financial Literacy Survey conducted in the U.S., 49 per cent of total 1071 adults do not have enough savings to cover three months of living expenses, 56 per cent do not have any money left at the end of the month, and 35 per cent do not have any savings for retirement.

Looking back to these few decades, even though the causes of crises vary, one common observation is obvious: not all the participants of global economy has equal and sufficient information. Some households invest in financial instruments, on which they have no idea, some investors do not take financial decisions consciously, or some portfolio managers create complex investment strategies without considering simple profit/loss analysis. The only way to prevent these cases is to ensure the financial knowledge of these participants. Putting aside the investors, households, managers or portfolio managers, who prefer to decide consciously irrationally, financial knowledge or literacy is the power at the individual level to tackle with high-level economic problems. It is not a coincidence that initiatives/global projects/institutions/regulations/nation-wide campaigns on financial literacy are formed over the same past few decades. Therefore, financial knowledge, literacy or education has gained importance as a solution to avoid making financial mistakes.

This chapter aims to clarify why financial inclusion matters to every individual, and through which channels it affects financial decision-making process. Considering that there is no single definition nor a standard measure to measure the level of financial knowledge, this chapter would first focus on previous attempts to conceptualize and develop measures. Then, a comprehensive definition would be introduced to understand what financial inclusion or literacy really refers. Additionally, this chapter would shed light on findings from different countries to demonstrate there is still way ahead not only for developing countries, but also developed economies. Last but not least, solutions in action and recommendations to individuals, policy makers, and/or any other supportive parties would be provided.

BACKGROUND

In contrary to other financial concepts, financial literacy does not have a single definition or even there is not a single phrase to express. Several terms are used interchangeably, such as financial education, inclusion, literacy, knowledge, or skills.

However, without a proper definition the gap between current situation and ideal or desired level of literacy cannot be set. Therefore, first question is to ask what the financial literacy is in order to be able to understand what has to be done.

What is The Definition of "Financial Literacy"?

The financial literacy covers knowledge, education or competence, even sometimes with a greater emphasis on mathematical abilities. In case one of these topics is prioritized, then the measure would be biased to that direction as well. As an illustration, a definition with more focus on mathematical skills would measure the financial literacy via calculation questions, and consequently any policy built on this measurement would also target improving numeracy skills. The financial literacy definition can differ for the audience as well (i.e., individuals versus organizations). For instance, for managers financial literacy may refer to financial decisions related to the future of a company, whereas for an individual personal budget making can make more sense.

Table 1 summarizes some definitions of financial literacy by different institutions. These definitions put emphasis on different aspects although they align on some common points as well. Considering that there is no single common wording, this chapter defines the financial literacy as the set of following items:

- Knowledge about financial concepts/products/services,
- Competence to use financial concepts/products/services,
- Ability to take financial decisions (i.e., transmission to behavior),
- Confidence in financial operations

A comprehensive definition, which would be applicable to both individuals and organizations, should include all these dimensions: knowledge, skills, attributes and actions. This concept includes not only intangible skill sets, but also actions or decisions, because the impact of knowledge on behavior is the complementary outcome of really absorbed information. Any definition lacking one of these dimensions would be incomplete or misleading. That explains why financial literacy, financial inclusion, financial education, or financial knowledge are used interchangeably. From onwards, the financial literacy or one of these terms would be used to refer this comprehensive definition.

How to Measure the Financial Literacy?

Unfortunately, there is no standard way of measurement and there is still room for further development (Schmeiser and Seligman, 2013). Similar to the differences

Table 1. Different definitions of financial literacy

Study/Institution	Definition
U.S. Department of the Treasury, The Financial Literacy and Education Commission (FLEC)	*"The Commission's vision is of sustained financial well-being for all individuals and families in the U.S. In furtherance of this vision, the Commission sets strategic direction for policy, education, practice, research, and coordination so that all Americans make informed financial decisions."*
Organization for Economic Cooperation and Development (OECD) the International Network on Financial Education (INFE)	*"A combination of awareness, knowledge, skill, attitude and behavior necessary to make sound financial decisions and ultimately achieve individual financial wellbeing"*
Organization for Economic Cooperation and Development (OECD) Programme for International Student Assessment (PISA)	*"Financial literacy is defined as knowledge and understanding of financial concepts and risks, and the skills, motivation and confidence to apply such a knowledge and understanding in order to make effective decisions across a range of financial contexts, to improve the financial well-being of individuals and society, and to enable participation in economic life"*
Financial Industry Regulatory Authority Inc. (FINRA)	*"FINRA Investor Education Foundation empowers underserved Americans with the knowledge, skills and tools to make sound financial decisions throughout life."*
The National Financial Educators Council (NFEC)	*"Possessing the skills and knowledge on financial matters to confidently take effective action that best fulfills an individual's personal, family, and global community goals."*
The Standard & Poor's Global Financial Literacy Survey by Global Financial Literacy Excellence Center (GFLEC, 2015)	*"People who are financially literate have the ability to make informed financial choices regarding saving, investing, borrowing, and more."*
Jump$tart Coalition for Personal Financial Literacy (2007)	*"the ability to use knowledge and skills to manage one's ðnancial resources effectively for lifetime ðnancial security"*

in the conceptualization, the measures for financial literacy also vary. In some of the questionnaires, the respondent is required to assess himself whereas in other cases questions with multiple choice are asked, or both methods are used in one questionnaire design. In general, questionnaires with multiple choices are used to collect data, and then summation of the correct answers are used to score financial literacy.

The surveys requesting a direct self-assessment of the respondent carries a risk of over/under-judgment of the respondent. The Financial Industry Regulatory Authority (2009) highlights that self-assessment responses can be disconnected from other responses. Previous studies also show that people would have a tendency to overrate themselves (Guiso and Jappelli, 2009; Lusardi and Mitchell, 2014). On the other hand, if self-assessment is requested together with other questions targeting actual knowledge, the advantage would be to understand the gap in the awareness of respondent: what actually is known versus what is thought to be known.

Other surveys with multiple choice also face some difficulties. First, multiple choices enable respondent to pick one answer even though they have no idea about the solution. The respondent might end up with the correct answer by luck. To mitigate this problem, "do not know", "not answered" kind of choices can be added to choices, so that the respondent would not be forced to throw a number. On the other hand, even after providing this alternative, the respondent may prefer to hide its actual knowledge level by randomly selecting a choice. In that case, another remedy can be not to use very few choices to lower the success probability of random selection. Last but not least, there are other crucial details in the design of questionnaires such as wording of questions, level of numeracy, etc. (for a detailed discussion see OECD, 2009 and Nicolini, 2019).

Assuming that all aforementioned details are handled carefully, the next step becomes the calculation of a measure, which would correctly capture the financial literacy level of the respondent. Unfortunately, the calculation methodology also varies from one study to another even though all previous steps including the respondents are the same. As an illustration, the studies of both Allgood and Walstad (2011) and Mottola (2013) rely on the exact same database of FINRA, whereas in the former one the financial literacy is measured by summation of correct answers and self-assessment score, and in the latter one only a dummy variable is used.

A comprehensive summary of literature in Table 2 illuminates the differences among studies in detail. 68 questionnaires or designs are first grouped based on the country coverage, and then compared based on the targeted audience, number of respondents, content or topics covered, number of questions, and measures. First, the content is classified in two categories: basic and advanced. In case a survey includes advanced topics such as money management, investment strategies, advanced financial instruments, then it is categorized under "advanced". The content limited with basic interest rate, present value, inflation, risk calculations and/or numeracy are grouped under "basic". Additionally, self-assessment questions, which are limited with "feelings" or "confidence" of respondent, are also categorized under "basic". For example, the questionnaire of Hira and Loibl (2005), which aims to evaluate the impact of financial education on workspace satisfaction, is classified under "basic". Second, in Table 2 number of questions are reported by giving a reference to the design of Lusardi and Mitchell (2011), which has been found out to be the widely-applied one. The Lusardi-Mitchell design included only three questions: one for interest rate calculation, one to understand the awareness of respondent on the impact of inflation, and the last one to test both knowledge about stocks versus stock mutual funds, and risk diversification. The two first questions were multiple choice questions, whereas last question was a true/false question, but all with a "refuse to answer" option. Then, the financial literacy level was evaluated based on the summation of correct answers and a dummy variable for the cases where all answers were correct. Therefore, this design seems to perform like a rule of thumb and enables to capture different dimensions in a compact form. Third, Table 2 provides the measure methodology of studies: self-assessment versus asking questions. Besides, in case of questions, possible measurement methodologies are classified: summation of correct answers, use of dummy variable in case of all answers are correct, measures depending on at least "n" out of total number of questions, treatment of each question one-by-one separately, use of instrumental variables (IVs), and number of "do not know" answers (i.e., illiteracy). The instrumental variables refer the variables, which are not directly representative of financial literacy, but highly correlated with it. In other words, instrumental variables are chosen due to their hidden or not directly observed correlation with the financial literacy. Lastly, in Table 2 number of questions are limited with financial literacy related section of questionnaires, which are extensively long and detailed.

Based on the summary in Table 2, there are both similarities and challenges faced by previous studies:

- **Country-coverage:** The history of financial education initiatives goes back to 1950s in the U.S. (Hastings et al., 2013). Therefore, it is not a coincidence to observe that the number of studies focusing on the U.S. is relatively higher than in any other country. On the other hand, there are several countries covered by studies, and the number is growing at an increasing pace. As a final point, the number of multi-country studies is still low. By all the means, the aforementioned challenges in the design of questionnaires contributes to the difficulties in country-wise implementations and comparisons.
- **Respondents, sample size and content**: The most obvious observation is that there is a tendency of using larger scaled databases to have a more representative sample. Depending on the research question or design, either adults or students are chosen as respondents, but even with the same targeted respondents, the topics covered differ. Some studies include more complex issues such as advanced financial instruments knowledge whereas some others limit the content with numeracy. Overall, common topics appear to be compound interest, inflation and risk diversification.
- **Importance of Lusardi and Mitchell (2011):** Number of questions vary significantly from 148 page-long survey of the U.K. Financial Services Authority to 3 questions of Lusardi and Mitchell (2011). 26 out of 67 the studies either directly use or add further questions to the design of Lusardi and Mitchell (2011). The questions of Lusardi and Mitchell were selected probably due to its simplicity, but relevance at the same time. However, it

is important to re-emphasize that fewer number of questions can result in classifying a respondent as financially illiterate based on limited information.
- **Self-assessment:** As previously discussed, most of the studies preferred not to rely on self-assessment surveys, and only 12 out of 67 studies included self-assessed measures, where in most of them these questions served as complementary measures.
- **Financial literacy measures:** Most of the studies used summation of correct answers, but in complimentary to other measures. Due to non-availability of a single question or a measure to quantify the financial literacy level, some studies also used instrumental variables. Attendance of primary school, family related information, macroeconomic conditions (Behrman et al., 2012), financial background of family (Alessie et al., 2011), number of universities and newspapers sold in the neighborhood (Klapper et al., 2013), or even proficiency in the language (Sekita, 2011) were used to estimate financial literacy. However, these results should be interpreted with caution since geography of the study, cultural differences or conceptualization of instrumental variable may influence the results (such as higher the family bonds, higher the impact of family in more eastern cultures, or artificially high number of universities due to online/distant education giving or very small-scaled institutions).

Last but not least, these observations indicate that every study puts its own angle, and it is a fact that the literature is expanding to contribute further and/or cover different parts of the world. This brings the next point of discussion: what is the financial literacy level in different countries? What does cross-country evidence tell?

FINANCIAL LITERACY IN DIFFERENT COUNTRIES

In a literature survey by Stolper and Walter (2017), the studies employing the Lusardi-Mitchell design were summarized by country. On the basis of their review, Figure 1 is derived to compare different financial literacy levels among various countries. In Figure 1, the size of each bubble changes with the number of participants, and on y-axis the percentage of respondents answering all three questions correctly is given. The visual evaluation clearly points out a clustering of upper-income countries versus middle-income group. Just as importantly, there is also a variation among the countries even within the same group: the literacy measure of Germany was found as 59 percent and 53 percent in two different studies whereas the score of Sweden was reported as 21 percent.

Table 2. Comparing different strategies to measure financial literacy

Author(s)	Targeted Respondents	Content Basic	Content Complex	# of Questions (*)	Self-assessment	Sum of correct	If all correct, dummy	At least "n" correct	One-by-one	Instrumental Variable (IV)	Number of "do not know"
Multi-country											
Atkinson and Messy (2012)	Adults (#19212, 14 countries)	x		22		x					
Jappelli and Padula (2011)	Adults (47 countries)	x		4						x	
Bucher-Koenen et al. (2017)	Adults (#5700, 3 countries)	x		18 (L-M)	x		x				
OECD – PISA (2018)	Students (#540000, 72 countries)	x		15		x					
Country-specific Studies from Australia & Oceania											
Agnew et al. (2013)	Adults (#1024, Australia)	x		3 (L-M)		x	x	x	x		x
Beal and Delpachitra (2003)	Students (#842, Australia)		x	25		x		x			
Worthington (2006)	Adults (#3548, Australia)		x	28		x					
Crossan et al. (2011)	Adults (#850, New Zealand)	x		3 (L-M)			x		x		
Country-specific Studies from Europe											
Bigot et al. (2011)	Adults (#1502, France)	x		10			x				
Muller and Weber (2010)	Adults (#3228, Germany)		x	8	x	x					
Bucher-Koenen and Lusardi (2011)	Adults (#2222, Germany)	x		3 (L-M)		x	x				
O'Donnell and Keeney (2009)	Adults (#1529, Ireland)		x	15 variables only for Factor Analysis						Factor analysis	
Monticone (2010)	Adults (#7977, Italy)	x		3 (L-M)		x					
Calcagno and Monticone (2011)	Adults (#1686, Italy)	x		8 (L-M+)		x				x	
Fornero and Monticone (2011)	Adults (#7977, Italy)	x		3 (L-M)		x		x	x		x
Beckman (2013)	Adults (#1030, Romania)	x		3 (L-M)		x	x		x		

continued on following page

Table 2 continued

Author(s)	Targeted Respondents	Content Basic	Content Complex	# of Questions (*)	Self-assessment	Sum of correct	If all correct, dummy	At least "n" correct	One-by-one	Instrumental Variable (IV)	Number of "do not know"
Country-specific Studies from Asia											
Song (2015)	Adults (#1000, China)	x		5		x					
Sekita (2011)	Adults (#5386, Japan)	x		3 (L-M)	x	x	x			x	
Klapper et al. (2011)	Adults (#1600, Russia)	x		4 (L-M)	x	x				x	
Klapper and Panos (2011)	Adults (#1600, Russia)	x		3 (L-M)			x		x		
Almenber and Save-Soderberg (2011)	Adults (#1302, Sweden)	x		3 (L-M)		x	x				x
Brown and Graf (2013)	Adults (#1500, Switzerland)	x		3 (L-M)			x		x		
Deuflhard et al. (2015)	Adults (#2000, Netherlands)	x		16						Factor analysis	
Alessie et al. (2011)	Adults (#2000, Netherlands)	x		3 (L-M)						x	
Van Rooij et al. (2011)	Adults (#2000, Netherlands)	x		16		x					
Van Rooij et al. (2011)	Adults (#2000, Netherlands)	x		16	x	x					
Van Rooij et al. (2011)	Adults (#1508, Netherlands)	x		16 (L-M+)		x					
Financial Services Authority of U.K. (2005)	Adults (#5328, U.K.)		x	8		x					
Atkinson et al. (2006)	Adults (#5328, U.K.)		x	148 pages (by Financial Services Authority)						Factor analysis	
Disney and Gathergood (2012)	Adults (#3041, U.K.)		x	3		x	x		x		
Country-specific Studies from America Region											
Behrman et al. (2012)	Adults (#13054, Chile)	x		12 (L-M+)						x	
Volpe et al. (1996)	Students (#454, US)	x		10		x					

continued on following page

Table 2 continued

Author(s)	Targeted Respondents	Content Basic	Content Complex	# of Questions (*)	Self-assessment	Sum of correct	If all correct, dummy	At least "n" correct	One-by-one	Instrumental Variable (IV)	Number of "do not know"
Chen and Volpe (1998)	Students (#924, US)	x		36		x					
Tennyson and Nguyen (2001)	Students (#1643, US)		x	31		x					
Volpe et al. (2002)	Adults (#530, US)	x		10		x			x	x	
Chen and Volpe (2002)	Students (#924, US)	x		36		x			x		
Bowen (2002)	Students (#64, US)		x	19					x		
Hilghert et al. (2003)	Adults (#1000, US)		x	28		x					
Agnew (2004)	Adults & Students (#395, US)		x	10		x					
Hira and Loibl (2005)	Adults (#1519, US)	x		4						x	
Perry and Morris (2005)	Adults (#10997, US)		x	4	x						
Baron-Donovan et al. (2005)	Adults (#42, US)		x	16		x					
Manton et al. (2006)	Students (#407, US)		x	20		x					
Danes and Haberman (2007)	Students (#5329, US)			4	x						
Mandell and Klein (2007)	Students (#5775, US)		x	31		x					
Robb and James (2008)	Students (#3525, US)		x	6		x					
Robb and Sharpe (2009)	Students (#3884, US)		x	6		x					
Borden et al. (2008)	Students (#93, US)		x	7		x					
Hill and Perdue (2008)	Students (#170, US)		x	50		x					
Lusardi (2011)	Adults (#1200, US)	x		5 (L-M+)	x					x	
Lusardi and Tufano (2009)	Adults (#1000, US)	x		3	x					x	

continued on following page

Table 2 continued

Author(s)	Targeted Respondents	Content Basic	Content Complex	# of Questions (*)	Self-assessment	Sum of correct	If all correct, dummy	At least "n" correct	One-by-one	Instrumental Variable (IV)	Number of "do not know"
Clark et al. (2010)	Adults (#1000, US)	x		14 (L-M+)		x					
Fonseca et al. (2012)	Adults (#2500, US)	x		23		x (used within a model)					
Yoong (2011)	Adults (#2500, US)	x		3 (L-M)						x	x
Lusardi and Mitchell (2011)	Adults (#1488, US)	x		3 (L-M)		x	x				
Utkus and Young (2011)	Adults (#900, US)	x		4		x					
Bumcrot et al. (2011)	Adults (#25000, US)	x		5 (L-M)		x					
de Bassa Scheresberg (2013)	Adults (#4500, US)	x		3 (L-M)	x	x		x			x
Huang et al. (2013)	Children (#2651, US)	x		3 (L-M)		x	x				
Lusardi and de Bassa Scheresberg (2013)	Adults (#25000, US)	x		5	x	x		x			
Mottola (2013)	Adults (#25000, US)	x		5 (L-M)		x					
Xiao et al. (2013)	Adults (#25000, US)	x		5	x	x					
Nye and Hillyard (2013)	Adults (#267, US)	x		13		x					
Moore (2003)	Adults (#1423, US)	x		21		x					
Gustman et al. (2012)	Adults (#3418, US)	x		3 (L-M)		x					
Knoll and Houts (2012)	Adults (#2539, US)	x		20 (L-M+)			x				
Jappelli and Padula (2015)	Adults (#18332, 14 countries)	x		5		x					

(*): L-M refers the three questions designed in Lusardi and Mitchell (2011), and L-M+ refers the surveys where further questions were added to the design of L-M.

Source: Author's calculations and Nicolini (2019)

Figure 1. Financial literacy in different countries based on Lusardi-Mitchell design
Source: Data retrieved from Stolper and Walter (2017)

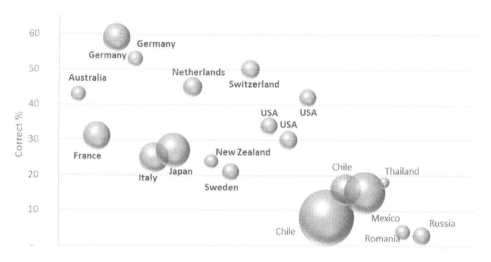

The heterogeneity among countries is also well noted by other surveys. The Standard & Poor's Global Financial Literacy Survey, conducted by Global Financial Literacy Excellence Center (GFLEC) of the George Washington University, shows that only 38 percent of account owning adults are classified as financially literate, varying from 57 percent in major advanced countries to 30 percent in emerging ones (GFLEC, 2015). Based on the International Survey of Adult Financial Literacy Survey of the OECD/INFE conducted over G20 countries, only 53% of respondents did not know what would happen to the purchasing power of money assuming flat inflation rate for another year (OECD, 2017). By utilizing the same database of OECD/INFE Survey, Cupak et al. (2018) correlated the unexplained of financial literacy gaps among the countries, which cannot be captured by the individual characteristics, with the variation in the macroeconomic and institutional country-level variables.

The evidence from different countries point out that the problem is not specific to a part of the world, and there is still need for initiatives to improve the situation in both developed and developing countries. The common findings highlight some important points that would be useful to enhance strategies to improve financial literacy:

- **Despite the fact that in all countries there is room to improve financial literacy level, there is also a difference between the major advanced economies and emerging ones, but even across the countries.** In the survey of GFLEC (2015), within the advanced economies the financial literacy rate varied from 37 percent in Italy to 68 percent in Canada. OECD/INFE (2017) also supported the variation among countries: financial knowledge scores vary from 9.6 in Saudi Arabia to 14.9 in France (out of full score of 20). In Australia, less than 50 percent of respondents were able to answer all 5 simple questions (University of Melbourne the Household, Income and Labor Dynamics in Australia, 2018) whereas financial knowledge score in Hong Kong was found out to be 5.9 out of 7.0 (Investor Education Center of Hong Kong, 2018).

- **The variations among country groups or countries is a result of several economic and financial circumstances, but it is not a simple causality.** The economic and financial environment of a country is an outcome of several other factors, so that it serves like an "instrumental variable" to understand financial literacy level. Naturally, any economy with a deeper financial market would signal that the citizens on average comparatively know more about the financial concepts and are more involved, or in a developed country it can be assumed that more resources allocated to financial education at national level that might support the numeracy skills, so the financial literacy. For instance; around 38 percent of the variation in financial literacy was explained by the differences in Gross Domestic Product (GDP) per capita of countries (GFLEC, 2015). Despite this correlation, the causality is not obvious. Financial literacy is not simply an outcome or output of the economic variables, but the interaction of economic variables with specific conditions, such as education or availability of financial systems. Therefore, better financial and economic climate would help to mitigate the problem, but the literacy level cannot be targeted in a cause-effect framework.

- **Country-specific experience affects the financial literacy measurement.** Cross-country evidence is hard to interpret especially due to aforementioned measure-related challenges. Whenever a global survey is applied to several countries simultaneously, the design of the questionnaire becomes even more important. Relevance of the wording and/or topic of the question to financial history of that country might affect the score. As an illustration, respondents from Argentina did better than world average in understanding inflation (GFLEC, 2015) due to their history with inflation. Therefore, both the measure and designs should be prepared cautiously in case multi-country results would be compared together, and interpretations should be derived accordingly.

FROM FINANCIAL LITERACY TO FINANCIAL DECISIONS

The interest of academics, policy makers, and authorities in financial literacy arises from the transmission channel of this awareness or knowledge to financial actions, and hence to general financial environment. Therefore, not the knowledge itself, but the link between financial literacy and financial decisions plays the crucial role. It is expected that higher the financial knowledge, better financial decisions would be taken since a financially literate person would process financial information, be aware of the consequences, and end up with financially reasonable decisions, and vice versa.

Unfortunately, the direct causality between higher literacy scores and better decisions does not seem to be obvious compared to the link between lower literacy and poor decisions. In other words, financial literacy cannot guarantee making the right decisions (Mason and Wilson, 2000). Even after having several courses, gaining an awareness on financial products, people may not be able to shape their behaviors in line with this knowledge. There can be several biases to explain the disconnectedness in knowledge and behaviors, such as not digested information, not paying attention to new knowledge, or choosing to rely on knowledge of family or friends. Besides, the definition of "financially better" decisions are a subjective outcome of personal risk aversion level, characteristics, cultural or social status, etc. Therefore, this chapter would limit the discussions with the situations where there is financial knowledge, but it is ignored or considered in decision-making process as putting aside the behavioral and personal biases. Any study focus on the transmission of financial literacy to financial actions should control the results for personal attributes as well. Another important thing is that the change in behavior requires time and effort, and there may not be a one-time measurement fitting all respondents. Like all other habits, one has to practice on this information, but when it comes to using this previous knowledge, this behavior can fall in place even after months. Therefore, one-time measurement may not work for all respondents as trying to quantify the effectiveness of financial literacy.

The review of Fernandes et al. (2013) including 188 studies supported the view that financial literacy cannot drive financial behavior. Especially after correcting behavioral biases, the financial literacy was found out to explain financial behavior in a very limited way. Willis (2008) even moved one step further by stating that financial literacy can result in dangerous decisions in case financially literate people would become overconfident by trusting their background. Willis (2008) also argued that due to fast changing financial environment, it is impossible to keep up the pace and reach financial literacy target.

Even there are only limited findings stating there is no significant transmission channel, these critics overlook the fact that financial literacy is regarded as complementary instead of replacing other financial services or resources. A person with financial knowledge is not expected to be a financial expert and depending on the needs one would still need the help of institutions or experts in the decision-making process. In other words, financial literacy would serve as a tool to improve the financial decision-making process. Financial knowledge is not a standalone tool to drive or guarantee people to make the best decision, but a person would well aware of his decision and potential behavioral biases.

That explains why financial literacy is the first important step; ensuring financial literacy would at least increase the probability of making financially reasonable decisions. This initial attempt would minimize any bad decisions given due to insufficient information, but of course not totally eliminate.

Following The Transmission Channels

Financial literacy would affect financial actions through different ways. Assuming that more financially literate person would know more about financial products and services, it can be expected that financial literacy can motivate people involve more in stock markets or riskier alternatives. However, it is not obvious what kind of other financial decisions can be influenced and whether always in a positive way. Previous studies help to shed light on these questions.

Use of credit cards and high-cost borrowing

It is expected that financially literate person would be aware of the possible consequences of borrowing or debt, and hence either use less debt or use borrowings under proper circumstances at a reasonable cost. The sample of Moore (2003) from Washington, U.S. supported that use of payday loans and withdrawal cash by credit cards is higher for lower financially literate people. For another sample composed of U.S. college students Robb (2011) also suggested that financial knowledge helps to use credit cards in a more responsible way, such as no delays in payments, and no use of cash advances. Even a larger dataset, 2009 National Financial Capability Study by FINRA, showed the same relationship between financial knowledge and credit card usage habits (Allgood and Walstad, 2011). A recent study by Harvey (2019) also verified that taking financial courses in high school helps to decrease the use of payday loan. Mottola (2013) also found positive relation between the low financial literacy and faulty credit card behavior.

Not only for credit cards but also for general cost of borrowing, evidence from U.K. showed that higher the financial literacy measure, lower the share of high cost credit items in a household's portfolio (Disney and Gathergood, 2013). In another study among the U.S. respondents, financial literacy improvement explained 20 percent reduction in the use of high-cost borrowing (Lusardi and de Bassa Scheresberg, 2013). Further evidence from the U.S. supported the relationship between financial literacy and the use of high-cost borrowing facilities such as student loans, payday loans, auto title loans (Lusardi and Tufano, 2015). Considering mortgage payments as a kind of borrowing for housing, a positive correlation between lower numerical ability group and mortgage delinquency was also noted (Gerardi et al., 2010).

Lastly, 2018 National Financial Capability Study (NFCS) released by the FINRA Investor Education Foundation found out a positive correlation between financial education and overdrawing the checking accounts, engagement in fee-generating credit card behaviors, or use of non-bank borrowing methods (NFCS, 2019).

Stock Market Participation and Advanced Financial Instruments

More financially literate people would know more about financial markets and products, and financial market participation is expected to increase with literacy. Financial sophistication can be associated with riskier share-holding-position, not only due to knowledge, but also learning from the investment experience. Previous studies proved the expectation of higher the financial literacy, higher participation in stock market (Christelis, et al., 2010; van Rooij, et al., 2011; Grinblatt et al., 2011; Yoong, 2011; Almenberg and Dreber, 2011; Arrondel et al., 2015; Balloch et al., 2015) and derivatives market (Hsiao and Tsai; 2018). Yoong (2011) also showed that financially literate individuals would more likely invest in stocks and mutual funds. Bianchi (2017) found that portfolio of the most literate households ended up with 0.4 percent higher annual returns than of the least literate households and added one more perspective to previous findings: the most literate people tend to hold riskier funds only if riskier alternatives offer higher returns. This finding is in line with the previous findings that highlighted a positive correlation between the financial literacy score and degree of portfolio diversification (Guiso and Jappelli, 2009).

Another important finding from Bianchi (2017) is that the more literate people can actively rebalance this risky position to keep risk exposure flattish over time. To be more specific; for the least literate group the passive changes in the portfolio is 64 percent of total change in the risky share whereas this rate goes down to 30 percent for the most literate group. This means that the financially literate people intervene in portfolio rebalancing more to keep their risk exposure stable. However, when it comes to the mutual funds, more financially literate people tend to rely more on passive funds whereas less sophisticated investors prefer active funds ignoring transaction fees/costs (Muller and Weber, 2010). Other studies also supported the view that financially sophisticated investors tend to do less investment mistakes (Feng and Seasholes, 2005; Bilias et al. 2010; Hoffmann et al. 2013; Bucher-Koenen and Ziegelmeyer 2014; Guiso and Viviano 2015).

Savings and returns

Previous findings found out that financial literacy positively affect interest rate on the saving accounts (Deuflhard et al., 2015), propensity to make a long-term financial plan (Arrondel et al., 2012), and holding precautionary savings (de Bassa Scheresberg, 2013).

There are findings from different countries supporting that the financial literacy is linked with retirement planning and savings (Lusardi and Mitchell, 2011; Hastings and Mitchell, 2011; Jappelli, 2011; Behrman et al., 2012; Beckmann, 2013; Brown and Graf, 2013). Utkus and Young (2011) even pointed out that people with more financial knowledge tend to borrow less from their saving plans. Nonetheless, Gustman et al. (2010) findings from the U.S. Health and Retirement Survey could not prove a significant impact of financial knowledge on the value of pension wealth even though better numeracy skills helps adults to have a better understanding of their pensions or social security. Song (2015) also could not conclude that the higher literacy the higher contributions to retirement saving plans, but only lower literacy would be related with lower contributions.

Lastly, for other saving purposes the positive impact of financial literacy was unveiled, such as for college saving plans (Huang et al., 2013), propensity to save or savings accumulation (Klapper et al., 2013; Jamison et al., 2014, Berry et al., 2018).

SOLUTIONS AND FUTURE DIRECTIONS

All aforementioned transmission channels indicate that an improvement in financial literacy would at least benefit decision-making processes in a positive way. Therefore, it is not surprising to see that several programs have been initiated in different parts of the world. Before structuring the solutions, it is important to specify the level of recommendations: younger people, individuals, and national level.

Younger People

One of the well-known measures to compare worldwide financial literacy among young people is the OECD's Programme for International Student Assessment (PISA). Latest available data of 2015 from 15 countries with 15-year-old subjects reveals the fact that on average 22 percent of students did not have basic financial skills (OECD, 2018). Interestingly, 56 percent of respondents had bank accounts referring that they were already a part of financial decision-making process whereas only 31 percent of this group had the skills to manage a bank account. In another survey conducted by EVERFI Inc. in 2018, college students could correctly answer only 2 out of 6 questions on average, but 84 percent of 104,000 respondents reported taking a personal finance course.

Unfortunately, this evidence from the world indicates that younger people are still lack of some important skills and knowledge. Especially considering that schoolchildren are increasingly taking financial decisions, such as mobile phone usages, university loans, younger people are starting to be a part of financial system at earlier ages compared to previous decades. The most efficient way to address this problem is to integrate financial knowledge and skills to the education system.

Tang and Peter (2015) found that number of states where the personal finance course is a part of high school curriculum has increased from 13 in 2009 to 17 in 2013. In other countries, financial education has already become a national level educational strategy. For example, in Czech Republic, Poland, Slovakia the integration to school curriculum is mandatory whereas in Hungary there is partial integration. To show the impact of these initiatives, Russia is a good example: together with the partnership of World Bank in 2011 financial literacy courses were initiated in schools and universities, and in 2017 Russian students ranked 4th versus 10th in 2012 in PISA.

Lastly, owing to recent financial crises, people became aware of the financial illiteracy, and hence understood the need for compulsory education. According to the 2019 April Equifax Financial Literacy Survey conducted in the U.S., 90 percent of total 1071 respondents also agreed that personal finance should be a part of graduate high school education. This means that any kind of compulsory training at schools would also be well perceived and accepted by citizens.

Individuals

At the individual level, gaining financial literacy needs time and effort. Especially, the return on this kind of self-investment is not so obvious. A person may be exposed to several trainings on financial concepts and spend time to really reflect this knowledge to his spending and investment behaviors, but might not quantify the cost and benefit of being financially literate. Therefore, it is really challenging to motivate individuals to participate in these educations voluntarily. In the beginning, people would not know what they do not know and how they can benefit from such a knowledge, and even after the completion they may not have a clear tangible benefit, which would elaborate the spread of financial literacy initiatives. Comparing to any other kind of self-invested training, such as language courses or software trainings, where the demand arises from the individual and benefit can be observable starting from the minute spent, it would definitely be harder to plant the need for financial training in individuals' minds. Last but not least, there is a well-documented gender gap at odds with females (Guiso and Jappelli, 2009; Fonseca et al., 2012; Almenberg and Dreber, 2015) referring that females should be specifically prioritized in all initiatives.

Figure 2. National financial literacy initiatives in different countries
Source: Banco de España (2018)

Countries with a national strategy at design phase
Argentina, Chile, China, Colombia, Costa Rica, El Salvador, France, Guatemala, Kenya, Kyrgyzstan, Lebanon, Malawi, Mexico, Pakistan, Paraguay, Peru, Poland, Romania, Saudi Arabia, Serbia, Tanzania, Thailand, Uganda, Uruguay, Zambia

Countries with a national strategy for the first time
Armenia, Belgium, Brazil, Canada, Croatia, Denmark, Estonia, Ghana, Hong Kong, China, India, Indonesia, Ireland, Israel, Korea, Latvia, Morocco, Nigeria, Portugal, Russia, Slovenia, South Africa, Sweden, Turkey

Countries with a national strategy that is under review, or with a second-strategy
Australia, Czech Republic, Japan, Malaysia, the Netherlands, New Zealand, Singapore, Slovakia, Spain, United Kingdom, United States

To achieve successful results, not only having a clear, specific larger-scaled strategies are enough, but it is also important to connect with audience. As an illustration, considering that family budget or controlling credit card expenditures would be an appealing topic and affect savings at national level, specific trainings or resources can be provided especially on this area. Even these topics can be considered as obvious or easy choices, it is important to remember that survey findings still indicate room for improvement. In the latest National Foundation for Credit Counseling (NFCC) 2019 Consumer Financial Literacy Survey among the U.S. adults, only two out of five adults report to have a budget and keep close track of their expenses (NFCC, 2019). One out of four admits that they do not pay their bills on time and even though nearly 2 out of 3 adults claim to save for their retirement, only 1 out of 5 adults feel very confident that the savings would be enough.

National Level

Due to the significance of the problem, many countries already have a strategy in action. Figure 2 classifies 60 countries based on their progress: (i) group of countries with a national strategy, which is currently being designed, (ii) another group of countries with a national strategy, which is currently pursued for the first time, (iii) last group, where the first strategy results are currently being reviewed or second-strategy is in action.

There are three main key takeaways from the current situation: first, the number of countries with a solid strategy is high and growing. Second, in most of the countries there are multiple involved institutions showing the need for joint effort. For example, in France the Central Bank, Ministry of Economy and Finance, Ministry of Agriculture, Ministry of Education, National Financial Counseling Association (ANACOFI), French Banking Federation (FBF), National Institute for consumer Affairs (INC), and several other parties (both from private sector and non-profit organizations) join their forces. Another example from Australia demonstrates that Australian Securities Investment Commission, Taxation Office, Financial Security Authority, Department of Agriculture and Water Resources, Reserve Bank of Australia, and other governmental bodies contribute to the National Financial Literacy Strategy. Finally, most of the programs are set for long-term since the investment in financial literacy needs enough time to observe its impact

CONCLUSION

Financial literacy has gained attention over the past decades. The average publication per year, with a title including financial literacy or financial knowledge, increased from 1 to 26 papers (from 2002-2004 to 2013-2015) (Stolper and Walter, 2017). Of course, considering the financial turbulence of the past few decades, this trend is not a coincidence. By increasing the financial knowledge, the aim was to help individuals, who are equipped with necessary tools to avoid making financial mistakes. Not only governmental bodies or non-profit organizations, but also private sector started to invest in financial education to reach this aim. In June 2017 in the Argentina-European Union Forum, Banco Bilbao Vizcaya Argentaria, S.A. (BBVA) Executive Director announced that they invested more than 67 million Euro to develop financial education programs for more than 9 million people.

Compared to the importance of topic, surprisingly there is still not a standard definition of financial education nor a common measure to quantify the literacy. In other words, currently available measures used to quantify the gap between current status and targeted literacy level is still subjective. Based on previous studies, financial knowledge is only enough to understand the concepts, but not sufficient to put actions into practice. In this regard, this chapter redefines financial literacy (or any other interchangeably used term) as the set of following items:

- Knowledge about financial concepts/products/services,
- Competence to use financial concepts/products/services,
- Ability to take financial decisions (i.e., transmission to behavior),
- Confidence in financial operations

Previous literature review on different attempts to measure financial literacy highlights that target groups (adults versus students), countries (single-country versus multi-country), the content of questionnaires/surveys (from basic topics to advanced financial calculations), number of questions, and financial measure methodology (self-assessment, summation of correct answers, instrumental variables, etc.) vary substantially. However, there are some similarities in: (i) the selection of basic topics, such as compound interest, inflation and risk diversification, (ii) the survey design, where three questions of Lusardi and Mitchell (2011) were widely used, (iii) tendency to have larger databases covering higher number of countries. Comparing the outcomes of these studies from different countries, the results indicate that financial literacy is a global issue. Owing to several economic and financial variations, there is a gap between the major advanced economies and emerging ones, but there is still a huge variation from country to country that cannot be explained by only macroeconomic and financial environment.

The interest of academics and policy makers in financial literacy arises from the transmission of financial knowledge to decisions, and hence to general financial environment. Therefore, the link between financial literacy and financial decisions plays the crucial role. The results of previous studies supported that financially literate people would (i) use less debt or use any kind of borrowings (including credit cards) under proper circumstances at a reasonable cost, (ii) participate in stock market more, tend to take riskier positions in the financial markets (only if accompanied with higher returns), do less investment mistakes, (iii) have higher propensity to save, participate in retirement funds, and make long-term financial plans. Even though there were some contradictory studies stating that "financial literacy cannot guarantee better decisions" or "findings are not enough to support a significant positive relationship", it is important to note that financial literacy is only a tool to improve the financial decision-making process. Ensuring financial literacy would at least increase the probability of making financially reasonable decisions and minimize any poor choices selected due to insufficient information, but of course cannot totally prevent unfavorable outcomes.

To utilize the benefit from financial literacy, there are three stages of action: younger ages, individual, and national level. By including financial topics as a part of compulsory education programmes, younger people would get familiar with basic topics. At individual level, trainings or long-term programmes should be prepared audience-specific with a clear language, and individuals should also make efforts to learn at least basic financial concepts to be aware of their rights and opportunities. Lastly, national financial literacy strategy should be in action and serve as an umbrella to guide and support all country-wise initiatives in the long-term.

REFERENCES

Agnew, J. (2004). *An analysis of how individuals react to market returns in one 401(k) plan.* Center for Retirement Research at Boston College, CRR WP 2004-13.

Agnew, J., Bateman, H., & Thorp, S. (2013). Financial Literacy and Retirement Planning in Australia. *Numeracy Advancing Education in Quantitative Literacy, 6*(2), article 7.

Alessie, R., van Rooij, M., & Lusardi, A. (2011). Financial Literacy, Retirement Preparation and Pension Expectations in the Netherlands. *Journal of Pension Economics and Finance, 10*(4), 527–545. doi:10.1017/S1474747211000461

Allgood, S., & Walstad, W. (2011). *The Effects of Perceived and Actual Financial Knowledge on Credit Card Behavior.* Networks Financial Institute at Indiana State University Working Paper, 2011-WP-15.

Almenberg, J., & Dreber, A. (2015). Gender, stock market participation and financial literacy. *Economics Letters, 137,* 140–142. doi:10.1016/j.econlet.2015.10.009

Almenberg, J., & Save-Soderberg, J. (2011). *Financial Literacy and Retirement Planning in Sweden.* NETSPAR Discussion Paper 01/2011–018.

Arrondel, L., Debbich, M., & Savignac, F. (2015). Stockholding in France: The role of financial literacy and information. *Applied Economics Letters, 22*(16), 1315–1319. doi:10.1080/13504851.2015.1026578

Atkinson, A., McKay, S., Kempson, E., & Collard, S. (2006). Levels of Financial Capability in the U.K.: Results of a Baseline Survey. Financial Service Authority, Consumer Research, 47.

Atkinson, A., & Messy, F. (2012). *Measuring Financial Literacy: Results of the OECD/ International Network on Financial Education (INFE) Pilot Study.* OECD Working Paper on Finance, Insurance and Private Pensions, No 15.

Balloch, A., Nicolae, A., & Philip, D. (2015). Stock market literacy, trust, and participation. *Review of Finance, 19*(5), 1925–1963. doi:10.1093/rof/rfu040

Banco de Espana. (2018) *Financial Education Plan 2018-2021.* Retrieved from https://www.bde.es/f/webbde/Secciones/Publicaciones/OtrasPublicaciones/educacionfinaciera/PlanEducacion2018en.pdf

Baron-Donovan, C., Wiener, R., Gross, K., & Block-Lieb, S. (2005). Financial literacy teacher training: A multiple-measure evaluation. *Journal of Financial Counselling and Planning, 16*(2), 63–75.

Beal, D., & Delpachitra, S. B. (2003). Financial Literacy among Australian University Students. *Economic Papers*, *22*(1), 65–78. doi:10.1111/j.1759-3441.2003.tb00337.x

Beckmann, E. (2013). Financial Literacy and Household Savings in Romania. *Numeracy Advancing Education in Quantitative Literacy*, *6*(2), Article 9.

Behrman, J., Mitchell, O. S., Soo, C., & Bravo, D. (2012). Financial Literacy, Schooling, and Wealth Accumulation. *American Economic Review Paper and Proceedings*, *102*(3), 300–304. doi:10.1257/aer.102.3.300 PMID:23355747

Berry, J., Karlan, D., & Pradhan, M. (2018). The Impact of Financial Education for Youth in Ghana. *World Development*, *102*, 71–89. doi:10.1016/j.worlddev.2017.09.011

Bianchi, M. (2017). Financial Literacy and Portfolio Dynamics. *The Journal of Finance*, *73*(2), 831–859. doi:10.1111/jofi.12605

Bigot, R., Croutte, P., Mueller, J., & Osier, G. (2011). *Middle Classes in Europe*. Research Center for the Study and Observation of Living (CREDOC) Working Paper, No 282.

Bilias, Y., Georgarakos, D., & Haliassos, M. (2010). Portfolio inertia and stock market ñuctuations. *Journal of Money, Credit and Banking*, *42*(4), 715–742. doi:10.1111/j.1538-4616.2010.00304.x

Borden, L. M., Lee, S. A., Serido, J., & Collins, D. (2008). Changing college students' financial knowledge, attitudes, and behavior through seminar participation. *Journal of Family and Economic Issues*, *29*(1), 23–40. doi:10.100710834-007-9087-2

Bowen, C. (2002). Financial Knowledge of Teens and Their Parents. *Journal of Financial Counselling and Planning*, *13*(2), 93–102.

Brown, M., & Graf, R. (2013). Financial Literacy and Retirement Planning in Switzerland. *Numeracy Advancing Education in Quantitative Literacy*, *6*(2), article 6.

Bucher-Koenen, T., & Lusardi, A. (2011). Financial literacy and retirement planning in Germany. *Journal of Pension Economics and Finance*, *10*(4), 565–584. doi:10.1017/S1474747211000485

Bucher-Koenen, T., Lusardi, A., Alessie, R., & van Rooij, M. (2017). How financially literate are women? An overview and new insights. *The Journal of Consumer Affairs*, *51*(2), 255–283. doi:10.1111/joca.12121

Bumcrot, C., Lin, J., & Lusardi, A. (2013). The Geography of Financial Literacy. *Numeracy Advancing Education in Quantitative Literacy*, *6*(2), article 2.

Calcagno, R., & Monticone, C. (2011). Financial Literacy and the Demand for Financial Advice. *Journal of Banking & Finance, 50*, 363–380. doi:10.1016/j.jbankfin.2014.03.013

Chen, H., & Volpe, R. P. (1998). An analysis of personal financial literacy among college students. *Financial Services Review, 7*(2), 107–128. doi:10.1016/S1057-0810(99)80006-7

Chen, H., & Volpe, R. P. (2002). Gender Differences in Personal Financial Literacy among College Students. *Financial Services Review, 11*, 289–307.

Christelis, D., Jappelli, T., & Padula, M. (2010). Cognitive abilities and portfolio choice. *European Economic Review, 54*(1), 18–39. doi:10.1016/j.euroecorev.2009.04.001

Clark, R., Sandler, M., & Mallen, S. (2010). *The Role of Financial Literacy in Determining Retirement Plans.* National Bureau of Economic Research Working Paper, No. 16612. Retrieved from www.nber.org/papers/w16612

Crossan, D., Feslier, D., & Hurnabard, R. (2011). Financial Literacy and Retirement Planning in New Zealand. *Journal of Pension Economics and Finance, 10*(4), 619–635. doi:10.1017/S1474747211000515

Cupak, A., Fessler, P., Silgoner, M., & Ulbrich, E. (2018). *Exploring differences in financial literacy across countries: the role of individual characteristics and institutions.* Oesterreichische National Bank Working Paper, 220.

Danes, S., & Haberman, H. (2007). Teen financial knowledge, self-efficacy, and behavior: A gender view. *Journal of Financial Counselling and Planning, 18*(2), 48–60.

de Bassa, S. C. (2013). Financial literacy and ðnancial behavior among young adults: Evidence and implications. *Numeracy, 6*(2), 1–21.

Deuflhard, F., Georgarakos, D., & Inderst, R. (2015). *Financial Literacy and Savings Account Returns.* European Central Bank Working Paper, No. 1852.

Disney, R., & Gathergood, J. (2012). *Financial literacy and consumer credit use.* Centre for Finance and Credit Markets (CFCM) Working Paper, No. 12/01.

Equifax Financial Literacy Survey. (2019). *2019 Equifax Consumer Solutions Financial Literacy Month Survey.* Retrieved from https://blog.equifax.com/credit/fast-facts-2019-equifax-financial-literacy-survey/

EVERFI. (2018). *Next Generation of Financial Capability: Young Adults in Higher Education.* Retrieved from https://everfi.com/press-releases/everfi-reveals-national-financial-knowledge-findings-based-survey-results-college-students-across-country/

Feng, L., & Seasholes, M. S. (2005). Do investor sophistication and trading experience eliminate behavioral biases in ðnancial markets? *Review of Finance, 9*(3), 305–351. doi:10.100710679-005-2262-0

Fernandes, D., Lynch, J. Jr, & Netemeyer, R. (2013). Financial Literacy, Financial Education and Downstream Financial Behaviors. *Management Science, 60*(8), 1861–2109. doi:10.1287/mnsc.2013.1849

Financial Industry Regulatory Authority. (2009). *Financial Capability in the United States National Survey Executive Summary.* FINRA Investor Education Foundation. Retrieved from https://www.usfinancialcapability.org/downloads/NFCS_2009_Natl_Exec_Sum.pdf

Financial Services Authority of U.K. (2005). *Financial Services Authority: Financial Capability baseline survey: questionnaire.* Retrieved from http://www.fsa.gov.uk/

Fonseca, R., Mullen, K. J., Zamarro, G., & Zissimopoulos, J. (2012). What explains the gender gap in financial literacy? The role of household decision making. *The Journal of Consumer Affairs, 46*(1), 90–106. doi:10.1111/j.1745-6606.2011.01221.x PMID:23049140

Fornero, E., & Monticone, C. (2011). Financial Literacy and Pension Plan Participation in Italy. *Journal of Pension Economics and Finance, 10*(4), 547–564. doi:10.1017/S1474747211000473

Gerardi, K., Goette, L., & Meier, S. (2010). *Financial Literacy and Subprime Mortgage Delinquency: Evidence from a Survey Matched to Administrative Data.* Federal Reserve Bank of Atlanta Working Paper, 2010–10.

Gerrans, P., & Heaney, R. (2016). The Impact of undergraduate personal finance education on individual financial literacy, attitudes and intentions. *Accounting and Finance, 59*(1), 177–217. doi:10.1111/acfi.12247

Global Financial Literacy Excellence Center. (2015). *GFLEC Financial Literacy around the World.* Retrieved from https://gflec.org/wp-content/uploads/2015/11/3313-Finlit_Report_FINAL-5.11.16.pdf?x37292

Grinblatt, M., Keloharju, M., & Linnainmaa, J. (2011). IQ and Stock Market Participation. *The Journal of Finance, 66*(6), 2121–2164. doi:10.1111/j.1540-6261.2011.01701.x

Guiso, L., & Jappelli, T. (2009). *Financial literacy and portfolio diversification.* Centre for Studies in Economics and Finance (CSEF) Working Paper, 212.

Guiso, L., & Viviano, E. (2015). How much can financial literacy help? *Review of Finance, 19*(4), 1347–1382. doi:10.1093/rof/rfu033

Gustman, A. L., Steinmeier, T. L., & Tabatabai, N. (2012). Financial Knowledge and Financial Literacy at the Household Level. *American Economic Review, 102*(3), 309–313.

Harvey, M. (in press). Impact of Financial Education Mandates on Younger Consumers' Use of Alternative Financial Services. *The Journal of Consumer Affairs.*

Hastings, J., & Mitchell, O. S. (2011). *How Financial Literacy and Impatience Shape Retirement Wealth and Investment Behaviors.* NBER Working Paper, No.16740.

Hastings, J., Mitchell, O. S., & Chyn, E. (2011). Fees, Framing, and Financial Literacy in the Choice of Pension Manager. In A. Lusardi & O. S. Mitchell (Eds.), *Financial Literacy – Implications for Retirement Security and the Financial Marketplace* (pp. 101–115). New York, NY: Oxford University Press. doi:10.1093/acprof:oso/9780199696819.003.0006

Hilghert, M. J., Hogarth, S., & Beverly, S. (2003). Household Financial Management: The Connection between Knowledge and Behavior. *Federal Reserve Bulletin,* 309–322.

Hill, R., & Perdue, G. (2008). A methodological issue in the measurement of financial literacy. *Journal of Economics and Economic Education Research, 9,* 150–162.

Hira, T. K., & Loibl, C. (2005). Understanding the Impact of Employer-Provided Financial Education on Workplace Satisfaction. *The Journal of Consumer Affairs, 39*(1), 173–194. doi:10.1111/j.1745-6606.2005.00008.x

Hoffmann, A. O. I., Post, T., & Pennings, J. M. E. (2013). Individual investor perceptions and behavior during the financial crisis. *Journal of Banking & Finance, 37*(1), 60–74. doi:10.1016/j.jbankfin.2012.08.007

Hsiao, Y., & Tsai, W. (2018). Financial literacy and participation in derivatives markets. *Journal of Banking & Finance, 88,* 15–29. doi:10.1016/j.jbankfin.2017.11.006

Huang, J., Nam, Y., & Sherraden, M. (2013). Financial Knowledge and Child Development Account Policy a Test of Financial Capability. *The Journal of Consumer Affairs, 47*(1), 1–26. doi:10.1111/joca.12000

Investor Education Center of Hong Kong. (2018). *The Investor Education Center (IEC) 2018 Financial Literacy Monitor*. Retrieved from https://www.ifec.org.hk/common/pdf/about_iec/iec-financial-literacy-monitor-2018.pdf

Jamison, J. C., Karlan, D., & Zinman, J. (2014). *Financial Education and Access to Savings Accounts: Complements or Substitutes? Evidence from Ugandan Youth Clubs*. NBER Working Paper, No. 20135.

Jappelli, T. (2011). Economic Literacy: An International Comparison. *Economic Journal (London)*, *120*(548), 429–451. doi:10.1111/j.1468-0297.2010.02397.x

Jappelli, T., & Padula, M. (2011). *Investment in Financial Literacy and Saving Decisions*. CSEF Centre for Studies in Economics and Finance.

Jappelli, T., & Padula, M. (2015). Investment in Financial Literacy, Social Security and Portfolio Choice. *Journal of Pension Economics and Finance*, *14*(4), 369–411. doi:10.1017/S1474747214000377

Jump$tart Coalition. (2007). National Standards in K-12 Personal Finance Education. *Jumpstart Coalition*. Retrieved from https://www.jumpstart.org/what-we-do/support-financial-education/standards/

Klapper, L., Lusardi, A., & Panos, G. (2011). *Financial Literacy and the Financial Crisis: Evidence from Russia*. SSRN Working Paper. Retrieved from https://ssrn.com/abstract=1786826

Klapper, L., Lusardi, A., & Panos, G. (2013). Financial Literacy and its Consequences: Evidence from Russia during the Financial Crisis. *Journal of Banking & Finance*, *37*(10), 3904–3923. doi:10.1016/j.jbankfin.2013.07.014

Klapper, L., & Panos, G. (2011). *Financial Literacy and Retirement Planning: The Russian Case*. University of Essex CER Working Paper No. 3. Retrieved from SSRN: https://ssrn.com/abstract=1984059

Knoll, M. A. Z., & Houts, C. R. (2012). The Financial Knowledge Scale: An Application of Item Response Theory to the Assessment of Financial Literacy. *The Journal of Consumer Affairs*, *46*(3), 381–410. doi:10.1111/j.1745-6606.2012.01241.x

Lusardi, A. (2011). *Americans' Financial Capability*. National Bureau of Economic Research Working Paper, 17103.

Lusardi, A., & de Bassa Scheresberg, C. (2013). *Financial Literacy and High-Cost Borrowing in the United States*. Global Financial Literacy Excellence Center (GFLEC) Research Paper. Retrieved from http://www.usfinancialcapability.org/downloads/HighCostBorrowing.pdf?utm_source=

Lusardi, A., & Mitchell, O. S. (2011). Financial literacy around the world: An overview. *Journal of Pension Economics and Finance*, *10*(04), 497–508. doi:10.1017/S1474747211000448 PMID:28553190

Lusardi, A., & Mitchell, O. S. (2014). The Economic Importance of Financial Literacy: Theory and Evidence. *Journal of Economic Literature*, *52*(1), 5–44. doi:10.1257/jel.52.1.5 PMID:28579637

Lusardi, A., & Tufano, P. (2009). *Debt Literacy, Financial Experiences, and Overindebtedness*. National Bureau of Economic Research Working Paper, No.14808. Retrieved from http://www.nber.org/papers/w14808

Lusardi, A., & Tufano, P. (2015). Debt Literacy, Financial Experiences, and Overindebtedness. *Journal of Pension Economics and Finance*, *14*(04), 332–368. doi:10.1017/S1474747215000232

Mandell, L., & Klein, L. (2007). Motivation and Financial Literacy. *Financial Services Review*, *16*, 105–116.

Manton, E. J., English, D. E., Avard, S., & Walker, J. (2006). What college freshmen admit to not knowing about personal ðnance. *Journal of College Teaching and Learning*, *3*(1), 43–54. doi:10.19030/tlc.v3i1.1758

Mason, C., & Wilson, R. (2000). *Conceptualizing Financial Literacy. Loughborough University Business School* Research Series Paper.

Monticone, C. (2010). How much does wealth matter in the acquisition of financial literacy? *The Journal of Consumer Affairs*, *44*(2), 403–422. doi:10.1111/j.1745-6606.2010.01175.x

Moore, D. (2003). *Survey of Financial Literacy in Washington State: Knowledge, Behavior, Attitudes and Experiences*. Washington State University Social and Economic Sciences Research Center, Technical Report 03–39.

Mottola, G. (2013). In Our Best Interest: Women, Financial Literacy, and Credit Card Behavior. Numeracy Advancing Education in Quantitative Literacy, 6(2), Article 4.

Muller, S., & Weber, M. (2010). Financial Literacy and Mutual Fund Investments: Who Buys Actively Managed Funds? *Schmalenbach Business Review*, *62*(2), 126–153. doi:10.1007/BF03396802

National Financial Capability Study. (2019). *The State of U.S. Financial Capability: the 2018 National Financial Capability Study (NFCS)*. Retrieved from http://www.usfinancialcapability.org/downloads/NFCS_2018_Report_Natl_Findings.pdf

National Foundation for Credit Counseling. (2019). *NFCC 2019 Consumer Financial Literacy Survey.* Retrieved from https://www.nfcc.org/2019-consumer-financial-literacy-survey/

Nicolini, G. (2019). *Financial Literacy in Europe.* New York: Routledge. doi:10.4324/9780429431968

Nye, P., & Hillyard, C. (2013). Personal Financial Behavior: The Influence of Quantitative Literacy and Material Values. *Numeracy Advancing Education in Quantitative Literacy, 6*(1), article 3.

O'Donnell, N., & Keeney, M. (2009). *Financial Capability: New Evidence for Ireland.* Central Bank of Ireland Research Technical Paper, 1/RT/09.

Organization for Economic Cooperation and Development. (2009). *Framework for the Development of Financial Literacy Baseline Surveys: A First International Comparative Analysis.* OECD Working Papers on Finance, Insurance and Private Pensions, No. 1. OECD Publishing.

Organization for Economic Cooperation and Development. (2017). *G20/OECD INFE report on adult financial literacy in G20 countries.* Retrieved from https://www.oecd.org/daf/fin/financial-education/G20-OECD-INFE-report-adult-financial-literacy-in-G20-countries.pdf

Organization for Economic Cooperation and Development. (2018). *The Programme for International Student Assessment (PISA) 2015 Results in Focus.* Retrieved from http://www.oecd.org/pisa/pisa-2015-results-in-focus.pdf

Perry, V., & Morris, M. (2005). Who is in Control? The Role of Self-Perception, Knowledge, and Income in Explaining Consumer Financial Behavior. *The Journal of Consumer Affairs, 39*(2), 299–313. doi:10.1111/j.1745-6606.2005.00016.x

Robb, C. A. (2011). Financial knowledge and credit card behavior of college students. *Journal of Family and Economic Issues, 32*(4), 690–698. doi:10.100710834-011-9259-y

Robb, C.A., & Russell, N. J. (2008). Personal Financial Knowledge among College Students: Associations between Individual Characteristics and Scores on an Experimental Measure of Financial Knowledge. *Consumer Interests Annual,* 54-144.

Robb, C. A., & Sharpe, D. L. (2009). Effect of personal financial knowledge on college students' credit card behavior. *Journal of Financial Counseling and Planning, 20*(1), 25–40.

Schmeiser, M., & Seligman, J. (2013). Using the Right Yardstick: Assessing Financial Literacy Measures by Way of Financial Well-Being. *The Journal of Consumer Affairs, 47*(2), 191–374. doi:10.1111/joca.12010

Sekita, S. (2011). Financial Literacy and Retirement Planning in Japan. *Journal of Pension Economics and Finance, 10*(4), 637–656. doi:10.1017/S1474747211000527

Song, C. (2015). *Financial Illiteracy and Pension Contributions: A Field Experiment on Compound Interest in China*. SSRN Working Paper. Retrieved from https://ssrn.com/abstract=2580856

Stolper, O. A., & Walter, A. (2017). Financial literacy, financial advice, and financial behavior. *Journal of Business Economics, 87*(5), 581–643. doi:10.100711573-017-0853-9

Tang, N., & Peter, P. (2015). Financial knowledge acquisition among the young: The role of financial education, financial experience, and parents' financial experience. *Financial Services Review, 24*(2), 119–137.

Tennyson, S., & Nguyen, C. (2001). State curriculum mandates and student knowledge of personal finance. *The Journal of Consumer Affairs, 35*(2), 241–262. doi:10.1111/j.1745-6606.2001.tb00112.x

University of Melbourne the Household, Income and Labor Dynamics in Australia. (2018). *The Household, Income and Labor Dynamics in Australia (HILDA) Survey*. The University of Melbourne, Melbourne Institute: Applied Economic & Social Research. Retrieved from https://melbourneinstitute.unimelb.edu.au/hilda

Utkus, S. P., & Young, J. A. (2011). *Financial Literacy and 401(k) Loans. In Financial Literacy Implications for Retirement Security and the Financial Marketplace* (pp. 59–75). New York, NY: Oxford University Press.

Van Rooij, M., Lusardi, A., & Alessie, R. (2011). Financial literacy and stock market participation. *Journal of Financial Economics, 101*(2), 449–472. doi:10.1016/j.jfineco.2011.03.006

Van Rooij, M., Lusardi, A., & Alessie, R. (2011). Financial literacy and retirement planning in the Netherlands. *Journal of Economic Psychology, 32*(4), 593–608. doi:10.1016/j.joep.2011.02.004

Volpe, R. P., Chen, H., & Pavlicko, J. J. (1996). Personal investment literacy among college students: A survey. *Financial Practice and Education, 6*(2), 86–94.

Volpe, R. P., & Willis, L. E. (2008). Against Financial Literacy Education. *Iowa Law Review, 94*, 197–285.

Willis, L. E. (2008). *Against financial literacy education*. University of Pennsylvania Law School, Public Law and Legal Theory Research Paper No. 08-10.

Worthington, A. (2006). Predicting Financial Literacy in Australia. *Financial Services Review, 15*, 59–79.

Xiao, J., Chen, C., & Chen, F. (2013). Consumer Financial Capability and Financial Satisfaction. *Social Indicators Research, 118*(1), 415–432. doi:10.100711205-013-0414-8

Yoong, J. (2011). *Financial Illiteracy and Stock Market Participation: Evidence from the RAND American Life Panel. In Financial Literacy Implications for Retirement Security and the Financial Marketplace* (pp. 76–10). New York, NY: Oxford University Press.

Zait, A., & Bertea, P. E. (2014). Financial Literacy – Conceptual Definition and Proposed Approach for a Measurement Instrument. *Journal of Accounting and Management, 4*(3), 37–42.

ADDITIONAL READING

Bianchi, M. (2017). Financial Literacy and Portfolio Dynamics. *The Journal of Finance, 73*(2), 831–859. doi:10.1111/jofi.12605

Clason, G. S. (1955). *The Richest Man in Babylon*. New York: Plume.

Graham, B. (2003). *The Intelligent Investor* (Revised edn.). New York: HarperCollins.

Lusardi, A., & Mitchell, O. S. (2011). Financial literacy around the world: An overview. *Journal of Pension Economics and Finance, 10*(04), 497–508. doi:10.1017/S1474747211000448 PMID:28553190

Lusardi, A., & Mitchell, O. S. (2011). *Financial Literacy – Implications for Retirement Security and the Financial Marketplace*. New York: Oxford University Press.

Malkiel, B. G. (2019). *A random walk down Wall Street: the time-based strategy for successful investing*. New York: W. W. Norton & Company.

Nicolini, G. (2019). *Financial Literacy in Europe*. New York: Routledge. doi:10.4324/9780429431968

Organization for Economic Cooperation and Development. (2014). *Financial education for youth: the role of schools*. Retrieved from https://www.oecd.org/education/financial-education-for-youth.htmf

Organization for Economic Cooperation and Development. (2018). *The Programme for International Student Assessment (PISA) 2015 Results in Focus*. Retrieved from http://www.oecd.org/pisa/pisa-2015-results-in-focus.pdf

KEY TERMS AND DEFINITIONS

Financial Decision Making: Any decision-making process that affects overall financial well-being of an individual.

Financial Literacy: Financial literacy is the set of following items: knowledge about financial concepts/products/services, competence to use financial concepts/products/services, ability to take financial decisions (i.e., transmission to behavior), confidence in financial operations.

Financial Literacy Measure: Any type of measurement used to quantify the financial literacy.

Instrumental Variable: Any variable, which is not directly representative of the variable in interest, but highly correlated with it.

Lusardi-Mitchell Design: Lusardi and Mitchell (2011) design included three questions: one for interest rate calculation, one to understand the awareness of respondent on the impact of inflation, and last one to test both knowledge about stocks versus stock mutual funds, and risk diversification.

Numeracy: The ability to understand and work with numbers.

Self-Assessment Questionnaire: The questionnaires that ask respondents to assess themselves.

Chapter 12
Evaluating Financial and Fiscal Knowledge for an Inclusive Society

Laura Varela-Candamio
https://orcid.org/0000-0001-9321-3280
Universidade da Coruña, Spain

Joaquín Enríquez-Díaz
https://orcid.org/0000-0001-8711-0795
Universidade da Coruña, Spain

ABSTRACT

Financial education and fiscal awareness are considered two fundamental branches of knowledge in the training of citizens from the first stages of learning. Thus, it is necessary to teach them in order to know the different savings products that can be acquired in a bank, to understand the basic information related to savings and the means of payment, or to differentiate between investment and risk. This work seeks to analyze the factors that determine the degree of financial knowledge and also fiscal knowledge of the current population. As a case study, the authors have selected a small sample of young people between 9 and 19 years at middle schools in the region of A Coruna (Spain). Findings reveal the low level of both financial and fiscal knowledge of the youngest population.

DOI: 10.4018/978-1-7998-2440-4.ch012

Evaluating Financial and Fiscal Knowledge for an Inclusive Society

INTRODUCTION

Financial inclusion is defined as the access to various financial products and services, both for individuals and businesses, useful and affordable that meet their needs (transactions, payments, savings, credit and insurance) provided in a responsible and sustainable way to improve the wealth generation and, essentially, social welfare.

According to the most recent data of the World Bank (2019), the level of financial inclusion in Spain reaches 98% of the population. An efficient and competitive banking sector is essential to explain this high financial inclusion. In comparative terms, it is the second highest percentage among the main countries of the euro zone, below 99% of Germany but by over 97% of France and 87% estimated for Italy. According to data from the Spanish Banking Association (in Spanish, Asociación Española de Banca, AEB), 75% of the Spanish population resides in municipalities with six or more credit institutions, and more than 92% of the population lives in villages with two or more different banks. This offers the customer the possibility to choose between them and therefore to benefit from healthy competition.

In addition, the density of bank offices in Spain is also one of the highest in Europe. According to the data from ECB, in Spain there is a bank branch for every 1,493 inhabitants compared to 2,170 inhabitants on average in the euro zone. The banks belonging to the AEB have extensive networks of offices that guarantee access to financial services to a significant majority of the population. In addition, they have been developing digital banking for years, accompanying the client in his demand for new digital services that complement the personal relationship through the traditional office. In the specific case of payments, using data from the Bank of Spain, the volume of card payments increased in 2017 by 10.75% compared to the previous year and cash withdrawals from ATMs by 3%. The number of ATMs grew 0.2% in 2016, while the number of payment terminals increased 4.1%. Therefore, digitalization is an unstoppable process as is the emergence of alternatives regarding payments methods.

However, despite this easy access to the banking system and even though consumers are engaged in financial market transactions daily, knowledge of the current financial sector is very limited among families as well as the consequences of these transactions when making financial decisions (Cardaci, 2018; Atkinson and Morelli, 2011). The enormous complexity of the current financial system and the low levels of financial information are the two fundamental causes of this lack of financial knowledge (Stiglitz, 2012). Thus, in developed countries it is observed that consumers do not know how to diversify risk and do not invest in those alternatives that would allow them to obtain a higher return (Lusardi, 2008). For example, in Japan, a recent study by the University of Osaka revealed that 71% of respondents lacked knowledge about bonds and stocks, about financial products in general (57%)

and about insurance and pensions (29%). Also, in Australia, 37% of individuals who had investments did not understand that their value could fluctuate, and although 67% indicated that they understood the concept of compound interest, but when asked to solve a problem using it, only 28% proved to have a good level of understanding (Lusardi and Mitchell, 2011).

On the other hand, in relation to the tax aspect, the payment of contributions worldwide is derived from the need for countries to raise tax collection to be reinvested in social welfare. In addition, after the economic crisis of 2008, the urgent need to resize the public sources has become apparent in Spain. This requires a greater and better tax culture on citizens because the fiscal instruments may have been poorly implemented and controlled, aggravating the deficit and increasing tax evasion.

This work seeks to analyze the factors that determine the degree of financial knowledge and also fiscal knowledge of the current population. The main strength of this study is that for first time we provide a case study, selecting a small sample of young people between 9 to 19 years at middle school in the region of A Coruna (Spain). Findings reveal the low level of both financial and fiscal knowledge of the youngest population. In addition, related to the financial issues, it is observed the large disparities among the individuals based on aspects such as financial income (financial mathematics) comprising liquidity, different payment methods, financial solvency, savings vs. investment, interest and inflation, commissions and financial risk as well as fiscal knowledge measured through knowledge about tax collection and public spending .

Similarly, it is shown that the tax culture also makes the interest in greater fiscal knowledge difficult. These results highlight the need to implement both financial and fiscal education at the most elementary academic levels in order to improve the general objectives of social inclusion and well-being.

After this introduction, the structure of the work is as follows. Section 2 defines the importance of the financial sector and the public sector today, highlighting the main difficulties that exist for the full achievement of the general objective of inclusion. Besides, Section 3 highlights the importance of financial and fiscal education for the improvement of the citizens' literacy and, therefore, of social inclusion. Section 4 performs a descriptive analysis of the determinants of the degree of financial literacy and also fiscal literacy for the case study here considered. Finally, the conclusions section summarizes the main contributions of the work.

BACKGROUND

The Importance of The Financial Sector And The Public Sector: Challenges And Difficulties

The access to a transaction account is a first step towards broader financial inclusion, as it allows people to save money and also send and receive payments. A transaction account can also serve as a gateway to other financial services. Therefore, ensuring that people around the world can access a transaction account is the focus of the Universal Access to Financial Services Initiative for 2020 (UFA2020) of the World Bank Group (GBM). Besides, the access to financial services makes everyday life easier and helps families and businesses to establish a planning for everything from long-term goals to unforeseen emergencies. People, as account holders, are more likely to use other financial services, such as credit and insurance, to start and expand business, invest in education or health, manage risks and overcome financial crises, all of which can improve their general quality of life.

Financial inclusion is becoming a priority for authorities, regulatory bodies and development agencies worldwide. It has been determined that financial inclusion is a factor that propitiates 7 of the 17 Sustainable Development Goals. In this regard, the Group of Twenty (G-20) pledged to promote financial inclusion worldwide and reaffirmed its commitment to apply the G-20 High Level Principles for Digital Financial Inclusion.

The countries that have made the most progress towards financial inclusion are those that have created a favorable regulatory environment and have encouraged competition by allowing banking and non-banking institutions to innovate and expand access to financial services (World Bank, 2018). However, the creation of this innovative and competitive space must be accompanied by appropriate regulations and other type of user protection measures to ensure the responsible provision of financial services.

Digital financial technology, and in particular the increase in the use of mobile phones worldwide, has facilitated the expansion of access for small businesses and hard-to-reach populations to financial services at a lower cost and with less risk. Thus, for example, digital ID make it easier than ever to open an account and, in general, the digitalization of payments methods has allowed more people to start using transaction accounts. On the other hand, mobile phone financial services allow access to be available even in the most isolated geographical areas. In turn, the greater availability of customer data allows suppliers to design digital financial products that are better suited to the needs of unbanked people.

As countries have accelerated their efforts towards financial inclusion, similar obstacles that prevent them from moving forward have become evident. Financial ignorance (as a simple example, the way in which interest is applied in a simple consumer loan) and the lack of provision for unforeseen expenses (for example, the repair of a damaged vehicle) in a current environment of high family indebtedness cause families to experience high levels of financial distress because of debt repayment and prevent consumers from making sound decisions. In other words, this financial distress make them vulnerable to debt repayment obligations and more likely to make suboptimal credit decisions (Lusardi and Mitchell, 2014).

This situation is even more worrying among those who meet all or at least one of the following conditions: low levels of education, higher levels of credit restriction, low income levels and limited liquidity access by the main service providers financial, that is, mainly commercial banks (Collins and Gjertson, 2013). Therefore, it is observed that financial innovation together with the expansion of access to financial services mentioned above are necessary but not sufficient conditions to guarantee financial resources by families in the commercial banks. This reality was especially aggravated by the sub-prime mortgage crisis in 2008, which showed the adverse effects of excessive family indebtedness on the welfare levels of this population that was not adequately prepared to assume unexpected financial emergencies (Brobeck, 2008).

It is necessary to be mentioned that these reflections should not be evaluated solely at the family level. The government and private sector regulatory systems should also contribute to reduce levels of fiscal distress and improving consumer knowledge and autonomous capacity in the financial market. In this sense, financial education can be an adequate solution to solve all these problems related to the financial management of families on a daily basis.

In relation to the public sector, the crisis erupted in 2008 had a deep negative impact on public revenues and governments suffer the debts of failing financial institutions. At the same time, the levels of tax evasion also rose due to the increase of household indebtedness derived from the crisis. Then, governments were aware of the serious risks of high and sharply increases in public debts. These risks refer, among others, to the loss of confidence of the citizens regarding the public administrations and, therefore, the risk of further increases in tax evasion (Cecchetti et al., 2010).

Financial and Fiscal Education for Social Inclusion

Numerous studies show that an improvement in knowledge within the world of finance favors greater financial results or, at least, is directly related to more positive financial behaviors in daily activities such as cash withdrawal, cash flow management and bank credit, investment in financial assets, among others (Tang et al., 2015). Moreover, a greater degree of knowledge in economics and finance improves the financial well-being of consumers (Gjertson, 2015; Telyukova, 2013). In particular, there are empirical investigations that positively relate financial knowledge to credit management. Thus, for instance, Hilgert et al. (2003) found that households with a good knowledge of credit were likely to be in the high credit management index level. Conversely, Disney and Gathergood (2013) demonstrated that respondents who borrowed on consumer credit and whose financial knowledge is poor exhibited high-cost debts, which caused them to be less confident in financial practices. In the same way, Rhine and Robbins (2012) indicated the importance of relevant financial knowledge in determining the choice of alternative financial services.

On the other hand, a recent branch of the literature has observed the differences between real (objective) financial knowledge and perceived (subjective) financial knowledge that can trigger an over-confidence problem. Therefore, empirical research has begun to include subjective measures related to self-assessment that complement other more traditional objective measures, mainly test scores. As a result, it has been proven that confidence in financial knowledge (that is, subjective financial knowledge) can help a person to engage in more positive financial behaviors (Courchane, 2005). Thus, for example, Allgood and Walstad, (2016) found that a combined measure including both actual and perceived financial literacy influences positive financial practices in five different dimensions: credit cards, loans, insurance, investment and even financial counseling. Other similar studies also suggest that objective financial knowledge is insufficient to ensure adequate financial behavior (Perry and Morris, 200; Braunstein and Welch, 2005). Specifically, Robb and Woodyard (2011) point out other even more decisive variables such as satisfaction or financial confidence. These authors also highlight the sociodemographic variables, especially the level of income, in addition to education. Thus, purchasing power is related to greater savings, on the one hand, because it is easier to cover basic needs, and with the need to manage these resources, on the other hand, which favors the use of financial products and, therefore, a learning based on their use.

Following this line, Raccanello and Herrera Guzmán (2014) establish a series of socio-cultural factors (in addition to the level of income) associated with the lack of financial education such as gender, age, education level and others related to the place of residence. Regarding gender, women have less financial knowledge than men, possibly because they use financial products less (Lycette and White, 1989). In relation to age, young people and those over 60 years of age tend to have major deficiencies in terms of basic knowledge of finance due to the lower experience in the use of financial products and services in the first case and due to the lack of learning in financial innovation, in the second case (Elan, 2011). If we look at the level of schooling, although the relationship between education and knowledge is positive in general terms, the degree of knowledge in society about financial education is low, even among the groups with the highest level of academic training. Therefore, the educational level is not a useful indicator to assess financial knowledge (Lusardi and Mitchell, 2011). Also, as regards the residential place of individuals, financial knowledge urban areas is usually greater than in rural areas (Agnew and Harrison, 2015).

Similarly, trust in the public administration is also essential to promote social inclusion. In this case, we cannot talk about tax inclusion since the payment of taxes is coercive and therefore of mandatory compliance for all citizens. In other words, all citizens are involved in paying taxes. The tax culture encompasses a set of values, beliefs and social representations that citizens attribute to the government actions, connoting their behavior as a taxpayer helping to improve social welfare. This construction of the positive link between citizens who pay taxes (fiscal obligation) and those who manage and use resources (fiscal solidarity) will avoid behaviors leading to tax evasion (Herrero and Monge, 2002). The lack of tax culture is the main cause of tax evasion and illicit, where the tax administration is immersed in general, resulting in the deterioration of the tax collection system and the existence of high rates of evasion and fiscal fraud, as well as the ignorance of the citizens regarding the fulfillment of the formal duties established in the different laws that govern the taxes (Golía, 2003). Therefore, the tax culture is encouraged by showing citizens that the effort made in paying taxes is directed to an adequate use of public services for the common goods (Méndez, 2004). This translates into a behavior manifested in the permanent fulfillment of tax duties based on reason, trust and affirmation of the values of personal ethics, respect for the law, citizen responsibility and social solidarity, both for the taxpayers as for the officials of the different tax administrations.

Consequently, alternative public policies such as the development of financial education programs should receive more attention from researchers, academics and policy makers to eliminate the problems arising from social exclusion and, at the same time, take advantage of the externalities it generates in terms of equality and well-being for society as a whole. Financial education is defined by the Organization for Economic Cooperation and Development (OECD), as: "the process by which individuals acquire a better understanding of financial concepts and products and develop the necessary skills to make informed decisions, evaluate financial risks and opportunities, and improve their well-being"(OECD, 2005, p. 26). Thus, policy makers can promote financial inclusion through their positive link with financial education through different ways: a) increasing the number of intermediaries and reducing the requirements for the commercialization of financial assets; b) increasing the coverage and access to financial products and services to the population and c) offering quality financial products that meet the needs of current and potential consumers (Raccanello and Herrera Guzmán, 2014).

An example of a successful reference in this regard is the combination of consumer financial education programs in the US; specifically, the National Endowment for Financial Education, the Cooperative Extension System, and the National Foundation for Consumer Credit, which cover three main aspects. First, the improvement of the financial management capabilities of consumers. Second, the promotion of an improvement in the behavior of family savings. Third, the improvement of asset-building behavior. The combination of these three measures has been shown to generate a great success in achieving the final objective of financial inclusion (Vitt et al., 2000).

Regarding the fiscal field, tax education is the transmission of values aimed at the civic fulfillment of the duties of every citizen by contributing to public expenses, which is achieved by accepting the responsibilities that correspond to the citizens participating in a democratic society (Mendoza Shaw, 2016).

This tax culture towards fiscal commitment must be encouraged from an early age, in order to correct entrenched tax evasion behaviors. Accordingly, it would be equally convenient to design teaching programs in tax culture to strengthen citizen values in students. This education would refer not only to fiscal knowledge but also to the promotion of a specific fiscal ethic based on public and social morals.

MAIN FOCUS OF THE CHAPTER

Data

This chapter analyzes the determinants of financial knowledge through 8 indicators divided into two groups: firstly, financial income (financial mathematics) comprising liquidity, different payment methods, financial solvency, savings vs. investment, interest and inflation, commissions and financial risk and, secondly, fiscal knowledge measured through knowledge about tax collection and public spending.

The data comprises 472 students from middle school in the region of A Coruna (Spain) between 9 to 19 years old. The proportion of women is 49.79%. The percentage of students living in urban areas is 59.96% while the rest are living in rural ones. This research, developed during the academic year 2017/2018, has been focused on students of vocational training education and pre-university education: primary education, compulsory secondary education (in Spain, called E.S.O) and high school studies. The distribution of the sample by education levels is shown below in Table 1:

The data show that the largest number of individuals in the sample corresponds to students who took 3rd and 4th years of Compulsory Secondary Education in Spain. These students represent people who either decide to study for High School, Vocational Training or directly to enter in the labor market confronting financial and fiscal knowledge for their daily life. This justifies the selection of the sample and the proportions established among students for these educational levels.

Table 1. Participants in the study by educational level

Educational level	No. Students	%
High school (1st course)	142	30.08%
High school (2nd course)	17	3.60%
Secondary education (3rd course)	132	27.97%
Secondary education (4th course)	113	23.94%
Primary education (5th course)	25	5.30%
Primary education (6th course)	40	8.47%
Vocational training education (trade)	3	0.64%

METHOD

In order to develop this study during the months of September and November, different professors from the Faculty of Economics and Business of the University of A Coruna contacted a total of 9 educational centers in different locations in the province of A Coruna (Spain). The number of participants in each center is reflected below in Table 2.

The aim of this analysis is to analyze the degree of financial and fiscal knowledge of pre-university and vocational training students as well as the possible relationship of these knowledge with certain sociodemographic variables. The field research is based on data collected directly from students through personal surveys conducted in the schools aforementioned. These interviews include different questions that we can classify in the following four groups: 1) socio-demographic questions, 2)

Table 2. Educational centers participating in the study

Centro	Area	No. students	%	Educational level
CEIP Cruceiro de Canido	Ferrol	65	13.77%	Primary
Colegio Hijas de Cristo Rey	A Coruna	39	8.26%	Secondary + High School
IES Fragas Do Eume	Pontedeume	27	5.72%	Secondary + High School
IES Punta Candieira	Cedeira	38	8.05%	Secondary + High School
IES Sofia Casanova	Ferrol	19	4.03%	Secondary + High School
IES Concepcion Arenal	Ferrol	143	30.30%	Secondary + High School
IES Canido	Ferrol	20	4.24%	Secondary + High School
IES Ferrol Vello	Ferrol	24	5.08%	Secondary
IES Santurino Montojo	Ferrol	97	20.55%	Secondary + High School

Table 3. Sociodemographic variables

Question	%
I live in a rural area	16.53%
I live in a city	59.96%
I live in both places (rural-city)	23.52%
My father has university studies	27.75%
My mother has university studies	35.38%
I pass mathematics last course	85.81%
I have my own PC	66.53%
There is at least one Smart Tv at home	73.73%
I have repeated course at least once	21.82%
I have studied Economics before	37.92%

questions about the use of financial instruments, 3) questions to evaluate financial knowledge and 4) questions to assess fiscal knowledge and awareness

Socio-Demographic Questions

Regarding the questions asked to obtain different sociodemographic variables, students have been asked about the area of residence (if they live in a country house or in the city), the educational level of the father and mother (if they have university studies or not), the most recent grade they obtained in the subject of mathematics (in order to know whether they had pass or not), whether or not they have their own computer to work and perform their tasks, if they have a television in their house with Internet connection or smart TV, if they have ever repeated a course as well as if they have previously studied some subject related to economic issues. The most relevant results obtained regarding these sociodemographic variables are shown below in Table 3:

These sociodemographic variables show that only 37.92% of the students surveyed affirm they have taken subjects with economic content. In addition, if we deepen in this variable we observe that there are slight differences if we take care of the gender or the residence of the students. Thus, more than half of women, 55.31%, have ever studied subjects related to economic issues, while only 44.69% of men say they have ever studied in their studies economic studies at school. If we look at the area where students live (city or rural area), 52.51% of the students who studied economics once live in the city while the percentage of those who study economics living in rural areas is less than half (47.49%).

Taking these results into account a priori it seems that women do not have a great exclusion when acquiring financial or fiscal knowledge, in fact we find that they are studying economic subjects in greater percentage than men. However, students living in rural areas are less likely to access subjects in which they can learn financial or fiscal knowledge.

Questions About the Use Of Financial Instruments

In the second part of the survey, students responded to a number of issues related to the use of financial instruments. Specifically, they were asked whether they had a bank account, some type of card (credit, debit or stored value cards) and if they had ever used or had access to the electronic banking of a financial entity. It should be noted that 63.56% of students claim to have a current account in a financial entity, 19.49% say they have some type of card while only 18.22% of the students surveyed say they have access or use electronic banking at some point.

Likewise, if we make a comparison between the rural area and the city, despite the fact that in rural areas the percentage of having a current account exceeds 70%, only 25.93% have electronic banking and just over 25% have some type of card (credit, debit or stored value cards type).

Questions To Evaluate Financial Knowledge

In order to evaluate the degree of financial knowledge of students, eight issues that refer to different areas of finance have been selected: saving, investment, risk, payment methods, among others. Specifically, we decide to focus on those issues we consider that students may need to know to be able to develop correctly activities related to the everyday financial practice, as well as when they need to go to a financial entity to contract a product.

The questionnaire is presented in a test type format with four possible responses of which only one was correct. Likewise, with the intention that students do not leave blank any question, a fifth possible response was incorporated under the heading "I do not know", in case the students did not understand what we were asking. With the intention of creating incentives for the students to try to answer the questions as much as possible, the questionnaire was made as a contest in which the answers correctly answered added points, and the wrong answers or the blank answers (in our case, "I do not know") they did not add either subtract (no points added). At the end of the contest, the student with better scores in each class received a small prize.

Next, we proceed to detail the content of each of the eight questions from the test performed:

- Question No. 1. In this question we raised a problem related to the concepts of financial income. Students had to respond by applying very basic knowledge of financial laws, namely simple and / or compound capitalization.
- Question No. 2. In this question we proposed a series of different financial assets (money in a deposit, in a checking account, a vehicle and a house), for students to choose what they considered was more liquid.
- Question No. 3. In this question we incorporate different payment methods. Specifically, we asked the students about the differences between credit cards, debit cards and stored value cards.
- Question No. 4. This question was related to the savings and the concept of financial solvency. For this, we present to the students different family situations of expenses, income and savings among which they have to choose the one that implies the greater financial solvency in terms of family budget.
- Question No. 5. This question incorporated the concept of financial risk. Students had to identify the concept of risk as the main difference between saving and investing.
- Question No. 6. In this question we incorporated the concepts of interest and inflation. Thus, we raised the students a situation in which an individual had to determine whether the final capital of a savings account would be greater or less than the initial one based on interest rate and inflation data.
- Question 7. In this question, we incorporated the concepts of banking commissions as well as those of the overdraft. To do this, students should respond on the possible consequences of an overdraft in a bank account.
- Question 8. In this question we introduced the concept of risk diversification. For this issue, we ask students about the relationship between the diversification derived from investing in different financial products and the evolution of the total risk assumed by the investor.

RESULTS

In Table 4 we collect the percentage of correct answers given by the group of students to each of the eight questions. Likewise, we have differentiated for each question among groups of students with different sociodemographic characteristics and their degree of correct answers.

The questions that generally present more problems for students are those related to income valuation (Q1), payment methods (Q3), as well as the relationship between the concepts of interest and inflation (Q6). From these three questions, it should be highlighted the question Q3 related to the differentiation between the different types of card. It is remarkable that, from the students that have a card, only 34%

Table 4. Survey about financial knowledge: results

	% Correct answers							
	Q1	Q2	Q3	Q4	Q5	Q6	Q7	Q8
Total	36%	61%	36%	72%	53%	39%	47%	51%
Urban area	40%	55%	31%	67%	49%	35%	40%	47%
Rural area (or both areas)	29%	70%	42%	80%	59%	44%	57%	59%
Men	32%	57%	36%	67%	55%	38%	43%	49%
Women	40%	66%	35%	78%	51%	40%	51%	54%
My father has university studies	40%	59%	29%	74%	56%	45%	37%	51%
My father has not university studies	34%	62%	38%	72%	52%	36%	51%	52%
My mother has university studies	38%	64%	33%	79%	66%	44%	44%	51%
My mother has not university studies	35%	60%	37%	69%	46%	36%	48%	51%
I pass mathematics last course	37%	61%	36%	74%	53%	39%	47%	52%
I fail mathematics last course	30%	60%	36%	66%	51%	36%	43%	46%
I have a bank card	33%	63%	34%	78%	59%	45%	51%	59%
I have a bank card	37%	61%	36%	71%	52%	37%	46%	50%
I have a bank account	36%	65%	37%	79%	57%	43%	52%	54%
I do not have a bank account	35%	55%	34%	62%	47%	31%	38%	48%
I have electronic banking	38%	70%	37%	81%	62%	48%	51%	59%
I do not have electronic banking	35%	59%	35%	70%	51%	37%	46%	50%
I have my own PC	35%	66%	38%	79%	58%	45%	52%	55%
I do not have my own PC	37%	52%	31%	59%	42%	26%	37%	45%
There is one Smart Tv at home	39%	62%	34%	73%	51%	39%	48%	53%
There is no Smart Tv at home	28%	60%	40%	72%	59%	39%	43%	48%
I have repeated course at least once	35%	59%	33%	66%	49%	30%	42%	50%
I have never repeated course	36%	62%	36%	75%	54%	41%	48%	52%
I have studied Economics before	37%	65%	44%	83%	64%	47%	55%	56%
I have not studied Economics before	35%	59%	31%	66%	46%	34%	42%	48%

respond correctly. On the other hand, among the students who do not have this financial instrument, the percentage of correct answers is greater. In short, financial instruments could be used with a high degree of ignorance in some cases.

On the other hand, according to the area of residence (urban or rural area), it is observed that in general, students living in rural areas get higher scores in almost all questions. However, when these questions refer to more technical and less intuitive aspects (i.e. less related to investment or savings (Q1)), the percentage of

Figure 1. In your opinion, which of these two behaviors would be more reprehensible?

■ Someone stop entering € 6,000 to the Public Treasury   ■ someone steals you € 100

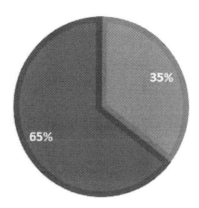

students who respond correctly decreases. This may be due to the fact that in the rural areas there is a greater awareness of the savings and a greater concern for the issues related to it.

The comparative analysis by gender shows that there are few differences among men and women, observing only a slighlyt greater percentage of correct answers in the case of women. This increased financial knowledge can be explained because, as discussed above, the sample also collected a larger percentage of women who had previously studied issues related to the economy.

Overall, the results obtained allow us to determine that those students who obtain better qualifications in mathematics, have their own computer to carry out their tasks, have a bank account in an entity, did not repeat course and previously studied economics responded better to all the issues contemplated in the survey.

Questions To Assess Fiscal Knowledge And Awareness

In this last part of the survey, we ask some questions about fiscal knowledge and awareness. In order to evaluate the degree of fiscal awareness, two questions are asked to the students. In the first question, they are asked to select what behavior they think it could be most reprehensible: "let someone stop paying € 6,000 of taxes" or "somebody steals you 100 €". Secondly, students are required to answer how fiscal responsible they considered themselves: very irresponsible, irresponsible,

Figure 2. In general, to what extent do you consider yourself a responsible person?

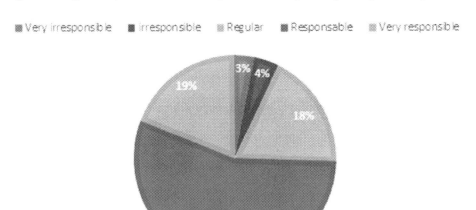

regular, responsible or very responsible. The results obtained from these questions are shown below in Figures 1 and 2.

On the one hand, despite the fact that in general 56% of the students say they are responsible and 19% very responsible in the fiscal field, it is very worrisome that one third of the students consider that "somebody steals you €100" is more reprehensive than "let someone stop adding € 6,000 to the Public Treasury", since this last action leads to a certain way of tax fraud behaviors.

Finally, to measure the degree of fiscal knowledge, and more specifically about the management of public spending, students were asked to relate a series of public services (hospitals, parks and gardens, defense, cleaning –in streets or garbage collection- and universities) with the public administrations responsible for its management (Central Administration, Regional Administration or Local Administration). The percentage of correct answers given for each of the services is reflected in Table 5 according to the different sociodemographic characteristics of students.

In general, we observe that students associate quite well the different services considered and the administration in charge of their management, having more difficulties when asked about the case of Hospitals (50% of correct answers) and Universities (65% of correct answers). In terms of gender or area of residence in this case we do not find large differences among students. Again, we verify that students who have their own computer and have previously studied economics have a higher percentage of correct answers in all the cases considered.

Table 5. Public services and Public administration: results

	Hospitals	Parks	Defense	Cleaning	Universities
Total	50%	89%	77%	79%	65%
Urban area	51%	87%	79%	76%	63%
Rural area (or both areas)	49%	92%	75%	82%	68%
Men	48%	87%	75%	75%	65%
Women	53%	91%	79%	82%	66%
My father has university studies	54%	90%	84%	78%	67%
My father has not university studies	49%	89%	75%	79%	65%
My mother has university studies	53%	89%	82%	77%	64%
My mother has not university studies	49%	89%	75%	80%	66%
I pass mathematics last course	53%	89%	79%	79%	67%
I fail mathematics last course	35%	92%	69%	77%	58%
I have a bank card	43%	90%	74%	81%	67%
I have a bank card	52%	89%	78%	78%	65%
I have a bank account	52%	90%	79%	81%	69%
I do not have a bank account	47%	87%	74%	75%	58%
I have electronic banking	51%	90%	79%	80%	67%
I do not have electronic banking	50%	89%	77%	78%	65%
I have my own PC	51%	91%	79%	81%	66%
I do not have my own PC	49%	85%	73%	73%	64%
There is one Smart Tv at home	48%	88%	77%	77%	64%
There is no Smart Tv at home	58%	94%	77%	82%	68%
I have repeated course at least once	38%	85%	69%	74%	58%
I have never repeated course	54%	91%	80%	80%	67%
I have studied Economics before	59%	92%	79%	79%	67%
I have not studied Economics before	44%	87%	76%	79%	64%

CONCLUSIONS

Adequate financial knowledge of financial products encourages financial inclusion aimed at achieving greater well-being in society. In Spain, the levels of access to financial services are certainly high, greatly favored by the development of electronic banking. However, the degree of financial knowledge is not yet sufficient to guarantee positive behavior in the financial decision making of consumers, according to their spending needs. This phenomenon is especially serious in the case of the most vulnerable groups in society, including those with low educational levels and reduced income levels. In the same way, the implementation of a tax culture among citizens aimed to avoid tax evasion and to increase the awareness directed towards greater tax liability would also result in a greater social welfare.

For this reason, the OECD together with other supranational institutions are dedicating a great effort aimed at improving financial inclusion. One of the most outstanding proposals lies in the implementation of financial education programs in the classrooms that favor the development of good financial practices from an early age. Financial inclusion accompanied by the development of adequate financial education can bring very positive benefits to consumers of financial products and services that result in a more efficient use of financial products and services, on the one hand, and in improving the well-being of society, on the other. The same should apply for the case of fiscal education.

For this purpose, in this work the degree of financial knowledge of the young population is evaluated from a series of indicators related to financial knowledge such as liquidity, different payment methods, saving, investment and financial risk as well as other information about fiscal knowledge related to tax collection and public spending.

Findings show that students have problems to calculate financial income, to know the characteristics of different payment methods, as well as the relationship between the concepts of interest and inflation. From these three aspects, we find especially worrying, above all, the fact that they often use financial instruments such as debit cards and, however, they do not have any knowledge about their characteristics and consequences. We also check that the students of the rural area have a greater fiscal knowledge, especially when they refer to aspects related to investment or savings. Therefore, these students may be more aware when they decide to save and invest in financial products. Besides, this study verifies that a priori there is no big difference for gender in terms of financial knowledge; in other words, women do not seem to suffer financial exclusion In fact, we observe that women take greater care of matters related to the economy in pre-university studies. On the other hand, the students who obtain better qualifications in mathematics have a higher probability to have a bank account, and those who studied economics at school tend to present a greater financial knowledge as well. With regard to fiscal knowledge and tax culture, despite the fact that the knowledge about public spending is not so low, there have been problems with regard to tax awareness and the repulsion of tax fraud.

Finally, these results justify the need to develop financial and also fiscal education programs from middle school to college that may help consumers to create enhanced financial habits and to avoid tax evasion behaviors at an early age in Spain. In order to achieve this goal, governments and financial intermediaries should provide the necessary tools to implement these educational issues in the classrooms. In this way, by understanding the main financial concepts and by creating a generalized tax culture, future societies will be able to make more accurate financial decisions about the products that are most convenient for their needs.

REFERENCES

Agnew, S., & Harrison, N. (2015). Financial literacy and student attitudes to debt: A cross national study examining the influence of gender on personal finance concepts. *Journal of Retailing and Consumer Services*, *25*, 122–129. doi:10.1016/j.jretconser.2015.04.006

Allgood, S., & Walstad, B. (2016). The effects of perceived and actual financial literacy on financial behaviors. *Economic Inquiry*, *54*(1), 675–697. doi:10.1111/ecin.12255

Atkinson, A. B., & Morelli, S. (2011). Economic crisis and inequality. *Human Development Research Paper*, *5*, 112-115.

Braunstein, S., & Welch, C. (2002). Financial literacy: An overview of practice, research, and policy. *Federal Reserve Bulletin*, 445–457.

Brobeck, S. (2008). *Understanding the emergency savings needs of low-and moderate-income households: a survey-based analysis of impacts, causes and remedies*. Washington, DC: Consumer Federation of America.

Bthutta, N., Skiba, P., & Tobacman, J. (2015). Payday loan choices and consequences. *Journal of Money, Credit and Banking*, *47*(2-3), 223–260. doi:10.1111/jmcb.12175

Cardaci, A. (2018). Inequality Household Debt and Financial Instability: An agent-based perspective. *Journal of Economic Behavior & Organization*, *149*, 434–458. doi:10.1016/j.jebo.2018.01.010

Cecchetti, S. G., Mohanty, M. S., & Zampolli, F. (2010). *The Future of Public Debt: Prospects and Implications*. Bank for International Settlements Working Paper No. 300.

Collins, J. M., & Gjertson, L. (2013). Emergency savings for low-income consumers. *Focus (San Francisco, Calif.)*, *30*(1), 12–17.

Courchane, M., & Zorn, P. (2005). *Consumer literacy and creditworthiness. In 950 Proceedings of Federal Reserve Bank of Chicago*. Federal Reserve Bank of Chicago.

Disney, R., & Gathergood, J. (2013). Financial literacy and consumer credit portfolios. *Journal of Banking & Finance*, *37*(7), 2246–2254. doi:10.1016/j.jbankfin.2013.01.013

Elan, S. (2011). Financial Literacy Among Retail Investors in the United States. Report prepared by the Federal Research Division. Library of Congress under an Interagency Agreement with the Securities and Exchange Commission.

Gjertson, L. (2015). Liquid savings patterns and credit usage among the poor. In J. M. Collins (Ed.), *A Fragile balance*. New York: Palgrave Macmillan.

Golia, J. (2003). Evasión Cero. *Revista Dinero 180*. Retrieved from: http://www.dinero.com.ve/180/portada/tributos

Herrero, F., & Monge, G. (2002). *Grandes Retos de la Política Tributaria*. Jaguar.

Hilgert, M. A., Hogarth, J. M., & Beverly, S. G. (2003). Household financial management: The connection between knowledge and behavior. *Federal Reserve Bulletin*, *89*, 309–322.

Lusardi, A. (2008). *Financial Literacy: An Essential Tool for Informed Consumer Choice?* Cambridge, MA: National Bureau of Economic Research. doi:10.3386/w14084

Lusardi, A., & Mitchell, O. S. (2011). *Financial Literacy Around the World: An Overview*. Cambridge, MA: National Bureau of Economic Research.

Lusardi, A., & Mitchell, O. S. (2014). The economic importance of financial literacy. *Journal of Economic Literature*, *52*(1), 5–44. doi:10.1257/jel.52.1.5 PMID:28579637

Lycette, M., & White, K. (1989). Improving Women's Access to Credit in Latin America and the Caribbean: Policy and Project Recommendations. In Women's Ventures (pp. 19-44). West Harford: Kumarian Press.

Méndez, M. (2004). *Cultura Tributaria, Deberes y Derechos*. Espacio Abierto.

Mendoza Shaw, F. A., Palomino Cano, R., Robles Encinas, J. E., & Ramírez Guardado, S. R. (2016). Correlación entre cultura tributaria y educación tributaria universitaria: Caso Universidad Estatal de Sonora. *Revista Global de Economía*, 4(1), 61–76.

OECD. (2005). *Improving Financial Literacy: Analysis of Issues and Policies*. Paris: OECD Publishing.

Perry, V. G., & Morris, M. D. (2005). Who is in control? The role of self-perception, knowledge, and income in explaining consumer financial behavior. *The Journal of Consumer Affairs*, 39(2), 299–313. doi:10.1111/j.1745-6606.2005.00016.x

Raccanello, K., & Herrera Guzmán, E. (2014). Educación e inclusión financiera. *Revista Latinoamericana de Estudios Educativos*, 44(2), 119–141.

Rhine, S. L. W., & Robbins, E. (2012). *FDCI survey of banks' efforts to serve the unbanked and underbanked*. Washington, DC: Federal Deposit Insurance Corporation. Retrieved from https://www.fdic.gov/unbankedsurveys/2011survey/2011execsummary.pdf

Robb, C. A., & Woodyard, A. (2011). Financial knowledge and best practice behavior. *Journal of Financial Counseling and Planning*, 22(1), 60–70.

Stiglitz, J. E. (2012). *The price of inequality*. New York: W.W. Norton & Company.

Tang, N., Baker, A., & Peter, P. C. (2015). Investigating the disconnect between financial knowledge and behavior: The role of parental influence and psychological characteristics in responsible financial behaviors among young adults. *The Journal of Consumer Affairs*, 49(2), 376–406. doi:10.1111/joca.12069

Telyukova, I. A. (2013). Household Need for Liquidity and the Credit Card Debt Puzzle. *The Review of Economic Studies*, 80(3), 1148–1177. doi:10.1093/restud/rdt001

Vitt, L. A., Carol, A., Kent, J., Lyter, D. M., Siegenthaler, J. K., & Ward, J. (2000). *Personal finance and the rush to competence: financial literacy education in the U.S*. Middleburg, VA: Institute for Socio-Financial Studies.

World Bank. (2018). *Gains in financial inclusion, gains for a sustainable world*. Retrieved from: https://www.worldbank.org/en/news/immersive-story/2018/05/18/gains-in-financial-inclusion-gains-for-a-sustainable-world

ADDITIONAL READING

Bongini, P., Trivellato, p., & Zenga, M. (2012). Measuring financial literacy among students: an application of rasch analysis. *Electronic journal of applied statistical analysis, 5*(3), 425-430.

Carpena, F., Cole, S., Shapiro, J., & Zia, B. (2017). The ABCs of financial education: Experimental evidence on attitudes, behavior, and cognitive biases. *Management Science, 65*(1), 346–369. doi:10.1287/mnsc.2017.2819

Chen, H., & Volpe, R. P. (1998). An analysis of personal financial literacy among college students. *Financial Services Review, 7*(2), 107–128. doi:10.1016/S1057-0810(99)80006-7

Ibrahim, D. I. D., Harun, R., & Isa, Z. M. (2010). A study on financial literacy of Malaysian degree students. *Cross-Cultural Communication, 5*(4), 51–59.

Lusardi, A. (2015). Financial literacy skills for the 21st century: Evidence from PISA. *The Journal of Consumer Affairs, 49*(3), 639–659. doi:10.1111/joca.12099

Thomson, S. (2014). Financing the future: Australian students' results in PISA 2012 Financial Literacy assessment. Retrieved from https://research.acer.edu.au/ozpisa/16/

KEY TERMS AND DEFINITIONS

Credit Card: A small plastic card issued by a bank, building society, etc., allowing the holder to purchase goods or services on credit.

Debit Card: Payment card that deducts money directly from a consumer's checking account to pay for a purchase.

Financial Knowledge: Understanding about the financial concepts and procedures as well as the use of this understanding to solve financial problems.

Financial Risk: The possibility that investors will lose money.

Fiscal Awareness: The individual behavior when tackling tax obligations.

Public Spending: Money spent by the state; government expenditure.

Saving: The money one has saved, especially through a bank.

Compilation of References

(1990, September). Circular 8/1990 del Banco de España: Circular 8/1990 de 7 de septiembre a entidades de crédito sobre transparencia de las operaciones y protección de la clientela, del Banco de España [BOE]. *Published in the Boletín Oficial del Estado, 20*(226), 27498–27508.

(1994, August). Circular 5/1994 del Banco de España: Circular 5/1994, de 22 de julio, a entidades de crédito, sobre modificación de la circular 8/1990 sobre transparencia de las operaciones y protección de la clientela. [BOE]. *Published in the Boletín Oficial del Estado, 3*(184), 25106–2511.

Abreu, M., & Mendes, V. (2010). Financial Literacy and Portfolio Diversification. *Quantitative Finance, 10*(5), 515–528. doi:10.1080/14697680902878105

Acemoglu, D., Ozdaglar, A., & Tahbaz-Salehi, A. (2015). Systematic risk and stability in financial networks. *The American Economic Review, 105*(2), 564–608. doi:10.1257/aer.20130456 PMID:29543414

Acharya, V., Drechsler, I., & Schnabl, P. (2014). A pyrrhic victory? Bank bailouts and sovereign credit risk. *The Journal of Finance, 69*(6), 2689–2739. doi:10.1111/jofi.12206

Acharya, V., & Rajan, R. (2013). Sovereign debt, government myopia and the financial crisis. *Review of Financial Studies, 26*(6), 1526–1560. doi:10.1093/rfs/hht011

Acharya, V., & Steffen, S. (2015). The "greatest" carry trade ever? Understanding Eurozone bank risks. *Journal of Financial Economics, 115*(2), 215–236. doi:10.1016/j.jfineco.2014.11.004

Acosta-González, E., Andrada-Félix, J., & Fernández-Rodríguez, F. (2016). Stock-bond decoupling before and after the 2008 crisis. *Applied Economics Letters, 23*(7), 465–470. doi:10.1080/13504851.2015.1083072

Adhami, S., Giudici, G., & Martinazzi, S. (2018). Why do businesses go crypto? An empirical analysis of initial coin offerings. *Journal of Economics and Business, 100*, 64–75. doi:10.1016/j.jeconbus.2018.04.001

Adrian, T., Colla, P., & Shin, H. S. (2012). Which financial frictions? Parsing the evidence from the financial crisis of 2007 to 2009. Working paper no.18335. National Bureau of Economic Research.

Compilation of References

Adrian, T., & Ashcraft, A. B. (2016). Shadow banking: a review of the literature. In G. Jones (Ed.), *Banking Crises* (pp. 282–315). London: Palgrave Macmillan.

AFI. (2013). *Empoderamiento del consumidor y conducta del mercado*. Nota de orientación, 8.

Agarwal, S. A.-D., Amromin, G., Ben-David, I., Chomsisengphet, S., & Evanoff, D. D. (2014). Predatory lending and the subprime crisis. *Journal of Financial Economics*, *113*(1), 29–52. doi:10.1016/j.jfineco.2014.02.008

Agarwal, S., Driscoll, J., Gabaix, X., & Laibson, D. (2009). The age of reason: Financial decisions over the lifecycle. *Brookings Papers on Economic Activity*, *2009*, 51–101. doi:10.1353/eca.0.0067

Agnew, J. (2004). *An analysis of how individuals react to market returns in one 401(k) plan*. Center for Retirement Research at Boston College, CRR WP 2004-13.

Agnew, J., Bateman, H., & Thorp, S. (2013). Financial Literacy and Retirement Planning in Australia. *Numeracy Advancing Education in Quantitative Literacy, 6*(2), article 7.

Agnew, S., & Harrison, N. (2015). Financial literacy and student attitudes to debt: A cross national study examining the influence of gender on personal finance concepts. *Journal of Retailing and Consumer Services*, *25*, 122–129. doi:10.1016/j.jretconser.2015.04.006

Ahrend, R., & Goujard, A. (2015). Global banking, global crises? The role of bank balance-sheet channel for transmission of financial crises. *European Economic Review*, *80*, 253–279.

Aït-Sahalia, Y., Andritzky, J., Jobst, A., Nowak, S., & Tamirisa, N. (2009). *How to stop a herd of running bears. Market response to policy initiatives during the global financial crisis*. IMF Working Paper, No. WP/09/204.

Akhtaruzzamn, M., & Shamsuddin, A. (2016). International contagion through financial versus non-financial firms. *Economic Modelling*, *59*, 143–163. doi:10.1016/j.econmod.2016.07.003

Alba, J., Lynch, J., Weitz, B., Janiszewski, C., Lutz, C., & Swyer, A. (2010). Interactive home shopping: Consumer, retailer, and manufacturer incentives to participate in electronic marketplaces. *Journal of Marketing*, *61*(3), 38–53. doi:10.1177/002224299706100303

Albertazzi, U., Ropele, T., Sene, G., & Signoretti, F. (2014). The impact of the sovereign debt crisis on the activity of Italian banks. *Journal of Banking & Finance*, *46*, 387–402. doi:10.1016/j.jbankfin.2014.05.005

Alessie, R., van Rooij, M., & Lusardi, A. (2011). Financial Literacy, Retirement Preparation and Pension Expectations in the Netherlands. *Journal of Pension Economics and Finance*, *10*(4), 527–545. doi:10.1017/S1474747211000461

Alfonso, A., Furceri, D., & Gomes, P. (2011). Sovereign credit ratings and financial markets linkages: Application to European data. *Journal of International Money and Finance*, *31*(3), 606–638. doi:10.1016/j.jimonfin.2012.01.016

Compilation of References

Allegret, J. P., Raymond, H., & Rharrabti, H. (2017). The impact of the European sovereign debt crisis on banks stocks. Some evidence of shift contagion in Europe. *Journal of Banking & Finance, 74*, 24–37. doi:10.1016/j.jbankfin.2016.10.004

Allgood, S., & Walstad, W. (2011). *The Effects of Perceived and Actual Financial Knowledge on Credit Card Behavior.* Networks Financial Institute at Indiana State University Working Paper, 2011-WP-15.

Allgood, S., & Walstad, B. (2016). The effects of perceived and actual financial literacy on financial behaviors. *Economic Inquiry, 54*(1), 675–697. doi:10.1111/ecin.12255

Almenberg, J., & Save-Soderberg, J. (2011). *Financial Literacy and Retirement Planning in Sweden.* NETSPAR Discussion Paper 01/2011–018.

Almenberg, J., & Dreber, A. (2015). Gender, stock market participation and financial literacy. *Economics Letters, 137*, 140–142. doi:10.1016/j.econlet.2015.10.009

Altman, E. (1977, Oct.). Some estimates of the cost of lending errors for commercial banks. *Journal of Commercial Bank Lending.*

Altman, E. (1968). Financial Ratios, Discriminant Analysis and Prediction of Corporate Bankruptcy. *The Journal of Finance, 23*(4), 589–609. doi:10.1111/j.1540-6261.1968.tb00843.x

Altman, E. (1969). Corporate bankruptcy potential, stockholder returns, and share valuation. *The Journal of Finance, 24*(5), 887–904. doi:10.1111/j.1540-6261.1969.tb01700.x

Altman, E. I. (2000). *Predicting Financial Distress of Companies: Revisiting the Z-Score and ZETA© Models.* NYU Salomon Center.

Altman, E. I., Haldeman, R. C., & Narayanan, P. (1977). ZETA Analysis. A New Model to Identify Bankruptcy Risk Corporations. *Journal of Banking & Finance, 1*(June), 29–54. doi:10.1016/0378-4266(77)90017-6

Altman, M. (2012). Implications of behavioural economics for financial literacy and public policy. *Journal of Behavioral and Experimental Economics, 41*(5), 677–690.

Álvarez García, B., & Abeal Vázquez, J. P. (2018). *Fragility of the Spanish banking System and Financial Exclusion. Lessons learned from the golbal crisis and new challenges for the Century Balnking Sector.* Hershey, PA: IGI Global.

Alvarez García, B., & Abeal Vázquez, J. P. (2019). Fragility of the Spanish Banking System and Financial Exclusion. Lessons Learned from the Global Crisis and New Challenges for the 21th Century Banking Sector. In S. Nayak & A. Behl (Eds.), *Maintaining Financial Stability in Times of Risk and Uncertainty* (pp. 69–91). Hershey, PA: IGI Global. doi:10.4018/978-1-5225-7208-4.ch004

Amit, R., & Shoemaker, P. (1993). Strategic Assets and Organizational Rent. *Strategic Management Journal, 14*(1), 33–46. doi:10.1002mj.4250140105

Amromin, G., Huang, J., Sialm, C., & Zhong, E. (2018). Complex Mortgages. *Review of Finance*, *22*(6), 1975–2007. doi:10.1093/rof/rfy016

Anderson, S. R., Auquier, A., Hauck, W. W., Oakes, D., Vandaele, W., & Weisberg, H. I. (2009). *Statistical Methods for Comparative Studies: Techniques for Bias Reduction*. New York: Wiley.

Andersson, M., Krylova, E., & Vähämaa, S. (2008). Why does the correlation between stock and bond returns vary over time? *Applied Financial Economics*, *18*(2), 139–151. doi:10.1080/09603100601057854

Andrieu, G., Staglianò, R., & van der Zwan, P. W. (2018). Bank debt and trade credit for SMEs in Europe: Firm-, industry-, and country-level determinants. *Small Business Economics*, *51*(1), 245–264. doi:10.100711187-017-9926-y

Annunziata, F. (2019). *Speak if you can. What are you? An alternative approach to the qualifications of tokens and Initial Coin Offerings*. Bocconi Legal Studies Research Paper Series, n 2636561.

Arezki, R., Candelon, B., & Sy, A. (2011). *Sovereign Rating News and Financial Market Spillovers: Evidence from the European Debt Crisis*. Working paper No. 11/68. International Monetary Fund.

Argenti, J. (1976). *Corporate Collapse: The Causes and Symptoms*. London: McGraw – Hill.

Arghyrou, M., & Kontonikas, G. (2012). The EMU-sovereign debt crisis: Fundamentals, expectations and contagion. *Journal of International Financial Markets, Institutions and Money*, *22*(4), 658–677. doi:10.1016/j.intfin.2012.03.003

Arnedo, L., Lizarraga, F., & Sánchez, S. (2008). Going-concern Uncertainties in Prebankrupt Audit Reports: New Evidence Regarding Discretionary Accruals and Wording Ambiguity. *International Journal of Auditing*, *12*(1), 25–44. doi:10.1111/j.1099-1123.2008.00368.x

Arrondel, L., Debbich, M., & Savignac, F. (2015). Stockholding in France: The role of financial literacy and information. *Applied Economics Letters*, *22*(16), 1315–1319. doi:10.1080/13504851.2015.1026578

Arroyo Amayuelas, E. (2017). La directiva 2014/17/UE sobre los contratos de crédito con consumidores para bienes inmuebles de uso residencial. *Revista para el análisis del derecho InDret*. Retrieved from www.indret.com

Ashcraft, A. B., & Schuermann, T. (2008). Understanding the Securitisation of Subprime Mortgage Credit. Foundations and Trends in Finance, 2(3), 191–309. doi:10.1561/0500000024

Ashcraft, A. (2005). Are banks really sepecial? New evidence from the FDIC-Induced failure of healthy banks. *The American Economic Review*, *94*(5), 1712–1730. doi:10.1257/000282805775014326

Association of Chartered Certified Accountants. (2016). Professional accountants – the future: Drivers of change and future skills. Retrieved October 7, 2019, from https://www.accaglobal.com/content/dam/ members-beta/docs/ea-patf-drivers-of-change-and-future-skills.pdf

Compilation of References

Atkinson, A. B., & Morelli, S. (2011). Economic crisis and inequality. *Human Development Research Paper*, *5*, 112-115.

Atkinson, A., & Messy, F. (2012). *Measuring Financial Literacy: Results of the OECD/ International Network on Financial Education (INFE) Pilot Study.* OECD Working Paper on Finance, Insurance and Private Pensions, No 15.

Atkinson, A., McKay, S., Kempson, E., & Collard, S. (2006). Levels of Financial Capability in the U.K.: Results of a Baseline Survey. Financial Service Authority, Consumer Research, 47.

Audretsch, D. B., Heger, D., & Veith, T. (2015). Infrastructure and entrepreneurship. *Small Business Economics*, *44*(2), 219–230. doi:10.100711187-014-9600-6

Audretsch, D. B., Keilbach, M. C., & Lehmann, E. E. (2006). *Entrepreneurship and economic growth*. Oxford, UK: Oxford University Press. doi:10.1093/acprof:oso/9780195183511.001.0001

Autio, E., Kenney, M., Mustar, P., Siegel, D., & Wright, M. (2014). Entrepreneurial innovation: The importance of context. *Research Policy*, *43*(7), 1097–1108. doi:10.1016/j.respol.2014.01.015

Ayadi, R. (2009). SME financing in Europe: Measures to improve the rating culture under the new banking rules. In M. Balling, B. Bernet, & E. Gnan (Eds.), *Financing SMEs in Europe*. SUERF – The European Money and Finance Forum.

Baele, L., Bekaert, G., & Inghelbrecht, K. (2010). The determinants of stock and bond return comovements. *Review of Financial Studies*, *23*(6), 2374–2428. doi:10.1093/rfs/hhq014

Bakk-Simon, K., Borgioli, S., Giron, C., Hempell, H. S., Maddaloni, A., Recine, F., & Rosati, S. (2011). Shadow Banking in the Euro Area: An Overview. ECB Occasional Paper No. 133. Retrieved from https://ssrn.com/abstract=1932063

Bakos, Y. (1991). A strategic analysis of electronic marketplaces. *Management Information Systems Quarterly*, *15*(3), 295–312. doi:10.2307/249641

Bakshi, G., Madan, D., & Xiaoling, F. (2006). Investigating the role of systematic and firm-specific factors indefault risk: Lessons from empirically evaluating credit risk models. *The Journal of Business*, *79*(4), 1955–1987. doi:10.1086/503653

Balloch, A., Nicolae, A., & Philip, D. (2015). Stock market literacy, trust, and participation. *Review of Finance*, *19*(5), 1925–1963. doi:10.1093/rof/rfu040

Balluck, K. (2015). Investment banking: linkages to the real economy and the financial system. *Bank of England Quarterly Bulletin*.

Baltagi, B. H. (2008). *Econometric analysis of panel data*. John Wiley & Sons.

Banca de las Oportunidades y Superintendencia Financiera de Colombia. (2014a). *Inclusión Financiera en Colombia: Estudio desde la Demanda*. Author.

Banca de las Oportunidades y Superintendencia Financiera de Colombia. (2014b). *Reporte de Inclusión Financiera: 2014*. Author.

Banca de las Oportunidades. (2015). *Reporte Trimestral de Inclusión Financiera: diciembre de 2015*. Author.

Banco de Espana. (2018) *Financial Education Plan 2018-2021*. Retrieved from https://www.bde.es/f/webbde/Secciones/Publicaciones/OtrasPublicaciones/educacionfinaciera/PlanEducacion2018en.pdf

Bank of Spain. (2017). *Informe sobre la Crisis Financiera y Bancaria en España, 2008-2014*. Retrieved from https://www.bde.es/f/webbde/Secciones/Publicaciones/OtrasPublicaciones/Fich/InformeCrisis_Completo_web.pdf

Bank of Spain. (2019). *Boletín económico 1/2019. Informe trimestral de la Economía española*. Retrieved from www.bde.es/secciones/publicaciones

Barney, J. (1991). Firm resources and sustained competitive advantage. *Journal of Management*, *17*(1), 99–120. doi:10.1177/014920639101700108

Baron-Donovan, C., Wiener, R., Gross, K., & Block-Lieb, S. (2005). Financial literacy teacher training: A multiple-measure evaluation. *Journal of Financial Counselling and Planning*, *16*(2), 63–75.

Barontini, C. & Holden, H. (2019). *Proceeding with caution – a survey on central bank digital currency*. BIS Papers No 101.

Barua, A., Konana, P., Whinston, A., & Yin, F. (2004). An empirical investigation of the Net-enabled business value. *Management Information Systems Quarterly*, *28*(4), 585–620. doi:10.2307/25148656

Basset, W. F., Chosak, M. B., Driscoll, J. C., & Zakrajsek, E. (2014). Changes in bank lending standards and the macroeconomy. *Journal of Money, Credit and Banking*, *62*, 23–40.

Baur, D. G. (2012). Financial contagion and the real economy. *Journal of Banking & Finance*, *36*(10), 2680–2692. doi:10.1016/j.jbankfin.2011.05.019

Baur, D., & Lucey, B. (2009). Flights and contagion – An empirical analysis of stock-bond correlations. *Journal of Financial Stability*, *5*(4), 339–352. doi:10.1016/j.jfs.2008.08.001

Baxter, N. (1967). Leverage, risk of ruin, and the cost of capital. *The Journal of Finance*, *22*, 395–404.

Bayar, M. Y., Sezgin, H. F., & Öztürk, O. F. (2017). Impact of Financial Literacy on Personal Savings: A Research on Usak University Staff. *Journal of Knowledge Management. Economics and Information Technology*, *7*(6), 1–19.

Beal, D., & Delpachitra, S. B. (2003). Financial Literacy among Australian University Students. *Economic Papers*, *22*(1), 65–78. doi:10.1111/j.1759-3441.2003.tb00337.x

Bech, M. L., & Garratt, R. (2017). Central Bank Cryptocurrencies. *BIS Quarterly Review*. Retrieved from SSRN: https://ssrn.com/abstract=3041906

Compilation of References

Becker, B., & Ivashina, V. (2014). Cyclicality of credit supply: Firm level evidence. *Journal of Monetary Economics*, *62*, 76–93. doi:10.1016/j.jmoneco.2013.10.002

Beckmann, E. (2013). Financial Literacy and Household Savings in Romania. *Numeracy Advancing Education in Quantitative Literacy*, *6*(2), Article 9.

Beckmann, E. (2013). Financial Literacy and Household Savings in Romania. *Numeracy*, *6*(2), 1–22. doi:10.5038/1936-4660.6.2.9

Beck, T., Demirguc-Kunt, A., & Martinez Peria, M. S. (2011). Bank financing for SMEs: Evidence across countries and bank ownership types. *Journal of Financial Services Research*, *39*(2), 35–54. doi:10.100710693-010-0085-4

Behrman, J., Mitchell, O. S., Soo, C., & Bravo, D. (2012). Financial Literacy, Schooling, and Wealth Accumulation. *American Economic Review Paper and Proceedings*, *102*(3), 300–304. doi:10.1257/aer.102.3.300 PMID:23355747

Beirne, J., & Fratzscher, M. (2013). The pricing of sovereign risk and contagion during the European sovereign debt crisis. *Journal of International Money and Finance*, *34*, 60–82. doi:10.1016/j.jimonfin.2012.11.004

Bekaert, G., Ehrman, M., Fratzscher, F., & Mehl, A. (2014). The global crisis and equity market contagion. *The Journal of Finance*, *69*(6), 2597–2649. doi:10.1111/jofi.12203

Bekiros, S. D. (2014). Contagion, decoupling and spillover effects of the US financial crisis: Evidence from the BRIC markets. *International Review of Financial Analysis*, *33*, 58–69. doi:10.1016/j.irfa.2013.07.007

Belleflamme, P., Lambert, Th., & Schwienbacher, A. (2014). Crowdfunding: Tapping the right crowd. *Journal of Business Venturing*, *29*(5), 585–609. doi:10.1016/j.jbusvent.2013.07.003

Benartzi, S., & Thaler, R. H. (2001). Naive Diversification Strategies in Defined Contribution Savings Plans. *The American Economic Review*, *91*(1), 79–98. doi:10.1257/aer.91.1.79

Bengtsson, E. (2013). Shadow banking and financial stability: European money market funds in the global financial crisis. *Journal of International Money and Finance*, *32*, 579–594. doi:10.1016/j.jimonfin.2012.05.027

Berges, A., & Ontiveros, E. (2013). Sistema bancario español: Una transformación sin precedentes. *Harvard Deusto Business Review*, *229*, 16–28.

Bernanke, B. (1983). Non-monetary effects of the financial crisis in the propagation of the Great Depression. *The American Economic Review*, *73*(3), 257–276.

Bernheim, D., Garrett, D., & Maki, D. (2001). Education and saving: The long-term effects of high school financial curriculum mandates. *Journal of Public Economics*, *85*(3), 435–565. doi:10.1016/S0047-2727(00)00120-1

Berry, J., Karlan, D., & Pradhan, M. (2018). The Impact of Financial Education for Youth in Ghana. *World Development*, *102*, 71–89. doi:10.1016/j.worlddev.2017.09.011

Bertoni, F., Colombo, M., & Grilli, L. (2011). Venture Capital and the Growth of High-tech Start-ups: Disentangling Treatment from Selection Effects. *Research Policy*, *40*(7), 1028–1043. doi:10.1016/j.respol.2011.03.008

Better than Cash. (2015). *Development Results Focused Research Program. Country Diagnostic: Colombia*. Bankable Frontier. Retrieved from https://btca-prod.s3.amazonaws.com/documents/5/english_attachments/Colombia-Diagnostic-Long-ENG-Jan-2015.pdf?1431983488

Bharadwaj, A. S. (2000). A resource-based perspective on information technology capability and firm performance: An empirical investigation. *Management Information Systems Quarterly*, *24*(1), 169–196. doi:10.2307/3250983

Bharadwaj, A., Bharadwaj, S., & Konsynski, B. (1999). Information Technology Effects on Firm Performance as Measured by Tobin's q. *Management Science*, *45*(7), 1008–1024. doi:10.1287/mnsc.45.7.1008

Bhatt, G., Emdad, A., Roberts, N., & Grover, V. (2010). Building and leveraging information in dynamic environments: The role of IT infrastructure flexibility as enabler of organizational responsiveness and competitive advantage. *Information & Management*, *47*(7–8), 341–349. doi:10.1016/j.im.2010.08.001

Bianchi, M. (2017). Financial Literacy and Portfolio Dynamics. *The Journal of Finance*, *73*(2), 831–859. doi:10.1111/jofi.12605

Bigot, R., Croutte, P., Mueller, J., & Osier, G. (2011). *Middle Classes in Europe*. Research Center for the Study and Observation of Living (CREDOC) Working Paper, No 282.

Bilias, Y., Georgarakos, D., & Haliassos, M. (2010). Portfolio inertia and stock market fluctuations. *Journal of Money, Credit and Banking*, *42*(4), 715–742. doi:10.1111/j.1538-4616.2010.00304.x

Bird, G., Du, W., Pentecost, E. J., & Willett, T. (2017). Was it different the second time? An empirical analysis of contagion during the crises in Greece, 2009-2015. *World Economy*, *40*(12), 1–14. doi:10.1111/twec.12553

Blandin, A., Cloots, A. S., Hussain, H., Rauchs, M., Saleuddin, R., Allen, J. G., . . . Cloud, K. (2019) *Global Cryptoasset Regulatory Landscape Study*. Retrieved from SSRN: https://ssrn.com/abstract=3379219

Blatt, D., Candelon, B., & Manner, H. (2015). Detecting contagion in a multivariate time series system: An application to sovereign bond markets in Europe. *Journal of Banking & Finance*, *59*, 1–13. doi:10.1016/j.jbankfin.2015.06.003

Bocola, L. (2016). The Pass-Through of Sovereign Risk. *Journal of Political Economy*, *124*(4), 879–926. doi:10.1086/686734

Compilation of References

Bonardo, D., Paleari, S., & Vismara, S. (2009). When academia comes to market: Does university affiliation reduce the uncertainty of IPOs? Working paper, Department of Economics and Technology Management, University of Bergam.

Bond, P. M., Musto, D. K., & Yilmaz, B. (2009). Predatory mortgage lending. *Journal of Financial Economics*, *94*(3), 412–427. doi:10.1016/j.jfineco.2008.09.011

Borden, L. M., Lee, S. A., Serido, J., & Collins, D. (2008). Changing college students' financial knowledge, attitudes, and behavior through seminar participation. *Journal of Family and Economic Issues*, *29*(1), 23–40. doi:10.100710834-007-9087-2

Boulding, W., & Staelin, R. (1990). Environment, market share and market power. *Management Science*, *36*(10), 1160–1177. doi:10.1287/mnsc.36.10.1160

Bourlakis, M., & Bourlakis, C. (2006). Integrating Logistics and Information Technology Strategies for Sustainable Competitive Advantage. *Journal of Enterprise Information Management*, *19*(4), 389–402. doi:10.1108/17410390610678313

Bowen, C. (2002). Financial Knowledge of Teens and Their Parents. *Journal of Financial Counselling and Planning*, *13*(2), 93–102.

Braunstein, S., & Welch, C. (2002). Financial literacy: An overview of practice, research, and policy. *Federal Reserve Bulletin*, 445–457.

Bravo, C., Maldonado, S., & Weber, R. (2010). Experiencias Prácticas en la medicion de riesgo crediticio de microempresarios utilizando modelos de Credit Scoring. *Revista Ingenieria de Sistemas*, *24*(20), 69–88.

Briozzo, A., Vigier, H., Castillo, N., Pesce, G., & Speroni, M. C. (2016). Decisiones de financiamiento en pymes: ¿existen diferencias en función del tamaño y la forma legal? Estudios Gerenciales, 32(138), 71–81. doi:10.1016/j.estger.2015.11.003

Brobeck, S. (2008). *Understanding the emergency savings needs of low-and moderate-income households: a survey-based analysis of impacts, causes and remedies*. Washington, DC: Consumer Federation of America.

Brockett, P., Golden, L., Jang, J., & Yang, C. (2006). A comparison of neural network, statistical methods, and variable choice for life insurers' financial distress prediction. *The Journal of Risk and Insurance*, *73*(3), 397–419. doi:10.1111/j.1539-6975.2006.00181.x

Brown, M., & Graf, R. (2013). Financial Literacy and Retirement Planning in Switzerland. *Numeracy Advancing Education in Quantitative Literacy, 6*(2), article 6.

Brown, M., Henchoz, C., & Spycher, T. (2018). Culture and Financial Literacy: Evidence from a within-country language border. *Journal of Economic Behavior & Organization*, *150*(1), 62–85. doi:10.1016/j.jebo.2018.03.011

Bruhn, M., & Love, I. (2014). The Real Impact of Improved Access to Finance: Evidence from Mexico. *The Journal of Finance*, *69*(3), 1347–1369. doi:10.1111/jofi.12091

Brune, L., Giné, X., Goldberg, J., & Yang, D. (2016). Facilitating Savings for Agriculture: Field Experimental Evidence from Malawi. *Economic Development and Cultural Change*, *64*(2), 187–220. doi:10.1086/684014

Brunnermeier, M. K. (2008). *Deciphering – The liquidity and credit crunch 2007–2008*. National Bureau of Economic Research (NBER), Working Paper No. 14612.

Brunnermeier, M. K., Garciano, L., Lane, P., Pagano, M., Reis, R., Santos, T., ... Vayanos, D. (2016). The sovereign-banking diabolical loop and ESBies. *The American Economic Review*, *106*(5), 508–512. doi:10.1257/aer.p20161107

Brynjolfsson, E., & Hitt, L. (1993). Is information systems spending productive? New evidence and new results. *International Conference on Information Systems*.

Brynjolfsson, E., & Hitt, L. (1996). Paradox lost? Firm-level evidence on the returns to information systems spending. *Management Science*, *42*(4), 541–558. doi:10.1287/mnsc.42.4.541

Brynjolfsson, E., Hitt, L., & Yang, S. (2002). Intangible assets: Computers and organizational capital. *Brookings Papers on Economic Activity*, *1*(1), 137–191. doi:10.1353/eca.2002.0003

Bthutta, N., Skiba, P., & Tobacman, J. (2015). Payday loan choices and consequences. *Journal of Money, Credit and Banking*, *47*(2-3), 223–260. doi:10.1111/jmcb.12175

Buch, C. M. (2018). *Financial Literacy and Financial Stability*. Speech prepared for the 5th OECD-GFLEC Global Policy Research Symposium to Advance Financial Literacy, Paris, France.

Bucher-Koenen, T., & Lusardi, A. (2011). Financial literacy and retirement planning in Germany. *Journal of Pension Economics and Finance*, *10*(4), 565–584. doi:10.1017/S1474747211000485

Bucher-Koenen, T., Lusardi, A., Alessie, R., & van Rooij, M. (2017). How financially literate are women? An overview and new insights. *The Journal of Consumer Affairs*, *51*(2), 255–283. doi:10.1111/joca.12121

Bueno Campos, E. (2001). *Evolución y Perspectivas de la banca española*. Madrid: Civitas.

Bumcrot, C., Lin, J., & Lusardi, A. (2013). The Geography of Financial Literacy. *Numeracy Advancing Education in Quantitative Literacy*, *6*(2), article 2.

Burgess, R., & Pande, R. (2005). Do Rural Banks Matter? Evidence from the Indian Social Banking Experiment. *The American Economic Review*, *95*(3), 780–795. doi:10.1257/0002828054201242

Burniske, C. (2017, Sep 24). *Cryptoasset valuation*. Retrieved from https://medium.com/@cburniske/cryptoasset-valuations-ac83479ffca7

Bustos, E., & Martínez, I. (2012). El MAB EE. In *El mercado alternativo bursátil* (pp. 35–60). Pamplona: Thomson Reuters.

Buterin, V. (2013). *Ethereum: A Next-Generation Smart Contract and Decentralized Application Platform*. Retrieved from https://github.com/ethereum/wiki/wiki/White-Paper

Butler, K. C., & Joaquin, D. C. (2002). Are the gains from international portfolio diversification exaggerated? The influence of downside risk in bear markets. *Journal of International Money and Finance*, *21*(7), 981–1011. doi:10.1016/S0261-5606(02)00048-7

Calcagno, R., & Monticone, C. (2015). Financial literacy and the demand for financial advice. *Journal of Banking & Finance*, *50*, 363–380. doi:10.1016/j.jbankfin.2014.03.013

Calvet, L. E., Campbell, J. Y., & Sodini, P. (2009). Measuring the financial sophistication of households. *The American Economic Review*, *99*(2), 393–398. doi:10.1257/aer.99.2.393 PMID:29504738

Calvo Bernardino, A., & Martín de Vidales Carrasco, I. (2014). Crisis y cambios estructurales en el sector bancario español: Una comparación con otros sistemas financieros. *Estudios de Economía Aplicada*, *32*(2), 535–566.

Campbell, J. Y. (2006). Household Finance. *The Journal of Finance*, *61*(4), 1553–1604. doi:10.1111/j.1540-6261.2006.00883.x

Campbell, J. Y., Jackson, H. E., Madrian, B. C., & Tufano, P. (2011). Consumer Financial Protection. *The Journal of Economic Perspectives*, *25*(1), 91–113. doi:10.1257/jep.25.1.91 PMID:24991083

Campbell-Kelly, M., & Garcia-Swartz, D. (2012). The Move to the Middle: Convergence of the Open-Source and Proprietary Software Industries. *International Journal of the Economics of Business*, *17*(2), 223–252. doi:10.1080/13571516.2010.483091

Campelo, M., Graham, J., & Harvey, C. R. (2009). *The real effects on financial constraints: evidence from a financial crisis.* Working paper no. 15552. National Bureau of Economic Research.

Cantner, U., & Goethner, M. (2011). Performance differences between academic spin-offs and non-academic star-ups: A comparative analysis using a non-parametric matching approach. *DIME Final Conference*.

Caporin, M., Pelizzon, L., Ravazzolo, F., & Rigobon, R. (2013). *Measuring Sovereign Contagion in Europe*. NBER Working paper 18741.

Cardaci, A. (2018). Inequality Household Debt and Financial Instability: An agent-based perspective. *Journal of Economic Behavior & Organization*, *149*, 434–458. doi:10.1016/j.jebo.2018.01.010

Carlin, B. I., & Manso, G. (2011). Obfuscation, learning, and the evolution of investor sophistication. *Review of Financial Studies*, *24*(3), 754–785. doi:10.1093/rfs/hhq070

Carrera, N. (2017). What Do We Know about Accounting in Family Firms? *Journal of Evolutionary Studies in Business*, *2*(2), 97–159. doi:10.1344/jesb2017.2.j032

Carr, N. (2003). IT doesn't matter. *Harvard Business Review*, *81*, 41–50. PMID:12747161

Carro Meana, D. (2012). La Pyme ante el reto de la cotización en los mercados. In *Pequeña y mediana empresa: impacto y retos de la crisis en su financiación* (pp. 215–234). Madrid: Fundación de Estudios Financieros.

Carroll, G. R. (1993). A sociological view on why firms differ. *Strategic Management Journal*, *14*(4), 237–249. doi:10.1002mj.4250140402

Casey, E., & O'Toole, C. M. (2014). Bank lending constraints, trade credit and alternative financing during the financial crisis: Evidence from European SMEs. *Journal of Corporate Finance*, *27*, 173–193. doi:10.1016/j.jcorpfin.2014.05.001

Casino, F., Dasaklis, T. K., & Patsakis, C. (2019). A systematic literature review of blockchain-based applications: Current status, classification and open issues. *Telematics and Informatics*, *36*, 55–81. doi:10.1016/j.tele.2018.11.006

Catalini, C., & Gans, J. S. (2019). *Initial Coin Offerings and the Value of Crypto Tokens*. NBER Working Paper No. w24418.

Cecchetti, S. G., Mohanty, M. S., & Zampolli, F. (2010). *The Future of Public Debt: Prospects and Implications*. Bank for International Settlements Working Paper No. 300.

Cetorelli, N., & Goldberg, G. (2011). *Global banks and international shock transmission: evidence from the crisis*. Working paper no 15974. National Bureau of Economic Research.

CGAP. (2013). *Incentivos para la Apertura de Corresponsales No Bancarios de la Banca de las Oportunidades en Colombia*. Retrieved from https://www.cgap.org/sites/default/files/colombia_agent_subsidy_program_spanish.pdf

Chang, C. L., & Hsueh, P. L. (2013). An investigation of the flight-to-quality effect: Evidence from Asia-Pacific countries. *Emerging Markets Finance & Trade*, *49*(sup4), 53–69. doi:10.2753/REE1540-496X4905S404

Chang, R., Chang, Y., & Paper, D. (2003). The effect of task uncertainty, decentralization and AIS characteristics on the performance of AIS: An empirical case in Taiwan. *Information & Management*, *40*(7), 691–703. doi:10.1016/S0378-7206(02)00097-6

Chartered Institute of Management Accountants – CIMA. (2011). Finance Transformation a Missed Opportunity for SMEs? Retrieved May 5, 2019, from https://www.cimaglobal.com/Research--Insight/Finance-transformation-a-missed-opportunity-for-SMEs

Chartered Institute of Management Accountants - CIMA. (2016). A CFO's Key Competencies for the Future. Retrieved October 15, 2019, from https://www.ifac.org/system/files/publications/files/Role%20of%20the%20CFO.pdf

Chatterjee, C., Grewal, R., & Sambamurthy, V. (2002). Shaping Up for e-commerce: Institutional enablers of the organizational assimilation of web technologies. *Management Information Systems Quarterly*, *26*(2), 65–89. doi:10.2307/4132321

Compilation of References

Chatterjee, D., Richardson, V., & Zmud, R. (2001). Examining the shareholder wealth effects of new CIO position announcements. *Management Information Systems Quarterly*, *25*(1), 43–70. doi:10.2307/3250958

Chava, S., & Purnanandam, A. (2010). CEOs versus CFOs: Incentives and corporate policies. *Journal of Financial Economics*, *97*(2), 263–278. doi:10.1016/j.jfineco.2010.03.018

Chen, H., & Volpe, R. P. (1998). An analysis of personal financial literacy among college students. *Financial Services Review*, *7*(2), 107–128. doi:10.1016/S1057-0810(99)80006-7

Chen, H., & Volpe, R. P. (2002). Gender Differences in Personal Financial Literacy among College Students. *Financial Services Review*, *11*, 289–307.

Chernenko, S., & Sunderam, A. (2014). Frictions in Shadow Banking: Evidence from the Lending Behavior of Money Market Mutual Funds. *Review of Financial Studies*, *27*(6), 1717–1750. doi:10.1093/rfs/hhu025

Chian, T. C., Nam, B., & Li, H. (2007). Dynamic correlation analysis of financial contagion: Evidence from Asian markets. *Journal of International Money and Finance*, *26*(7), 1206–1228. doi:10.1016/j.jimonfin.2007.06.005

Choe, J. M. (1998). The effects of user participation on the design of accounting information systems. *Information & Management*, *34*(3), 185–198. doi:10.1016/S0378-7206(98)00055-X

Choy, K., Lau, H., Kwok, S., & Stuart, C. (2007). Using Radio Frequency Identification Technology in Distribution Management: A Case Study on Third-Party Logistics. *International Journal of Manufacturing Technology and Management*, *10*(1), 19–32. doi:10.1504/IJMTM.2007.011399

Christelis, D., Jappelli, T., & Padula, M. (2010). Cognitive abilities and portfolio choice. *European Economic Review*, *54*(1), 18–39. doi:10.1016/j.euroecorev.2009.04.001

Cicarelli, M., Maddaloni, A., & Peidró, J. L. (2013). *Heterogeneous transmisión mechanism monetary policy and financial regulity in the euro area*. Working paper no. 1527. European Central Bank.

CIIFC. (2016). *Estrategia Nacional de Inclusión Financiera en Colombia*. Bogotá: Comisión Intersectorial para la Inclusión Financiera. Retrieved from https://www.superfinanciera.gov.co/descargas/institucional/pubFile1030467/estrategia_nacional_inclusion_financiera.pdf

Cintra, M. A. M., & Farhi, M. (2008). A crise financeira e o global shadow banking system. Novos Estudos CEBRAP, (82): 35–55. doi:10.1590/S0101-33002008000300002

Circular 2/2018, of 4 December, on admission and removal of securities in the Alternative Fixed Income Market (MARF). (n.d.). Retrieved from: http://www.bmerf.es/docs/ing/normativa/circulares/2018/Circular_2_2018_de_4_December,_on_admision_and_removal_of_securities_i.pdf

Circular 5/2012 del Banco de España: Circular 5/2012, de 27 de junio, del Banco de España, a entidades de crédito y proveedores de servicios de pago, sobre transparencia de los servicios bancarios y responsabilidad en la concesión de préstamos. Published in the Boletín Oficial del Estado (BOE), No. 161, 6 July 2012.

Circular 5/2017, rates applicable to the Alternative Equity Market. (n.d.). Retrieved from: https://www.bolsasymercados.es/mab/docs/normativa/ing/circulares/2017/Tarifas_MAB_Circular_5-2017_eng.pdf

Circular 9/2013, of 18 December, on Alternative Fixed Income Market fees. (n.d.). Retrieved from: http://www.bmerf.es/docs/ing/normativa/circulares/2013/Circular%209-2013.pdf

Circular 13/1993 del Banco de España: Circular 13/1993 de 21 de diciembre, a Entidades de crédito, sobre modificación de la circular 8/1990, sobre transparencia de las operaciones y protección a la clientela. Published in the Boletín Oficial del Estado (BOE), No. 313, 31 December 1993.

Claessens, S., Tong, H., & Zuccardi, I. (2011b). *Did the Euro crisis affect non-financial firm stock prices through a financial or trade channel?* Working paper no. 11/227. International Monetary Fund.

Claessens, S., Tong, H., & Wei, S. (2011a). From the financial crisis to the real economy: Using firm-level data to identify transmission channels. *Journal of International Economics, 88*(2), 375–387. doi:10.1016/j.jinteco.2012.02.015

Claeys, P., & Vasicek, B. (2014). Measuring bilateral spillover and testing contagion on sovereign bond markets in Europe. *Journal of Banking & Finance, 46*, 151–165. doi:10.1016/j.jbankfin.2014.05.011

Clark, R., Sandler, M., & Mallen, S. (2010). *The Role of Financial Literacy in Determining Retirement Plans*. National Bureau of Economic Research Working Paper, No. 16612. Retrieved from www.nber.org/papers/w16612

Clemons, E. K., & Row, M. C. (1991). Sustaining IT advantage: The role of structural differences. *Management Information Systems Quarterly, 15*(September), 275–292. doi:10.2307/249639

Cocco, J., Gomes, F., & Maenhout, P. (2005). Consumption and portfolio choice over the lifecycle. *Review of Financial Studies, 18*(2), 490–533. doi:10.1093/rfs/hhi017

Coindesk. (n.d.). Retrieved from https://www.coindesk.com/ico-tracker

Coinschedule. (n.d.). Retrieved from https://www.coinschedule.com/stats

Collin-Dufresne, P., & Goldstein, R. (2001). Do credit spreads reflect stationary leverage? Reconciling structural and reduced-form frameworks. *The Journal of Finance, 56*(5), 1929–1957. doi:10.1111/0022-1082.00395

Collins, J. M., & Gjertson, L. (2013). Emergency savings for low-income consumers. *Focus (San Francisco, Calif.), 30*(1), 12–17.

Compilation of References

Colombo, M., & Grilli, L. (2010). On Growth Drivers of High-tech Start-ups: Exploring the Role of Founders' Human Capital and Venture Capital. *Journal of Business Venturing*, *25*(6), 610–626. doi:10.1016/j.jbusvent.2009.01.005

Coluzzi, Ch., Ferrando, A., & Martinez-Carrascal, C. (2015). Financing obstacles and growth: An analysis for Euro area non-financial firms. *European Journal of Finance*, *21*(10-11), 773–790. doi:10.1080/1351847X.2012.664154

Conceição, O., Faria, A. P., & Fontes, M. (2017). Regional variation of academic spinoffs formation. *The Journal of Technology Transfer*, *42*(3), 654–675. doi:10.1007/s10961-016-9508-1

Conefrey, T., & Cronin, D. (2015). Spillover in Euro area sovereign bond markets. *The Economic and Social Review*, *46*(2), 197–231.

Cong, L., Li, Y., & Wang, N. (2019). *Tokenomics: Dynamic Adoption and Valuation*. Columbia Business School Research Paper No. 18-46.

Connolly, R., Stivers, C., & Sun, L. (2005). Stock market uncertainty and the relation between stocks and bond returns. *Journal of Financial and Quantitative Analysis*, *40*, 161–194. doi:10.1017/S0022109000001782

Cooper, R., & Nikolov, K. (2018). Government debt and banking fragility: The spreading of strategic uncertainty. *International Economic Review*, *59*(4), 1905–1925. doi:10.1111/iere.12323

Courchane, M., & Zorn, P. (2005). *Consumer literacy and creditworthiness. In 950 Proceedings of Federal Reserve Bank of Chicago*. Federal Reserve Bank of Chicago.

Coval, J., Jurek, J., & Stafford, E. (2009). The economics of structured finance. *The Journal of Economic Perspectives*, *23*(1), 3–25. doi:10.1257/jep.23.1.3

Covitz, D., Liang, N., & Suarez, G. (2012). The Evolution of a Financial Crisis: Collapse of the Asset-Backed Commercial Paper Market. *The Journal of Finance*, *68*(3), 815–848. doi:10.1111/jofi.12023

Cronin, D., Flavin, T. J., & Sheenan, L. (2016). Contagion in Eurozone sovereign bond markets? The good, the bad and the ugly. *Economics Letters*, *143*, 5–8. doi:10.1016/j.econlet.2016.02.031

Cron, W. I., & Sobol, M. G. (1983). The relationship between computerization and performance: A strategy for maximizing the economic benefits of computerization. *Journal of International Management*, *6*, 171–181.

Crossan, D., Feslier, D., & Hurnabard, R. (2011). Financial Literacy and Retirement Planning in New Zealand. *Journal of Pension Economics and Finance*, *10*(4), 619–635. doi:10.1017/S1474747211000515

Crowe, Ch., Dell'Ariccia, G., Deniz, I., & Rabanal, P. (2013). How to deal with real estate booms: Lessons from country experiences. *Journal of Financial Stability*, *9*(3), 300–319. doi:10.1016/j.jfs.2013.05.003

Cupak, A., Fessler, P., Silgoner, M., & Ulbrich, E. (2018). *Exploring differences in financial literacy across countries: the role of individual characteristics and institutions.* Oesterreichische National Bank Working Paper, 220.

Daft, R. L., & Lengel, R. H. (1986). Organizational Information Requirements. Media Richness and Structural Design. *Management Science, 32*(5), 554–571. doi:10.1287/mnsc.32.5.554

Daft, R. L., Lengel, R. H., & Trevino, L. K. (1987). Message Equivocality, Media Selection, and Manager Performance: Implications for Information Systems. *Management Information Systems Quarterly, 11*(3), 355–366. doi:10.2307/248682

Damanpour, F., & Evan, W. M. (1984). Organizational Innovation and Performance: The Problem of Organizational Lag. *Administrative Science Quarterly, 29*(3), 392–409. doi:10.2307/2393031

Dambolena, I., & Khoury, S. (1980). Ratio stability and corporate failure. *The Journal of Finance, 35*(4), 1017–1026. doi:10.1111/j.1540-6261.1980.tb03517.x

DANE. (2019). *Empleo informal y seguridad social.* Retrieved July 15, 2019, from https://www.dane.gov.co/index.php/estadisticas-por-tema/mercado-laboral/empleo-informal-y-seguridad-social. http://microdatos.dane.gov.co/index.php/catalog/599/get_microdata

Danes, S., & Haberman, H. (2007). Teen financial knowledge, self-efficacy, and behavior: A gender view. *Journal of Financial Counselling and Planning, 18*(2), 48–60.

David, P. A. (1989). *Computer and dynamo: the modern productivity paradox in a not-too-distant mirror.* Stanford, CA: Center for Economic Policy Research.

de Bassa, S. C. (2013). Financial literacy and ðnancial behavior among young adults: Evidence and implications. *Numeracy, 6*(2), 1–21.

De Bruyckere, V., Gerhardt, M., Schepens, G., & Vander Vennet, R. (2013). Bank/sovereign risk spillovers in the European debt crisis. *Journal of Banking & Finance, 37*(12), 4793–4809. doi:10.1016/j.jbankfin.2013.08.012

de Meza, D., Irlenbusch, B., & Reyniers, D. (2008). *Financial capability: a behavioural economics perspective.* FSA Consumer Research Paper 69.

De Santis, R. (2012). *The Euro Area Sovereign Debt Crisis: Safe Haven, Credit Rating Agencies and the Spread of the Fever from Greece, Ireland and Portugal.* Working paper No. 1419. European Central Bank.

De Santis, G., & Gerard, B. (1997). International asset pricing and portfolio diversification with time-varying risk. *The Journal of Finance, 52*(5), 1881–1912. doi:10.1111/j.1540-6261.1997.tb02745.x

Deeg, R. (2009). The rise of internal capitalist diversity? Changing patterns of finance and corporate governance in Europe. *Economy and Society, 38*(4), 552–579. doi:10.1080/03085140903190359

Compilation of References

Dees, S., Mauro, F., Pesaran, M., & Smith, V. (2007). Exploring the international linkages of the euro area: A global VAR analysis. *Journal of Applied Econometrics*, *22*(1), 1–38. doi:10.1002/jae.932

Dehning, B., & Richardson, V. (2002). Returns on investments in information technology: A research synthesis. *Journal of Information Systems*, *16*(1), 7–30. doi:10.2308/jis.2002.16.1.7

Dehning, B., Richardson, V., & Stratopoulos, T. (2005). Information technology investments and firm value. *Information & Management*, *42*(7), 989–1008. doi:10.1016/j.im.2004.11.003

Delavande, A., Rohwedder, S., & Willis, R. (2008). *Preparation for Retirement, Financial Literacy and Cognitive Resources*. University of Michigan Retirement Research Center Working Paper 2008-190.

Demary, M., Hornik, J., & Watfe, G. (2016). *SME Financing in the EU: Moving beyond one-size-fits-all*. Bruges European Economic Policy Briefings 40/2016.

Demirguc-Kunt, A., Klapper, L., & Singer, D. (2017). *Financial Inclusion and Inclusive Growth – A Review of Recent Empirical Evidence*. World Bank Policy Research Paper, No. 8040.

Demirgüç-Kunt, A., Klapper, L., Singer, D., Ansar, S., & Hess, J. (2018). *The Global Findex Database 2017: Measuring Financial Inclusion and the Fintech Revolution*. Washington, DC: World Bank. doi:10.1596/978-1-4648-1259-0

Demyanyk, Y., & Van Hemert, O. (2011). Understanding the Subprime Mortgage Crisis. *Review of Financial Studies*, *24*(6), 1848–1880. doi:10.1093/rfs/hhp033

Denis, D. J. (2004). Entrepreneurial finance: An overview of the issues and evidence. *Journal of Corporate Finance*, *10*(2), 301–326. doi:10.1016/S0929-1199(03)00059-2

Deuflhard, F., Georgarakos, D., & Inderst, R. (2015). *Financial Literacy and Savings Account Returns*. European Central Bank Working Paper, No. 1852.

Deuflhard, F., Georgarakos, D., & Inderst, R. (2018). Financial literacy and savings account returns. *Journal of the European Economic Association*, *17*(1), 131–164. doi:10.1093/jeea/jvy003

DeWit, G., & de Kok, J. (2014). Do small businesses create more jobs? New evidence for Europe. *Small Business Economics*, *42*(2), 283–295. doi:10.100711187-013-9480-1

Dierickx, I., & Cool, K. (1989). Asset Stock Accumulation and Sustainability of Competitive Advantage. *Management Science*, *35*(12), 1504–1511. doi:10.1287/mnsc.35.12.1504

Dimitrou, D., Kenourgios, D., & Simos, T. (2013). Global financial crisis and emerging stock market contagion: A multivariate FIAPARCH-DCC approach. *International Review of Financial Analysis*, *30*, 46–56. doi:10.1016/j.irfa.2013.05.008

Directive 2014/17/EU of the European Parliament and of the Council of 4 February 2014 on credit agreements for consumers relating to residential immovable property and amending Directives 2008/48/EC and 2013/36/EU and Regulation (EU), No. 1093/2010 Text with EEA relevance. (n.d.). Retrieved from http://data.europa.eu/eli/dir/2014/17/oj

Disney, R., & Gathergood, J. (2012). *Financial literacy and consumer credit use.* Centre for Finance and Credit Markets (CFCM) Working Paper, No. 12/01.

Disney, R., & Gathergood, J. (2013). Financial literacy and consumer credit portfolios. *Journal of Banking & Finance, 37*(7), 2246–2254. doi:10.1016/j.jbankfin.2013.01.013

Djokovic, D., & Souitaris, V. (2008). Spinouts from academic institutions: A literature review with suggestions for further research. *The Journal of Technology Transfer, 33*(3), 225–247. doi:10.1007/s10961-006-9000-4

Domínguez Martínez, J. (2019). *El sistema bancario en España: evolución reciente, situación actual, y problemas y retos planteados.* Madrid: Instituto Universitario de Análisis económico y social, Universidad de Alcalá.

dos Santos, B. L., Peffers, K., & Mauer, D. C. (1993). The impact of information technology investment announcements on the market value of the firm. *Information Systems Research, 4*(1), 1–23. doi:10.1287/isre.4.1.1

Drucker, P. (1988). The Coming of the New Organization. *Harvard Business Review, 66*(1), 3–11.

Dungey, M., Flavin, T. J., & Sheenan, L. (2019). *Banks and sovereigns: Did adversity bring them closer?* (Unpublished manuscript). Maynooth University.

Dungey, M., Dwyer, G., & Flavin, T. (2013). Systematic and liquidity risk in suprime-mortgage backed securities. *Open Economies Review, 24*(1), 5–32. doi:10.100711079-012-9254-4

Dungey, M., Flavin, T., & Lagoa-Varela, D. (2018). Are banking shocks contagious? Evidence from the Eurozone. *Journal of Banking & Finance,* 105386. doi:10.1016/j.jbankfin.2018.07.010

Dungey, M., & Gajurel, D. (2014). Equity market contagion during the global financial crisis: Evidence from the world's eight largest economies. *Economic Systems, 38*(2), 161–177. doi:10.1016/j.ecosys.2013.10.003

Dupas, P., & Robinson, J. (2013). Savings Constraints and Microenterprise Development: Evidence from a Field Experiment in Kenya. *American Economic Journal. Applied Economics, 5*(1), 163–192. doi:10.1257/app.5.1.163

Duréndez Gómez-Guillamón, A., García Pérez de Lema, D., & Mariño Garrido, T. (2014). El Mercado Alternativo Bursátil: Una novedosa oportunidad para las empresas familiares. *Revista de Empresa Familiar, 4*(2), 37–46.

Dwyer, G. P., Devereux, J., Baier, S., & Tamura, R. (2013). Recessions, growth and banking crises. *Journal of International Money and Finance, 38,* 18–40. doi:10.1016/j.jimonfin.2013.05.009

Compilation of References

Dwyer, G., & Tkac, P. (2009). The financial crisis of 2008 in fixed-income markets. *Journal of International Money and Finance*, *28*(8), 1293–1316. doi:10.1016/j.jimonfin.2009.08.007

ECB. (2019). *Crypto-Assets: Implications for financial stability, monetary policy, and payments and market infrastructures*. Occasional Paper Series, 223.

Eisenhardt, K. M., & Martin, J. (2000). Dynamic Capabilities: What Are They? *Strategic Management Journal*, *21*(10-11), 1105–1121. doi:10.1002/1097-0266(200010/11)21:10/11<1105::AID-SMJ133>3.0.CO;2-E

Elan, S. (2011). Financial Literacy Among Retail Investors in the United States. Report prepared by the Federal Research Division. Library of Congress under an Interagency Agreement with the Securities and Exchange Commission.

Engel, D., & Keilbach, M. (2007). Firm-level implications of early stage venture capital investment— An empirical investigation. *Journal of Empirical Finance*, *14*(2), 150–167. doi:10.1016/j.jempfin.2006.03.004

Equifax Financial Literacy Survey. (2019). *2019 Equifax Consumer Solutions Financial Literacy Month Survey*. Retrieved from https://blog.equifax.com/credit/fast-facts-2019-equifax-financial-literacy-survey/

ESMA. (2019). *Advice. Initial Coin Offerings and Crypto-Assets*. ESMA50-157-1391. Retrieved from https://www.esma.europa.eu/sites/default/files/library/esma50-157-1391_crypto_advice.pdf

Esquivel, G., León, R., & Arley, V. (2013). *Modelo CREDIT SCORING PYMES para la medición del riesgo de morosidad de pequeña y mediana empresa: Un caso de aplicación en Entidad financiera (Unpublished End-of- Degree Project)*. Instituto Técnico de Costa Rica, San José de Costa Rica.

European Systemic Risk Board. (2018). EU Shadow Banking Monitor, No 3, September 2018. Retrieved from https://www.esrb.europa.eu/pub/pdf/reports/esrb.report180910_shadow_banking.en.pdf

EVERFI. (2018). *Next Generation of Financial Capability: Young Adults in Higher Education*. Retrieved from https://everfi.com/press-releases/everfi-reveals-national-financial-knowledge-findings-based-survey-results-college-students-across-country/

Facebook. (2019). *Facebook Q2 Earnings Release*. Retrieved from https://s21.q4cdn.com/399680738/files/doc_financials/2019/Q2/FB-Q2-2019-Earnings-Release.pdf

Fahri, E., & Tirole, J. (2018). Deadly embrace: Sovereign and financial balance sheets doom loops. *The Review of Economic Studies*, *85*(3), 1781–1823. doi:10.1093/restud/rdx059

Fama, E. F. (1980). Banking in the theory of finance. *Journal of Monetary Economics*, *6*(1), 39–57. doi:10.1016/0304-3932(80)90017-3

Fama, E., & French, K. R. (1988). Permanent and temporary components of stock prices. *Journal of Political Economy*, *96*(2), 246–273. doi:10.1086/261535

Fargher, N. L., & Weigand, R. A. (1998). Changes in the stock price reaction of small firms to common information. *Journal of Financial Research*, *21*(1), 105–121.

FCA. (2019). *Guidance on Cryptoassets.* Consultation paper CP19/3. Retrieved from https://www.fca.org.uk/publication/consultation/cp19-03.pdf

Feng, L., & Seasholes, M. S. (2005). Do investor sophistication and trading experience eliminate behavioral biases in ðnancial markets? *Review of Finance*, *9*(3), 305–351. doi:10.100710679-005-2262-0

Fernandes, D., Lynch, J. Jr, & Netemeyer, R. (2013). Financial Literacy, Financial Education and Downstream Financial Behaviors. *Management Science*, *60*(8), 1861–2109. doi:10.1287/mnsc.2013.1849

Fernández de Lis, S., & Rubio, A. (2013). *Tendencias a medio plazo en la banca española* (BBVA Working Paper No. 13/33). Retrieved from BBVA website: https://www.bbvaresearch.com/publicaciones/tendencias-a-medio-plazo-en-la-banca-espanola/

Fernández, C., & Pérez, R. (2005). El modelo logístico: Una herramienta estadística para evaluar el riesgo de crédito. *Revista Ingenierías Universidad de Medellín*, *4*(6), 1–22.

Ferrando, A., & Griesshaber, N. (2011). *Financing obstacles among Euro area firms. Who suffers the most?* European Central Bank. Working Paper Series n° 1293. Retrieved from https://www.ecb.europa.eu/pub/pdf/scpwps/ecbwp1293.pdf

Fiaschi, D., Kondor, I., Marsili, M., & Volpati, V. (2014). The Interrupted Power Law and the Size of Shadow Banking. *PLoS One*, *9*(4), e94237. doi:10.1371/journal.pone.0094237 PubMed

Fichman, R. (2004). Real Options and IT Platform Adoption: Implications for Theory and Practice. *Information Systems Research*, *15*(2), 132–154. doi:10.1287/isre.1040.0021

Fiegenbaum, A., & Thomas, H. (1988). Attitudes Toward Risk and the Risk-Return Paradox: Prospect Theory Explanations. *Academy of Management Journal*, *31*, 85–106.

Financial Industry Regulatory Authority. (2009). *Financial Capability in the United States National Survey Executive Summary.* FINRA Investor Education Foundation. Retrieved from https://www.usfinancialcapability.org/downloads/NFCS_2009_Natl_Exec_Sum.pdf

Financial Services Authority of U.K. (2005). *Financial Services Authority: Financial Capability baseline survey: questionnaire.* Retrieved from http://www.fsa.gov.uk/

Financial Stability Board. (2018). Global shadow banking monitoring report 2017. Retrieved from https://www.fsb.org/wp-content/uploads/P050318-1.pdf

Finoa. (2018, Oct 27). *The Era of tokenization – market outlook on a $24trn business opportunity.* Retrieved from https://medium.com/finoa-banking/market-outlook-on-tokenized-assets-a-usd24trn-opportunity-9bac0c4dfefb

Compilation of References

Flavin, T. J. (2019). From bulls to bears: Analysing the stock-bond relationship of European countries across different market regimes. In S. Boubaker & D. K. Nguyen (Eds.), *Handbook of Global Financial Markets: Transformations, Dependence, and Risk Spillovers.* World Scientific Publishing. doi:10.1142/9789813236653_0002

Flavin, T. J., & Lagoa-Varela, D. (2019). On the stability of Stock-bond comovements across market conditions in the Eurozone periphery. *Global Finance Journal*, 100491. doi:10.1016/j.gfj.2019.100491

Flavin, T. J., Morley, C. E., & Panopoulou, E. (2014). Identifying safe haven assets for equity investors through an analysis of the stability of shock transmission. *Journal of International Financial Markets and Money*, *33*, 137–154. doi:10.1016/j.intfin.2014.08.001

Flavin, T. J., & Sheenan, L. (2015). The role of U.S. subprime mortgage-backed assets in propagating the crisis: Contagion or interdependence? *The North American Journal of Economics and Finance*, *34*, 167–186. doi:10.1016/j.najef.2015.09.001

Fleming, J., Kirby, C., & Ostdiek, B. (1998). Information and volatility linkages in the stock, bond, and money markets. *Journal of Financial Economics*, *49*(1), 111–137. doi:10.1016/S0304-405X(98)00019-1

Florackis, C., & Sainani, S. (2018). How do chief financial officers influence corporate cash policies? *Journal of Corporate Finance*, *52*, 168–191. doi:10.1016/j.jcorpfin.2018.08.001

Fonseca, R., Mullen, K. J., Zamarro, G., & Zissimopoulos, J. (2012). What explains the gender gap in financial literacy? The role of household decision making. *The Journal of Consumer Affairs*, *46*(1), 90–106. doi:10.1111/j.1745-6606.2011.01221.x PMID:23049140

Forbes, K. J., & Rigobon, R. J. (2002). No contagion, only interdependence: Measuring stock market comovements. *The Journal of Finance*, *57*(5), 2223–2261. doi:10.1111/0022-1082.00494

Fornero, E., & Monticone, C. (2011). Financial Literacy and Pension Plan Participation in Italy. *Journal of Pension Economics and Finance*, *10*(4), 547–564. doi:10.1017/S1474747211000473

Fox Gotham, K. (2009). Creating Liquidity out of Spatial Fixity: The Secondary Circuit of Capital and the Subprime Mortgage Crisis. *International Journal of Urban and Regional Research*, *33*(2), 355–371. doi:10.1111/j.1468-2427.2009.00874.x

Frydman, H., Altman, E., & Kao, D. (1985). Introducing Recursive Partitioning for Financial Classification: The Case of Financial Distress. *The Journal of Finance*, *XL*(1), 269–291. doi:10.1111/j.1540-6261.1985.tb04949.x

Fry-McKibben, R. A., & Hsiao, C. Y. (2015). *Extremal dependence tests for contagion.* CAMA Working paper 40/2015. Australian National University.

FUNCAS-ODF. (2018a). *Informe Criptomercados y Blockchain, primer trimestre.* Retrieved from www.funcas.es/_obsdigi_/DownLoadObs.aspx?Id=1177

FUNCAS-ODF. (2018b). *Informe Criptomercados y Blockchain, cuarto trimestre.* Retrieved from www.funcas.es/_obsdigi_/DownLoadObs.aspx?Id=1237

FUNCAS-ODF. (2019). *Informe Criptomercados y Blockchain, primer semestre.* Retrieved from www.funcas.es/_obsdigi_/DownLoadObs.aspx?Id=1290

Galesi, A., & Sgherri, S. (2009). *Regional financial spillovers across Europe: A global VAR analysis.* Working paper no 09/23. International Monetary Fund.

Galvis, L. (2012). *Informalidad Laboral en las áreas urbanas de Colombia.* Documentos de Trabajo sobre Economía Regional, 164, Banco de la República, Cartagena, Colombia. Retrieved from https://www.banrep.gov.co/sites/default/files/publicaciones/archivos/DTSER-164_0.pdf

Gamba-Santamaria, S., Gomez-Gonzalez, J. E., Hurtado Guarin, J. L., & Melo-Velandia, L. F. (2017). Stock market volatility spillovers: Evidence for Latin America. *Finance Research Letters, 20*, 207–216. doi:10.1016/j.frl.2016.10.001

García Delgado, J. M. (2013). *Lecciones de Economía española.* Thomson- Civitas.

García-Vaquero, V., & Roibás, I. (2018). *Recent developments in non-bank financing of Spanish firms.* Economic Bulletin, 4/2018, Banco de España. Retrieved from https://www.bde.es/f/webbde/SES/Secciones/Publicaciones/InformesBoletinesRevistas/ArticulosAnaliticos/2018/T4/descargar/Files/beaa1804-art32e.pdf

Garfield, M., & Dennis, A. (2012). Toward an Integrated Model of Group Development: Disruption of Routines by Technology-Induced Change. *Journal of Management Information Systems, 29*(3), 43–86. doi:10.2753/MIS0742-1222290302

Gatti, S. (2013). *Project finance in theory and practice. Designin, structuring, and financing private and public proyect* (2nd ed.). San Diego, CA: Academic Press.

Gennaioli, N., Martin, A., & Rossi, S. (2014). Sovereign defaults, domestic banks, and financial institutions. *The Journal of Finance, 69*(2), 819–866. doi:10.1111/jofi.12124

Georgoutsos, D., & Moratis, G. (2017). Bank-sovereign contagion in the Eurozone: A panel VAR approach. *Journal of International Financial Markets, Institutions and Money, 48*, 146–159. doi:10.1016/j.intfin.2017.01.004

Gerardi, K., Goette, L., & Meier, S. (2010). *Financial Literacy and Subprime Mortgage Delinquency: Evidence from a Survey Matched to Administrative Data.* Federal Reserve Bank of Atlanta Working Paper, 2010–10.

Gerardi, K., Goette, L., & Meier, S. (2013). Numerical ability and mortgage default. *Proceedings of the National Academy of Sciences of the United States of America, 110*(28), 11267–11271. doi:10.1073/pnas.1220568110 PMID:23798401

Gerrans, P., & Heaney, R. (2016). The Impact of undergraduate personal finance education on individual financial literacy, attitudes and intentions. *Accounting and Finance, 59*(1), 177–217. doi:10.1111/acfi.12247

Compilation of References

Gharavi, H., Love, P., & Cheng, E. (2004). Information and Communication Technology in the Stockbroking Industry: An Evolutionary Approach to the Diffusion of Innovation. *Industrial Management & Data Systems, 104*(9), 756–765. doi:10.1108/02635570410567748

Ghosh, S., González del Mazo, I., & Ötker-Robe, İ. (2012). *Chasing the Shadows: How Significant is Shadow Banking in Emerging Markets? Economic Premise, No. 88.* Washington, DC: World Bank; Retrieved from https://openknowledge.worldbank.org/handle/10986/17088

Gileborg, R. (2018). *Initial token offerings, friend or foe?* (Master of Science Thesis Dissertation). TRITA-ITM-EX; 2018:445.

Giralt, A., & González Nieto, J. (2012). Financiación de la Pyme en el mercado financiero español. La experiencia y proyección del MAB. In *Pequeña y mediana empresa: impacto y retos de la crisis en su financiación* (pp. 235–258). Madrid: Fundación de Estudios Financieros.

Gjertson, L. (2015). Liquid savings patterns and credit usage among the poor. In J. M. Collins (Ed.), *A Fragile balance*. New York: Palgrave Macmillan.

Global Financial Literacy Excellence Center. (2015). *GFLEC Financial Literacy around the World*. Retrieved from https://gflec.org/wp-content/uploads/2015/11/3313-Finlit_Report_FINAL-5.11.16.pdf?x37292

Golia, J. (2003). Evasión Cero. *Revista Dinero 180*. Retrieved from: http://www.dinero.com.ve/180/portada/tributos

Gompers, P., & Lerner, J. (1999). *The Venture Capital Cycle*. Cambridge, MA: MIT Press.

Gordon, M. (1971). Towards a theory of financial distress. *The Journal of Finance, 25*(2), 347–356. doi:10.1111/j.1540-6261.1971.tb00902.x

Gorton, G., Metrick, A., Shleifer, A., & Tarullo, D. K. (2010). Regulating the Shadow Banking System. Brookings Papers on Economic Activity, 2010(Fall), 261–312. doi:10.1353/eca.2010.0016

Gorton, G. (2009). Information, liquidity and the (ongoing) panic of 2007. *The American Economic Review, 99*(2), 567–572. doi:10.1257/aer.99.2.567

Grammatikos, T., & Vermeulen, R. (2012). Transmission of the financial and sovereign debt crises to the EMU: Stock prices, CDS spreads and exchange rates. *Journal of International Money and Finance, 31*(3), 517–533. doi:10.1016/j.jimonfin.2011.10.004

Grant, E. (2016). *Exposure to international crises: trade versus financial contagion*. Working Paper no 30/2016. European Systematic Risk Board.

Gratzer, M., & Winiwarter, W. (2003). A Framework for Competitive Advantage in eTourism. In *Proceedings of the 10th International Conference on Information Technology and Travel and Tourism*. Berlin: Springer-Verlag.

Grimsey, D., & Lewis, M. K. (2004). *Public private partnerships. The worldwide revolution in infrastructure provision and project finance*. Edward Elgar Publishing, Inc.

Grinblatt, M., Keloharju, M., & Linnainmaa, J. (2011). IQ and Stock Market Participation. *The Journal of Finance*, *66*(6), 2121–2164. doi:10.1111/j.1540-6261.2011.01701.x

Grohmann, A., Klühs, T., & Menkhoff, L. (2018). Does financial literacy improve financial inclusion? Cross country evidence. *World Development*, *111*, 84–96. doi:10.1016/j.worlddev.2018.06.020

Gropp, R., Lo Duca, M., & Vesala, J. (2009). Cross-border bank contagion in Europe. *International Journal of Central Banking*, *5*(1), 97–139.

Grossman, G. M., & Helpman, E. (1992). *Innovation and growth in the global economy*. Cambridge, MA: MIT Press.

Grover, V., & Kohli, R. (2012). Cocreating IT value: New capabilities and metrics for multiform environments. *Management Information Systems Quarterly*, *36*(1), 225–232. doi:10.2307/41410415

Guercio, M. B., Martinez, L. B., & Vigier, H. (2017). Las limitaciones al financiamiento bancario de las pymes de alta tecnología. Estudios Gerenciales, 33(142), 3-12. DOI: . 2017.02.001 doi:10.1016/j.estger

Guidolin, M., Hansen, E., & Pedio, M. (2019). Cross-asset contagion in the financial crisis: A Bayesian time-varying parameter approach. *Journal of Financial Markets*, *45*, 83–114. doi:10.1016/j.finmar.2019.04.001

Guidolin, M., & Timmermann, A. (2006). An econometric model of nonlinear dynamics in the joint distribution of stock and bond returns. *Journal of Applied Econometrics*, *21*(1), 1–22. doi:10.1002/jae.824

Guinard, F., Trifa, V., Mattern, F., & Wilde, E. (2011). From the Internet of Things to the Web of Things: Resource-oriented Architecture and Best Practices. In D. Uckelmann, M. Harrison, & F. Michahelles (Eds.), *Architecting the Internet of things* (pp. 97–129). New York: Springer – Verlag. doi:10.1007/978-3-642-19157-2_5

Guiso, L., & Jappelli, T. (2009). *Financial literacy and portfolio diversification*. Centre for Studies in Economics and Finance (CSEF) Working Paper, 212.

Guiso, L., & Viviano, E. (2015). How much can ðnancial literacy help? *Review of Finance*, *19*(4), 1347–1382. doi:10.1093/rof/rfu033

Gu, J., & Jung, H. (2013). The effects of IS resources, capabilities, and qualities on organizational performance: An integrated approach. *Information & Management*, *50*(2-3), 87–97. doi:10.1016/j.im.2013.02.001

Gul, F. A., & Chia, Y. M. (1994). The effect of management accounting systems, perceived environment uncertainty and decentralization on managerial performance: A test of three-way interaction. *Accounting, Organizations and Society*, *19*(4), 413–426. doi:10.1016/0361-3682(94)90005-1

Guo, F., Chen, C., & Huang, Y. S. (2011). Markets contagion during financial crisis: A regime switching approach. *International Review of Economics & Finance*, *20*(1), 95–109. doi:10.1016/j.iref.2010.07.009

Gustman, A. L., Steinmeier, T. L., & Tabatabai, N. (2012). Financial Knowledge and Financial Literacy at the Household Level. *American Economic Review*, *102*(3), 309–313.

Guttmann, R. (2016). Finance-Led Capitalism: shadow banking, re-regulation, and the future of global markets. Hampshire, UK: Palgrave MacMillan; doi:10.1057/9781137529893.

Habib, A., & Hossain, M. (2013). CEO/CFO characteristics and financial reporting quality: A review. *Research in Accounting Regulation*, *25*(1), 88–100. doi:10.1016/j.racreg.2012.11.002

Hacker, P., & Thomale, C. (2018). Crypto-Securities Regulation: ICOs, Token Sales and Cryptocurrencies under EU Financial Law. *European Company and Financial Law Review*, *15*(4), 645–696. doi:10.1515/ecfr-2018-0021

Hagsten, E., & Kotnik, P. (2017). ICT as facilitator of internationalisation in small- and medium-sized firms. *Small Business Economics*, *48*(2), 431–446. doi:10.1007/s11187-016-9781-2

Hameed, M., Counsell, S., & Swift, S. (2012). A meta-analysis of relationships between organizational characteristics and IT innovation adoption in organizations. *Information & Management*, *49*(5), 218–232. doi:10.1016/j.im.2012.05.002

Hand, D., & Henley, W. (1997). Statistical Classification Methods in Consumer Credit Scoring: a Review. Journal of the Royal Statistical Society, 160(3), 523-541.

Hargrave, J., Sahdev, N., & Feldmeier, O. (2019). How value is created in tokenized assets. In M. Swan, J. Potts, S. Takagi, F. Witte, & P. Tasca (Eds.), *Blockchain economics: Implications of distributed ledgers* (pp. 125–143). London: World Scientific. doi:10.1142/9781786346391_0007

Harris, S. E., & Kaatz, L. (1989). Predicting organizational performance using information technology managerial control ratios. *Proceedings of the 22nd Hawaiian International Conference on System Science*. 10.1109/HICSS.1989.48122

Harutyunyan, A., Massara, A., Ugazio, G., Amidzic, G., & Richard Walton, R. (2015). Shedding Light on Shadow Banking. IMF Working Paper, WP/15/1. Retrieved from https://www.imf.org/external/pubs/ft/wp/2015/wp1501.pdf

Harvey, M. (in press). Impact of Financial Education Mandates on Younger Consumers' Use of Alternative Financial Services. *The Journal of Consumer Affairs*.

Hastings, J., & Mitchell, O. S. (2011). *How Financial Literacy and Impatience Shape Retirement Wealth and Investment Behaviors.* NBER Working Paper, No.16740.

Hastings, J. S., Madrian, B. C., & Skimmyhorn, B. (2013). Financial Literacy, Financial Education, and Economic Outcomes. *Annual Review of Economics*, *5*(1), 347–373. doi:10.1146/annurev-economics-082312-125807 PMID:23991248

Hastings, J., Mitchell, O. S., & Chyn, E. (2011). Fees, Framing, and Financial Literacy in the Choice of Pension Manager. In A. Lusardi & O. S. Mitchell (Eds.), *Financial Literacy – Implications for Retirement Security and the Financial Marketplace* (pp. 101–115). New York, NY: Oxford University Press. doi:10.1093/acprof:oso/9780199696819.003.0006

Hayter, C. S. (2013). Conceptualizing knowledge-based entrepreneurship networks: Perspectives from the literature. *Small Business Economics*, *41*(4), 899–911. doi:10.1007/s11187-013-9512-x

Helfat, C. E., & Raubitscek, R. S. (2000). Product sequencing: Co-evolution of knowledge, capabilities and products. *Strategic Management Journal*, *21*(10-11), 961–979. doi:10.1002/1097-0266(200010/11)21:10/11<961::AID-SMJ132>3.0.CO;2-E

Hellmann, T., & Puri, M. (2002). On the fundamental role of venture capital. *Economic Review (Federal Reserve Bank of Atlanta)*, *87*(4), 19–24.

Hernández-Cánovas, G., & Martínez-Solano, P. (2010). Relationship lending and SME financing in the continental European bank-based system. *Small Business Economics*, *34*(4), 465–482. doi:10.100711187-008-9129-7

Herrero, F., & Monge, G. (2002). *Grandes Retos de la Política Tributaria*. Jaguar.

Hiebl, M., Gärtner, B., & Duller, C. (2017). Chief financial officer (CFO) characteristics and ERP system adoption: An upper-echelons perspective. *Journal of Accounting & Organizational Change*, *13*(1), 85–111. doi:10.1108/JAOC-10-2015-0078

Hiebl, M., Neubauer, H., & Duller, C. (2013). The Chief Financial Officer's Role in Medium-Sized Firms: Exploratory Evidence from Germany. *Journal of International Business & Economics*, *13*(2), 83–92. doi:10.18374/JIBE-13-2.8

Hilgert, M., Hogarth, J., & Beverly, S. (2003). Household financial management: The connection between knowledge and behavior. *Federal Reserve Bulletin*, 309–322.

Hilghert, M. J., Hogarth, S., & Beverly, S. (2003). Household Financial Management: The Connection between Knowledge and Behavior. *Federal Reserve Bulletin*, 309–322.

Hill, R., & Perdue, G. (2008). A methodological issue in the measurement of ðnancial literacy. *Journal of Economics and Economic Education Research*, *9*, 150–162.

Hindle, K., & Yencken, J. (2004). Public Research Commercialisation, Entrepreneurship and New Technology Based Firms: An Integrated Model. *Technovation*, *24*(10), 793–803. doi:10.1016/S0166-4972(03)00023-3

Hing-Ling, A. (1987). A five-state financial distress prediction model. *Journal of Accounting Research*, *25*(1), 127–138. doi:10.2307/2491262

Hippler, W. J. III, Hossain, S., & Hassan, M. K. (2019). Financial crisis spillover from Wall Street to Main Street: Further evidence. *Empirical Economics*, *56*(6), 1893–1938. doi:10.100700181-018-1513-9

Compilation of References

Hira, T. K., & Loibl, C. (2005). Understanding the Impact of Employer-Provided Financial Education on Workplace Satisfaction. *The Journal of Consumer Affairs*, *39*(1), 173–194. doi:10.1111/j.1745-6606.2005.00008.x

Hoffmann, A. O. I., Post, T., & Pennings, J. M. E. (2013). Individual investor perceptions and behavior during the ðnancial crisis. *Journal of Banking & Finance*, *37*(1), 60–74. doi:10.1016/j.jbankfin.2012.08.007

Holsapple, C., & Wu, J. (2011). An elusive antecedent of superior firm performance: The knowledge management factor. *Decision Support Systems*, *52*(1), 271–283. doi:10.1016/j.dss.2011.08.003

Hotchkiss, E., & Mooradian, R. (1997). Vulture investors and the market for control of distressed firms. *Journal of Financial Economics*, *43*(3), 401–432. doi:10.1016/S0304-405X(96)00900-2

Howell, S. T., Niessner, M., & Yermack, D. (2019). *Initial Coin Offerings: Financing Growth with Cryptocurrency Token Sales*. NBER Working Paper No. 24774.

Hsiao, Y., & Tsai, W. (2018). Financial literacy and participation in derivatives markets. *Journal of Banking & Finance*, *88*, 15–29. doi:10.1016/j.jbankfin.2017.11.006

Huang, J. (2018). Banking and shadow banking. *Journal of Economic Theory*, *178*, 124–152. doi:10.1016/j.jet.2018.09.003

Huang, J., Nam, Y., & Sherraden, M. (2013). Financial Knowledge and Child Development Account Policy a Test of Financial Capability. *The Journal of Consumer Affairs*, *47*(1), 1–26. doi:10.1111/joca.12000

Huang, X., Zhou, H., & Zhu, H. (2012). Assessing the systematic risk of heterogeneous portfolio of banks during the recent financial crisis. *Journal of Financial Stability*, *8*(3), 193–205. doi:10.1016/j.jfs.2011.10.004

Huberman, G., & Jiang, W. (2006). Offering versus Choice in 401(k) Plans: Equity Exposure and Number of Funds. *The Journal of Finance*, *61*(2), 763–801. doi:10.1111/j.1540-6261.2006.00854.x

IBM Institute for Business Values. (2010), APQC Webinar: Chief Financial Officer Global Study 2010. Retrieved May 7, 2019, from https://www.apqc.org/sites/default/files/files/WebinarPDFs/IBMCFOStudy 2010APQCJuly13Webinar.pdf

Icobench. (2019). *ICO market analysis 2018*. Retrieved from https://icobench.com/reports/ICO_Market_Analysis_2018.pdf

Icodata. (n.d.). Retrieved from https://www.icodata.io/ stats/2018

Im, K., Dow, V., & Grover, V. (2001). Research Report: A Re-examination of IT Investment and the Market Value of the Firm - An Event Study Methodology. *Information Systems Research*, *12*(1), 103–117. doi:10.1287/isre.12.1.103.9718

Infelise, F. (2014). *Supporting Access to Finance by SMEs: Mapping the Initiatives in Five EU Countries*. ECMI Research Report No. 9. Retrieved from https://ssrn.com/abstract=2430116

Ingham, G. (2013). Revisiting the Credit Theory of Money and Trust. In J. Pixley (Ed.), New Perspectives on Emotions in Finance (pp. 121-139). London: Routledge.

International Federation of Accountants - IFAC. (2013). The Role and Expectations of a CFO. A Global Debate on Preparing Accountants for Finance Leadership. Retrieved May 9, 2019, from https://www.ifac.org/system/files/publications/files/Role%20of%20the%20CFO.pdf

International Federation of Accountants - IFAC. (2018a). The Crucial Roles of Professional Accountants in Business in Mid-Sized Enterprises. Retrieved Octuber 12, 2019, from https://www.ifac.org/system /files/publications /files/the-crucial-roles-of-pro.pdf

International Federation of Accountants – IFAC. (2018b). Information and Communications Technology Literature Review. Retrieved October 4, 2019, from https://www.ifac.org/system/files/publications /files/IAESB-Information-Communications-Technology-Literature-Review.pdf

International Federation of Accountants. (2002). The Role of the Chief Financial Officer in 2010. IFAC. Retrieved May 9, 2019, from https://www.icjce.es/images/pdfs/ TECNICA/C01%20-%20 IFAC/C.01.073%20-%20PAIB%20-%20Other/PAIB-CFO_2010.pdf

Investor Education Center of Hong Kong. (2018). *The Investor Education Center (IEC) 2018 Financial Literacy Monitor.* Retrieved from https://www.ifec.org.hk/common/pdf/about_iec/iec-financial-literacy-monitor-2018.pdf

Inwara. (2019). *Half-Yearly Report. H1 2019. Deciphering token offerings – IEOs, STOs and ICOs.* Retrieved from https://www.inwara.com

Itami, I., & Roehl, R. (1991). *Mobilizing Invisible Assets.* Cambridge, MA: Harvard University Press.

Jacobson, R. (1990). What really determines business performance? Unobservable effects – The key to profitability. *Management Science*, *9*, 74–85.

Jamison, J. C., Karlan, D., & Zinman, J. (2014). *Financial Education and Access to Savings Accounts: Complements or Substitutes? Evidence from Ugandan Youth Clubs.* NBER Working Paper, No. 20135.

Jammazi, R., Tiwari, A., Ferrer, R., & Moya, P. (2015). Time-varying dependence between stock and government bond returns: International evidence with dynamic copulas. *The North American Journal of Economics and Finance*, *33*, 74–93. doi:10.1016/j.najef.2015.03.005

Janulek, P. (2018). *Tokenization as a Form of Payment and Valuation Professional, Scientific, Specialist and Technical Activities.* Available at SSRN: https://ssrn.com/abstract=3307180

Jappelli, T. (2011). Economic Literacy: An International Comparison. *Economic Journal (London)*, *120*(548), 429–451. doi:10.1111/j.1468-0297.2010.02397.x

Jappelli, T., & Padula, M. (2011). *Investment in Financial Literacy and Saving Decisions.* CSEF Centre for Studies in Economics and Finance.

Compilation of References

Jappelli, T., & Padula, M. (2013). Investment in Financial Literacy and Saving Decisions. *Journal of Banking & Finance, 37*(8), 2779–2792. doi:10.1016/j.jbankfin.2013.03.019

Jappelli, T., & Padula, M. (2015). Investment in Financial Literacy, Social Security and Portfolio Choice. *Journal of Pension Economics and Finance, 14*(4), 369–411. doi:10.1017/S1474747214000377

Jarvenpaa, S. L., & Ives, B. (1991). Executive involvement and participation in the management of information technology. *Management Information Systems Quarterly, 15*(2), 205–227. doi:10.2307/249382

Jiang, Y., Yu, M., & Mohsin, S. (2017). The financial crisis and co-movement of global stock markets-a case of six major economics. *Sustainability, 9*(2), 1–19. doi:10.3390u9020260

Jordà, O., Schularick, M., & Taylor, A. M. (2015a). Leveraged bubbles. *Journal of Monetary Economics, 76*(S), 1-20.

Jordan, E. (1994). Information strategy and organization structure. *Information Systems Journal, 4*(4), 253–270. doi:10.1111/j.1365-2575.1994.tb00055.x

Judge, K. (2017). Information gaps and shadow banking. *Virginia Law Review, 103*(3), 411–480.

Jump$tart Coalition. (2007). National Standards in K-12 Personal Finance Education. *Jumpstart Coalition*. Retrieved from https://www.jumpstart.org/what-we-do/support-financial-education/standards/

Kahl, M. (2002). Economic Distress, Financial Distress, and Dynamic Liquidation. *The Journal of Finance, 57*(1), 135–168. doi:10.1111/1540-6261.00418

Kahneman, D., & Tversky, A. (1979). Prospect Theory: An Analysis of Decision Under Risk. *Econometrica, 47*(2), 263–291. doi:10.2307/1914185

Kanchana, V., & Sri Ranjini, S. (2018). Investigation and Study of Vital Factors in Selection, Implementation and Satisfaction of ERP in Small and Medium Scale Industries. *Iranian Journal of Electrical and Computer Engineering, 81*(2), 1150–1155. doi:10.11591/ijece.v8i2.pp1150-1155

Kaousar Nassr, I., & Wehinger, G. (2016). Opportunities and limitations of public equity markets for SMEs. *OECD Journal: Financial Market Trends, 2015*(1). doi:10.1787/fmt-2015-5jrs051fvnjk

Kenourgios, D., & Padhi, P. (2012). Emerging markets and financial crises: Regional, global or isolated shocks? *Journal of Multinational Financial Management, 22*(1-2), 24–38. doi:10.1016/j.mulfin.2012.01.002

Kessler, O., & Wilhelm, B. (2013). Financialization and the Three Utopias of Shadow Banking. *Competition & Change, 17*(3), 248–264. doi:10.1179/1024529413Z.00000000036

Keynes, J. M. (2011). *A Treatise on Money*. Martino Fine Books. (Original work published 1930)

Kim, S., Sarin, A., & Virdi, D. (2018). *Crypto-Assets Unencrypted*. Retrieved from SSRN: https://ssrn.com/abstract=3117859

Kim, D., Ow, T., & Jun, M. (2008). SME strategies. An assessment of high vs. low performers. *Communications of the ACM*, *51*(11), 113–117. doi:10.1145/1400214.1400237

King, M., & Wadhawani, S. (1990). Transmission of volatility between Stock Markets. *Review of Financial Studies*, *3*(1), 5–33. doi:10.1093/rfs/3.1.5

King, R. G., & Levine, R. (1993). Finance and growth: Schumpeter might be right. *The Quarterly Journal of Economics*, *108*(3), 717–737. doi:10.2307/2118406

Klapper, L., & Panos, G. (2011). *Financial Literacy and Retirement Planning: The Russian Case*. University of Essex CER Working Paper No. 3. Retrieved from SSRN: https://ssrn.com/abstract=1984059

Klapper, L., El-Zoghbi, M., & Hess, J. (2016). *Achieving the Sustainable Development Goals – The Role of Financial Inclusion*. CGAP Working Paper.

Klapper, L., Lusardi, A., & Panos, G. (2011). *Financial Literacy and the Financial Crisis: Evidence from Russia*. SSRN Working Paper. Retrieved from https://ssrn.com/abstract=1786826

Klapper, L., Lusardi, A., & van Oudheusden, P. (2015). *Financial Literacy around the World. Insights from the Standard & Poors Ratings Services Global Financial Literacy Survey*. Retrieved from https://responsiblefinanceforum.org/wp-content/uploads/2015/12/2015-Finlit_paper_17_F3_SINGLES.pdf

Klapper, L., Lusardi, A., & Panos, G. (2013). Financial Literacy and its Consequences: Evidence from Russia during the Financial Crisis. *Journal of Banking & Finance*, *37*(10), 3904–3923. doi:10.1016/j.jbankfin.2013.07.014

Klausner, A. (2005). Biotech venture capital—It's not too late to be early. *Nature Biotechnology*, *23*(4), 417–418. doi:10.1038/nbt0405-417 PubMed

Klein, N. (2014). *Small and medium size enterprises, credit supply shocks and economic recovery in Europe*. Working Paper no 14/98. International Monetary Fund.

Knapp, G. F. (1973). *The State Theory of Money*. Clifton, NY: Augustus M. Kelley. (Original work published 1924)

Knight, F. H. (1921). *Risk, uncertainty and profit*. Boston: Houghton Mifflin.

Knoll, M. A. Z., & Houts, C. R. (2012). The Financial Knowledge Scale: An Application of Item Response Theory to the Assessment of Financial Literacy. *The Journal of Consumer Affairs*, *46*(3), 381–410. doi:10.1111/j.1745-6606.2012.01241.x

Konstantinidis, I., Siaminos, G., Timplalexis, C., Zervas, P., Peristeras, V., & Decker, S. (2018). *Blockchain for Business Applications: A Systematic Literature Review*. BIS.

Kortum, S., & Lerner, J. (2000). Assessing the contribution of venture capital to innovation. *The Rand Journal of Economics*, *31*(4), 674–692. doi:10.2307/2696354

Compilation of References

Kudyba, S., & Diwan, R. (2002). Research report: Increasing returns to information technology. *Information Systems Research*, *13*(1), 104–111. doi:10.1287/isre.13.1.104.98

Kunreuther, H., Pauly, M. V., & McMorrow, S. (2013). *Insurance and Behavioral Economics: Improving Decisions in the Most Misunderstood Industry*. Cambridge University Press.

Lado, A., & Wilson, M. (1994). Human resource system and sustained competitive advantage: Competency-based perspective. *Academy of Management Review*, *19*(4), 699–727. doi:10.5465/amr.1994.9412190216

Laeven, L., & Valencia, F. (2013). The real effects of financial sector interventions during crises. *Journal of Money, Credit and Banking*, *45*(1), 147–177. doi:10.1111/j.1538-4616.2012.00565.x

Lajili, K., & Zéghal, D. (2011). Corporate governance and bankruptcy filing decisions. *Journal of General Management*, *35*(4), 3–26. doi:10.1177/030630701003500401

Langfield, S., & Pagano, M. (2016). Bank bias in Europe: Effects on systemic risk and growth. *Economic Policy*, *31*(85), 51–106. doi:10.1093/epolic/eiv019

Lasch, F., Le Roy, F., & Yami, S. (2007). Critical growth factors of ICT start-ups. *Management Decision*, *45*(1), 62–75. doi:10.1108/00251740710718962

Lee, B., Barua, A., & Whinston, A. (1997). Discovery and representation of causal relationships: A methodological framework. *Management Information Systems Quarterly*, *12*(1), 109–136. doi:10.2307/249744

Lehner, J. M. (2000). Shifts of Reference Points for Framing of Strategic Decisions and Changing Risk-Return Associations. *Management Science*, *46*(1), 63–76. doi:10.1287/mnsc.46.1.63.15130

Lehr, W., & Lichtenberg, F. (1998). Computer use and productivity growth in US Federal Government agencies. *The Journal of Industrial Economics*, *XLVI*(2), 257–279. doi:10.1111/1467-6451.00071

Leifer, R. (1988). Matching computer – based information systems with organizational structures. *Management Information Systems Quarterly*, *12*(1), 63–73. doi:10.2307/248805

Lennox, C. (2000). Do companies successfully engage in opinion - shopping? Evidence from the UK. *Journal of Accounting and Economics*, *29*(3), 321–337. doi:10.1016/S0165-4101(00)00025-2

Levine, R. (1997). Financial development and economic growth: Views and agenda. *Journal of Economic Literature*, *35*(2), 688–726.

Ley 2/2011: Ley 2/201 de 4 de marzo, de Economía sostenible. *Published in the Boletín Oficial del Estado, No.*, *55*, 5.

Ley 26/1988: Ley 26/1988 de 29 de julio, sobre Disciplina e Intervención de las entidades de crédito, published in the Boletín Oficial del Estado, No. 182, 30 July 1988, 23524-23534.

Ley 5/2019: Ley 5/2019, de 15 de marzo, reguladora de los contratos de crédito inmobiliario. *Published in the Boletín Oficial del Estado*, *16*(65), 26319–26399.

Li, F. (1995). *The Geography of Business Information*. Chichester, UK: John Wiley and Sons.

Lin, H., & Paravisini, D. (2012). The effect of financial constraints on risk. *Review of Finance*, *17*(1), 229–259. doi:10.1093/rof/rfr038

Livdan, D., Sapriza, H., & Zhang, L. (2009). Financially constrained stock returns. *The Journal of Finance*, *64*(4), 1827–1862. doi:10.1111/j.1540-6261.2009.01481.x

Lo Petre, A. (2013). Economic literacy, inequality, and financial development. *Economics Letters*, *118*(1), 74–76. doi:10.1016/j.econlet.2012.09.029

Lockett, A., Siegel, D., Wright, M., & Ensley, M. D. (2005). The creation of spin-off firms at public research institutions: Managerial and policy implications. *Research Policy*, *34*(7), 981–993. doi:10.1016/j.respol.2005.05.010

Loerwald, D., & Stemmann, A. (2016). Behavioral Finance and Financial Literacy: Educational Implications of Biases in Financial Decision Making. In International Handbook of Financial Literacy. Springer Verlag. doi:10.1007/978-981-10-0360-8_3

London Stock Exchange. (2015). *A guide to AIM*. Retrieved from https://www.londonstockexchange.com/companies-and-advisors/aim/for-companies/companies.htm

Longstaff, F. (2010). The subprime credit crisis and contagion in financial markets. *Journal of Financial Economics*, *97*(3), 436–450. doi:10.1016/j.jfineco.2010.01.002

Longstaff, F., & Schwartz, E. (1995). A simple approach to valuing risky fixed and floating rate debt. *The Journal of Finance*, *50*(3), 789–819. doi:10.1111/j.1540-6261.1995.tb04037.x

Loveman, G. W. (1994). An assessment of the productivity impact on information technologies. In T. J. Allen & M. S. Morton (Eds.), *Information Technology and the Corporation of the 1990s*. Cambridge, MA: Information Technology Press.

Lucas, D. J., Goodman, L. S., & Fabozzi, F. J. (2007). Collateralized Debt Obligations and Credit Risk Transfer. Yale ICF Working Paper No. 0706. Retrieved from SSRN http://depot.som.yale.edu/icf/papers/fileuploads/2503/original/07-06.pdf

Luchtenberg, K., & Viet, Q. (2015). The 2008 financial crisis: Stock market contagion and its determinants. *Research in International Business and Finance*, *33*, 178–203. doi:10.1016/j.ribaf.2014.09.007

Luck, S., & Schempp, P. (2015). Banks, Shadow Banking, and Fragility. ECB Working Paper No. 1726. Retrieved from https://ssrn.com/abstract=2479948

Lusardi, A. (2011). *Americans' Financial Capability*. National Bureau of Economic Research Working Paper, 17103.

Lusardi, A., & de Bassa Scheresberg, C. (2013). *Financial Literacy and High-Cost Borrowing in the United States*. Global Financial Literacy Excellence Center (GFLEC) Research Paper. Retrieved from http://www.usfinancialcapability.org/downloads/HighCostBorrowing.pdf?utm_source=

Compilation of References

Lusardi, A., & Tufano, P. (2009). *Debt Literacy, Financial Experiences, and Overindebtedness.* National Bureau of Economic Research Working Paper, No.14808. Retrieved from http://www.nber.org/papers/w14808

Lusardi, A. (2008). *Financial Literacy: An Essential Tool for Informed Consumer Choice?* Cambridge, MA: National Bureau of Economic Research. doi:10.3386/w14084

Lusardi, A. (2019). Financial literacy and the need for financial education: Evidence and implications. *Schweizerische Zeitschrift für Volkswirtschaft und Statistik, 155*(1).

Lusardi, A., Michaud, P. C., & Mitchell, O. S. (2017). Optimal Financial Knowledge and Wealth Inequality. *Journal of Political Economy, 125*(2), 431–477. doi:10.1086/690950 PMID:28555088

Lusardi, A., & Mitchell, O. (2007a). Baby boomers retirement security: The role of planning, financial literacy and housing wealth. *Journal of Monetary Economics, 54*(1), 205–224. doi:10.1016/j.jmoneco.2006.12.001

Lusardi, A., & Mitchell, O. (2007b). Financial literacy and retirement preparedness: Evidence and implications for financial education. *Business Economics (Cleveland, Ohio), 42*(1), 35–44. doi:10.2145/20070104

Lusardi, A., & Mitchell, O. (2011). Financial literacy around the world: An overview. *Journal of Pension Economics and Finance, 10*(4), 497–508. doi:10.1017/S1474747211000448 PMID:28553190

Lusardi, A., & Mitchell, O. (2014). The Economic Importance of Financial Literacy: Theory and Evidence. *Journal of Economic Literature, 52*(1), 5–44. doi:10.1257/jel.52.1.5 PMID:28579637

Lusardi, A., & Mitchell, O. S. (2011). *Financial Literacy Around the World: An Overview.* Cambridge, MA: National Bureau of Economic Research.

Lusardi, A., & Tufano, P. (2015). Debt Literacy, Financial Experiences, and Overindebtedness. *Journal of Pension Economics and Finance, 14*(4), 332–368. doi:10.1017/S1474747215000232

Lu, Y. (2017). Industry 4.0: A survey on technologies, applications and open research issues. *Journal of Industrial Information Integration, 6*, 1–10. doi:10.1016/j.jii.2017.04.005

Lu, Y., Guo, H., Kao, E. H., & Fung, H. G. (2015). Shadow banking and firm financing in China. *International Review of Economics & Finance, 36*, 40–53. doi:10.1016/j.iref.2014.11.006

Lycette, M., & White, K. (1989). Improving Women's Access to Credit in Latin America and the Caribbean: Policy and Project Recommendations. In Women's Ventures (pp. 19-44). West Harford: Kumarian Press.

Lysandrou, Ph., & Nesvetailova, A. (2015). The role of shadow banking entities in the financial crisis: A disaggregated view. *Review of International Political Economy, 22*(2), 257–279. doi:10.1080/09692290.2014.896269

Mahoney, J. T., & Pandian, J. R. (1992). The Resource-based View within the Conversation of Strategic Management. *Strategic Management Journal, 13*(5), 363–380. doi:10.1002mj.4250130505

Mandelbrot, B., & Hudson, R. (2004). *The (mis)behavior of markets. A fractal view of risk, ruin & reward*. New York: Basic Books.

Mandell, L., & Klein, L. (2007). Motivation and Financial Literacy. *Financial Services Review, 16*, 105–116.

Manton, E. J., English, D. E., Avard, S., & Walker, J. (2006). What college freshmen admit to not knowing about personal ðnance. *Journal of College Teaching and Learning, 3*(1), 43–54. doi:10.19030/tlc.v3i1.1758

Mao, E., & Palvia, P. (2008). Exploring the effects of direct experience on IT use: An organizational field study. *Information & Management, 45*(4), 249–256. doi:10.1016/j.im.2008.02.007

Marulanda Consultores. (2013). *Propuestas de Reforma al Sistema de Financiamiento Agropecuario*. USAID - Programa de Políticas Públicas.

Mason, C., & Wilson, R. (2000). *Conceptualizing Financial Literacy. Loughborough University Business School* Research Series Paper.

Mata, F., Fuerst, W., & Barney, J. (1995). Information technology and sustained competitive advantage: A resource-based analysis. *Management Information Systems Quarterly, 19*(4), 487–505. doi:10.2307/249630

Maudos, J. (2012). El impacto de la crisis en el sector bancario español. *Cuadernos de Información Económica, 226*, 155–163.

Mbuyisa, B., & Leonard, A. (2017). The Role of ICT Use in SMEs Towards Poverty Reduction: A Systematic Literature Review. *Journal of International Development, 29*(2), 159–197. doi:10.1002/jid.3258

Melville, N., Kraemer, K., & Gurbaxani, V. (2004). Information Technology and Organizational Performance: An Integrative Model of IT Business Value. *Management Information Systems Quarterly, 28*(2), 283–322. doi:10.2307/25148636

Méndez, M. (2004). *Cultura Tributaria, Deberes y Derechos*. Espacio Abierto.

Mendoza Shaw, F. A., Palomino Cano, R., Robles Encinas, J. E., & Ramírez Guardado, S. R. (2016). Correlación entre cultura tributaria y educación tributaria universitaria: Caso Universidad Estatal de Sonora. *Revista Global de Economía, 4*(1), 61–76.

Mensi, Q., Hammoudeh, S., Nguyen, D., & Hoon, S. (2016). Global financial crises and spillover effects among the U.S. and BRIC stock markets. *International Review of Economics & Finance, 42*, 257–276. doi:10.1016/j.iref.2015.11.005

Compilation of References

Mercieca, S., Schaeck, K., & Wolfe, S. (2009). Bank Market Structure, Competition, and SME Financing Relationships in European Regions. *Journal of Financial Services Research*, *36*(2-3), 137–155. doi:10.100710693-009-0060-0

Merediz-Solá, I., & Barriviera, A. F. (2019). A bibliometric analysis of Bitcoin scientific production. *Research in International Business and Finance*, *50*, 294–305. doi:10.1016/j.ribaf.2019.06.008

Merton, R. (1974). On the pricing of corporate debt. The risk structure of interest rates. *The Journal of Finance*, *29*, 449–470.

Merton, R. C., Billio, M., Getmansky, M., Gray, D., Lo, A. W., & Pelizzon, L. (2013). On a new approach for analyzing and managing macrofinancial risks. *Financial Analysts Journal*, *69*(2), 22–33. doi:10.2469/faj.v69.n2.5

Metiu, N. (2012). Sovereign risk contagion in the Eurozone. *Economics Letters*, *117*(1), 35–38. doi:10.1016/j.econlet.2012.04.074

Metrick, A., & Yasuda, A. (2010). *Venture Capital and the Finance of Innovation* (2nd ed.). John Wiley and Sons, Inc.

Michaud, P. C. (2017). The value of financial literacy and financial education for workers. *IZA World of Labor*, *2017*, 400.

Milgrom, P., & Roberts, J. (1995). Complementarities and Fit Strategy, structure, and organizational change in manufacturing. *Journal of Accounting and Economics*, *19*(2-3), 179–208. doi:10.1016/0165-4101(94)00382-F

Mingfang, L., & Ye, R. (1999). Information technology and firm performance: Linking with environmental, strategic and managerial contexts. *Information & Management*, *35*(1), 43–51. doi:10.1016/S0378-7206(98)00075-5

Mink, M., & de Haan, J. (2013). Contagion during the Greek sovereign debt crisis. *Journal of International Money and Finance*, *34*, 102–113. doi:10.1016/j.jimonfin.2012.11.006

Minsky, H. P. (2008). *Stabilizing an unstable economy*. Mc Graw Hill.

Minzer, R. (2011). *Las instituciones microfinancieras en América Latina: factores que explican su desempeño*. CEPAL, Serie Estudios y Perspectivas, 128. Retrieved from https://repositorio.cepal.org/bitstream/handle/11362/4910/1/S2011012_es.pdf

Modigliani, F., & Miller, M. (1958). The cost of capital, corporation finance, and the theory of investment. *The American Economic Review*, *48*(3), 261–297.

Modigliani, F., & Miller, M. (1963). Corporate Income Taxes and the Cost of Capital: A correction. *The American Economic Review*, *53*(3), 433–443.

Mody, A., & Sandri, D. (2012). The Eurozone crisis: How banks and sovereigns came to be joined at the hip. *Economic Policy*, *27*(70), 199–230. doi:10.1111/j.1468-0327.2012.00281.x

Mollah, S., Zafifov, G., & Shahiduzzama, A. (2014). *Financial market contagion during the Global Financial Crisis.* Working Paper, no 2014/5. Center for Innovation and Technology Research.

Mollick, E. (2014). The dynamics of crowdfunding: An exploratory study. *Journal of Business Venturing, 29*(1), 1–16. doi:10.1016/j.jbusvent.2013.06.005

Montañez Núñez, M., Rubio González, A., Ruesta Baselga, M., & Ulloa Ariza, C. (2015). La financiación de las pymes españolas. *ICE, 885,* 133–149.

Monticone, C. (2010). How much does wealth matter in the acquisition of financial literacy? *The Journal of Consumer Affairs, 44*(2), 403–422. doi:10.1111/j.1745-6606.2010.01175.x

Moore, D. (2003). *Survey of Financial Literacy in Washington State: Knowledge, Behavior, Attitudes and Experiences.* Washington State University Social and Economic Sciences Research Center, Technical Report 03–39.

Moore, D. (2003). *Survey of Financial Literacy in Washington State: Knowledge, Behavior, Attitudes, and Experiences.* Washington State University Social and Economic Sciences Research Center Technical Report 03-39.

Morales, L., & Afreosso-O'Callaghan, B. (2014). The global financial crisis: World market or regional contagion effects? *International Review of Economics & Finance, 29,* 108–131. doi:10.1016/j.iref.2013.05.010

Morrison, C. J., & Berndt, E. R. (1990). *Assessing the productivity of information technology equipment in the US manufacturing industries.* National Bureau of Economic Research Working Paper No. 3.582.

Mottola, G. (2013). In Our Best Interest: Women, Financial Literacy, and Credit Card Behavior. Numeracy Advancing Education in Quantitative Literacy, 6(2), Article 4.

Mottola, G. R. (2013). In Our Best Interest: Women, Financial Literacy, and Credit Card Behavior. *Numeracy, 6*(2). Available at: http://scholarcommons.usf.edu/numeracy/vol6/iss2/art4

Mouna, A., & Anis, J. (2017). Financial literacy in Tunisia: Its determinants and its implications on investment behavior. *Research in International Business and Finance, 39,* 568–577. doi:10.1016/j.ribaf.2016.09.018

Muhanna, W., & Stoel, M. (2010). How Do Investors Value IT? An Empirical Investigation of the Value Relevance of IT Capability and IT Spending Across Industries. *Journal of Information Systems, 24*(1), 43–66. doi:10.2308/jis.2010.24.1.43

Mukhopadhyay, T., Kekre, S., & Kalathur, S. (1995). Business Value of Information Technology: A Study of Electronic Data Interchange. *Management Information Systems Quarterly, 19*(2), 137–156. doi:10.2307/249685

Muller, P., Mattes, A., Klitou, D., Lonkeu, O-K., Ramada, P., Aranda Ruiz, F., … Steigertahl, L. (2018). *Annual report on European SMEs 2017/2018.* European Commission.

Compilation of References

Müller, J. M., Buliga, O., & Voigt, K. (2018). Fortune favors the prepared: How SMEs approach business model innovations in industry 4.0. *Technological Forecasting and Social Change*, *132*, 2–17. doi:10.1016/j.techfore.2017.12.019

Muller, S., & Weber, M. (2010). Financial Literacy and Mutual Fund Investments: Who Buys Actively Managed Funds? *Schmalenbach Business Review*, *62*(2), 126–153. doi:10.1007/BF03396802

Muratori, U. (2014). Contagion in the Euro Area Sovereign Bond Market. *Social Sciences*, *4*(1), 66–82. doi:10.3390ocsci4010066

Nakamoto, S. (2008). *Bitcoin: A peer-to-peer electronic cash system*. Retrieved from https://Bitcoin.org/Bitcoin.pdf

National Financial Capability Study. (2019). *The State of U.S. Financial Capability: the 2018 National Financial Capability Study (NFCS)*. Retrieved from http://www.usfinancialcapability.org/downloads/NFCS_2018_Report_Natl_Findings.pdf

National Foundation for Credit Counseling. (2019*). NFCC 2019 Consumer Financial Literacy Survey*. Retrieved from https://www.nfcc.org/2019-consumer-financial-literacy-survey/

Neirotti, P., & Paolucci, E. (2012). Assessing the importance of industry in the adoption and assimilation of IT: Evidence from Italian enterprises. *Information & Management*, *48*(7), 249–259. doi:10.1016/j.im.2011.06.004

Nersisyan, Y., & Wray, L. R. (2010). The Global Financial Crisis and the Shift to Shadow Banking. Levy Economics Institute Working Paper No. 587. Retrieved from https://ssrn.com/abstract=1559383 or doi:10.2139srn.1559383

Nevo, S., & Wade, M. (2010). The formation and value of IT-enabled resources: Antecedents and consequences of synergistic relationships. *Management Information Systems Quarterly*, *34*(1), 163–183. doi:10.2307/20721419

Newman, K. L. (2000). Organizational transformation during institutional upheaval. *Academy of Management Review*, *25*(3), 602–619. doi:10.5465/amr.2000.3363525

Nicolini, G. (2019). *Financial Literacy in Europe*. New York: Routledge. doi:10.4324/9780429431968

Nonaka, I., & Takeuchi, H. (1995). *The Knowledge-Creating Company*. Oxford, UK: Oxford University Press.

Noyelle, T. (1990). *Skills, wages and productivity in the service sector*. Boulder, CO: Westview Press.

Nye, P., & Hillyard, C. (2013). Personal Financial Behavior: The Influence of Quantitative Literacy and Material Values. *Numeracy Advancing Education in Quantitative Literacy*, *6*(1), article 3.

O'Shea, R. P., Chugh, H., & Allen, T. J. (2008). Determinants and consequences of university spinoff activity: A conceptual framework. *International Journal of Technology Transfer, 33*(6), 653–666. doi:10.1007/s10961-007-9060-0

O'Donnell, N., & Keeney, M. (2009). *Financial Capability: New Evidence for Ireland.* Central Bank of Ireland Research Technical Paper, 1/RT/09.

OECD INFE. (2011). *Measuring Financial Literacy: Core Questionnaire in Measuring Financial Literacy: Questionnaire and Guidance Notes for conducting an Internationally Comparable Survey of Financial literacy.* Paris: OECD.

OECD. (2003). *A Proposed Classification of ICT Goods.* Paris: OECD Working Party on Indicators for the Information Society.

OECD. (2005). *Improving Financial Literacy: Analysis of Issues and Policies.* Paris: OECD Publishing.

OECD. (2017). *G20/OECD INFE report on adult financial literacy in G20 countries.* Paris: OECD.

Olson, E. (2006). Not by Technology Alone: Sustaining Winning Strategies. *The Journal of Business Strategy, 27*(84), 33–42. doi:10.1108/02756660610701003

Orden de 5 de mayo de 1994: Orden de 5 de mayo de 1994, sobre transparencia de las condiciones financieras de los préstamos hipotecarios. Published in the Boletín Oficial del Estado (BOE), No. 112, 11 May 1994.

Orden del 12 de diciembre de 1989: Orden del 12 de diciembre de 1989, sobre información de tipos de interés y comisiones, normas de actuación, información a clientes y publicidad de las entidades de crédito. Published in the Boletín Oficial del Esado (BOE), No. 303, 19 December 1989.

Orden EHA/2899/2011: Orden EHA/2899/2011, de 28 de octubre, de transparencia y protección del cliente de servicios bancarios. Published in the Boletín Oficial del Estado (BOE), No. 261, 29 October 2011.

Ordóñez, G. (2018). Sustainable Shadow Banking. American Economic Journal. Macroeconomics, 10(1), 33–56. doi:10.1257/mac.20150346

Organization for Economic Cooperation and Development. (2009). *Framework for the Development of Financial Literacy Baseline Surveys: A First International Comparative Analysis.* OECD Working Papers on Finance, Insurance and Private Pensions, No. 1. OECD Publishing.

Organization for Economic Cooperation and Development. (2017). *G20/OECD INFE report on adult financial literacy in G20 countries.* Retrieved from https://www.oecd.org/daf/fin/financial-education/G20-OECD-INFE-report-adult-financial-literacy-in-G20-countries.pdf

Organization for Economic Cooperation and Development. (2018). *The Programme for International Student Assessment (PISA) 2015 Results in Focus.* Retrieved from http://www.oecd.org/pisa/pisa-2015-results-in-focus.pdf

Compilation of References

Ortín, P., & Vendrell, F. (2010). University spin-off vs. other NTBFs: Productivity Differences at the Outset and Evolution. Searle Center Working Paper.

Ortín, P., Salas, V., Trujillo, M. V., & Vendrell, F. (2007). *El spin-off universitario en España como modelo de creación de empresas intensivas en tecnología, Estudio DGPYME, Ministerio de Industria Turismo y comercio*. Secretaría General de Industria, Dirección General de Política de la Pyme.

Ortín, P., Salas, V., Trujillo, M. V., & Vendrell, F. (2008). La creación de spin-off universitarios en España. Características, determinantes y resultados. *Economía Industrial, 368*, 79–95.

Osterman, P. (1991). Impact of IT on Jobs and Skills. In M. S. Scott Morton (Ed.), *The Corporation of the 1990's. Information Technology and Organizational Transformation* (pp. 221–243). Oxford, UK: Oxford University Press.

Otim, S., Dow, K., Grover, V., & Wong, J. (2012). The Impact of Information Technology Investments on Downside Risk of the Firm: Alternative Measurement of the Business Value of IT. *Journal of Management Information Systems, 29*(1), 159–193. doi:10.2753/MIS0742-1222290105

Paltalidis, N., Gounopoulos, D., Kizys, R., & Koutelidakis, Y. (2015). Transmission of systematic risk and contagion in Europe. *Journal of Banking & Finance, 61*, 536–552. doi:10.1016/j.jbankfin.2015.03.021

Parramón Jimenez, E. (2014). Claves para entender la banca en la sombra: Shadow Banking. *Análisis Financiero, 125*, 67–76.

Pellegrina, L. D., Frazzoni, S., Rotondi, Z., & Vezulli, A. (2017). Does ICT adoption improve access to credit for small enterprises? *Small Business Economics, 48*(3), 657–679. doi:10.1007/s11187-016-9794-x

Peña Cuenca, I. (2015). Situación y futuro de la renta fija y la financiación alternativa en España y Europa. *Anuario sobre renta fija y financiación alternativa IEB-Axesor*, 20-58. Retrieved from: https://www.axesor.es/docs/default-source/estudios/anuario_axesor_ieb_2018.pdf

Penrose, E. T. (1959). *The theory of the growth of the firm*. Oxford, UK: Basil Blackwell.

Pentecost, E. J., Du, W., Bird, G., & Willett, T. (2019). Contagion from the crises in the Eurozone: Where, when and why? *European Journal of Finance, 25*(14), 1309–1327. doi:10.1080/1351847X.2019.1589552

Pereira, M. J. (2003). Impacts of information systems and technology on productivity and competitiveness of the Portuguese banking sector: An empirical study. *International Transactions in Operational Research, 11*(1), 43–62. doi:10.1111/j.1475-3995.2004.00439.x

Pericoli, M., & Sbracia, M. (2003). A Primer on Financial Contagion. *Journal of Economic Surveys, 17*(4), 571–608. doi:10.1111/1467-6419.00205

Perry, V., & Morris, M. (2005). Who is in Control? The Role of Self-Perception, Knowledge, and Income in Explaining Consumer Financial Behavior. *The Journal of Consumer Affairs*, *39*(2), 299–313. doi:10.1111/j.1745-6606.2005.00016.x

Peteraf, M. (1993). The Cornerstones of Competitive Advantage: A Resource-based View. *Strategic Management Journal*, *14*(3), 179–191. doi:10.1002mj.4250140303

Peters, E. (1991). *Chaos and order in capital markets. A new view of cycles, prices, and market volatility*. New York: Wiley.

Phan, D. D. (2003). E-business development for competitive advantages: A case study. *Information & Management*, *40*(6), 581–590. doi:10.1016/S0378-7206(02)00089-7

Philippas, D., & Siriopoulos, C. (2013). Putting the 'C' Into Crisis: Contagion, Correlations and Copulas on EMU Bond Markets. *Journal of International Financial Markets, Institutions and Money*, *27*, 161–176. doi:10.1016/j.intfin.2013.09.008

Piñeiro, C., de Llano, P., & Rodríguez, M. (2012). Evaluation of the likelihood of financial failure. Empirical contrast of the informational content of the audit of accounts. *Spanish Journal of Finance and Accounting*, *XLI*(156), 565–588.

Pirnay, F., Surlemont, B., & Nlemvo, F. (2003). Toward a typology of spin-offs. *Small Business Economics*, *21*(4), 355–369. doi:10.1023/A:1026167105153

Plantin, G. (2015). Shadow Banking and Bank Capital Regulation. *Review of Financial Studies*, *28*(1), 146–175. doi:10.1093/rfs/hhu055

Poon, S., & Swatman, P. (1995). The Internet for Small Business: an enabling infrastructure for competitiveness. INET'95 Proceedings.

Porter, M. (1999). Creating advantage. *Executive Excellence*, *6*(1), 13–14.

Poterba, J. M., & Summers, L. H. (1988). Mean reversion in stock prices: Evidence and implications. *Journal of Financial Economics*, *22*(1), 27–59. doi:10.1016/0304-405X(88)90021-9

Pozsar, Z. (2014). Shadow Banking: The Money View. Office of Financial Research Working Paper. Retrieved from https://ssrn.com/abstract=2476415

Pozsar, Z., Adrian, T., Ashcraft, A., & Boesky, H. (2010). *Shadow banking, Staff Report, No. 458*. New York, NY: Federal Reserve Bank of New York.

Pragidis, I. C., Aielli, G. P., Chionis, D., & Schizas, P. (2015). Contagion effects during financial crisis: Evidence from the Greek sovereign bonds market. *Journal of Financial Stability*, *18*, 127–138. doi:10.1016/j.jfs.2015.04.001

Prahalad, C. K., & Hamel, G. (1990). The core competence of the corporation. *Harvard Business Review*, *68*(3), 79–91.

Prasad, A., Green, P., & Heales, J. (2013). On Governing Collaborative Information Technology (IT). A Relational Perspective. *Journal of Information Systems*, *27*(1), 237–259. doi:10.2308/isys-50326

Prusty, S. (2011). Household Saving Behaviour: Role of Financial Literacy and Saving Plans. *Journal of World Economic Review*, *6*(1), 75–86.

Qosasi, A., Permana, E., Muftiadi, A., Purnomo, M., & Maulina, E. (2019). Building SMEs' Competitive Advantage and the Organizational Agility of Apparel Retailers in Indonesia: The role of ICT as an Initial Trigger, Gadjah Mada International. *The Journal of Business*, *21*(1), 69–90.

Quan, J., Hu, Q., & Hart, P. J. (2003). Information Technology Investments and Firms' Performance: A Duopoly Perspective. *Journal of Management Information Systems*, *20*(3), 121–158. doi:10.1080/07421222.2003.11045773

Quinn, S., & Roberds, W. (2015). Responding to a Shadow Banking Crisis: The Lessons of 1763. *Journal of Money, Credit and Banking*, *47*(6), 1149–1176. doi:10.1111/jmcb.12240

Raccanello, K., & Herrera Guzmán, E. (2014). Educación e inclusión financiera. *Revista Latinoamericana de Estudios Educativos*, *44*(2), 119–141.

Rai, A., Patnayakuni, R., & Patnayakuni, N. (1997). Technology investment and business performance. *Communications of the ACM*, *40*(7), 89–97. doi:10.1145/256175.256191

Ravinchandran, T., & Lertwongsatien, C. (2005). Effect of Information Systems Resources and Capabilities on Firm Performance: A Resource-Based Perspective. *Journal of Management Information Systems*, *21*(4), 237–276. doi:10.1080/07421222.2005.11045820

Real Decreto 309/2019: Real Decreto 309/2019, de 26 de abril, por el que se desarrolla parcialmente la Ley 5/2019, de 15 de marzo, reguladora de los contratos de crédito inmobiliario y se adoptan otras medidas en materia financiera. *Published in the Boletín Oficial del Estado*, *29*(102), 43114–43128.

Red OTRI. (2011). Informe Red OTRI de Universidades, 2011. Madrid: Conferencia de Rectores de las Universidades Españolas, CRUE.

Regulation of the Mercado Alternativo de Renta Fija. (2018). Retrieved from: http://www.bmerf.es/docs/esp/Documentos/REGLAMENTO_ES_MARF.pdf

Reinhart, C. M., & Rogoff, K. S. (2009). The aftermath of financial crises. *The American Economic Review*, *99*(2), 466–472. doi:10.1257/aer.99.2.466

Revest, V., & Sapio, A. (2013). Does the alternative investment market nurture firm growth? A comparison between listed and private companie. *Industrial and Corporate Change*, *22*(4), 953–979. doi:10.1093/icc/dtt021

Rhine, S. L. W., & Robbins, E. (2012). *FDCI survey of banks' efforts to serve the unbanked and underbanked*. Washington, DC: Federal Deposit Insurance Corporation. Retrieved from https://www.fdic.gov/unbankedsurveys/2011survey/2011execsummary.pdf

Ricks, M. (2010). Shadow Banking and Financial Regulation. Columbia Law and Economics Working Paper No. 370. Retrieved from https://ssrn.com/abstract=1571290

Riegelmen, R. K. (2005). *Studying a Study and Testing a Test: How to Read the Medical Evidence*. Philadelphia: Lippincott Williams & Wilkins.

Roach, S. S. (1991). Services under siege – The restructuring imperative. *Harvard Business Review*, *69*(5), 82–91. PMID:10113914

Robb, C.A., & Russell, N. J. (2008). Personal Financial Knowledge among College Students: Associations between Individual Characteristics and Scores on an Experimental Measure of Financial Knowledge. *Consumer Interests Annual*, 54-144.

Robb, C. A. (2011). Financial knowledge and credit card behavior of college students. *Journal of Family and Economic Issues*, *32*(4), 690–698. doi:10.100710834-011-9259-y

Robb, C. A., & Sharpe, D. L. (2009). Effect of personal financial knowledge on college students' credit card behavior. *Journal of Financial Counseling and Planning*, *20*(1), 25–40.

Robb, C. A., & Woodyard, A. (2011). Financial knowledge and best practice behavior. *Journal of Financial Counseling and Planning*, *22*(1), 60–70.

Rodríguez Fernández, F. (2017). El sector bancario español. Foto de una reestructuración en movimiento. *Mediterráneo Económico*, *29*, 35–47.

Rodríguez-Gulías, M. J., Rodeiro-Pazos, D. & Fernández-López, S. (2015). The regional effect on the innovative performance of University spin-offs: a multilevel approach. Journal of the Knowledge Economy, 1-21.

Rodríguez-Gulías, M. J., Rodeiro-Pazos, D., & Fernández-López, S. (2016). Impact of venture capital on the growth of university spin-offs. In Multiple Helix Ecosystems for Sustainable Competitiveness (pp. 169–183). Springer International Publishing; doi:10.1007/978-3-319-29677-7_11.

Rodríguez-Gulías, M. J., Rodeiro-Pazos, D., & Fernández-López, S. (2017). The growth of university spin-offs: A dynamic panel data approach. *Technology Analysis and Strategic Management*, *29*(10), 1181–1195. doi:10.1080/09537325.2016.1277580

Rodríguez-Gulías, M. J., Rodeiro-Pazos, D., Fernández-López, S., Corsi, C., & Prencipe, A. (2018). The role of venture capitalist to enhance the growth of Spanish and Italian university spin-offs. *The International Entrepreneurship and Management Journal*, *14*(4), 1111–1130. doi:10.1007/s11365-017-0489-9

Roldán, J. Y. (2015). *Las entidades financieras en España. Un sistema en evolución al servicio de la sociedad*. Madrid: Fundación de Estudios Financieros.

Rose, P. S., Andrews, W. T., & Giroux, G. A. (1982). Predicting Business Failure: A Macroeconomic Perspective. *Journal of Accounting, Auditing & Finance*, *6*(1), 20–31.

Compilation of References

Rumelt, R. P. (1991). How much does industry matter? *Strategic Management Journal, 12*(3), 167–185. doi:10.1002mj.4250120302

Saardchom, N. (2012). Expert Judgment Based Scoring Model. *Journal of Business and Economics, 3*(3), 164–175. doi:10.15341/jbe(2155-7950)/03.03.2012/002

Samarakoon, L. (2011). Stock market interdependence, contagion and the US financial crisis: The case of emerging frontier markets. *Journal of International Financial Markets, Institutions and Money, 21*(5), 724–742. doi:10.1016/j.intfin.2011.05.001

Sambamurthy, V., Bharadwaj, A., & Grover, V. (2003). Shaping agility through digital options: Reconceptualizing the role of information technology in contemporary Firms. *Management Information Systems Quarterly, 27*(2), 237–263. doi:10.2307/30036530

Santero Sánchez, R., De la Fuente-Cabrero, C., & Laguna Sánchez, P. (2016). Efectos de la crisis sobre la financiación bancaria del emprendimiento. Un análisis de las microempresas españolas desde el sector de las Sociedades de Garantía Recíproca. *European Research on Management and Business Economics, 22*(2), 88–93. doi:10.1016/j.iedee.2015.10.006

Savelyev, A. (2018). Some risks of tokenization and blockchainizaition of private law. *Computer Law & Security Review, 34*(4), 863–869. doi:10.1016/j.clsr.2018.05.010

Sawyer, S., & Tapia, A. (2005). The sociotechnical nature of mobile computing work: Evidence from a study of policing in the United States. *International Journal of Technology and Human Interaction, 1*(3), 1–14. doi:10.4018/jthi.2005070101

Schereiner, M. (2000). A Scoring Model of the Risk Costly Arreals from Loans from Afiliates Womens World Banks in Colombia. Report to Women's World Banking, Bogotá, Colombia.

Schmeiser, M., & Seligman, J. (2013). Using the Right Yardstick: Assessing Financial Literacy Measures by Way of Financial Well-Being. *The Journal of Consumer Affairs, 47*(2), 191–374. doi:10.1111/joca.12010

Schnitzer, M., & Watzinger, M. (2017). Measuring the spillovers of venture capital. CESifo Working Paper.

Schreiner, M. (2002). *Ventajas y desventajas del scoring estadistico para las microfinanzas.* Retrieved November 2, 2019, from http://www.microfinance.com/Castellano/Documentos/Scoring_Ventajas_Desventajas.pdf

Schreiner, M., Clancy, M., & Sherraden, M. (2002). *Saving Performance in the American Dream Demonstration: A National Demonstration of Individual Retirement Accounts," Final Report.* St. Louis, MO: Center for Social Development, University of Washington.

Schröder, C. (2013). Regional and company-specific factors for high growth dynamics of ICT companies in Germany with particular emphasis on knowledge spillovers. *Papers in Regional Science, 92*(4), 741–772. doi:10.1111/j.1435-5957.2012.00457.x

Schwarz, M., & Takhteyev, Y. (2010). Half a Century of Public Software Institutions: Open Source as a Solution to Hold-Up Problem. *Journal of Public Economic Theory, 12*(4), 609–639. doi:10.1111/j.1467-9779.2010.01467.x

Scott, J. Jr. (1977). Bankruptcy, secured debt, and optimal capital structure. *The Journal of Finance, 32*(1), 1–19. doi:10.1111/j.1540-6261.1977.tb03237.x

SEC. (2017). Report of investigation pursuant to Section 21(a) of the Securities Exchange Act of 1934: The DAO. *Release No., 81207*(July), 25.

Sekita, S. (2011). Financial Literacy and Retirement Planning in Japan. *Journal of Pension Economics and Finance, 10*(4), 637–656. doi:10.1017/S1474747211000527

Shane, S. A. (2004). *Academic Entrepreneurship: University Spinoffs and Wealth Creation.* Edward Elgar Publishing. doi:10.4337/9781843769828

Sharma, M., & Zeller, M. (1997). Repayment performance in group-based credit programs in Bangladesh: An empirical analysis. *World Development, 25*(10), 1731–1742. doi:10.1016/S0305-750X(97)00063-6

Siegel, D., & Griliches, Z. (1991). *Purchased services, outsourcing, computers and productivity in manufacturing.* National Bureau of Economic Research Working Paper No. 3.678.

Skagerlund, K., Lind, T., Strömbäck, C., Tinghög, G., & Västfjäll, D. (2018). Financial literacy and the role of numeracy-How individuals' attitude and affinity with numbers influence financial literacy. *Journal of Behavioral and Experimental Economics, 74*, 18–25. doi:10.1016/j.socec.2018.03.004

Slusarczyk, M., Pozo, J.M., & Perurena, L. (2015). Estudio de aplicación de las TIC en las pymes. 3C Empresa, 4(1), 69-87.

Song, C. (2015). *Financial Illiteracy and Pension Contributions: A Field Experiment on Compound Interest in China.* SSRN Working Paper. Retrieved from https://ssrn.com/abstract=2580856

Sorenson, O., Assenova, V., Li, G. C., Boada, J., & Fleming, L. (2016). Expand innovation finance via crowdfunding. *Science, 35*(6319), 1526–1528. doi:10.1126/science.aaf6989 PubMed

Sosa-Padilla, C. (2018). Sovereign defaults and banking crises. *Journal of Monetary Economics, 99*, 88–105. doi:10.1016/j.jmoneco.2018.07.004

Šoškić, D. (2011, September 15). *Financial literacy and financial stability.* Retrieved from https://www.bis.org/review/r110929e.pdf?ql=1

Souder, W. E., & Jenssen, S. A. (1999). Management practices influencing new product success and failure in the United States and Scandivavia: A cross-cultural comparative study. *Journal of Product Innovation Management, 16*(2), 183–203. doi:10.1111/1540-5885.1620183

Sprague, R. H. (1980). A Framework for the Development of Decision Support Systems. *Management Information Systems Quarterly, 4*(4), 1–26. doi:10.2307/248957

Compilation of References

Stango, V., & Zinman, J. (2007). *Fuzzy math and red ink: When the opportunity cost of consumption is not what it seems*. Working Paper, Dartmouth College.

Stango, V., & Zinman, J. (2009). Exponential Growth Bias and Household Finance. *The Journal of Finance*, *64*(6), 2807–2849. doi:10.1111/j.1540-6261.2009.01518.x

Stanko, M. A., & Henard, D. H. (2017). Toward a better understanding of crowdfunding, openness and the consequences for innovation. *Research Policy*, *46*(4), 784–798. doi:10.1016/j.respol.2017.02.003

Stein, J. (2010). Securitisation, Shadow Banking, and Financial Fragility. *Daedalus*, *139*(4), 41–51. doi:10.1162/DAED_a_00041

Steurs, G. (1994). Spillovers and Cooperation in Research and Development (Doctoral dissertation). KU Leuven.

Stiglitz, J. E. (2012). *The price of inequality*. New York: W.W. Norton & Company.

Stock, T., & Seliger, G. (2016). Opportunities of sustainable manufacturing in industry 4.0. Procedia CIRP, 40, 536–541. doi:10.1016/j.procir.2016.01.129

Stolper, O. A., & Walter, A. (2017). Financial literacy, financial advice, and financial behavior. *Journal of Business Economics*, *87*(5), 581–643. doi:10.100711573-017-0853-9

Strassman, P. A. (1990). *The business value of computers*. Information Economics Press.

Strategic Hub for Innovation and Financial Technology. (2019). *Framework for "Investment Contract" Analysis of Digital Assets*. Retrieved from https://www.sec.gov/corpfin/framework-investment-contract-analysis-digital-assets

Strategy. (2019). *5th ICO/STO Report. A strategic perspective*. Retrieved from https://www.pwc.ch/en/insights/fs/5th-ico-sto-report.html

Straub, D. W., & Watson, R. T. (2001). Research Commentary: Transformational issues in Researching IS and Net-Enabled Organizations. *Information Systems Research*, *12*(4), 337–345. doi:10.1287/isre.12.4.337.9706

Sunderam, A. (2015). Money Creation and the Shadow Banking System. *Review of Financial Studies*, *28*(4), 939–977. doi:10.1093/rfs/hhu083

Tajadura Garrido, C. (2015). El sistema financiero español tras la crisis: Menor en tamaño, más seguro y menos rentable. *Análisis Financiero*, *127*, 1–19.

Tam, K. (1998). The Impact of Information Technology Investments on Firm Performance and Evaluation: Evidence from Newly Industrialized Economies. *Information Systems Research*, *9*(1), 85–98. doi:10.1287/isre.9.1.85

Tan, L. (2019). *Token economics framework*. Retrieved from SSRN: https://ssrn.com/abstract=3381452

Tang, N., Baker, A., & Peter, P. C. (2015). Investigating the disconnect between financial knowledge and behavior: The role of parental influence and psychological characteristics in responsible financial behaviors among young adults. *The Journal of Consumer Affairs*, *49*(2), 376–406. doi:10.1111/joca.12069

Tang, N., & Peter, P. (2015). Financial knowledge acquisition among the young: The role of financial education, financial experience, and parents' financial experience. *Financial Services Review*, *24*(2), 119–137.

Tavakoli, J. M. (2008). Structured finance and collateralized debt obligations. New developments in cash and synthetic securitization (2nd ed.). Jon Wiley & Sons, Inc.; doi:10.1002/9781118268230.

Teece, D. J., Pisano, G., & Shuen, A. (1997). Dynamic Capabilities and Strategic Management. *Strategic Management Journal*, *18*(7), 509–533. doi:10.1002/(SICI)1097-0266(199708)18:7<509::AID-SMJ882>3.0.CO;2-Z

Teece, D., & Pisano, G. (1994). The dynamic capabilities of firms: An introduction. *Industrial and Corporate Change*, *3*(3), 537–556. doi:10.1093/icc/3.3.537-a

Telyukova, I. A. (2013). Household Need for Liquidity and the Credit Card Debt Puzzle. *The Review of Economic Studies*, *80*(3), 1148–1177. doi:10.1093/restud/rdt001

Tennyson, S., & Nguyen, C. (2001). State curriculum mandates and student knowledge of personal finance. *The Journal of Consumer Affairs*, *35*(2), 241–262. doi:10.1111/j.1745-6606.2001.tb00112.x

Teo, T. S., & Pian, Y. (2003). A contingency perspective on Internet adoption and competitive advantage. *European Journal of Information Systems*, *12*(2), 78–92. doi:10.1057/palgrave.ejis.3000448

The Federal Council. (2018). *Legal framework for distributed ledger technology and blockchain in Switzerland: An overview with a focus on the financial sector*. Federal Council Report.

The Tokenist. (2018). *Security tokens explained*. Retrieved from https://thetokenist.io/security-tokens-explained/

Thiemann, M., Birk, M., & Friedrich, J. (2018). Much Ado About Nothing? Macro-Prudential Ideas and the Post-Crisis Regulation of Shadow Banking. KZfSS Kölner Zeitschrift für Soziologie und Sozialpsychologie, 70(S1), 259–286. doi:10.100711577-018-0546-6

Tokenization Standards Association. (2019). *Tokenization standards*. Retrieved from https://bettertokens.org/pdf/Tokenization%20Standards.pdf

Tong, H., & Wei, S.-J. (2009). *The misfortune of non-financial firms in a financial crisis: Disentangling finance and demand shocks*. CEPR Discussion paper no. 7208. National Bureau of Economic Research.

Compilation of References

United Nations. (2004). *UN Social Economic Council's Report of the International Telecommunication Union on information and communication technologies statistics*. United Nations, Economic and Social Council.

University of Melbourne the Household, Income and Labor Dynamics in Australia. (2018). *The Household, Income and Labor Dynamics in Australia (HILDA) Survey*. The University of Melbourne, Melbourne Institute: Applied Economic & Social Research. Retrieved from https://melbourneinstitute.unimelb.edu.au/hilda

Uría, F. (2017). La regulación financiera y su efecto sobre el negocio bancario. *Mediterráneo económico*, 101-122.

Utkus, S. P., & Young, J. A. (2011). *Financial Literacy and 401(k) Loans. In Financial Literacy Implications for Retirement Security and the Financial Marketplace* (pp. 59–75). New York, NY: Oxford University Press.

Van den Heuvel, J., Van Gils, A., & Voordeckers, W. (2006). Board roles in small and medium-sized family businesses: Performance and importance. *Corporate Governance*, *14*(5), 467–485. doi:10.1111/j.1467-8683.2006.00519.x

Van Rooij, M., Lusardi, A., & Alessie, R. (2011). Financial literacy and retirement planning in the Netherlands. *Journal of Economic Psychology*, *32*(4), 593–608. doi:10.1016/j.joep.2011.02.004

van Rooij, M., Lusardi, A., & Alessie, R. (2011). Financial literacy and stock market participation. *Journal of Financial Economics*, *101*(2), 449–472. doi:10.1016/j.jfineco.2011.03.006

van Rooij, M., Lusardi, A., & Alessie, R. (2012). Financial Literacy, Retirement Planning, and Household Wealth. *Economic Journal (London)*, *122*(560), 449–478. doi:10.1111/j.1468-0297.2012.02501.x

Vinig, T.; Blocq, R.; Braafhart, J. & Laufer, O. (1998). Developing a successful information and communication technology industry: the role of venture capital, knowledge, and the government. ICIS 1998 Proceedings. doi:10.1145/353053.353070

Vitt, L. A., Anderson, C., Kent, J., Lyter, D. M., Siegenthaler, J. K., & Ward, J. (2000). *Personal finance and the rush to competence: Financial literacy education in the U.S.* Middleburg, VA: Institute for Socio-Financial Studies.

Vitt, L. A., Carol, A., Kent, J., Lyter, D. M., Siegenthaler, J. K., & Ward, J. (2000). *Personal finance and the rush to competence: financial literacy education in the U.S.* Middleburg, VA: Institute for Socio-Financial Studies.

Volpe, R. P., Chen, H., & Pavlicko, J. J. (1996). Personal investment literacy among college students: A survey. *Financial Practice and Education*, *6*(2), 86–94.

Volpe, R. P., & Willis, L. E. (2008). Against Financial Literacy Education. *Iowa Law Review*, *94*, 197–285.

von Gaudecker, H. M. (2015). How Does Household Portfolio Diversification Vary with Financial Sophistication and Advice? *The Journal of Finance*, *70*(2), 489–507. doi:10.1111/jofi.12231

Wade, M., & Hulland, J. (2004). The Resource-Based View and Information Systems Research: Review, Extension, and Suggestions for Future Research. *Management Information Systems Quarterly*, *28*(1), 107–142. doi:10.2307/25148626

Wang, N., Liang, H., Zhong, W., Xue, Y., & Xiao, J. (2012). Resource Structuring or Capability Building? An Empirical Study of the Business Value of Information Technology. *Journal of Management Information Systems*, *29*(2), 325–367. doi:10.2753/MIS0742-1222290211

Weill, P. (1992). The relationship between investment in information technology and firm performance: A study of the value manufacturing sector. *Information Systems Research*, *3*(4), 307–333. doi:10.1287/isre.3.4.307

Wennberg, K., Wiklund, J., & Wright, M. (2011). The effectiveness of university knowledge spillovers: Performance differences between university spinoffs and corporate spinoffs. *Research Policy*, *40*(8), 1128–1143. doi:10.1016/j.respol.2011.05.014

Whited, I. M., & Wu, G. (2006). Financial constraints risk. *Review of Financial Studies*, *19*(2), 531–559. doi:10.1093/rfs/hhj012

Willis, L. E. (2008). *Against ðnancial literacy education*. University of Pennsylvania Law School, Public Law and Legal Theory Research Paper No. 08-10.

Wood, G. (2014). *Ethereum: A secure decentralized generalized transaction ledger*. Retrieved from https://gavwood.com/paper.pdf

World Bank. (2013). *Capacidades financieras en Colombia: resultados de la encuesta nacional sobre comportamientos, actitudes y conocimientos financieros*. Author.

World Bank. (2018). *Gains in financial inclusion, gains for a sustainable world*. Retrieved from: https://www.worldbank.org/en/news/immersive-story/2018/05/18/gains-in-financial-inclusion-gains-for-a-sustainable-world

World Economic Forum. (2015). *Deep Shift. Technology tipping points and societal impact*. Survey Report.

Worthington, A. (2006). Predicting Financial Literacy in Australia. *Financial Services Review*, *15*, 59–79.

Wright, M., Lockett, A., Clarysse, B., & Binks, M. (2006). University spin-out companies and venture capital. *Research Policy*, *35*(4), 481–501. doi:10.1016/j.respol.2006.01.005

Xiang, B. (1993). The choice of return-generating models and cross-sectional dependence in event studies. *Contemporary Accounting Research*, *9*(2), 365–394. doi:10.1111/j.1911-3846.1993.tb00887.x

Xiao, J., Chen, C., & Chen, F. (2013). Consumer Financial Capability and Financial Satisfaction. *Social Indicators Research*, *118*(1), 415–432. doi:10.100711205-013-0414-8

Yagüe-Perales, R. M., & March.Chordà, I. (2011). Performance analysis of research spin-offs in the Spanish biotechnology industry. *Journal of Business Research*, *65*(12), 1782–1789. doi:10.1016/j.jbusres.2011.10.038

Yang, J., Zhou, Y., & Wang, Z. (2009). The stock-bond correlation and macroeconomic conditions: One and a half centuries of evidence. *Journal of Banking & Finance*, *33*(4), 670–680. doi:10.1016/j.jbankfin.2008.11.010

Yescombe, E. R. (2002). *Principles of project finance*. San Diego, CA: Academic Press.

Yoong, J. (2011). *Financial Illiteracy and Stock Market Participation: Evidence from the RAND American Life Panel. In Financial Literacy Implications for Retirement Security and the Financial Marketplace* (pp. 76–10). New York, NY: Oxford University Press.

Zahra, S. A., Van de Velde, E., & Larrañeta, B. (2007). Knowledge conversion capability and the performance of corporate and university spin-off. *Industrial and Corporate Change*, *16*(4), 569–608. doi:10.1093/icc/dtm018

Zait, A., & Bertea, P. E. (2014). Financial Literacy – Conceptual Definition and Proposed Approach for a Measurement Instrument. *Journal of Accounting and Management*, *4*(3), 37–42.

Zamora, D. (2017). *Guia para elaborar un scoring de credito para reinsertados del postconflicto colombiano* (Unpublished End-of-Degree Project). Universidad Autónoma de Occidente, Santiago de Cali, Colombia. Retrieved from http://red.uao.edu.co:8080/bitstream/10614/9780/1/T07448.pdf

Zeffane, R. (1992). Patterns of structural control in high and low computer user organizations. *Information & Management*, *23*(3), 159–170. doi:10.1016/0378-7206(92)90040-M

Zeng, S., & Ni, X. (2018). *A Bibliometric Analysis of Blockchain Research. Intelligent Vehicles Symposium (IV)*, Changshu, China.

Zhang, J. (2009). The performance of university spin-offs: An exploratory analysis using venture capital data. *The Journal of Technology Transfer*, *34*(3), 255–285. doi:10.1007/s10961-008-9088-9

Zoni, L., & Pippo, F. (2017). CFO and finance function: What matters in value creation. *Journal of Accounting & Organizational Change*, *13*(2), 216–238. doi:10.1108/JAOC-12-2014-0059

Zorn, D. M. (2004). Here a Chief, There a Chief: The Rise of the CFO in the American Firm. *American Sociological Review*, *69*(3), 345–364. doi:10.1177/000312240406900302

About the Contributors

Begoña Álvarez-García is a lecturer in the Department of Business at the Universidade da Coruña (Spain). She has also been a lecturer at the University of Paris IX-Dauphine (France) and the Coordinator of the Master in Banking and Finance at the Universidade da Coruña. She holds a PhD degree in Economy and Management from the Universidade da Coruña and she was given an Extraordinary Doctorate Award. She has completed several research stages in the Universities of Paris-Dauphine and the Massachusetts Institute of Technology (MIT). She has participated in several European and national research projects and she has published several books related to financial topics.

José Pablo Abeal-Vázquez is a lecturer in the area of Financial Economics and Accounting of the Department of Business of the Universidade da Coruña (Spain). He has also taught at several University Schools linked to the Universidade da Coruñaand other Private Universities. He holds a PhD Degree in Economics from the Universidade da Coruña. He completed a Management Development Program by IESE Business School and he holds a Master in Commercial Management and Marketing from the Caixanova Business School. He frequently collaborates in economic studies for companies and institutions, and as a speaker in courses and specialized seminars. He has various publications in journals and congresses in the economic field.

* * *

Oscar Arcos is a DPhil in Economic Sciences, Universidad Nacional de Colombia, Specialist in Latin American Studies, Université Paris VIII. Professor in Economics, Universidad Santo Tomás.

Natália Barbosa is an associate professor of economics (with Habilitation) at the University of Minho (Portugal). She holds a PhD in Economics from the University of Manchester (United Kingdom), a Master in International Trade from the

About the Contributors

University of Minho (Portugal), and a first degree in Economics from the University of Porto (Portugal). Her research interests are in the fields of business dynamics, innovation, and foreign direct investment. She has published in journals such as Research Policy, International Journal of Industrial Organization, Journal of Small Business Management, International Business Review, Industrial and Corporate Change, Review of Industrial Organization, Growth and Change, and, among others, Economic Letters.

Ulkem Basdas, after graduating Middle East Technical University (METU) Economics Department (with a minor degree in Industrial Engineering on Operational Research), earned M.A. degree in Economics, Bilkent University, and Ph.D. in Finance, METU. She continued her research in finance as Visiting Scholar at the University of Michigan, Ann Arbor, Ross Business School. She started her professional career in Siemens as Project Commercial Manager in 2005, and between 2009 and 2010 she worked as Economic Policy Analyst in the Economic Policy Research Institute of Turkey. Following her experience in Borsa İstanbul over 2010-2016, she joined Philip Morris International, Leaf Planning Department. She has given lectures on financial markets and financial instruments, and her research interests are behavioral decision-making and financial anomalies. She also took a volunteer role in a nation-wide program under the Turkish Capital Markets Association, executing the goal of increasing the awareness of investment options in Turkey and nudging citizens to increase their savings.

Lucía Boedo is a teacher of Finance at the Universidade da Coruña, Spain. She teaches in the degree as well as in the post-graduate program of Finance. She is specialized in business finance, specifically in the topic of the optimal capital structure (subject of her PhD thesis), and in the cost and convenience of the different sources of financing available for a company, topic on which he has published several textbooks and scientific articles.

Pablo de Llano-Monelos is a Professor of Finance at the Universidade da Coruña. He served with IBM as internal controller and administration manager. He has published over 35 referred papers on financial economics, operations research and management science, and several books. Dr. De Llano's research concentrates in bankruptcy forecasting, financial options modelling, and corporate valuation

Gustavo Diaz has a B.A. in Economics, MPhil in Rural Economics, DPhil in Economics, Universidad Nacional de Colombia. Professor in Economics, Research Group: Economics and Humanism, Universidad Santo Tomas.

Joaquín Enríquez-Díaz is assistant professor in the Department of Business of the Universidade da Coruña. He is a BSc in Economics and MSc in Banking and Finance. Joaquín is currently a PhD student at the Universidade da Coruña. His research interests include: Economic and financial analysis of innovation barriers and drivers, financial economic education and teaching Innovation

Sara Esclapes-Membrives is a Senior Consultant, Grant Thornton. Member of the blockchain lab. Lawyer.

Ana Paula Faria is Director of the Industrial Economics Master and member of the EEG Pedagogical Council. She published in international scientific journals like: Research Policy, Industrial and Corportae Change, Journal of Technology Transfer, Economics of Innovation and New Technology, International Journal of Innovation Management, Growth and Change, Empirica, Economics Letters and Applied Economcis. Visiting Professor at the University of Berkeley, California, USA and participated in various research projects not only with the University of Inland, The Netherlands, at the University of Binus Nusantara in Jacarta, Indonesia, and Bank of Portugal.

Carlos Fernández Herraiz is a Senior Advisor, Grant Thornton. Member of the Blockchain Lab. PhD in Applied Economics.

Sara Fernández-López joined the Universidade de Santiago de Compostela (Spain) as associate professor in 2006, after 11 years of working as a lecturer and researcher. Her research interests are in two main areas: household finance and academic entrepreneurship. She has around 50 internationally refereed papers. Recently, she has published in the journals Business Services, European Journal of Finance, Feminist Economist, Spanish Journal of Finance and Accounting or Academia Revista Latinoamericana de Administración, all of them included in JCR.

Thomas Flavin is an Associate Professor in Financial Economics at Maynooth University (Ireland). Thomas completed his D.Phil on 'Tactical Asset Allocation' at University of York, under the supervision of Michael Wickens. His main research interests are in financial market linkages and shock transmission, financial contagion, and in empirical models of asset allocation. He has published in leading peer-reviewed academic journals such as Journal of International Money and Finance, Journal of Banking and Finance, Economics Letters, Emerging Markets Review, Journal of Forecasting, International Review of Finance among others. He has held visiting positions at University of York, University of Cambridge and the Federal Reserve Bank of Atlanta.

About the Contributors

Olga Garcia has an MPhil in Rural Development, Universidad Santo Tomás, DPhil in History. Finance specialist and Professor in Economics, Research group: Economics and Humanism, Universidad Santo Tomás.

Antonio Javier Grandío Dopico is a Professor in Department of Economics, Faculty of Economics and Business, Universidade da Coruña (Spain).

Carlos Pineiro Sanchez is a Permanent Lecturer at the Faculty of Economics of the Universidade da Coruña. He obtained his Ph. D. degree in Business Economics at the Universidade da Coruña. His research interests include financial valuation, bankruptcy, intangible assets, and the evaluation of IT investments. He has published over 30 referred papers and 15 books, along with a large number of contributions to international academic conferences on Finance and MIS. He has also acted as a consultant for a variety of Spanish Public Administrations and commercial companies.

Antonio Javier Prado-Dominguez is a Full Professor, Universitiy of A Coruña, Applied Economics. PhD in Public Economics. A specialist in financial and monetary economics and financial system.

David Rodeiro-Pazos joined Universidade de Santiago de Compostela (Spain) as associate professor in 2009, after 7 years of working as a lecturer and researcher. He has his PhD. from the University of Santiago in 2008. His research interests are academic entrepreneurship, university spin-offs, technology transfer and venture capital. He is author and co-author of several books on entrepreneurship. He has around 40 internationally refereed papers published in journal as Technology Analysis & Strategic Management, Journal of the Knowledge Economy, Journal of Management Development or Service Business, included in JCR. Recently, he and has been involve in European projects "Citizenergy" and "FANBEST".

María Jesús Rodríguez-Gulías joined the Universidade da Coruña (Spain) as lecturer in 2015. Previously, she combined her work as technician in the Technology Transfer Office of Universidade de Santiago de Compostela (Spain) and the development of her PhD and worked for Universidade de Vigo. Dissertation on university spin-offs, defended in January 2014. Her research interests are in two main areas: intellectual property valuation and academic entrepreneurship. Recently, she has published in different journals as International Journal of Innovation and Learning, International Journal of Globalisation and Small Business, Technology Analysis & Strategic Management, Journal of International Entrepreneurship or Journal of the Knowledge Economy.

José Manuel Sánchez Santos is a Senior Lecturer in the Department of Economics at the Universidade da Coruña. He holds a PhD in Economics and Business Sciences and he teaches a Monetary Policy and the Financial System course in the Economics degree.

Laura Varela-Candamio is an Assistant Professor in the Department of Economics at the Universidade da Coruña (Spain) and Tutor in the Associate Centre of Lugo at the Spanish National Open University (UNED). She is also a member of Jean Monnet Research Group of Competition and Development. She got her Bachelor in Economics in 2007 and her PhD also in Economics in 2011. His research interest include public economics such as public finance, taxation and public policies; sustainable economic development and behavioral economics. She has published its research outcomes in numerous international conferences and in scientific journals such as Journal of Cleaner Production, Journal of Policy Modeling, Empirica, Economics Letters, Applied Economics, Computers in Human Behavior, El Trimestre Económico, Sustainability, among others. She has been a visiting professor in American universities: Andrew Young School (Georgia State University) (2015), REAL (University of Illinois) (2013), Suffolk University (2012) and also European institutions: University of Porto (2014, 2011 and 2010) and IRPET, Italy (2018). She has been member of the technical committee of Globe Conference and WorldCist. She has also been invited as keynote speaker in international conferences, such as the 2016 International Conference "Information Society and Sustainable Development" – ISSD in Pologravi (University Targu-Jiu - Romania).

Andres Vernazza has an MPhil in Bank and Finances, Universidad de la Coruña, Spain, MPhil in Economic Sciences, Universidad Santo Tomás, DPhil in Economics, Universidad de la Coruña, Spain. Director of the Master programme in Economic Sciences, Universidad Santo Tomás.

Index

A

AIM 5, 33, 35, 48, 51, 66-67, 75, 84, 111-112, 122, 125, 153-154, 167, 201, 211, 214, 216, 231, 241, 267, 288
alternative markets 106-112, 121-122, 124-125
Annual Percentage Rate (APR) 172
Asset Tokens 36, 41-42, 46-48, 51-52, 57

B

Bank Financing 108, 110, 122, 129, 176, 187
Bank of Opportunities 232
banking system 108, 110, 131-132, 136, 138-141, 146-147, 151, 177, 208, 231, 281
Behavioral Bias 223
Blockchain 33-44, 46-49, 52, 57-58, 60, 66, 73

C

collateralized debt obligations 135, 174
collateralized loan obligations 141
Consensus 32, 50, 83, 174, 187, 217
Consumer Protection 161, 205-206, 217
Contagion Effects 178, 180, 185-187
Corporate Structure 10
Credit Card 208, 262-263, 266, 300
Credit Constraints 178, 187, 197
credit default swaps 136
Credit Scoring 227, 229-231, 238-239, 242-243

Crisis Period 174, 176, 180, 183, 186
Cross-Country 97, 254
cryptocurrencies 35-37, 39, 41-42, 47, 50, 57, 61, 249

D

Debit Card 211, 300
Debt Market 106-107, 112, 116, 125, 129
Decision making 66, 166, 205-207, 216, 279, 296
De-Coupling 197
Default Interest 157, 172
Digitalization 60, 79, 281, 283
Disruptive Technology 79
Drop by Drop 229

E

Economic Downturns 176, 186, 197
Equity Market 107, 112, 116, 130, 180
European Standardised Information Sheet (ESIS) 162, 172
European Systemic Risk Board (ESRB) 137, 151
Eurozone 139, 172, 174-175, 179, 181-187

F

FEIN 162, 165, 172
FiAE 165, 172
Ficha de Información Precontractual (FIPRE) 161, 172
Financial Contagion 173-174, 181, 185, 197
financial decision-making 205, 207, 216, 248-249, 262, 264, 268, 279, 296

Financial Director 59
Financial Distress 6, 10, 12, 14, 16, 31, 176, 186, 284
Financial Education 165, 201-202, 206, 209, 212-217, 248-250, 252, 263, 265, 267, 280, 284-286, 296
Financial Function 59-61, 63, 66-67, 69, 73-75, 79
Financial Inclusion 51, 201, 205, 211-212, 215-216, 223, 227-229, 232, 243, 248-250, 281, 283, 286-287, 296
Financial Knowledge 168, 200-202, 204, 207, 209-210, 212-217, 248-250, 261-262, 264-265, 267-268, 280-282, 285-287, 289-290, 293, 296-297, 300
Financial Literacy 199-202, 204-217, 224-225, 248-254, 259, 261-268, 279, 282, 285
Financial Literacy Measure 262, 279
Financial Regulation 39, 177, 214-215, 217, 224
Financial Risk 1-2, 8, 10, 15-16, 18, 282, 287, 296, 300
Financial Stability 1, 131, 138, 151, 162, 176, 201, 205, 212-213, 215, 224
Financial Stability Board (FSB) 131, 151
Financial Tool 231, 243
financing problems 106-107, 110
FINRA 252, 262-263
Firm Growth 83, 85, 87, 94, 96
Fiscal Awareness 280, 293, 300
Fiscal Knowledge 280, 282, 287-290, 293-294, 296-297
Flight to Safety 183, 197
Floor-Ceiling Clause 172
Foreign Currency Loan 172

G

Global Financial Crisis 155, 168, 173, 175, 178-181, 186-187, 197, 200, 208, 212, 214

H

Housing Bubble 248

I

ICT-USOs 82-98
Industry 4.0 61, 63, 65-67, 75
INFE 201, 259
Informal Economy 246-247
Informal Retailers 227-231, 235-239, 242-243, 247
Information and Communication Technologies (ICT) 82-84, 103
Information and Communication Technology Industry 83
Information Technology 1, 63
Initial Coin Offering (ICO) 57
Initial Exchange Offering (IEO) 57
Instrumental Variable 279
International Diversification 180
IRPH 157, 172

L

Legal Liability 51
Loan Sharks 243
Lusardi-Mitchell Design 252, 254, 259, 279

M

MAB 107, 112-115, 121-122, 124-125
MARF 107, 116-120, 123-125
Market Challenge 43, 46, 48-49, 52, 57
Market Downturns 185, 197
Market Failure 224
Means of Payment 32-35, 37, 39, 42, 50, 52, 57, 280
Megatrends 59, 63, 74
Mortgage loan 152, 157, 160-161, 163, 167, 172

N

Numeracy 202, 213, 224-225, 250, 252, 264, 279

O

OECD 103, 201, 204, 252, 259, 264, 286, 296

Index

Official Market 111, 116, 120, 122, 130

P

Panel Data 90
Performance 1, 4-7, 31, 65, 68, 79, 84, 87-89, 95, 98, 116, 167, 178, 200, 207, 238-239, 242
PISA 264-265
Product Challenge 41, 46-48, 52, 58
Project Finance 144-145, 151
Public Spending 282, 287, 294, 296-297, 300

R

Reliability 32, 51, 121
repo 133-134
Representative Tokens 36, 46, 48-49, 51-52, 58

S

Safe Haven Asset 197
Saving 129, 200-201, 205, 209-211, 264, 290, 296, 300
Securitization 117, 120, 133-134, 143, 151
Security Token Offering (STO) 58
Self-Assessment Questionnaire 279
Shadow Banking 131-133, 135, 137-141, 146-147, 151
SMEs 1, 8-10, 59, 61, 63-69, 71, 73-75, 106-112, 116, 121, 124-125, 178, 216, 230, 232-233, 238
Sources of Finance 107, 130, 179
Sovereign Debt Crisis 183-186, 248

Spain 83-85, 92, 95, 97, 107-110, 112, 116, 122, 124-125, 152-157, 160-161, 166, 168, 172, 181-183, 204, 249, 280-282, 287-288, 296-297
Spillover 173, 176-177, 179-181, 186-187, 197
Spillover Effects 173, 176-177, 179-181, 186-187, 197
Start-Up 103
Strategic Thinking 80
subprime mortgages 135-136, 141, 174
synthetic CDO 135-136
Systemic Risk 132, 137, 139, 141, 151, 224

T

Token 33, 35, 38-50, 52, 58
Tokenization 32, 35-38, 40-44, 47, 51-52, 58
Transparency 32, 51, 73, 107, 110, 113, 121-122, 125-126, 138, 167-168, 214

U

Uncertainity 80
Uncertainty 63, 73, 80, 179, 205, 210
Unfair Terms 152, 156, 159, 172
university spin offs 82, 96, 103

V

Value Chain 62, 65, 69, 71, 80
Venture Capital 82, 84, 93, 103, 110, 112, 137, 142, 144
Volatility 10, 45, 63, 80, 108, 174, 178, 181, 185, 238

Purchase Print, E-Book, or Print + E-Book

IGI Global's reference books can now be purchased from three unique pricing formats:
Print Only, E-Book Only, or Print + E-Book.
Shipping fees may apply.

www.igi-global.com

Recommended Reference Books

ISBN: 978-1-5225-6201-6
© 2019; 341 pp.
List Price: $345

ISBN: 978-1-5225-7262-6
© 2019; 360 pp.
List Price: $215

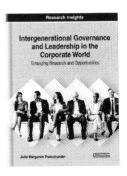

ISBN: 978-1-5225-8003-4
© 2019; 216 pp.
List Price: $205

ISBN: 978-1-5225-5763-0
© 2019; 304 pp.
List Price: $205

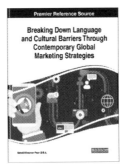

ISBN: 978-1-5225-6980-0
© 2019; 325 pp.
List Price: $235

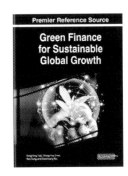

ISBN: 978-1-5225-7808-6
© 2019; 397 pp.
List Price: $215

Looking for free content, product updates, news, and special offers?
Join IGI Global's mailing list today and start enjoying exclusive perks sent only to IGI Global members.
Add your name to the list at **www.igi-global.com/newsletters**.

Publisher of Peer-Reviewed, Timely, and Innovative Academic Research

www.igi-global.com   Sign up at www.igi-global.com/newsletters   facebook.com/igiglobal   twitter.com/igiglobal

Ensure Quality Research is Introduced to the Academic Community

Become an IGI Global Reviewer for Authored Book Projects

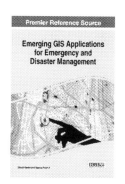 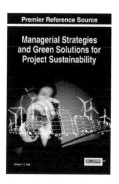  

The overall success of an authored book project is dependent on quality and timely reviews.

In this competitive age of scholarly publishing, constructive and timely feedback significantly expedites the turnaround time of manuscripts from submission to acceptance, allowing the publication and discovery of forward-thinking research at a much more expeditious rate. Several IGI Global authored book projects are currently seeking highly-qualified experts in the field to fill vacancies on their respective editorial review boards:

Applications and Inquiries may be sent to:
development@igi-global.com

Applicants must have a doctorate (or an equivalent degree) as well as publishing and reviewing experience. Reviewers are asked to complete the open-ended evaluation questions with as much detail as possible in a timely, collegial, and constructive manner. All reviewers' tenures run for one-year terms on the editorial review boards and are expected to complete at least three reviews per term. Upon successful completion of this term, reviewers can be considered for an additional term.

If you have a colleague that may be interested in this opportunity, we encourage you to share this information with them.

IGI Global Proudly Partners With eContent Pro International

Receive a 25% Discount on all Editorial Services

Editorial Services

IGI Global expects all final manuscripts submitted for publication to be in their final form. This means they must be reviewed, revised, and professionally copy edited prior to their final submission. Not only does this support with accelerating the publication process, but it also ensures that the highest quality scholarly work can be disseminated.

English Language Copy Editing

Let eContent Pro International's expert copy editors perform edits on your manuscript to resolve spelling, punctuaion, grammar, syntax, flow, formatting issues and more.

Scientific and Scholarly Editing

Allow colleagues in your research area to examine the content of your manuscript and provide you with valuable feedback and suggestions before submission.

Figure, Table, Chart & Equation Conversions

Do you have poor quality figures? Do you need visual elements in your manuscript created or converted? A design expert can help!

Translation

Need your documjent translated into English? eContent Pro International's expert translators are fluent in English and more than 40 different languages.

Hear What Your Colleagues are Saying About Editorial Services Supported by IGI Global

"The service was very fast, very thorough, and very helpful in ensuring our chapter meets the criteria and requirements of the book's editors. I was quite impressed and happy with your service."

– Prof. Tom Brinthaupt,
Middle Tennessee State University, USA

"I found the work actually spectacular. The editing, formatting, and other checks were very thorough. The turnaround time was great as well. I will definitely use eContent Pro in the future."

– Nickanor Amwata, Lecturer,
University of Kurdistan Hawler, Iraq

"I was impressed that it was done timely, and wherever the content was not clear for the reader, the paper was improved with better readability for the audience."

– Prof. James Chilembwe,
Mzuzu University, Malawi

Email: customerservice@econtentpro.com   www.igi-global.com/editorial-service-partners

Celebrating Over 30 Years of Scholarly Knowledge Creation & Dissemination

www.igi-global.com

InfoSci®-Books

A Database of Over 5,300+ Reference Books Containing Over 100,000+ Chapters Focusing on Emerging Research

GAIN ACCESS TO **THOUSANDS** OF REFERENCE BOOKS AT **A FRACTION** OF THEIR INDIVIDUAL LIST **PRICE**.

InfoSci®-Books Database

The **InfoSci®-Books** database is a collection of over 5,300+ IGI Global single and multi-volume reference books, handbooks of research, and encyclopedias, encompassing groundbreaking research from prominent experts worldwide that span over 350+ topics in 11 core subject areas including business, computer science, education, science and engineering, social sciences and more.

Open Access Fee Waiver (Offset Model) Initiative

For any library that invests in IGI Global's InfoSci-Journals and/or InfoSci-Books databases, IGI Global will match the library's investment with a fund of equal value to go toward **subsidizing the OA article processing charges (APCs) for their students, faculty, and staff** at that institution when their work is submitted and accepted under OA into an IGI Global journal.*

INFOSCI® PLATFORM FEATURES

- No DRM
- No Set-Up or Maintenance Fees
- A Guarantee of No More Than a 5% Annual Increase
- Full-Text HTML and PDF Viewing Options
- Downloadable MARC Records
- Unlimited Simultaneous Access
- COUNTER 5 Compliant Reports
- Formatted Citations With Ability to Export to RefWorks and EasyBib
- No Embargo of Content (Research is Available Months in Advance of the Print Release)

*The fund will be offered on an annual basis and expire at the end of the subscription period. The fund would renew as the subscription is renewed for each year thereafter. The open access fees will be waived after the student, faculty, or staff's paper has been vetted and accepted into an IGI Global journal and the fund can only be used toward publishing OA in an IGI Global journal. Libraries in developing countries will have the match on their investment doubled.

To Learn More or To Purchase This Database:
www.igi-global.com/infosci-books

eresources@igi-global.com • Toll Free: 1-866-342-6657 ext. 100 • Phone: 717-533-8845 x100

www.igi-global.com